Space and Time under Persecution

Space and Time under Persecution

THE GERMAN-JEWISH EXPERIENCE IN THE THIRD REICH

Guy Miron

Translated by Haim Watzman

The University of Chicago Press CHICAGO AND LONDON

The University of Chicago Press, Chicago 60637
The University of Chicago Press, Ltd., London

Published 2023
Printed in the United States of America

32 31 30 29 28 27 26 25 24 23   1 2 3 4 5

ISBN-13: 978-0-226-82732-2 (cloth)
ISBN-13: 978-0-226-82815-2 (paper)
ISBN-13: 978-0-226-82814-5 (e-book)
DOI: https://doi.org/10.7208/chicago/9780226828145.001.0001

Originally published in Hebrew as להיות יהודי בגרמניה הנאצית

Library of Congress Cataloging-in-Publication Data

Names: Miron, Gai, author. | Watzman, Haim, translator.
Title: Space and time under persecution : the German-Jewish experience in the Third Reich / Guy Miron ; translated by Haim Watzman.
Other titles: Li-heyot Yehudi be-Germanyah ha-natsit. English
Description: Chicago : The University of Chicago Press, 2023. | Includes bibliographical references and index.
Identifiers: LCCN 2023001762 | ISBN 9780226827322 (cloth) | ISBN 9780226828152 (paperback) | ISBN 9780226828145 (ebook)
Subjects: LCSH: Jews—Germany—History—1933–1945. | Jews—Germany—History—1933–1945—Sources. | Space perception—Social aspects. | Time perception—Social aspects.
Classification: LCC DS134.255 .M5713 2023 | DDC 943/.004924009043—dc23/eng/20230123
LC record available at https://lccn.loc.gov/2023001762

♾ This paper meets the requirements of ANSI/NISO Z39.48-1992 (Permanence of Paper).

Contents

Introduction

"The world has expanded for each of us. What was close has become distant. . . . We live in accelerated and changing times. Each year is like a historical era."[1] The quote is from a Jewish newspaper in Germany in September 1937, on the eve of Rosh Hashanah, the Jewish New Year, nearly five years after the Nazis came to power. It comes from a greeting for the New Year from the National Representation of the Jews in Germany (Reichsvertretung der Juden in Deutschland). The Nazi regime was escalating its anti-Jewish policies, aimed at excluding Jews from the German public space. Notably, the author of this message from the country's leading Jewish organization framed the effect of the regime's policies in terms of how they had changed the way Jews experienced space and time. The close and distant were now confused, and the flow of time was much more intense than in the past. These changes, which up to this point have remained at the margins of historical study, stand at the center of this work.

The lives of Germany's Jews underwent radical and rapid metamorphoses with the inception of the Nazi regime in January 1933, changes that challenged the manner in which Jews lived and perceived space and time. This book addresses how Jews coped with this challenge and how they reshaped their view of their world in the face of exclusion and social and economic decline. It happened while they were in rapid motion—as they migrated within Germany, emigrated in large numbers, and later suffered the expropriation of their homes, conscription into forced labor, and expulsion to their deaths in the east. Given the intensity of the lives of German Jews at this moment in history, with its specific social and economic backdrop, this history can serve as a useful case study of how human beings contend with changing space and time and the intricate relations between these fundamental experiences and individuals and communities. A more profound understanding of the experience of space and time in such a complex quotidian context illuminates elemental questions that the study of history has always sought to clarify—how human beings, in the shadow of momentous historical events, perceive the world around them, their own identities, and the fabric of social relations that connects them.

Space and time are the most basic features of being human in the world. No human existence is possible outside of them. The nature of space and time, like the way human beings relate to them and the ways in which they experience them, as individuals and communities, raise complex and profound questions that have interested thinkers since the dawn of history. They constitute the raw material from which our daily experience is constructed. In normal times and more placid periods in the lives of individuals and communities, space and time can seem to be transparent. Space can be imagined as an empty and neutral receptacle and time as linear, flowing forward at a constant rate. But in periods of crisis and distress these factors become dynamic, shaping human existence. In such circumstances a deeper aspect of them comes to the fore—both in the broader public discourse and in the lives of families and individuals. The late Boaz Neumann proposed that "being-in-the-world," a concept deriving from Heidegger's concept of *Dasein*, could be harnessed to the study of history. Historians who do so focus largely on recreating space and time as experienced by people in the past, based on documentation of everyday lives. Such sources reflect the world of people living in a past era.[2]

This book will cast light on these fundamental issues through the use of contemporary sources: a rich array of personal diaries, correspondence, autobiographical accounts, and articles from the press. The discussion will be based on the insights and conceptualizations of thinkers and scholars from different fields in the social sciences and humanities, among them cultural anthropology, environmental psychology, human geography, and the sociology of time. The world of German Jews under the Nazi regime offers exceptional opportunities to examine the way in which these people experienced their being-in-the-world against the background of the historical circumstances in which they found themselves, using the bountiful capacities for self-expression that were available to many of them.

A broad range of studies has been published on the lives of Jews during the early years of the Nazi regime, from a variety of perspectives. Many of these studies have surveyed the way Jews responded to Nazi policies, others the Jewish organizations that continued to operate openly during these years. Still others have looked at the profuse Jewish public discourse about issues of the day, or at Jewish activities in areas such as education, social assistance, emigration, and religious life.[3] During the 1990s, Marion Kaplan offered an overview of Jewish life during the Nazi era, broadly addressing issues of gender and the world of adolescents, while Saul Friedländer proposed a narrative that combined a chronicle of Nazi policies of exclusion and oppression with the lives of Jews in Germany.[4] A range of notable studies has appeared since then, illuminating this period using the tools of social history and the history of everyday life, while relating to gender and the point of view of adolescents. New conceptualizations have also been proposed for examining the ways Jews responded to and protested against the Nazi government.[5] More recently, cultural history has entered the field, one example being Alon Confino's book *A World without Jews*, which highlights new aspects of Jewish life using fresh theoretical perspectives and comparative analysis.[6]

The end of the last century, the field of history underwent what has been called the "spatial turn." It was heralded by Henri Lefebvre's book *The Production of Space*. Lefebvre, a philosopher and sociologist, argued that space was not neutral, transparent, and empty. Its ostensible transparency, he argued, was an illusion that needed to be replaced by a broader and more complex conception that would relate to the ways in which space was perceived and shaped as a product of social construction.[7] Lefebvre's conceptualization of space, along with the thinking of Michel Foucault and others, served as a basis for the work of the geographer Edward Soja, who, in addition to his theoretical development of the spatial turn, also produced empirical studies focused on the urban environment.[8] In recent decades the spatial turn has been influential in the fields of Jewish history and Jewish studies. Scholars in these fields have reexamined phenomena in Jewish history in Europe in general and in Germany in particular, using the concept of space to offer new insights.[9]

Likewise, scholars from the social science and cultural studies fields, and historians as well, have in recent decades focused on time, the way it is organized in human society, and its role in historical changes. A variety of studies have transformed time from a present absence in historical events into a factor with significance for the way human beings experience and shape society. These insights have been systematized with the help of scholars such as Norbert Elias and Eviatar Zerubavel in their work on the sociology of time.[10] In historical work, the concept of time has been used to probe questions about the different ways in which time is experienced, the shaping of memory, and the changing relationship to the past.[11] Historians have also considered the shaping of public time and its role in the formation of modern collective identities.[12]

Many studies have shown that the manners in which humans exist in time and space are the main shapers of their self-awareness and the way they accord meaning to the world. What sets this book apart is its attempt to offer a systematic examination, on the basis of these universal ideas, of the life circumstances and worldviews of German Jews during the Nazi period. By means of a new and fresh reading of the plentiful and diverse corpus of source material, I will show how Jews formulated their experiences for themselves by means of perceptions of space and time. I will also examine how their coping with the difficult challenges of Nazi exclusion policies was based on the way they thought about and experienced space and time. This discussion will help develop a broad discourse that combines the sensitivities of social and cultural history and breaks through the accepted boundaries of Jewish historiography in the Nazi era.

The book has two parts. The first looks at different aspects of the Jewish experience of space, and the second focuses on time.

The Bourgeois Space: The City and the Home

Jewish integration into Germany during the age of emancipation, the nineteenth century and the beginning of the twentieth century, was characterized largely by entry into the German middle class, the bourgeoisie. In joining the German bourgeoisie, the Jews adopted not only the economic profile of the middle class, but also its mores and values—its lifestyle, or more precisely its habitus.[13] This process involved, in part, a profound change in the vocational profile of Jewish society, the adoption of German culture, and rapid migration into Germany's cities. The latter was particularly notable in Berlin, which on the verge of the twentieth century was home to about a third of the country's Jews. Joining the German bourgeoisie was partly a process of secularization that also involved a reshaping of Jewish religion, and changes and innovations in consumer culture. With adoption of the bourgeois lifestyle, the home lives of German Jews changed radically: the types of dwellings they lived in, the gendered division of labor between men and women, the structure and size of families, and the way children were educated.[14] These processes had a very real effect on the ways in which Jews experienced space and time and constituted them in their consciousness: lived space and lived time.

Chapter 1 of this book covers the lives of Jews in the public space, especially in the cities. The opening of German public space to Jews, as a result of the revocation of the constraints on their movement and the completion of the process of emancipation, made the German environment available to them. No less important than the change in their legal status was the enormous impact of the age of the railroad. For middle-class Europeans in the second half of the nineteenth century, the train system created a new spatial experience.[15] Due to the impact of the industrial age in general and the railroads in particular, the experience of space in Germany during the late nineteenth century was marked by increased mobility and accelerated urbanization. These processes were even more pronounced for Jews, beyond their proportion in the population.[16] As German burghers, the Jews took part in the new "travel cultures" that emerged in Germany. This included both going out into nature and the development of an active connection to it as part of the process by which Germany became their homeland (*Heimat*).[17] The advent of the private automobile at the beginning of the twentieth century, which marked another stage in the development of the culture of travel, influenced Jews prior to the Nazi era, but made its biggest impact precisely in the challenging circumstances they faced after January 1933.

Nature and the city were not the only venues that opened to Jews during the age of emancipation in Germany. They were also accepted into a growing number of institutions and places, both in their occupations and in their cultural and leisure lives, that became key elements in the constitution of their bourgeois customs. Jews' experience of space in this age was shaped not only by the move into cities and augmented mobility, but by their ability to frequent new public spaces such as cafés, theaters, opera houses, museum, public libraries, sports facilities, and vacation spots. By gaining access to these spaces, each of which offered the individual a range of new activities, Jews also gained access to German society, took part in the shaping of bourgeois consumer culture, and had experiences that laid the foundations for expressing and reshaping their identities and selfhoods.[18] The ways Jews coped with exclusion in such spaces will also be discussed in chapter 1.

Chapter 2 is devoted to Jewish sites and spaces: synagogues, cemeteries, and other communal spaces. A central feature of the structuring of the bourgeois space in the pre-Nazi era might be called the "separation of spheres." Each new public space was shaped according to specific rules, devoted to specific activities, and accessible at fixed times. Each imposed on its users a particular dress and behavioral code. The spatial principle of the separation of spheres also reshaped Jewish spaces—first and foremost the synagogue, which metamorphosed during the nineteenth century from a place in which a wide variety of social, cultural, and even economic activities took place into a house of prayer devoted solely to religious activity. In the Nazi period, this separation between the secular and sacred realms was severely eroded by the exclusionary regime imposed on Jews. Nazi strictures forced them into newly restricted spaces that, step by step, became the only places in which they could live and gather.

Chapter 3 is devoted to the concept of the home. The separation of spheres typical of the bourgeois lifestyle was particularly pronounced in the partitioning of spaces of production and consumption, and even more so between private and public spaces of various kinds. The age of Jewish emancipation in Germany was also the age in which the modern home and the domesticity associated with it became foundational to life in the West as a whole, and to the middle class in particular. Starting at the end of the nineteenth century, the bourgeois home in Germany, as in other industrialized countries, became an important class symbol, "a shrine to German domesticity and to middle-class gentility."[19] For many, the home became more spacious, and transformed into, above all else, a warm and intimate (*gemütlich*) emotional space, the realm of the mistress of the house. This was the sort of woman Marion Kaplan terms a "lady of leisure," responsible for cultivating the home and family as a unit of consumption detached from the world of work and production, for which the man of the family was responsible. This bourgeois ideal, internalized by the great majority of German Jews, brought the separation of spheres into the home itself, in the form of a clear internal division between spaces devoted to distinct needs and purposes.

The rapid erosion of the economic position of German Jews during the initial years of the Nazi regime, followed by the exclusionary policies that drove many Jews out of their large homes into much more restricted private spaces, made it increasingly difficult for them to maintain a domestic bourgeois lifestyle. It led to a lively and incisive debate on the significance of the home as a concept.

The discussion of how Jews grappled with the experience of space during the Nazi era is tied, of course, to the regime's own attitude toward it. *Raum*, the German word for space, was a fundamental concept in the Nazi *Weltanschauung*. The slogan "people without space" (*Volk ohne Raum*) was coined by the novelist Hans Grimm in his work of that name to express the plight of the German nation. The German need for living space (*Lebensraum*) became a foundational element of Nazi ideology. This Nazi obsession with space led to the aggressive pursuit of territorial expansion, especially to the east. But it was no less evident in the Nazification of German space, in which the German urban and rural landscapes were reshaped in a process that included the policy of excluding Jews from them.[20]

Bourgeois Time: The Annual Cycle and the Pace of Time

The socialization of Jews into Germany's bourgeoisie and its national culture, as it developed during the age of emancipation, could clearly be seen in the shaping of their experience of time. Freedom of movement, urbanization and industrialization, and integration into the capitalist economic system were accompanied by a standardization of the measure of time, and the adoption of the time regime of the surrounding society. The Jews also accommodated themselves to the German national annual cycle as it emerged in the imperial age. Many of them adopted certain customs and observances of Christmas, which began to transform during this period into a German national holiday with manifestly consumerist domestic elements.[21] At the same time, many Jews maintained their connection to the cycle of the traditional Jewish calendar. The appropriation of the German national calendar by the Nazi regime involved imbuing national holidays with Nazi meaning and the creation of new holidays. As chapter 4 shows, this led to the Jews' alienation from the synchronization of their lives with the German cycle of time and to the need to formulate new approaches to shaping the annual cycle.

The bourgeois worldview and habits also affected the way in which Germany's Jews perceived and experienced the flow of time. The standardization of the uniform flow of time brought on the by railroad age, the rise of clock time, and above all the awareness that people ought to plan and exploit their time efficiently to advance their careers and the achievement of their goals, were central features of the way Germany's Jews came to experience time during the age of emancipation. Linear time flowed at a uniform pace and was thus amenable to division and to planning. As such, it could be seen as requiring a person to use it to the best purpose and in the most efficient way. This view of time became particularly characteristic of the world of bourgeois men, an outgrowth of the broad space for action that opened to them in the age of emancipation. Chapter 5, devoted to the flow of time, shows how the strictures imposed by the Nazi regime seriously fractured this attribute. It created states in which Jews experienced time as creeping or even standing in place, along with others in which time was experienced as speeding forward uncontrollably.

Another aspect of how time was shaped for Jews has to do with their attitude toward the past. During the age of emancipation, alongside the consolidation of the experience of forward-flowing linear time, the public discourse and political culture of Germany's Jews was characterized by a new historical consciousness and a clear inclination to create a "usable past" that could help them cope with the challenges of the present.[22] The central status of historical discourse and its importance for the picture of German Jewish public space seems to have reflected broader trends in the German and European national discourse of the nineteenth and early twentieth centuries. But it also bore traces of Jewish cultural memory. The crisis that faced Jews under Nazi rule considerably reinforced, as chapter 6 will show, their need to turn to the past, both as a communities and as individuals.

Like space, Jewish time took on a new shape under the Nazis as a result of its aggressive policies. The regime Nazified time by reconstituting the German calendar, instituting holidays marking events and people from the party's heritage, while at the same time downgrading or eliminating commemorations associated with the Weimar regime and the German liberal tradition. It also sought to replace a political heritage based on negotiation and gradual change with one that engaged in rapid and determined action. The Nazi obsession with time also found expression in a constant attempt to remold German memory in the spirit of the movement's ideology, as well as to proclaim the new imagined future embodied in the proclamation of a thousand-year Reich (*Tausendjährige Reich*).[23] These processes changed the milieu in which the Jews lived, and sometimes their daily lives.

Sources

The presentation and analysis of the shaping of the way German Jews experienced space and time under the Nazi regime is based on two principal types of sources: personal ones, such as diaries, letters, and memoirs; and public ones, principally the contemporary Jewish press. The historian Peter Fritzsche has argued that life under the Third Reich prompted, for many, "intensified self-scrutiny" and encouraged the self-expression of inner life in writing, more so than in other eras. "Letters and diaries," he claims, "provide valuable insights into the efforts Germans made to come to terms with National Socialism."[24] In the same spirit, Janosch Steuwer, in his work on the keeping of diaries in Nazi Germany, has recently pointed out how the circumstances of the era made the personal journals of many Germans, including those with no political orientation, more reflective, rich, and profound.[25] The diaries of Jews who lived under Nazi rule, in Germany and throughout Europe, have recently been treated in research as centrally important not only to recreating the daily lives of Jews, in the spirit of social history, but to the analysis of the representation of their self-consciousness, in the spirit of cultural history.[26]

Prominent among the diarists on whose work this book rests are older and educated men of the middle class, such as the literary scholar Victor Klemperer of Dresden and the historian and teacher Willy Cohn of Breslau, both of whom documented their daily lives in great detail and with considerable reflection. I also perused the diaries of women, as well as those of young people and adolescents of different backgrounds, when I was able to locate such documents. In addition to diaries, my study is also based on personal and family correspondence conducted by German Jews, especially those with close family members who had emigrated. These letters, like the diaries, fall under the rubric of egodocuments—autobiographical documentation in the first person singular. Because of the needs of these writers to present their worlds to people living outside Nazi Germany, such texts sometimes provide noteworthy details and insights that touch on the issues of time and space.[27] Like diaries, letters are written in real time. Both are fragmentary in content and form, and precisely for that reason they respond to the challenge of reconstructing the experiences of space and time that constituted the being-in-the-world of their authors.

The use of letters, a large part of which were written by women, such as the poet Gertrud Kolmar, of Berlin, and Jeanette Schocken, a widow who lived in Wesermünde in northern Germany, provides a gender balance to the sources for my work. Another genre of first-person documentation is one that is also more gender-balanced than the available diaries: autobiographies and memoirs written by Jews after leaving Germany. While such writing after the event must be treated with caution because of its retrospective nature, the autobiographical passages used here also contribute to the reconstruction of certain aspects of their writers' experience of space and time. One example is the memoir penned by an active member of the Central Association of German Citizens of Jewish Faith (Centralverein deutscher Staatsbürger jüdischen Glaubens) in Berlin, Hans Reichmann, who wrote it in London in the summer of 1939, a few months after his release from the Sachsenhausen concentration camp. Another is that of Elisabeth Freund, also of Berlin, who managed to get out of Germany in October 1941 and composed a personal history as soon as she arrived as a refugee in Havana, Cuba, in November 1941. Both these documents are useful because they were written just a short time after their authors' emigration, when the experience of Nazi Germany was still fresh in their minds.

That there was a Jewish press under Nazi rule, and that in the regime's early years its activity and circulation were on the rise, is hardly something to be taken for granted. In practical terms it was a result of the regime's inclination, during these years, to seek to confine Jews to their own intracommunal world while allowing them to live within it with a certain modicum of freedom of action, under state oversight.[28] Under these circumstances, the Jewish press in Nazi Germany served, at least until the November 1938 pogrom ("Kristallnacht" in Nazi parlance), as a major force in the constitution and activity of the Jewish public sphere. As the historian Michael Nagel put it, it was "a kind of cover, a layer of protection between the Nazi regime and the isolated individual."[29] Over the course of these years, dozens of nationwide and local Jewish publications appeared, providing platforms for a wide range of political, cultural, and religious views, a kind of pluralism that continued to be characteristic of German Jewry at this time. The most important of these periodicals were *CV- Zeitung*—published by the Central Association and affiliated with the large centrist camp with which most German Jews, non-Orthodox and liberal in their social outlook, identified—the Zionist newspaper *Jüdische Rundschau*, and the nonpartisan *Israelitisches Familienblatt*. All three were distributed nationally and serve in this book as major sources for understanding currents in the German Jewish world and the way in which space and time were experienced. They represented different political and social camps in German Jewry, with their writers offering a socially and religiously liberal, Zionist, or other point of view. But the fact is that they all shared a fundamental affiliation with the bourgeois way of life and a profound connection to German culture. As such, when it came to issues touching on space and time, they were much more alike than they were different. Their representations of space and time can be found in editorials, announcements, and the opinion pieces that appeared on the front pages of newspapers, as well as in the publications' sports, children's, and especially women's supplements, which offer fresh and original insights. Occasionally even the advertisements offer conceptions of space and time. It is important to note that state surveillance of the Jewish press tightened over time and, as Thomas Pegelow Kaplan has shown, anti-Jewish linguistic violence increased. It was especially notable after the summer of 1935, when two of the most important papers were shut down by order of the Gestapo, and it grew even more severe after the promulgation of the Nuremberg Laws.[30] But most of the severe restrictions related to political issues and manners of identification, and as such the Jewish press, even under these strictures, is of great value in the study of lived space and time.

Both egodocuments and articles in the press reflect primarily the experiential world of the middle class, the members of which, both men and women, were much more inclined to write reflectively and were also readers of these publications. As most German Jews belonged to the middle class, and as much discourse in the press focused on the challenges presented by the wearing down of the bourgeois habitus, these sources are especially useful for this book.

Egodocuments, diaries in particular, may not necessarily be representative of the entire German Jewish population, but when used carefully they provide evidence of a complex range of Jewish experiences in the areas under discussion here. They also provide evidence about the ways Jews grappled with the new challenges they faced and the changes in their self-awareness. They offer exposure to the variety in the worlds of different social groups and classes and of different ages, both men and women, living in different parts of Germany. In contrast with these individual records, which depict personal experiences, the newspaper articles generally present views and offer readers ways of contending with new realities. For example, they show how writers, especially women writing in women's supplements, called on readers to cope with the challenges of shaping the experience of home under problematic conditions, and they offer different perspectives with regard to the annual cycle.

The study of the complex world of German Jews in the Nazi era, presented here through their being-in-the-world in space and time, exposes readers to issues of broad historical significance. It also touches on core issues of human existence everywhere. The way Jews coped with the oppressive system that pushed them out of German public space and robbed them of time is linked to the question of the way a society subject to forces far stronger and more arbitrary than itself can nevertheless have agency in the shaping of the fundamental life experiences of its members.

PART 1

Space

* CHAPTER ONE *

Public Space

Breslau was not the same city Willy Cohn had been born in forty-seven years earlier, as the historian and teacher wrote in his diary in August 1935. "Nazi party broadsides are blazoned all over the city, with *Der Stürmer*," he commented, referring to the Nazi newspaper notorious for its obscene antisemitic caricatures. "I no longer see them, in a really *bildich* [pictorial] sense."[1] This odd depiction by an educated man consciously choosing to disregard something happening before his eyes testifies to the fundamental challenge that many German Jews faced in the initial years of Nazi rule, and to their endeavors to cope with it. Cohn and others like him depicted profound and sweeping political and social changes by referring to their spatial manifestations. They attempted to comprehend their new circumstances in reference to the spatial changes that were the direct result of the new regime's explicit policy of seeking to entrench its rule by means of rapid transformations in the configuration of the public space. Newspapers disseminating propaganda, Nazi billboards, and the strident and proliferating presence of Sturmabteilung (SA) militiamen and other Nazi organizations in the street were only part of the regime's spatial strategy. On top of it came prohibitions preventing Jewish entry into specific urban and rural spaces and the construction of new towns and suburbs. This Nazification of public space not only put Nazi ideology on display but shaped a new type of social power relations.

About a year later, in September 1936, a new segment of highway was opened in the Breslau area. It was part of the Third Reich's freeway (*Reichsautobahn*) project, aimed at connecting the German nation and making the German landscape accessible to the masses.[2] Cohn, who had previously displayed a lively interest in the changes taking place around him, put down an account of the road's dedication ceremony, but said that he and other Jews avoided attending such formal events not out of fear but "so as to maintain the necessary distance. It barely touches us inside."[3] Such conscious choices demonstrate how the change in the space around him came to be reflected in his daily activity and in the meaning he assigned to his behavior.

In this chapter I examine the way German Jews depicted the Nazification of German public space, and the range of their reactions to it. I will open with a brief discussion of the refashioning of public space in Nazi Germany. I will then illuminate the way these processes were reflected in the reshaping of the experienced space of German Jews—in city streets and squares, public institutions of different kinds, and in open spaces and nature. The chapter presents the experiences, and the modes of response, of Jews as users of public spaces—among other ways, as pedestrians, drivers, visitors to institutions and sites, and vacationers—based both on personal diaries and correspondence and on the discourse in contemporary German Jewish newspapers.

The bulk of this chapter will focus on what I will refer to, following the philosopher and sociologist Henri Lefebvre, as the "lived space" (*espace vécu*) of the Jews.[4] In his book *The Production of Space*, Lefebvre noted how the hegemonic ruling power constitutes the space under its rule and regulates the way in which individuals living in its realm experience that space. While this perspective, which views the experience of space as being shaped from the top down, is not sufficient to encompass all complexities, it can serve as a good starting point for analysis of the spatial aspect of the Nazi regime's policy of excluding Jews. Because of their exclusion from many public spaces designated as Aryan, and their restriction to ever-shrinking closed Jewish spaces, their world was reordered as a narrow and delimited one.

Michel de Certeau, considering the production of space by the hegemonic power in *The Practice of Everyday Life*, places at the center the individuals who constitute their space through daily practices.[5] De Certeau's stress on the regime's strategic exclusion of the individual highlights the agency exercised by German Jews in shaping their lived space and time in the face of the increasingly severe restrictions imposed on them. Many of them shaped and even expanded the boundaries of their daily lives to the full extent that circumstances permitted, and to the full extent to which they were able to challenge the restrictions placed on them. It is reasonable to presume that such conduct applies to all historical situations, but in the present context it was realized under more extreme conditions and in a more deliberate way.

"Threatening Public Spaces": The Production of Nazi Public Space and the Exclusion of Jews

As soon as it took power, the new regime launched an intensive Nazification of public spaces, both by government regulation and by means of the activities of party organizations in the field. City streets were flooded with Nazi flags and military parades. Torchlight processions wended through the streets at night, and Nazism seized control of both visual and aural spaces.[6] Contemporary German letters and diaries testify to the intensity of the open display of Nazi symbols and people in Nazi uniforms in the street, their use in photography, and their pervasion of radio broadcasts and cinema newsreels. All these served to reconstitute the German collective and the public space.[7] "Hitler's voice is heard everywhere on loudspeakers, even if you walk on relatively empty streets," Cohn wrote in his diary on August 18, 1934. A year later, he noted the huge racket made by the Hitler Youth as they marched, with large drums, while he was writing in his diary.[8] Another means of appropriating the public space was the bloody street violence, principally by SA storm troopers against opponents of the regime and Jews. Beyond the immediate political goals it sought to achieve, this aggression had a symbolic and expressive significance; it was meant to be seen and heard, and to reshape consciousness.[9]

Just how rapidly this change took place is brought home by the political novel *Our Street*, which the Communist activist Jan Petersen wrote in the underground in Berlin in 1933–34. Petersen chronicles the rapid transformation in the early months following the Nazi rise to power on a single working-class street, Wallstrasse, in the city's Charlottenburg quarter. He writes of the sudden disappearance of the symbols of labor movements, which were replaced by swastikas. He also notes the closure of workers' pubs and clubs, and the opening of an SA Brown House. Arrests and brutal street violence became routine, as did an atmosphere of suspicion and denunciations among the street's inhabitants. In the end, the street's name was changed to commemorate Hans Maikowski, a storm trooper who was killed in a riot when the Nazis were striving to gain power.[10] The conquest of the German street, not only in Berlin and in other large cities but in provincial cities and rural areas, laid the foundation for the Nazi ascendance.

The Nazification of the public space was important to the new regime not only as part of its process of taking over Germany politically, but also as a central component of its policy of social engineering for the purpose of establishing the German "People's Community" (*Volksgemeinschaft*). Recent historical work has seen this process as key to understanding the nature of Nazism, because of its enormous effect on the daily lives of individual Germans.[11] Michael Wildt, who portrays the establishment of the people's community on the ruins of German bourgeois society as a project of manifestly territorial dimensions, shows that the transformation of German public space into one free of Jews was a leading principle in creating this imagined community.[12] The process, which in fact began in the years preceding 1933 by means of systematic Nazi party and SA activity to push the Jews out of the German lived space, redoubled in 1933 when signs began appearing at various sites declaring that Jews were not wanted. The Nazi regime, Alon Confino argues, pursued a series of symbolic activities to distance Jews from public space and to enable the establishment of a space without Jews in practice, first in small settlements and provincial cities and later on a much larger scale.[13] This created a situation in which, as Marion Kaplan recounts, the Jews were compelled to navigate their way through "increasingly menacing public spaces."[14]

The personal writings of German Jews of this time document a broad range of exclusions from public spaces of various sorts, due both to the top-down policy of the regime and to the behavior of social organizations and individuals who internalized the new attitudes. Siegfried Neumann, for example, recounted, beginning in March and April 1933, the process by which three Jewish jurists were pushed out of the courts in Berlin, while Victor Klemperer, during those same months, wrote about how Jewish students and instructors were denied entry to the students' club at the Dresden University of Technology.[15] Heinemann Stern of Berlin wrote in his memoirs that taking in a show at a German theater swiftly turned into an experience that Jews had to do without, almost without question. Some of them instead went to the Jewish Kulturbund—an organization founded by unemployed Jewish performers. Walter Tausk, born in 1890, had in the 1920s drifted away from the Jewish community in Breslau and affiliated with Buddhist groups. In early April 1933 he recorded in his diary how Schutzstaffel (SS) and SA patrols entered cafés and bakeries and asked the people there to identify themselves. Then they ejected anyone who looked Jewish to them. The café-bakery, which was a favorite haunt for bourgeois Germans of all kinds, became increasingly off-limits for many Jews, who instead had to patronize Jewish establishments.[16] Jews' memberships in trade unions and social organizations were suspended, and a wide range of Nazi daily practices and manifestations of hostility marked out for Jews the boundaries of their space. In 1933 a comment like "What are Jewish women doing here?" was enough to cause a Jewish mother who took her children to the traditional children's festival (*Kinderfest*) in the provincial city of Eichwald to leave, while a German pharmacist's cry of "Heil Hitler" in response to a parting greeting of "Auf Wiedersehen" was enough to tell a Jewish boy from Leipzig that in the future he should patronize a different pharmacy.[17] Above all, under the Nazi regime's refashioning of space, the street itself, the public space, turned largely into hostile territory that Jews found themselves being pushed out of.

The process of driving Jews out of public spaces was rapid and sweeping, but nevertheless the pace differed in different parts of the country. In large cities, Berlin above all, some public spaces remained open to Jews until at least the end of the 1930s, and Jews could use them at least at certain times. This was notably different from the case in provincial cities and rural areas, where the barring of Jews from public spaces already made their lives difficult during the Third Reich's early years.[18] The exclusion of Jews was much more visually apparent in peripheral areas, according to Michael Wildt. Anti-Jewish signs were impossible to avoid in small towns. In contrast with the situation in large cities, the boycott of Jews was relentless.[19] In provincial cities during the initial years of the regime, Jewish businesses, which exemplified their presence in the public space, were transferred to so-called Aryans, the term the Nazis used to refer to the German race. This contrasted with the situation in large cities, Berlin in particular, where Aryanization—the transfer of Jewish-owned property to non-Jews—went into high gear only in 1938.[20] In 1935, Hans Winterfeldt wrote in his memoir, the few dozen Jews who lived in Lippehne, Pomerania, could not show their faces in the city's guesthouses, in bathhouses, at the train station restaurant, or in parks. They did not dare encroach on the city's central square, the name of which was changed to Adolf Hitler Square. Invited to stay with a Jewish family in Berlin during Christmas 1935 and again in 1936, Winterfeldt, born in 1926, was astounded by how much liberty Jewish children had in the Third Reich's capital. They felt free to play in the city's open spaces.[21]

The acute plight of Jews in Germany's outlying areas was addressed by a series of articles in the Jewish press at the time.[22] Social and spatial isolation was much more suffocating for Jews in these areas, which were emptying of Jewish inhabitants, according to a report that appeared in May 1934 in *Jüdische Rundschau*. Daily connection to their surroundings was enormously significant to people living in small social settings and communities. They were very troubled when German neighbors stopped greeting them in the street.[23] Notably, the report's author used the term *eng* (narrow, confined) to denote—disapprovingly—the constricted lives of these Jews. He called on the members of large communities to maintain close contact with their counterparts in the provinces. Two-thirds of Germany's Jews lived outside Berlin, stated an article in the Central Association's *CV-Zeitung* two months later. There, in the provinces, the article reported, Jews encountered problems that could sometimes be disregarded in Berlin. For all their differences, the anonymous author claimed, the Jews in the provinces were much closer to the "time," as he called the new political circumstances—and Berlin's Jews thus needed to attend to their suffering.[24]

In 1935 Willy Cohn, who frequently visited Jewish communities in outlying parts of Silesia, addressed in his diary the increasing isolation of these Jews and the contraction of their public space, compared to the relatively benign conditions in his own city of Breslau.[25] This incongruence between the relative spatial freedom of Jews in the big city and the much more rigid spatial exclusion in remote cities appears also in the diaries of Klemperer, a literary scholar born in 1881 in Dresden who had converted to Christianity and married an "Aryan" woman. Klemperer, unlike all the other diarists cited here, neither emigrated nor was deported to the east, but survived in Nazi Germany until its fall. He wrote of the much more severe situation at the beginning of 1944, after the vast majority of Germany's Jews had already been deported and murdered:

> Einsenmann, already much recovered, visited us yesterday at about midday. Previously he was a considerable pessimist. He was now very optimistic. . . . He also said, about Berlin, that there one saw no Jews' stars on the street. They were covered up or not worn at all. He himself had used the tram and underground with his star covered—one simply could not get around Berlin in any other way, also in this huge mass of people it was not a risk, it was impossible for the Gestapo to recognize individuals, as they did here in the "village of Dresden."[26]

Levels of spatial exclusion differed not only geographically. The shunting of Jews out of German public spaces grew more extreme and violent in circumstances and at times of special importance in the Nazi symbolic order. Hitler's visit to Breslau in March 1936, recounted in Tausk's and Cohn's diaries, is a good example. The city was festooned with masses of flags and the police presence was boosted. The Nazi leader appeared in the city, according to Tausk, as a kind of messiah. The city streets through which his convoy passed were blocked off, and the Jews living on them were forbidden to leave their homes or even open windows facing the street throughout the event.[27] Even before they were forbidden to leave their homes, Cohn and his family shut themselves in because of the huge commotion on the streets. "We live our private lives," he wrote.[28] Hitler's appearance, it could be said, turned the city into a kind of Nazi sacred space, inevitably intensifying Jewish exclusion from it. Notably, this practice of marking out a sacred space by excluding Jews at the time of a formal ceremony, whether religious or royal, was in some ways a reversion to a pre-emancipation procedure. Something similar can be seen in the memoirs of Johann Wolfgang von Goethe, in his account of the election of the Holy Roman emperor in Frankfurt at the beginning of 1764. "On the evening before the day of the election," Goethe wrote following a long account of the meticulous preparations and formalities, "all the foreigners were removed from the city, the Jews were confined to their street, while the Frankfurt citizen's heart soared because only he was given leave to witness such an important ceremony."[29]

The pogrom of November 9, 1938, and the measures imposed in its wake—most importantly the incarceration of tens of thousands of Jewish men in concentration camps and a ream of new regulations and laws—marked a new stage in the regime's anti-Jewish policy. Many restrictions on the presence of Jews in the economy and public space were ensconced in law and made official policy.[30] About half of the approximately half-million Jews who had been living in Germany in 1933 managed to emigrate before World War II broke out, but those who remained faced much worse strictures. During the war's early years, many German Jews were forced to live in crowded "Jewish houses" (*Judenhäuser*). They were conscripted for forced labor, and in the end most of them were deported to the east. The German public space soon became, in practice, a space without Jews.

In the big picture, Jews reacted to their growing banishment from the public space in two principal ways, both of which found expression both in their personal writing and in public discourse. The first of these can be seen in the passage from Cohn with which I began this chapter. Cohn's response was one of detachment, abstention, seclusion, and alienation from the German public space. Different rationales for this response were offered, often by the very same writers. Sometimes it was presented as the inevitable result of the situation they faced, sometimes as a conscious choice to conduct a possible and even honorable way of life. In other cases, they framed it as a consequence of fear and as the manifestation of an unbearable situation.

The second response was one of resistance, of Jews tenaciously battling for their place in the public space. Jews used a range of tactics, in de Certeau's sense, to extricate themselves, if only in part, from the isolation and spatial suffocation that had been forced on them, and to continue to hold onto their daily routines to every extent possible. The two patterns are hardly binary opposites. Indeed, nearly all the writers quoted here availed themselves of both, and maneuvered between them in different circumstances, as part of how they grappled with the shaping of their lived space even as the policy of exclusion escalated.

"We Have Become Detached, We Have Lost the Ground from under Our Feet": Detachment, Abstention, Seclusion, and Alienation

"Between the sky and the earth" was how Alfred Wiener described the lives of the Jews around him in an article in *CV-Zeitung* in June 1933. Wiener addressed the disparity between their self-awareness of belonging to the public space and of being rooted in the German soil and the changes in their legal and economic status, which had detached them from German space. The Jews were in a "floating state" (*Schwebenzustand*) that they could not endure much longer.[31] Wiener's personal story reflects this instability. He called on his readers not to rush into ill-advised emigration from Germany, but he emigrated just months later, apparently because his political activity put him in danger.[32] About half a year later, Julie Meyer of Nuremberg offered Albrecht Dürer's engraving *Das grosse Glueck* (*The Great Luck*, also known as *Nemesis*), as a metaphor for the state of Germany's Jews, whose secure bourgeois world was crumbling. This work by Dürer, the renowned artist who had lived and worked in Nuremberg, depicts Fortuna, the goddess of luck, "in an empty space standing on a sphere without any outside source of support" (figure 1). Germany's Jews, Meyer wrote, could trust only their internal sense of balance.[33]

Wiener and Meyer, who came from the centrist camp, each called in their own way for readers to find a way to continue to keep their foothold in Germany. But their metaphors also depicted the spatial experience of many other German Jews who sensed that they were losing their grip in the country. As a result, they came to feel disengaged, empty, and caged in.

The diarists and memoirists tell of situations in which they at their own initiative avoided spaces of different kinds. One example came on Potsdam Day, March 21, a traditional Prussian event. In 1933 it was charged with new significance, as it marked the transfer of power from the conservative elites to the Nazi Party. Willy Cohn and his wife decided that it would best not to go through downtown Breslau that day, a tough emotional choice.[34] As I will show, in the years that followed Cohn was cut off from ever larger parts of his city. Hermann Klugmann, a high school teacher who generally spent part of his time in Wiesenbronn, the Bavarian village where he had been born, recounts in his memoirs the unbearable situation in the village on Sundays, when schoolchildren and adolescents roamed the streets. The harassment he suffered from them led him not to go out in public on this day. As pressure on the village's Jews increased, he relates, Jews increasingly had to retreat into "the tranquility of home."[35] Marta Appel of Dortmund wrote in her memoirs that, while she did not herself experience harassment in open public spaces, the fear of it led her to shut herself up at home. "I was not eager to leave home. . . . Actually, I never experienced such harassment in stores and on the street, but I anticipated them at every moment and the anxiety plagued me endlessly."[36] Appel's choice not to go to the theater or the cinema, she remarked, meant that when Jews were in fact formally barred from these places, it did not actually affect her. The view of Frieda Hirsch, an openly Zionist writer from Heidelberg, was that it was a mark of Jewish honor to stay away from German public spaces, including removing her children from their school at the beginning of April 1933, despite the fact that this was not yet required by the authorities.[37] An even more emphatic account of spatial withdrawal can be found in the diary of the Berlin physi-

Figure 1. Albrecht Dürer, *Nemesis*, ca. 1501–2. Courtesy of National Gallery of Art, Rosenwald Collection.

cian Herta Nathorff. In July 1933, when she was thirty-eight years old, she entered a shoe store and asked straight out whether it was a Jewish store. When the salesperson replied that "the entire staff is Aryan," Nathorff told him that she only patronized Jews and walked out.[38]

Voluntary disengagement from the Nazifying surroundings also involved avoidance of exposure to the German media. The historian Benedict Anderson has shown how exposure to newspapers, once they began to come out daily and were distributed to mass readerships, created a common experience through news reports that were read simultaneously and at regular intervals by large groups of people. This experience, Anderson argues, was of the utmost importance in consolidating solidarity among large numbers of readers spread over a large space, transforming them into "imagined communities," a key concept he proposed for the understanding of modern nationalism.[39] The decision by Victor Klemperer and his wife to stop reading newspapers, reported in his diary in June 1935, can be understood as a conscious attempt to sever ties with the Nazifying German imagined community. In other words, it can be seen as a choice to restrict their space. A few months later, when Klemperer felt he needed to know what was happening in the world, his renewed encounter with the German press caused revulsion. "It makes me physically sick," he wrote.[40] As the position of Jews grew ever more severe and as they felt more menaced, they tended to close themselves off and impose spatial restrictions on themselves. "There are Jews who no longer take the subway or the bus," Hans Reichmann reported in 1938 on Germany's cities. This was long before Jews were in fact forbidden to use public transportation, but middle-class Jews preferred to spend money on cabs so as to avoid confrontations.[41]

The experience of these writers extended beyond such self-isolation, the sense of suffocation and confinement that it produced, and the changes it caused in their personal experience of their space. Two feelings that come up again and again in their diaries, from the early years of the Nazi regime, are of increasing desolation and constriction. Kurt Rosenberg, a thirty-three-year-old Jewish attorney in Hamburg, portrayed his feeling that he and the members of his circle lacked any real connection to Judaism. "We are situated . . . in empty space. We remain in a quarantine of 'individualism.'"[42] This sense of emptiness was amplified by the disappearance of familiar anchors—institutions, objects, and people—from the bourgeois Jewish world they had known prior to 1933. Klemperer offered this account of shopping at the Tietz department store in January 1934. The emporium was owned by Jews and was about to shut down. The walls were bare, the tables half-empty, and the people crowding around them gave him the feeling of a space under evacuation.[43] Willy Cohn was shaken by the Night of the Long Knives, the bloody purge orchestrated by the Nazi regime at the beginning of July. It neutralized the political power of the SA and ratcheted up the atmosphere of political violence in Breslau's streets. He wrote of the emigration plans of many of his Jewish friends in Breslau. "It is becoming ever more empty around us," he wrote.[44] The palpable emptiness that Cohn experienced as a result of the thinning out of his social group seems to have become part of his inner experience. He was not spared it despite the fact that, unlike Rosenberg and Klemperer, he maintained an active connection to Judaism.

The sense of emptiness was accompanied by an increasingly powerful sense that the world was shrinking. Klemperer wrote in his diary in December 1933 that "recently, almost everything always seems small to me."[45] At this point, it should be noted, Klemperer's living conditions were much better than those he would have to cope with a few years later. He was still residing in his own home—indeed, he was about to move into a larger house—and was still teaching and earning a living, thanks to his standing as a World War I veteran who had served at the front. Nevertheless, his daily life worsened considerably during the first year of Nazi rule. His security about his future and his purchase on the space in which he lived quickly dwindled. During the years that followed, Klemperer frequently used the adjective *eng* (narrow) to describe how his living space continuously contracted.[46] Kurt Rosenberg wrote in the same vein that "the circumference of our lives is growing ever smaller."[47] Clearly, the emptying and narrowing of space outside individuals resonated in their internal mental spaces, and reshaped their views of their world.

This experience of rarefied and contracting space sometimes involved a conscious decision by Jews to disconnect mentally from their surroundings. "I have no heart for these things," Willy Cohn wrote in November 1934 in the face of the Nazi symbols that were taking over Breslau's public urban space. "A person lives best within their individual existence," he added.[48] In Cohn's case, as noted at the start of this chapter, his disengagement sometimes reached a sensual level: "I no longer see them, in a really *bildich* [pictorial] figurative sense."[49] The difficulties individuals have in coping with the huge quantity of sensory impressions that the modern city produces, according to sociologist Georg Simmel, leads them to filter them and to foster emotional indifference.[50] The context of Cohn's experiences in Breslau's public spaces was a different one, of course; but Simmel's insights can be of help in understanding his response. Cohn developed a defense mechanism against the surfeit of menacing sensory impressions that he encountered. The space he experienced was thus empty to a large extent because he consciously chose to empty it of the intimidating perceptions produced by the Nazi effort to refashion the German public arena.

Even so, a deliberate decision to turn their backs on the German space and turn their attention inward could not entirely obviate the feelings of pain and humiliation that many Jews experienced. "It is really bad to live in an environment inundated with such invective," Cohn wrote in his diary in September 1935 about the way the constant presence of *Der Stürmer* on billboards affected him. This was a statement that exposed the limitations of his mental and sensory disengagement. And what he consciously blocked out sometimes seeped into his unconscious. "Even though I try to give as little internal attention as possible to such things, I cannot avoid dreaming about them at night."[51]

Another response to spatial exclusion was a process of accumulative alienation. The city and region in which Jews had been born, in which they lived and acted, and where buildings and other sites figured in precious memories, now became alien and intimidating under Nazification. Hertha Nathorff was dismissed from her position at a Berlin hospital in 1933, compelling her to work with her husband at an improvised clinic in their home. In her diary she wrote much about coping with the changing conditions in Berlin's public spaces. At first, Nathorff tried to fight to maintain her foothold in the public space, but in the mid-1930s her diary evinced a process of alienation from the city, which, she wrote, had become "depressing."[52] Here, for example, is her description of Unter den Linden, the city's main boulevard, as a space that had been vandalized. It became tolerable only for a brief moment during the Olympic Games of the summer of 1936, when "the boxes with *Der Stürmer* with their disgusting photographs" were removed from the street.[53] "I go out to the street only when I absolutely must; everything repels me," Nathorff wrote, summing up her approach in November 1936. About a month later, on Christmas, she rode with her husband one morning through the posh Grunewald neighborhood. "It all seemed foreign, it's no longer 'mine,'" she wrote.[54] From time to time, for example during October 1938, Nathorff recalled that Berlin locations which "had once seemed to me to be the apotheosis of all that was wonderful and good."[55] But now the city's streets and many of its buildings, especially the police headquarters at Alexanderplatz, were more and more ominous.[56]

Kerstin Schoor, a German literary scholar, has collected and analyzed hundreds of literary works written by German Jews under the Nazi regime. She finds that, as the spatial restrictions imposed on Jews grew more severe, urban spaces in these works came to be described as nameless, foreign, and alien.[57] One example is a children's book, *Spatz macht sich* (Spatz makes do), by Meta Samson, published in 1938.[58] In contrast with the protagonists of children's books of the Weimar period, such as the bands of children in Erich Kästner's stories, the Jewish heroine of Samson's book did not experience the streets of her city as safe spaces that spurred her curiosity. Spatz's dominant experience in her encounters with the Nazified city was one of confusion, helplessness, and alienation.[59]

The experience of detachment and alienation from the public space, like the tactic of abstention and self-isolation, were imbued with new contexts by the Jews who remained in Germany after the November 1938 pogrom and during the war. "It is impossible to sit anywhere, it is impossible to enter anywhere," Willy Cohn wrote of the way he felt two days after the pogrom. He described the circumstances that led him to impose home detention on himself, out of fear that he would be arrested and sent to a concentration camp, as had happened to many others.[60] While Cohn gave in to his wife's importuning that he go out for a short walk, when it was over he continued to hole up in his home for many days thereafter. Cohen's deepening alienation from the city of his birth was evident a few weeks later, when he went out to the market to buy his youngest daughter an orange. "I felt like a foreigner. People are doing their last-minute Christmas shopping. We live outside that."[61] "We have become detached," Hans Reichmann wrote, attempting to sum up the Jew's existential experience a short time after he emigrated from his homeland in the spring of 1939. "We have lost the ground under our feet, we have been banished from the security of bourgeois life—without work, without a home, without a homeland."[62]

A curfew was imposed on those Jews who remained in Germany when World War II broke out. They were forbidden in the winter to leave their homes after 8 p.m. and in the summer after 9 p.m., exacerbating the sense of isolation and alienation.[63] When Victor Klemperer and his wife missed the last bus home one night in November 1940, they feared they would not get home in time. "I felt as if I were a hunted animal," he wrote in his diary.[64]

The regulation requiring German Jews to wear yellow stars on their clothing came into force on September 19, 1941. It was an especially harsh stricture for Klemperer. A day earlier, he had gone for a walk with his wife in Dresden, which felt to him like a final vacation before a long incarceration. On the day the badge became mandatory, he imposed on himself an even stricter isolation in the *Judenhaus* he had lived in since May 1940, to avoid the humiliation of being seen with it.[65] Surveying the year that had passed on December 31, he wrote that, since the imposition of the edict, he had been "completely cut off . . . sitting at home for days on end."[66] Further incidents of harassment led him to resolve that he would no longer go far from the *Judenhaus*. He would take only a few needed steps to take in some fresh air.[67]

In contrast, Philipp Manes, a sixty-four-year-old Jewish businessman in Berlin, responded much more tranquilly to the yellow star. "As of today we are marked [*ausgezeichnet*]," he punned on the day the rule came into effect—the German word can also mean "outstanding." Two days later, he calmly proposed taking a wait-and-see approach about how the yellow star would affect the attitude of Germans on the street to Jews.[68]

Elisabeth Block, fifteen years old, lived with her family in the Bavarian town of Niedernburg. She seldom wrote of political matters in her diary, but she was distraught about the prohibition against leaving home without the yellow star on her clothing. She experienced the obligation primarily as a limitation on her freedom of movement in rural public spaces, in particular hikes in the mountains.[69] But her diary describes nothing of the self-isolation and deliberate disengagement from public spaces of the type that Klemperer recounted. Instead, she tried to keep a hold on her freedom of movement, something she was able to do because she worked for farmers in the adjacent village of Benning. About a month later, she went so far as to note that, because of the difficult atmosphere at home, she deliberately avoided going there in the evening, preferring to sleep over with the farmers.[70]

These different reactions, even at the beginning of the 1940s, reflect to a large measure the different diarists' attitudes toward their Jewish backgrounds. Klemperer, the Christian convert, was humiliated when his Jewish origins were put on display. Manes suffered a great deal from other spatial restrictions, but was more relaxed about his origins and felt less embarrassed by the badge. Block, for her part, wanted most of all to maintain her daily experience of space. She was deported with her family at the end of March 1942 in a transport to Lublin, where they were almost certainly murdered. Manes and his wife were deported from Berlin in July of that year to the Theresienstadt ghetto, where he continued to keep his diary for more than two years. He and his wife were sent to Auschwitz and murdered in October 1944. Klemperer was not deported to the east, largely because his Christian wife was classified as an Aryan. To every extent he could, he continued to carry on his closed-off life in the *Judenhaus* in Dresden until the Allied bombing of the city in February 1945, at which time he removed the yellow star from his clothes and survived until the end of the war while concealing his Jewish origins.[71]

"I So Enjoy Going to the Cinema; It Takes Me Out of Myself": Daily Battles over Public Spaces

Isolation—whether by choice, by compulsion, or by self-alienation from the German public space—was not the only way Jews responded. Another way can best be understood with the help of Michel de Certeau's spatial theses. Jews—acting in this context as persons in the street facing the hegemonic Nazi system that shaped the rules for the production of space—tried to act in different ways to produce for themselves a tenable experience of space and to imbue their daily lives, which grew narrower and narrower, with meaning. This was not general "resistance" in the usual sense of the word, but rather something closer to what the Israeli Holocaust scholar Yehuda Bauer terms *amidah*, a Hebrew concept that might be rendered as "resilience," but which Bauer admits is "almost impossible to translate." It has nevertheless become an accepted term in Israeli historiography of the Holocaust. Another possibility is "defiance," the term recently discussed in Wolf Gruner's studies of the individual responses of German Jews.[72]

On February 24, 1933, during the violent election campaign conducted under Nazi rule, an article on the political violence of the ruling party appeared in *Jüdische Rundschau*. In many places, it claimed, Jewish gatherings had been scheduled in halls adjacent to Nazi rallies, and many were well attended despite the difficult atmosphere. This manner of maintaining a hold on the public space was linked by the author to Jewish dignity (*Würde*).[73] Autobiographical texts and diaries, especially from the earlier period of the Nazi regime, document assertive efforts to test and even challenge the restrictions imposed on Jewish space. Walter Tausk, for example, recounted in his diary his entry into the Breslau courthouse in March 1933, despite the SA guards stationed there to keep out Jewish interlopers. According to Tausk, this was a kind of battle for space, during which he mocked "the soldiers of the Third Reich."[74] He also reacted to the Nazification of the public space, which was flooded with swastika flags, by hanging a Prussian flag from the window of his room, to show that he was no less patriotic than anyone else.[75] But such acts, which involved making political statements and constituted a direct challenge to the Nazi spatial strategy, seem to have been few and far between. They were largely restricted to the regime's initial months. Once the regime had established itself firmly in power, this sort of defiance became extremely rare.

An interesting example of such conduct comes from the memoirs of Gerta Pfeffer, a young Jewish woman from a provincial city in southwest Germany.[76] Pfeffer recounted her fears of being seen in the street with her non-Jewish friends, but stressed that she did not allow herself to be shut up at home. She went out every night and stayed out until late, and was not deterred from frequenting cafés. On weekends and holidays, she wrote, she felt a need to be in a different environment. She dared to hitch rides, asking to be taken a long way outside the city. Pfeffer's memoirs offer a good account of her dread of the onerous spatial restrictions that life in a provincial city imposed. Among other things, she mentions the opening of an SS office in the building she lived in, and her apprehensions each evening when she returned home, fearing that she would run into the black-uniformed Nazis. She was also perturbed by the "Jews unwanted" signs and graffiti that she encountered in areas through which she she walked. Nevertheless, her need to express her selfhood by moving through space and maintaining a hold on it overcame her fears and compelled her to go on dangerous outings so as to shape her life more freely.

The act of creating one's consciousness of self via the extent of one's living space involved more than freedom of movement. This sense of self also emerged from the use of specific spaces that Jews shaped in their daily lives, and from the class identities they had acquired during the age of emancipation. Mirjam Zadoff conceptualized it in an interesting way in her book on Jews at German spa resorts, which she termed as one of a range of types of bourgeois experiential spaces.[77] Spa sites in Central European resort towns—as well as other spaces in which German Jews stayed, and which they used daily in the cities where they lived, such as cafés, theaters, cinemas, public libraries, and museums—enabled Jews to take part in the modern bourgeois culture of consumption.[78] In the age of emancipation, attending such sites and participating in the activities they offered, according to the rules of each, had played an important role in German Jews' creation of the bourgeois self. When Jews were pushed out of these sites, it thus affected not only their daily routines but the way they experienced their selves. This is essential for understanding their daily struggles to maintain their presence at these sites as part of their fight to shape their identities in a time of crisis.

Visits to cinemas, which can serve as an example of holding onto this type of space, are recounted from time to time in Victor Klemperer's diary as an activity that brought some relief to him and his wife in their struggle with the difficulties of the world in which they found themselves. "I so enjoy going to the cinema," he wrote on March 20, 1933, after seeing a film for the first time after a long hiatus. "It takes me out of myself."[79] Such visits had once been routine but now took on great significance; they enabled Klemperer to continue imagining himself, at least to a certain extent, as part of the community around him. They helped him experience a small measure of continuity. In subsequent years the couple went to the cinema less frequently, but these excursions were noted in the diary as events of great importance, part of their larger struggle to maintain their way of life and imbue their drab days with meaning. For example, in July 1937 Klemperer related that he had "rediscovered" a cinema that "was cheaper than the other cinemas." It was, he wrote, "a real haven." A few months later, he described further visits there as a kind of solace.[80] The effort that Jews had to put out just to maintain even a bit of their moviegoing can also be seen in a comment by Hertha Nathorff in her diary about Jewish acquaintances of hers in southern Germany. To see a film in 1935 they made a special trip to another city so that they would not be identified as Jews.[81] Under much more severe conditions, Cäcilie Lewissohn, who lived in Berlin throughout the war under an assumed identity, continued to go the movies from time to time. She also sometimes dined at the Kempinski restaurant (which had in the past been under Jewish proprietorship) on Berlin's west side during the years 1943 and 1944. In some cases she described these visits as festive occasions, holidays she made for herself.[82] At the end of 1944 Lewissohn's identity was revealed, and she was deported to Auschwitz and murdered. It is important to remember that visits to the cinema did more than simply provide a way for Jews to maintain a foothold in the public space and normal bourgeois practice, and an escape from the harsh circumstances. It also exposed them to the Nazi appropriation of the public space, in the form of newsreels that served as a central tool of Nazi propaganda.[83]

Another way Jews found to shape for themselves, even if only for a time, a less oppressive experience of space than what the Nazis sought to impose on them was to take vacations, both outside and inside Germany. In previous decades the annual vacation had become an important part of the bourgeois culture of travel, one that many German Jews adopted as a standard component of their spatial experience.[84] The economic consequences of the Nazi rise to power made a vacation abroad less manageable in light of shrinking family budgets, but also magnified, for those who could still afford one, the need to get outside the Third Reich, at least for a time. Those who did so not only bought themselves an "illusion of a normal middle-class existence,"[85] but expressed a certain measure of agency in shaping their spatial experience. Siegfried Neumann, who lost his position as a notary—in Germany a prestigious profession that required academic training—and who ran into difficulties in his efforts to emigrate, described in his memoirs the experience of traveling to Prague with his wife for Christmas in 1933 as "getting out of jail." About a year and a half later, the two went by boat for a vacation in Italy, and felt a sense of liberation and serenity as soon as they crossed the border.[86] Kurt Rosenberg, who made frequent trips abroad, described them in 1933 in his diaries as "breathing breaks" that allowed him to experience, from time to time, the "normal" bourgeois life that had been taken from him in his homeland.[87] In a similar spirit, the Berlin physician Erich Seligmann, who also made occasional trips abroad, portrayed a vacation in Italy in August 1937 as "five weeks in which we did not feel the weight of the German handcuffs."[88] His account of his return from this vacation was highly charged: it was like going back to prison. Because of the importance of these trips for Seligmann, he was extremely anxious about the prospect that he might lose his passport, or that it might not be renewed because he was Jewish. This anxiety, he wrote, was like a rope tightening around his neck.[89] The delay in processing his passport each time he needed to renew it heightened his apprehension, which was far from being unjustified. As early as September 1935, the German secret police had proposed restricting travel of Jews outside the country by not issuing them passports.[90] Measures of this sort were, however, only put into force about two years later.

More Jewish families traditionally took vacations within Germany. They continued to do so during the initial years of the Nazi regime, but the nature of these outings changed in a very real way. Like other public spaces in Germany, many vacation spots began excluding Jews, accelerating a trend that had already begun toward the end of the Weimar Republic, and which escalated considerably in 1933. They were thus left to patronize Jewish vacation spots.[91] In an article that appeared in a special supplement that *Israelitisches Familienblat* devoted to the subject in June 1936, Arno Herzberg stressed the need for a calmer spell from time to time, to distract the mind from quotidian concerns. He referred to the Jewish resorts still operating in Germany, which under the circumstances had transformed into isolated Jewish enclaves, places in which Jewish vacationers could form transitory communities free of the troubles of these times.[92] A few months later, in an article he wrote for the Frankfurt Jewish newspaper, Eduard Schreiber likened Jewish vacations to leaving constrictedness (*Enge*) space for spaciousness (*Weite*). He tried to characterize the disparity between the significance of vacations for Jews prior to the Nazi period and that which emerged under the new regime.[93] While he acknowledged the continuity, he also noted a change in the experience. Vacationers traveled no longer as individuals but as Jews, a change that reflected the restrictions on their choice of destinations as well as on the scope of their activities. "We have lost a great deal," Schreiber wrote toward the end of his article, "but have we gained something? Are the things that we now experience during our vacations not of greater value than the pleasures of vacations in the past?"[94] He left it to his readers to answer the question.

"Auto, Auto über Alles": Jews, Automobiles, and Driving in Nazi Germany

Victor Klemperer began learning how to drive in December 1935, and decided to cash in his life insurance policy to pay for a car. The decision ran contrary to all financial logic or long-range planning. Klemperer and his wife had moved at the end of 1934 to their new home, which they had purchased and renovated painstakingly, and had endured relentless economic tension that was exacerbated when he was dismissed from his job in May 1935, obtaining a deeply disappointing pension settlement. His decision to become a driver at the end of 1935, which he summed up in his diary as "our most sedentary year," was explicitly intended to restore to him and his wife something of their sense of open space. "The car will give us a little bit of life and of the world again," he wrote.[95] In January 1936 he passed his driving test, which was for him "a victory over my own nature . . . and a matter of the utmost importance."[96] Klemperer and other Jews who drove on German roads penned interesting and novel accounts of how they coped with the challenge of having their space restricted, and the agency they exercised in shaping for themselves their experience of open space, to the extent that they could do so under the new circumstances.

Klemperer had made his decision because he saw "cars all around." In a diary entry, he explained that "nearly all the quite ordinary people on our new streets have their garage."[97] According to Rudy Koshar, the private automobile became the principal symbol of the new culture of travel that characterized Germany in the 1920s, and even more so in the 1930s. Hitler's vision of a "nation on wheels," the basis of the great project of paving high-speed roads, spurred a sixfold increase in German automobile production between 1933 and 1939. Automobiles became a principal component of German popular culture. They featured in new games, and in magazines devoted to them.[98]

The increasing popularity of traveling by private car, including among Jews, was clearly evident from the mid-1930s in advertisements in the Jewish press that touted Jewish driving schools, car rentals for Jews, garages serving Jews, and other such services.[99] More and more Jews of all ages and genders were taking driving lessons, reported *Israelitisches Familienblatt* in February 1937. Many of them, according to the newspaper, did so as part of their preparations for leaving Germany. Some planned to be cab or truck drivers in their new countries.[100]

Friedrich Solon, a Jewish attorney of Klemperer's age from Berlin, recounted in his memoirs the purchase of an automobile in 1936, using money obtained from the sale of a family asset. "This car played an important role in my life," he wrote. "Driving it gave me enormous pleasure . . . and it was also vital for me on the professional level."[101] Indeed, in some cases driving was essential to economic survival. A traveling Jewish salesman who applied to a Jewish aid organization for assistance that would enable him to carry on his work in Germany's peripheral regions, which were growing more hostile, received a commercial vehicle. As more and more wayside inns stopped catering to Jews, he also slept in his vehicle during his sales trips.[102]

While the Nazi regime allowed Jews to drive in Germany during its initial years, exclusionary spatial practices were soon evident. The German Automobile Club, founded in 1933 as part of the regime's *Gleichschaltung* (coordination) process, decided in 1935 to expel all its "non-Aryan" members. This compelled Jewish drivers to form Auto-Club 1927, which became for all intents and purposes a Jewish organization. At the end of 1936 the Gestapo forced it to change its name to the Jüdischer Auto-Club.[103] These decisions had no immediate impact on Jewish drivers, but they heralded changes to come.

The experience of driving took a central place in Klemperer's diary in the years 1936 to 1938, and made a big change in his routine. In May 1936 he went so far as to parody the German national anthem by exclaiming: "Auto, Auto über alles, erster und letzter Gedanke" (Car, car over all, it is the first and last thing we think of).[104] His initial dealings with the car were frustrating, mostly because of technical difficulties, but it took only a few months for him to find driving a great pleasure, opening up new spaces for him and his wife. He frequently documented his trips in his diary, recording the distances he traveled and the landscapes he took in. Despite the constant need to economize on gasoline, which greatly limited his use of the car, Klemperer drove to Berlin in May 1937 and raved about driving its avenues.[105] To put it in the terms of contemporary sociology, Klemperer, like other Jews who continued to use their private vehicles despite and perhaps precisely because of the political circumstances, merged with their automobiles to become "driver-cars," autonomous selves that were more liberated and mobile than they had been before.[106]

The space that opened before Klemperer thanks to his driving had other implications, however. Passing through villages and provincial cities exposed him again and again to the intensity with which German space was undergoing Nazification. In Kipsdorf, for example, he enjoyed fine vistas but also noted that the main street had been named after Adolf Hitler, and that *Der Stürmer* was prominently displayed in public. In the autumn of 1936, while traveling on the new autobahn in the region of Dresden and relishing the opportunity to drive at fifty miles per hour, he was also bombarded with Nazi propaganda. About two years later, when his brother sent him money that enabled him to make a trip with his wife and two friends to Leipzig, the travelers stopped at a truck stop restaurant (*Fernfahrerrestaurant*), where they had to endure the very loud broadcast of a speech by Hermann Göring at a Nazi Party Congress.[107] But beyond all this, at the bottom of Klemperer's experience as a driver during these years lay the question he posed to himself back on March 29, 1936, when Germany held elections in which he could not vote because he was a Jew: "Is a Jewish professor allowed to have a car, to be 'noticeable' in any way?"[108] The query encapsulated the inherent tension between, on the one hand, the tactic Klemperer used to broaden his lived space, as de Certeau would have it, and perhaps even empower his selfhood by means of a daily practice of driving, and on the other hand his awareness that, fundamentally, the strategic power system that produced the space around him would not permit that in the long term. Klemperer was not the only Jew to feel this way. At the beginning of the summer of 1938, just before his emigration to the United States, Frederick Weil, a wine merchant from Frankfurt, took a road trip several weeks long throughout Germany. While the principal part of his experience was his encounter with the country's varied natural settings, that could not be separated from the experience of driving itself. Long, slow drives were a way for him and his wife to bid farewell to the beloved landscapes of their homeland. Some two years later Weil wrote, "I often had the feeling of enjoying a last meal."[109]

Indeed, the escalation of anti-Jewish pressure in Germany in 1938 transformed the presence of Jews in the German transport system to an increasingly fraught issue. For example, about a third of the 1,500 Jews who were branded "asocial" and sent to concentration camps in the roundup of June 1938 were arrested because of traffic violations.[110] A secret directive, issued by Berlin's chief of police on July 20, 1938, mandated particularly strict standards in granting driver's licenses to Jews, and authorized revoking them immediately in cases in which Aryans would have first received a warning. At every opportunity, it ordered, Jewish vehicles were to be searched "extremely thoroughly for specific shortcomings . . . and if necessary they are to be impounded until further notice."[111] Furthermore, a Joint Distribution Committee report on the condition of the Jews in Germany stated a few weeks later that "cars belonging to Jews were recently given special numbers . . . from 300,000 on. Thus, they are known to be owned by Jews. Such cars are not given any petrol on the autostrades [autobahns]."[112] For Friedrich Solon, a fine he received after an automobile accident in which he was involved took on critical significance. In his memoirs, he recounted how the initiative to mark Jewish cars quickly impelled him to sell his automobile, out of fear that he might find himself the victim of violence or blackmail. Arthur Samuel, a Jewish physician from Bonn, was stranded when his car broke down on the road on a winter night. He was so apprehensive of receiving a severe punishment that he abandoned his car on the roadside.[113]

Victor Klemperer's period as a driver reached its end in early December 1938, with the promulgation of an edict that revoked the driver's licenses of Jews forthwith.[114] This order, according to Klemperer's account, proclaimed that Jewish driving was detrimental to the German transportation community (*deutsche Verkehrsgemeinschaft*), stressing in particular the Jews' insolence in daring to use the new highways built by the hard work of German laborers. This aggressive act cut short the efforts of Klemperer and other Jewish drivers to expand their spaces, and thus to augment their sense of self by means of driving. "Until December more or less I still had use of the car and we were mobile," he wrote in his appraisal of 1938. "It was a little bit of freedom and life after all—no matter how pitiable it may have been."[115] From this point onward, his experiential space narrowed a great deal. Significantly, he continued to think and dream about his car and his experience as a driver for many years thereafter, when his living conditions in general, and the spatial restrictions imposed on him, grew much more severe.[116]

"I [Am] Always Dependent on What I Happen to Be Able to Borrow": The Library as a "Production Space" in the World of Intellectuals

In December 1938, during which Klemperer was deprived of his ability to drive around Germany, he was also denied access to the institution that was perhaps the most central to his everyday professional activity: the library. Public libraries of different types—municipal and academic, for example—were spaces of practice of critical importance to the constitution of modern bourgeois selfhood, which achieved its striving for the accumulation of knowledge and experience largely through reading.[117] Libraries were all the more important to Jewish scholars like Klemperer and Cohn, who also used them as their regular work spaces. The centrality of libraries in the lives of these two men only increased during the early years of the Nazi regime. These were people who engaged in research and writing, and who devoted themselves to these activities all the more intensively after having been dismissed from their teaching positions. As such, their presence in a library, and their access to books they needed, was a vital element in their daily experience, one that granted it meaning. As the streets, workplaces, and other spaces turned menacing and exclusionary, libraries continued for a time to function as open and neutral spaces, inclusive enclaves that continued to operate in the spirit of the values of the waning liberal era. So Cohn recounted his regular visits to the municipal library and to that of the University of Breslau as experiences that at times could distract him from harsh events and the hostile atmosphere in the street. Klemperer, in September 1935, just a few months after his dismissal from his job, portrayed the library as the only place he went to outside his home, other than when shopping for essentials.[118]

Klemperer recounted that, in October 1936, he was given notice that, not being an Aryan, he was no longer permitted to use the library's reading room. His borrowing privileges remained in force, as well as his access to the catalogue room, but the reading room was out of bounds. A few days later a librarian informed him that the books he had authored had been removed from the reading room, another symbolic sign of his exclusion.[119] Two years later, at the beginning of December 1938, as part of the strict spatial constraints imposed on Germany's Jews after the November pogrom, Klemperer was banned from the library entirely. The decree, he wrote, caused him "utter paralysis." Cohn, who frequently wrote in his diary about how he struggled to find time for intellectual endeavors and about his devotion to his scholarly projects, noted a few weeks later that the interdict against Jews using the municipal library in Breslau, where he had been a regular since 1904, made it enormously difficult for him to carry on with his work.[120]

For Cohn and Klemperer, research and writing were vital practices that imbued their lives with meaning. It freed them from the menace of a routine of proletarian nature, one focused solely on production and consumption—what Hannah Arendt would later term in her book *The Human Condition* as "mere labor." It was a peril that they both frequently complained about. Scholarship opened before them a higher plane of creativity or work, to use Arendt's terms.[121] How, then, did these two men respond to their exclusion from the library as a space, a harsh restriction that threatened to put an end to their research activity? Their entire diary of the months and years that followed shows that they found ways to shape their daily lives under these new circumstances, and to create a space that would provide for this vital need.

In February 1939, a few weeks after the municipal library closed its doors to him, Cohn reported in his diary a dream in which he was again at the library, reading the journal *Historische Zeitscrhrift*, and another dream in which he was as riding a horse. These, he wrote, were dreams about what he had lost. He continued to work on an article on the Jewish community in Berlin, and to amass material on the subject from every possible source.[122] A few months later he received permission from the Catholic authorities in Breslau to work in the Church archives and library in the city, and to borrow books.[123] The Breslau Church archive was a sort of gray zone, the status of which had not been formally defined by the authorities. Already during his initial days working there, Cohn was aware of the lack of clarity over the legitimacy of his presence. On June 5, 1939, he wrote that "each day I once again offer thanks." The next day, he added that "the Catholic authorities need to be wary of unpleasant consequences. I work in a state of great strain to collect as much material as possible."[124] Cohn continued to work in the Church library and archive on an almost regular basis for more than two years, until his deportation at the end of 1941. His presence there enabled him to carry on, to some extent, the research work that had been so significant for his routine and for his experience of selfhood. "I went to the Church archive," he wrote in March 1941. "Something is missing for me if I don't go there."[125]

Cohn's admittance to this space, which he called a "sleepy institution," after being excluded from the municipal library, can serve as a good example of how Jewish individuals shaped their daily routines by making use of their connections from "below" (in this case the administrators of the Church archives), despite the severe restrictions imposed from "above." The time Cohn spent in the Church library was for him an opportunity to mingle, on a daily basis, with "Aryan" Germans. Most, if not all, treated him warmly, saw to his needs, and regretted his absence when he did not show up for a few days. They also tried to help him. "I experienced there a great deal of love that restores my faith in humankind," he wrote.[126] He also continued to visit a private lending library, at least until the end of 1940, and to avail himself of the assistance of non-Jews in obtaining volumes from the university library.[127]

Klemperer, who unlike Cohn did not manage to find an alternative library in Dresden, redefined his creative space in a different way. Being barred from the Dresden library forced him to halt his research on the French Enlightenment in the eighteenth century, and created a situation in which "I am now literally without work." On December 6, 1938, just three days after the ban went into effect, he reported in his diary that he had decided to devote himself to writing an autobiography, later published under the title *Curriculum Vitae: Erinnerungen*.[128] Beginning at this point, and for more than two years, he cast his writing of *Curriculum Vitae* as a research project, the most significant focus of his activity. The move toward writing his own life story, along with his inclination to look to the past (which will be discussed in chapter 6) was in practical terms a way of circumventing the necessary connection between the library as a space and the access to books that it provided, and the research and writing practice that was so vital for him. Turning his life into the object of his study largely freed him from his dependence on sources. He even developed a capacity for working in his home and, later, in the much less comfortable conditions of the crowded *Judenhaus*. In his devotion to this project, Klemperer constructed for himself a creative space that was largely independent of the space from which he had been excluded.

Nevertheless, the increasingly harsh restrictions imposed on his daily life detrimentally affected this initiative as well. Klemperer was compelled at the end of 1941 to hand over his typewriter. He resolved to continue the project by hand.[129] In the end, the Gestapo's invasive search policy meant that his home lost all privacy. Writing an autobiography at home exposed him and those close to him to mortal danger. So he stopped working on it in March 1942 and, with the help of a non-Jewish friend, moved all the material connected to it out of his house.[130] Klemperer's commitment to his research work, so vital a part of his selfhood, did not stop even here. From this point on, he devoted himself to reading books, getting them from every possible source, and jotting down notes in them that would serve him when he resumed writing his memoir. Again and again in his diary he recorded attempts to gain entry to different libraries, such as the Jewish library, a lending library (*Leihbibliothek*), and even the private libraries of Jews who had been deported to the east. He sought to obtain almost any available book so as to carry on with his work. "I [am] always dependent on what I happen to be able to borrow," he wrote. To express his anxiety, Klemperer evoked the term "*leere*," meaning "empty," which in this context served as a metaphor for his experience of both space and time. In light of this terror, it could be said that his constant attempts to obtain and peruse books, along with his continual writing in his diary, expressed his ongoing search for gray areas that would enable him to actualize his habits, at the center of which stood his research.[131]

"The Year of Summer Rambles": Everyday Struggles in German Space during World War II

The prohibitions against driving and going to libraries were only a few of the restrictions imposed on what remained of Jews' freedom of movement after the November pogrom and especially after World War II began. The nighttime curfew imposed on them when the war broke out and the policy of forcing them into *Judenhäuser*, which intensified at that time, aggravated their situation. As the pressure increased from the outside to limit the space allowed to Jews, it intensified their need to get out of their homes and to try to stretch to the greatest possible extent the boundaries of that space. Willy Cohn's diary includes many accounts of walks he took by himself, with his wife, and with his daughters in their urban environment and out in nature, for the most part in the evenings and at night. These walks continued despite the tightening limitations on their movements. On a long walk he took around Breslau in June 1940 with his daughter Tamara, a toddler, he systematically searched for benches that were not marked "prohibited to Jews." Whenever they found one, the two of them sat on it. A few weeks later, when ever more park benches around the city were marked in this way, they sat on the benches where passengers waited for the streetcar, as had not yet been officially forbidden. Cohn also wrote of his efforts to take maximum advantage of the ability to remain outside until the curfew began at 9 p.m. summer time.[132]

Cohn's evening walks carried on a habit that dated back to 1933 and even before. The Klemperers, in contrast, were shut up in their home for long periods and began going out for long walks only in 1940, after they were forced in May of that year to leave their spacious home and move into a crowded *Judenhaus*. "A series of extended walks have been added to our usual activities," Klemperer wrote in his diary at the end of August 1940. Following a bus ride, the couple strolled for three hours in the countryside, where Klemperer recorded encountering sights he had not known as a driver.[133] While walking, he fantasized that in the future when he would again be allowed to drive, he would combine driving and walking, seeing them as two ways of coming to know this kind of space that he was coming to experience only under the conditions imposed on him by the Nazi regime. Being compelled to move to a *Judenhaus* had its advantages, he wrote in his diary, summing up 1940: "For the first time in years Eva learnt to walk again, even to go for long walks."[134]

These evening walks, which displayed a craving to experience freely as much of the urban environment as possible, may be understood in the spirit of the *flaneur*, of which Franz Hessel and Walter Benjamin wrote.[135] Like these two writers, both Cohn and Klemperer expressed their hold on the city by walking casually around it, despite the onerous constraints. To this end, they used, among other things, the major resource that remained to them: free time. It was a manifest expression of the use by individuals of practice from "the bottom up," as de Certeau calls it.

The battle to maintain a hold on space continued under even harsher circumstances, and when there was no free time. Such was the case with Elisabeth Freund, an economist born in 1898 who had published books on home economics (the field now known as family and consumer sciences). In April 1941 she was conscripted into forced labor in a laundry, and afterward in an arms factory in Berlin. Freund and her husband, who had sent their three children out of Germany in 1939, were waiting for an emigration visa that eventually enabled them to go to Cuba in October 1941, just a short time before the remaining Jews were forbidden to leave Germany. As soon as they reached Havana in November, Freund wrote for her children an account of her and her husband's final six months in Berlin.[136] She recounted in detail her daily life as a forced laborer under severe conditions, the contraction of their living space, and the terrors of Nazi Berlin.

Central to Freund's life during these months were her long work hours, from the early morning until nearly midnight. Nevertheless, after an exhausting day in the spring of 1941, when the workers had left the factory, she and two friends chose to take a long detour:

> The ways we took home were magnificent. They were wonderful nights, full of May stars! The scent of lilacs wafted from all the gardens. In the sky

> the lights of the air defense flashed. We found a path that passed through gardens and a meadow. Kaethe, Omi, and I walked there every night. Others walked in a large group by a shorter way. But we liked the long way. To see the moon floating above the black poplars and the stars twinkling and shining—that was an experience that they could not take from us even with that slave labor [*Sklavenarbeit*].[137]

Freund and her friends needed these broad vistas as compensation for their shrunken and unfree lives as forced laborers, and made an effort to take them in even when they were exhausted. They created for themselves the best way to do this: a spatial tactic they developed to cope with their difficult life circumstances. On Sundays, Freund even went out with her husband, when they could, to see the vistas around Potsdam.[138]

"Nature Does Not Change According to Any Political Wind": The Experience of German Natural Landscapes

The question of their relation to nature and the nonurban landscape around them preoccupied German Jews greatly, both in their public discourse and in their personal experience. The great majority of German Jews were urban, but despite or perhaps precisely because of that, the country's natural surroundings were for them a significant element that shaped their relationship with their homeland (*Heimat*). From the end of the nineteenth century, Jews had to cope with Germans of *völkisch* approaches and antisemitic tendencies who, maintaining that the Jews were an element foreign to the German nation, sought to exclude them, on both the symbolic and sometimes the practical level, from German nature. Even as they underwent rapid urbanization, Jews acted to counter these tendencies by deepening their connection to nature, including through initiatives taken by Jewish groups to settle as farmers in rural regions.[139] The Nazi period brought this tension to its height. Against this background, the Jews' attitude toward nature played an important role in shaping their lived space and maintaining their hold on their homeland.

Like the German urban space, community life, and German culture, the perception of German landscape and nature, a key element in the construction of German nationalism during the nineteenth century, was subordinated to the Nazi "coordination" policy. Light has recently been cast on these processes by scholars who have considered Nazi Germany from the perspective of environmental history. The blood-and-soil concept that was the foundation of the Nazi people's community made its way also into the regime's environmental policy, both on the propaganda level and in legislation and policy making. The landscape (*Landschaft*), as one of these scholars has depicted it, became an element in the Nazi doctrine of "living space" (*Lebensraum*).[140] The German forest in particular became an element in the Nazi perception of the homeland, and gradually crystalized into the regime's new forestation policy.[141] The paving of the autobahns, which, as already noted, served as a central element in the production of the Nazi space, involved a discourse on landscape and nature.[142] All these things quite naturally influenced Germany's Jews. The regime's exclusion policy was evident also in this area.

The question of how Jewish youth could access the countryside came up for discussion in the community's press with the approach of the summer of 1933. The expulsion of Jewish groups from the Reich Committee of German Youth Organizations (Reichausschuss der deutschen Jugendverbände) made it harder for Jewish teenagers and youngsters to lodge at German youth hostels and to receive discounts on train rides. This was seen as detrimental to their connection with Germany's nature sites. A brief article in the *CV-Zeitung* noted the great importance of travel throughout Germany for instilling in young Jews a love of the German landscape. The author expressed his concern that removing adolescents from the "landscape of the homeland" (*heimatlicher Landschaft*) would lead them to remain in the cities and turn them into "asphalt people."[143] In one response to the situation, a law student argued that young Jews had a profound need to hike outside the city. He called on Jewish organizations to do everything in their power to enable such trips.[144] Another article, appearing at the beginning of the autumn of that year in *Israelitisches Familienblatt*, discussed the worrying contraction, throughout Germany, in the number of sites where German Jews could lodge, and called on young people to take responsibility for themselves and to establish connections with Jews in provincial areas who could put them up.[145] Notably, this writer addressed the Jewish significance of the landscape, calling on Jewish hikers to use it as a way of connecting to German Jewish history and through it to their Jewish identity, through visits to sites of Jewish historical interest.

During the early years of the Nazi regime, the activities of Jewish youth and children's organizations throughout Germany, in particular those devoted to Hachsharah, agricultural training toward settlement in Palestine, strove to instill a sense of belonging to the German natural landscape even as the great majority of them sought to prepare young people for emigration.[146] It demonstrated a tension between their patriotic devotion to the German homeland and its natural beauty, and Zionism, which created its own connection to these symbols, as will be discussed in chapter 2.

Maintaining a grip on the German landscape was not just a problem for young people. It was also widely addressed in diaries and articles written by adult urban Jews as part of the more general question of their connection to German space. Kurt Rosenberg, for example, who wrote frequently about the pain of exclusion from the German public space, referred in his diary to the German countryside as a refuge from such feelings. "This morning I was with Theklein [his nickname for his eldest daughter, Thekla] in the Botanical Gardens. Blooms on top of blooms—which always awakens the recognition that nature does not change according to any political wind—and that caused a wonderful serenity."[147] About a year later, on May 1, 1934, as a Nazified National Labor Day was being celebrated in the streets, Rosenberg and his family decided to escape the ruckus in the city and went out into the countryside. "A walk together from Friedrichsruhe to Schwarzenbach," he recounted. "We are staying away from the instances in which huge crowds gather, and ponder, in quiet forests under a bright spring sky, that which is human and remains close to nature but is not subordinated to politics."[148]

But this perception of nature as a place of refuge from political vicissitudes and a sanctuary of humanity, which can also be found in the writing of Willy Cohn and others,[149] was shaken as the condition of German Jews worsened. Shortly after returning to Germany in July 1935 from a vacation in Switzerland, when he was again exposed to the burgeoning political pressures, Rosenberg again addressed his connection to the German landscape. But this time his tone was different.

> Fundamentally, the same doubt always awakens within me. This entire country, with which I have an intimate and ongoing acquaintance in all its particulars, was mine. There are long familiar sights which I reencountered with a sense of joy over and over again and ensconced in my memory. I was rooted in this land, in the country and in the city, I belonged to it in a boundless way. . . . The southern regions evoked the notes and rhythms of a soothing and placid harmony. Has all this now become foreign because, for more than two years, they have been preaching the racial gospel? Has the landscape turned its back on me, or have I disappointed it, in that I was too worn down to again trace its image within me?[150]

Rosenberg did not achieve a final resolution of this question. He went on to address his soul's aspiration to again connect with the timeless (*Zeitlos*) dimension of his homeland's landscapes, but also noted the difficulty of achieving this state because his soul was weighed down by contemporary events. This difficulty in connecting caused him, by his account, great suffering and a loss of his feeling of value. While Rosenberg did not divorce himself from his ties to the German landscape, it seems that from this point onward, until his emigration in 1937, he experienced the connection in a more intermittent way, as if living on borrowed time.[151]

The destabilization of the connection with the German landscape that Rosenberg felt as a painful personal matter of doubt was addressed publicly in a speech given by a young rabbi, Joachim Prinz, in the spring of 1935. Prinz belonged to what was called the Liberal denomination, which advocated a modernized approach to religious practice and belief, less radical than the much smaller Reform denomination. To avoid confusion, I will use the capitalized term Liberal to refer to this denomination, reserving the lower case to designate the political and social sense of the term. Prinz's speech was published in the Zionist newspaper *Jüdische Rundschau*. Prinz had come to the notice of German Jews in 1933, when he gave a series of popular lectures that were later published in book form as *We the Jews* (*Wir Juden*). In these talks he challenged the accepted interpretation of the age of emancipation, and proposed a new view of the concept of the ghetto.[152] In the spring of 1935 Prinz returned to the concept of the ghetto from a different perspective, arguing that the lives of Jews in Germany—especially of those in provincial cities who were forcefully experiencing the alienation from their neighbors—were turning into a life in an "inner ghetto." In the age that preceded emancipation, the Jewish ghetto had been a discrete geographical area, but now it was a manner of existence in a "neighborless" public space that became a ghetto. "In the marketplaces, on the country roads, in the restaurants, the ghetto is everywhere," he proclaimed.[153] Prinz also pointed to two other aspects of the changing world of Germany's Jews: their marginalization and exclusion from German culture and, in the context of the subject of this book, the change in their attitude toward the German landscape that came as a direct result of their experience of exclusion:

> We only need to walk through the German countryside once a day, now in spring, when everything is coming back to life, and fresh green is covering the meadows, the streams are shining like silver in the mountains, the trees are blossoming, and the woods are young and fresh on the mountains. That is all we need, and we feel it with all certainty and an elemental force that is as strong as an axiom: that we are bound to this landscape, bound for all time, and the longing of many Jews who leave Germany for karstic Palestine, the longing for the rustling forests and the luxuriant meadows, is genuine and robust. . . . And yet over the last two years it has been transformed. For there is no landscape without people. . . . But if that is so, then the face of the landscape in which we are living is gradually beginning to change. For where on earth could the bond remain undisturbed when this landscape is full of [sign]posts. Barriers, signs that forbid me as

someone living in this landscape to enter it . . . in fact *this also transforms the landscape itself, its objective image, its appearance, not only my feelings.* And mountains, rivers, trees, and meadows begin to grimace at us, in a transformation that was never anticipated nor believed. By this unmasking of a landscape that is also ours, our ghetto state is revealed once again.[154]

According to Prinz, the Jewish sense of estrangement from the German landscape is an objective and, in his view, inevitable result of the German attitude toward the Jews. The estrangement is part of the experience of the new ghetto.

Prinz's depiction served his Zionist message, in which he called on Jews to begin to form an active connection to the new mode of Jewish life taking form in Palestine. In practice, as in Rosenberg's case, the political atmosphere and policy of exclusion undermined the connection to the German landscape felt by non-Zionist Jews, although these processes were less clear-cut than they were among Zionists.

The diaries and personal documentation composed by German Jews at the end of the 1930s and in the early 1940s show that nature continued to serve some of them as a place of refuge from their day-to-day lives and from the growing sense of suffocation they felt in German public spaces as these were increasingly restricted by Nazi policy. Martha Wertheimer, a journalist and author from Frankfurt, recounted in a letter she wrote in July 1939 a weekend trip she had taken with her sister in the countryside. She remarked in particular on the quiet, the open air, and "forests empty of humankind."[155] The teenaged Elisabeth Bloch wrote that going out into open rural spaces made her happy. Her diary gives the impression that the forced agricultural labor imposed on her in 1941, which required her to spend time in the outdoors during the last year of her life, raised her spirits.[156]

Gertrud Kolmar, the poet, was compelled to move with her father in 1939 from the green suburb of Finkenkrug, west of Berlin, to the family apartment in the city's Schöneberg borough. In her letters from 1939 to 1943 she wrote longingly of Finkenkrug's rural surroundings and countryside as a lost paradise; it was for her a symbol of freedom.[157] During her last years in the city, Kolmar had difficulty finding an experience that would recall, even a little, the natural surroundings she had lost. But paradoxically, her final letters to her brother from the end of 1942, just before her deportation to Auschwitz, tell a different story. Her forced labor site had moved to Charlottenburg, and she described her morning walk to work as a "surrogate for nature" (*Naturersatz*), and a source of joy.[158]

The Nazi policy of excluding Jews from public spaces and curtailing their freedom of movement increasingly restricted the use Jews could make of natural spaces. The emotional connection some Jews felt with German nature was also damaged, as is evident in Rosenberg's ambiguity and Prinz's position. Nevertheless, even under these most difficult circumstances, Jews were sometimes able to discover tactics or options that enriched their shrinking lived spaces, if only for a bit.

Conclusion: Narrowness, Wideness, and Emptiness

In this chapter I have cast light on the exclusion of German Jews from public space, and the ways they coped with it. There were considerable differences between the large cities and provincial cities, and among individuals of different ages, classes, and circumstances. Furthermore, major changes took place during which the Nazification of space deepened. Especially after the pogrom of November 1938 and even more after war broke out, the exclusion of Jews from public space intensified, and their room for maneuver narrowed. This range of circumstances and timing meant that Jews made use of a variety of tactics for shaping their lived space.

One of the central concepts in Jewish lived space during this period is *Enge*, which may be translated as "narrowness" or "crowding." It evoked not only the physical experience of shrinking space but an inner experience, a feeling. As the following chapter will show, this experience also characterized the way in which Jews conducted their lives during the Nazi period in more interior spaces—within the Jewish communities and at home. While these difficulties prompted them to remain closed up in their own personal spaces, this chapter has adduced a variety of their attempts to break out and experience "spaciousness" (*Weite*). Another central concept that applies to the Jewish experience in this period is "emptiness" (*Leere*). It refers to the fact that the public space was emptied of people and experiences that had positive significance for Jews, many of whom thus chose, at least from time to time, to avoid and disengage themselves from public places. In contrast with this tendency to self-isolate, however, there were attempts by Jews to maintain a foothold in the bourgeois experiential space, as it filled their lives with meaning. This was the case with libraries, the cinema, and the German countryside. Physical experiences with their source in the external world—narrowness, wideness, and emptiness—made an imprint on the inner mental worlds of Jewish diarists. It meant that their battles to maintain a grip on different spaces were in fact battles to maintain their own identities.

In 1983 the environmental psychologists Harold Proshansky, Abbe Fabian, and Robert Kaminoff introduced the terms "place-identity" and "spatial identity" to denote important parts of the inner worlds of individuals. The spaces in which individuals spend their daily lives shape, though not always consciously, their patterns of behavior and the way they perceive the world.[159] Human beings, they argued, require "stability of place and space" to give meaning to their actions. Extreme changes in their physical surroundings are liable to be menaces to their identities. These three scholars also noted the importance of the human capacity for reshaping the relationship to space when it does not answer to their expectations. Their work demonstrates the importance of agency—the human ability to choose to shape one's fate even in harsh circumstances.

The concept of spatial identity would seem consistent with the way the historian Moritz Föllmer describes, in his book *Individuality and Modernity in Berlin*, the effect Jewish exclusion from the city during the Nazi period had on consciousness of the self. The sense of growing alienation from Berlin's urban space, he argues, led Jews to experience "a reduced form of individuality stripped of most economic, social and psychological resources."[160] Their search for agency, he adds, was indeed a way of coping with the situation, but as Nazi policy grew more extreme at the beginning of the 1940s, the Jews who remained in Berlin found themselves facing a situation that for all practical purposes denied them any possibility of exercising agency.[161] This chapter's discussion, including the part that takes de Certeau's approach to the small person struggling from below for a daily space against the hegemonic power, can be summed up differently. Yes, the spatial identities of German Jews faced a crisis that grew ever worse, but it looks as though in these extreme circumstances there were some who found a way to exercise agency of a sort, and to shape a spatial experience that had at least some meaning. Another aspect of this spatial experience—the reshaping of Jewish spaces—will be at the center of the next chapter.

* CHAPTER TWO *

Jewish Places and Spaces

In January 1937 the Central Association of Jews in Germany issued a copiously illustrated map of the city of Berlin (figure 2).[1] The regime's anti-Jewish exclusion policy had grown ever more severe over the previous few years, its effects felt most acutely in small and medium-sized towns and cities. In response, many Jews had moved from Germany's periphery to the capital. The map was meant to guide these newcomers around the city. But it also documented just how much the city had changed in a short time, obliging its longtime Jewish inhabitants to adopt a different attitude, a different way of imagining it. "The person who devotes a few minutes to studying the network of streets [presented on the map] will notice that this guide does not only offer the streets' external appearances," advised an article about the map in the Central Association's newspaper, explaining that it also accurately portrayed how Jews in Berlin lived, what they did, and how the community had changed.[2] The map depicted a rich network of old and new Jewish spaces, among them synagogues, cemeteries, hospitals, schools, sports facilities, and cultural centers. Many people, said the article's author, had not until recently been acquainted with the Jewish institutions that many of them now needed to frequent or seek out. The purpose of the map was to help them find these places. Perhaps, until just a few years earlier, some Jews might have opposed putting out a map specifically for Jews, the author acknowledged, "but in our times, when we are becoming accustomed to leafing through atlases and gazing at maps of foreign countries as if they were entrancing family pictures, it is certainly understandable that people will take an interest in a map that . . . does not portray the expanses between Rio de Janeiro and São Paulo or between Palestine and Italy, but between the Community House and the National Representation [building]."

According to the historian Karl Schlögel, maps should be read as

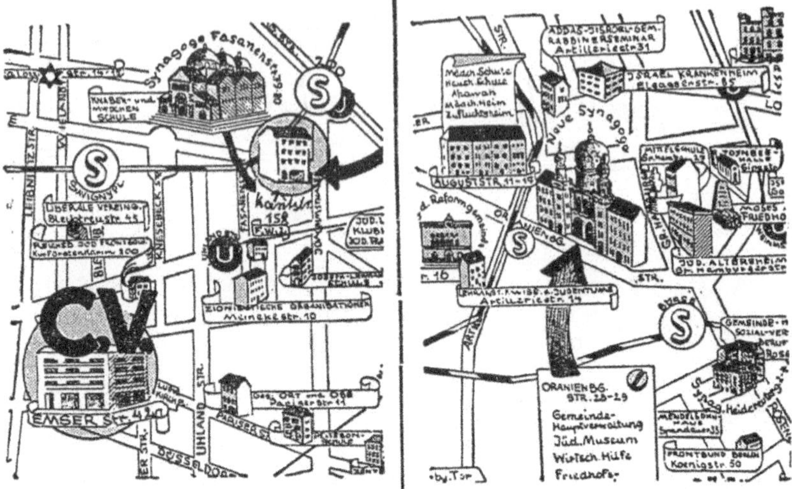

Figure 2. Sections of a map of Jewish Berlin. *CV-Zeitung* 16, no. 4, January 28, 1937. Digitized by Johann Christian Senckenberg University Library, Goethe University.

historical documents which document dramas of changing space, the rise and fall of different places and regions. Every map has an explicit or implicit purpose, and to that end its editors—individuals or groups—make choices about what will stand out. Likewise, they disregard spaces that do not serve their purposes, and even distort space for their own ends. After all, the cartographic ideal is usability.[3] Consistent with that pattern, the Central Association's map did not show important streets and institutions belonging to non-Jewish Berlin, but highlighted the extensive undertakings of the German Jewish organizations that operated in Berlin during the Nazi regime's initial years. From the point of view of the city's Jews, both long-time residents and newcomers, the map reflected the understanding that the experience of exclusion and alienation from the public space was accompanied by another spatial experience: the emergence of a swathe of new Jewish spaces.

Jacob Borut has shown that the creation and growth of Jewish spaces in Nazi Germany was a response both to the needs of Jews, who sought sites where they could feel safe from humiliation and oppression, and the Nazi aspiration to isolate the Jews and separate them from what it called the Aryan population. Borut argues that the process of concentrating Jewish community activity in Jewish locations and spaces in Germany had begun already in the 1920s, as social antisemitism burgeoned in Weimar Germany. That decade saw an upswing in the activities conducted in synagogues and, in many cases, the establishment of community houses (*Gemeinde-*

häuser). As might be expected, there was an upsurge in this phenomenon following the political turning point of 1933. The Nazi authorities, Borut notes, tended to allow a broad variety of Jewish public activities as long as they were "closed events" (*gescholssene Veranstaltungen*), out of sight of German spaces.[4]

Yi-Fu Tuan's use of the terms "place" and "space" has been influential, but has not achieved consensus among historians. For Tuan, a human geographer, "place" is a neutral marker of a location, site, or structure, not charged with meaning and depth, while "space" is a more laden concept imbued with memories, meanings, and ideologies.[5] Notably, the Hebrew word for "place," *makom*, is problematic because it comes with connotations from Jewish tradition that make it inappropriate for labeling something neutral in character. I have thus preferred to follow Borut in reversing Tuan's use of the terms.[6] I will use "place" to label sites charged with history and consciousness for Jews, serving for distinctly Jewish activity. "Space," in this work, will refer to the more general analytic metaconcept. Synagogues and cemeteries are thus Jewish places, while a wide range of sites where Jews conducted other activities and which were less imbued with tradition are thus, in this usage, spaces. But I should stress that the places discussed here may also be characterized and analyzed as spaces, and I will sometimes make use of that concept in my discussion.

In this chapter I look at some Jewish places and spaces and the way they were used by German Jews. I will combine an organizational-community perspective, documented principally in the contemporary press, with that of the lived space of individuals. Focusing on the German Jewish encounter with synagogues and cemeteries, the two most notable and oldest Jewish places, I will show that the need for and use of them took on new meanings for Jews as the political and social environment in which they found themselves and their living conditions changed. I will then address a range of additional spaces that characterized German Jewish community life: community houses, museums, cultural centers, and training farms. And, as a case study, I will offer a more detailed account of Jewish athletic spaces.

The article on the illustrated map of Berlin referred to the increasing use of maps and atlases by German Jews and their growing interest in far-flung destinations. Simone Lässig and Miriam Rürup have recently called for an examination of the question of Jewish space from new perspectives, and to include *imagined* space. These two historians advocate breaking free of binary distinctions between Jewish and non-Jewish spaces, arguing that the gray zones in the middle must also be examined.[7] Using these insights, I will, in the last part of this chapter, consider the way German Jews experienced, perceived, and imagined global geography at a time when emigration had become a major item on their agendas. For this reason, trains and train stations also became significant places for them, and are an example of the sort of liminal space that was experienced in one way by Jews and in quite a different way by non-Jews.

"There His Sense of Loneliness Passes": Synagogues as Revitalizing Community Spaces

Prior to the age of emancipation, synagogues served the Jews of Central Europe not only as places of worship but as sites of public assembly and study. Rabbinic courts conducted their sessions there, and in practice synagogues served also as places of social, economic, cultural, and administrative activity. The high frequency with which Jews met each other in the synagogue made it the most convenient place for a variety of interactions among members of the community in a wide variety of spheres of life. Scholars of the early modern age have noted that this multipurpose use of the space of the synagogue and the yard around it was often condemned by the religious elite, but to no avail.[8]

The adoption of the bourgeois habitus by German Jews in the age of emancipation led to an increasing division between the religious and secular spheres, and to the confinement of practices connected to these spheres to separate spaces. Michael Meyer has shown how, over the course of the nineteenth century, the German synagogue underwent a functional transformation from a place of assembly (the original meaning of the Greek word *synagogue*), for a variety of purposes of which prayer and study were just two, into a sacred space that came to be referred to as a house of God (*Gotteshaus*), a holy place (*Heligtum*), and a sanctuary (*Tempel*). The transformation of the synagogue into a place of a more manifestly religious character, in its sacred aura and architecture, followed in the wake of a similar process that had taken place earlier in Christianity. "The entry into a synagogue," asserts Meyer, "was now seen as a step from the realm of the secular into that of the sacred."[9] The social, economic, and cultural activities that were removed from the synagogue were transferred into new spaces that opened up to Jews under emancipation. The separation of these spheres, which could be seen as a spatial manifestation of the secularization undergone by Jewish communities in Germany during this period, led in practical terms to lower attendance at synagogues, especially those in liberal middle-class urban areas, most days of the year, including the Sabbath, the exception being the High Holidays of Rosh Hashanah and Yom Kippur.[10]

The age of emancipation also saw a change in the location and visibility of synagogues. Until the nineteenth century, synagogues were hidden from public sight, so that they would not come under the gaze of Christian outsiders. Now they were erected without any barrier between themselves and the outside world, and were even dedicated at impressive public ceremonies, in the presence of non-Jewish public figures. The synagogue thus manifested the Jewish presence in the public space. Andreas Gotzmann has recently argued that the German synagogue of this period was designed according to the Jews' picture of their own future. The choice of location, the architecture and interior design, the dedication ceremonies, and the nature of the worship were principally, he claims, the Jews' aspiration to see themselves as part of the German nation.[11]

The new circumstances that Jews faced under the Nazi regime, and their exclusion from public spaces, quickly changed the ways they needed to use this traditional Jewish space, and thus changed the way it operated. Willy Cohn's life, as evidenced by his diary, illustrates the change in the way the synagogue figured in shaping the lived space of German Jews. Cohn, dismissed in June 1933 from his position at the Breslau gymnasium high school, noted a few days later that he now had more free time, which enabled him to attend synagogue more frequently. Three months later, when he reported on a visit to Breslau's new synagogue immediately following time spent at the municipal library, he added, "I now sometimes have a stronger need than in the past to go there."[12] Like the library, discussed in the previous chapter, the synagogue thus became more significant in Cohn's daily life following the loss of his job.

These two spaces seem, however, to have answered different needs of his. The library, which he went to as an individual, was a neutral space where he endeavored to adhere to bourgeois habits and to his reading and research practices. The communal and family experience of the synagogue was for Cohn a gaze back into his family history. So, for example, when he went to synagogue with his daughter Ruth, he showed her "our old places," where he had sat thirty years before with his father.[13] Gathering there for prayers with other Jews in the House of God, he wrote in his diary, was a way of achieving "inner concentration" (*inneren Sammlung*). The experience of gazing inward (*innere Besinnung*) had for him become linked to Jewish spaces as early as March 1933, when he depicted how Jews gathered for a lecture in Breslau's community house, against the background of the Nazification of the public space—the inundation of the street with swastika flags.[14]

The increasing attraction of synagogues and their evocation of previous generations was also evident in writing by women. An issue of the periodical published by the League of Jewish Women in Germany (*Blätter des Jüdischer Frauenbundes*) in the fall of 1933, during the High Holidays that began the Jewish year of 5694, featured a poem by Suzanne Auerbach expressing the warmth she experienced in synagogue and the concept of the ghetto: "The bittersweet narrowness of the ghetto speaks clearly through this holy site: I feel my mother's arm comforting me and embracing me and the others."[15] The term "narrowness," which elsewhere often has negative connotations, is imbued in Auerbach's poem with warmth and intimacy.

In February 1934 the Berlin supplement to the Zionist newspaper *Jüdische Rundschau* printed a news item on an innovation in the Friday night services at a synagogue on Rykestrasse. The synagogue, the supplement reported, had reverted to using popular traditional melodies and chants instead of modern ones. The result was a special atmosphere, a Jewish "sound world" that caused those who heard it to feel as if "we are in *Schul*." "This is valuable, important, and vital today more than ever," the correspondent wrote, clearly alluding to the political situation in Nazi Germany and the exclusion of the Jews.[16] The word *Schul*, placed in quotation marks in the original, was the traditional Yiddish term for synagogue, one that modern German Jews had sought to distance themselves from. It clearly harked back to Ashkenazi Judaism of pre-emancipation times, evoking a world of meaning entirely different from that of the Liberal synagogues where organs were used (*Orgelsynagogen*), which the article also mentions. The latter were largely intended to serve as a means of integration into German society. But under Nazi rule, the article indicates, it was the turn to the past, as represented by the *Schul*, that met the needs of the worshippers, who packed it from wall to wall. In Berlin, which was quickly becoming the home of an ever larger percentage of Germany's Jews, the growing presence of newcomers from provincial cities, many of whom were more traditional than their established coreligionists in the city, helped augment the attendance at synagogues. The fact that significant numbers of worshippers filled Berlin synagogues not just on Sabbaths and holidays but also on weekdays, as a press report from the beginning of 1937 indicates, was to a large extent a result of this process.[17]

In her book on the festivals of the French Revolution, Mona Ozouf distinguishes between those observed outdoors and those celebrated in enclosed spaces. Outdoors, she argues, represented for the revolutionaries the fall of social distinctions, a breaking down of the barriers that had closed off the spaces of aristocrats. Moreover, the open air constituted a "space without memory," a symbol of entrance into the new world.[18] Nazism, which proclaimed a set of values entirely different from and in fact diametrically opposed to those of the French Revolution, sought to structure outside spaces politically. The party and regime organized a gamut of outdoor ceremonies and events, such as mass flag marches and torchlight processions, and used large open stadiums as means of cementing the masses into the German people's community.[19] In both the French Revolution and Nazism, despite their many differences, the open air represented both the consciousness of a boundless prospect and the conquest of the future. This experience provides the foil for understanding the closed spaces to which Jews like Cohn and Auerbach turned with increasing frequency during the early years of the Nazi regime. This is especially true of the synagogue and the experience of gazing inward. Auerbach's use of the concepts of "narrowness" and "ghetto" to underline this illustrates the connection between closed spaces and the gaze into the past. The Rykestrasse Berlin synagogue also reversed the horizon of time, from orientation toward a future based on integration into the German state to an attempt to connect to the pre-emancipation Ashkenazi Jewish past.

The rise in attendance at urban synagogues and the widening of the range of Jews of different backgrounds who appeared in them led to an erosion in another characteristic of the post-emancipation German synagogue: the spatial separation between the religious and secular spheres. The difficulties created by the new circumstances impelled many synagogues to become the sites of all kinds of nonreligious activities, and the main place where Jews assembled. In September 1933 at the start of a concert held at a synagogue in an outlying community near Breslau, one community leader said the synagogue was once more fulfilling its original purpose of being "the house of Jewish community life," in keeping with the original meaning of the term "synagogue."[20] "As far as my memory serves," wrote Marta Appel, the wife of the rabbi of the Dortmund community, "we have never had such bustle and tumult in our community building as we did in those days. In every single corner, from the basement to the attic, some course was being held."[21]

The transformation of the synagogue into a Jewish community center, another expression that gained currency at this time, led to changes in its routines and created new needs. For example, some communities decided to leave their synagogue buildings open all day, not just at the times of public prayer, so that people interested in "inner concentration" could enter. The participation of Jewish schoolchildren in a series of events held at synagogues in Berlin following prayer services raised questions about the boundaries of the use of the synagogue space, and the extent to which it should be adapted to different groups and events.[22] An especially interesting discussion around the mixture of religious and secular practices in the synagogue appeared in the Jewish press beginning in September 1933, following the refusal of one community leader in Berlin to cover his head during a secular community event conducted in the synagogue on Oranienburger Strasse in Berlin. Following this incident, which ended in the speaker's capitulation to pressure from the public, a writer for *Israelitisches Familienblatt* declared that it was necessary to create a clear distinction between prayer services and events of a secular nature held in synagogues. He gave the example of the custom at one Liberal synagogue in Berlin to cover the ark in which the Torah scrolls were housed with a curtain, so as to "neutralize" the space when secular events were held, thus allowing the men present to refrain from covering their heads.[23]

By the second half of the 1930s, such situations, which in the autumn of 1933 had been controversial and required solutions, now became routine. The number of sites where Jewish community events could be held had shrunk. By this time it was routine for synagogues to host secular cultural events and presentations on political issues, Jewish emigration from Germany, and vocational training.[24] The organizers of Jewish athletics, constantly searching for spaces appropriate for their activities, used the foyers and basements of synagogues and refashioned them as sports facilities.[25] In time it became the norm for many Jews to go to synagogue for social reasons and not necessarily to engage in religious worship or rituals. Religious Jews and leaders set aside their initial objections and accepted that their secular counterparts needed a replacement for secular public spaces from which they had been excluded.[26] The situation was depicted in an article headlined "The Lonely Man," which appeared in the summer of 1938 in *Israelitisches Familienblatt*'s current events forum. It told the story of a Jew who had lost his work and whose circle of close friends shrank inexorably until he was left all alone. The only place where he could feel that he belonged, so the article claimed, was the synagogue. "We encounter this lonely man in synagogues and houses of worship. . . . There his sense of loneliness passes, he feels close to the people sitting next to him at least for a few hours, he feels that the larger community of the Jewish people is embracing him."[27]

At the same time that synagogue activities were increasing in number and intensity, especially in the large cities, the Jewish communities in the provinces were declining as their communities dispersed. Synagogues in these places were abandoned. As Joachim Prinz recounted as early as November 1935, these transformed from functioning components of Jewish society to museumlike spaces devoid of all contemporary meaning.[28] The process reached its climax in 1938. On November 5 of that year, a few days before the November pogrom, Willy Cohn reported in his diary that several synagogues in which he had once given lectures had been disbanded, and that some of the buildings had been sold. Two days later he wrote of the dwindling and decline of the Jewish sector in Germany.[29]

German synagogues, once closed Jewish spaces that offered a certain measure of protection from the violent Nazification of the public space, now became places under siege, and in the end disappeared from the German space, as the Nazi regime's anti-Jewish policy intensified. It was a transition from Jewish self-isolation from "Aryan" society to the German government forcing them to leave Germany, which was in turn followed by their deportation from Germany to the east.

The demolition of synagogues, which reached its height during the November 1938 pogrom, began several months before that.[30] An account of the destruction of a prominent Munich synagogue in June of that year appears in Hans Reichmann's memoir: "There are reports from Munich of an order to demolish the synagogue. The Führer refused to speak at the German Art Day in Munich 'as long as that ugly disgrace' continues to stand there."[31] In previous years, Nazification in general and Hitler's presence in particular had required forcing the Jews out of public spaces and concealing them in closed spaces. Now, however, it required utterly expunging the symbol of their presence in the sacred space created by the Nazi leader's presence. It was, for all intents and purposes, the beginning of a process that would lead to the systematic demolition of synagogues in the November pogrom, as well as to the immolation of Torah scrolls throughout Germany. The purpose was to transform Germany into a space clean of Jews (*Judenrein*).[32]

Nevertheless, the pogrom did not bring an utter end to the synagogue as a functioning institution in the lives of Germany's Jews. Cohn documents the continuation of public worship in Breslau even after the destruction of the city's central synagogue. However, access to the synagogues that remained was severely restricted by the authorities.[33] On the holiday of Rosh Hashanah in September 1939, the authorities permitted public prayers for men only in the Abraham Mugdan synagogue, and even that with many restrictions. Cohn felt this to be not only a religious insult but a blow to the very existence of a Jewish public sphere. "Our one remaining way of being together has been taken from us," he wrote. A few days later, the authorities forbade Yom Kippur services even there. "It is the first time in centuries that prayers are not being held [in the synagogue] on this day," he told his diary. "I will try to pray at home."[34]

Over the two years that followed, until he was deported and murdered, Cohn continued to attend public worship from time to time, whenever he could, in those synagogues that remained in Breslau. Following the destruction of the central Liberal synagogue in the November pogrom, the police seized the entire compound, including a smaller synagogue that had been used until then for weekday services. Ironically, Cohn was summoned for interrogation in that structure. "The shades of the men and women I had seen there in the past passed before my eyes when I entered that space," he confided. "The ark that held the Torah scrolls remains there."[35]

On the last Yom Kippur of his life, just two months before he was transported to the east, he went to pray at the crowded "Concert House," as he referred to the home of the Breslau's Jewish Friends Association, a social group, which was one of the last two Jewish public buildings remaining in the city. He sought "elation of the soul" and yearned to be allowed on the next Yom Kippur to pray more comfortably.[36] Less than two months later, the building and the lot on which it stood became one of the two deportation depots from which the Jews of Breslau, Cohn's family among them, were deported to their deaths.

"Here Is Where Jews Are Wanted": Cemeteries as Places of Connection and Refuge

Cemeteries served Jewish communities as spaces that were, understandably, associated with transgenerational Jewish memory. In medieval Jewish culture there was a complex tension between the aversion to cemeteries and an attraction to them, and between the views that they were marginal spaces or central ones, as Avriel Bar-Levav has shown. He argues that in Jewish culture, death and mourning rituals were meant to establish but also to limit the connection between the living and the dead. According to Bar-Levav, it has been a common Jewish practice at least since the Middle Ages to visit the graves of loved ones and spiritual leaders.[37] These customs continued and were institutionalized in Ashkenazi Jewish communities in the early modern age, when Jews made a practice of visiting cemeteries on the eve of Rosh Hashanah and of Yom Kippur, on Tisha B'Av (the fast of the Ninth of Av), and at the time of community memorial events.[38]

It is difficult to estimate to what extent German Jews visited cemeteries during the emancipation period, but it seems reasonable to presume that such practices grew less frequent as a result of urbanization, secularization, and the erosion of traditional observance. The bourgeois ethos also no doubt expanded the gap between the dead and the living. "Death disappears from daily life," writes Silvie-Anne Goldberg, "and . . . the attention paid by Jews in past centuries to the hereafter is supplanted by a concentration on the here and now."[39] Nevertheless, cemeteries continued to be important in Jewish life. But if synagogues were refashioned in the age of emancipation with an orientation toward the future, cemeteries, argues Andreas Gotzmann, continued to lie on the opposite time horizon, oriented to the past. As Gotzmann sees it, the continuation of traditional burial practices even in Liberal contexts symbolized the alienation the Jews felt from their Christian surroundings. The cemetery remained a space of Jewish presence beyond time. But this orientation to the past also had an integrative element to it. The cemetery's foothold in the soil exemplified the idea of the continuity of Jewish settlement in Germany, and became an element in the consolidation of emancipated Jewry's historical consciousness.[40] So, for example, Nils Roemer describes the Jewish cemetery of Worms, built in 1034, a symbol of the Jewish presence in Germany over many generations, as a place that offered Jewish visitors of the late nineteenth and early twentieth centuries "the solace of the permanence of the past."[41]

The crisis German Jews faced in the wake of the events of 1933 intensified the standing of cemeteries, which attracted visitors, especially those who needed to make symbolic contact with Jews of previous generations. These visitors took comfort there or, alternatively, took stock of their situation there. The memoirs of Edwin Landau of Deutsch Krone offer a dramatic account of his pilgrimage to the graves of his ancestors a few days after the economic boycott in April 1933:

> I went to the graves of my parents, grandparents, and great grandparents, and spoke with them. I returned to them everything German that I have received from three generations, and that I have absorbed and cultivated. I cried into their graves: "You were mistaken. I, too, have been misled. I now know that I am no longer a German. And what will my children be? The question remained open. . . . The gravestones remained silent.[42]

The contemporary press also depicted cemeteries as important Jewish sites. Jewish publications were concerned about the increasing vandalism of cemeteries as part of the rising antisemitic tension,[43] and adduced them as a way of expressing different views of alarming current phenomena. Hilda Marx, a liberal Jewish poet and journalist active in Berlin in the 1930s, depicted in January 1935 the old Jewish cemetery in Walsdorf, near the place of her family's origin, as an integral part of the Franconian space. It was, she said, a site that tied all the Jews buried there over centuries to the landscape of the German homeland. Her emphasis on the tranquility of the cemetery as an open space can be seen as an experience that ran counter to the transformation of other public Jewish spaces into closed and narrow ones. "The cemetery has only the spaces of land around it and the infinity of sky above it."[44]

The romantic view of the cemetery as an open space of Jewish memory and a site of refuge and security is clearly evident in two articles in *Israelitisches Familienblatt*. The first, "Sun on the Graves" by Erich Cohn-Beuthen, appeared in July 1936. He depicted the cemetery in a small German city as "a place of refuge," a kind of hidden paradise. First Cohn-Beuthen described it from the perspective of himself as a boy who, wandering through the city where he lives, comes upon this magical spot. Thirty years later, the boy, now grown up, returns to the landscape of his childhood many years after leaving the city. As an adult he again feels inner peace at the cemetery, but is far more aware of the chain of generations the site symbolizes. Alluding to the political situation, Cohn-Beuthen remarked that "if the fate of the Jewish people becomes mine," that is, if he were compelled to leave Germany, he could take with him the image of the cemetery in the city of his birth.[45]

Martha Wertheimer's essay, "Snow on the Graves," which appeared about half a year later, reads like a response to Cohn-Beuthen's piece. It depicts the cemetery in winter as the last place Jews visit before they emigrate.[46] It elicits thoughts on life and death, and is the complete opposite of noisy city life. Writing of how the overcast sky blended with the snow-covered graves, Wertheimer painted the site as a place outside normal space and beyond time. The cemetery is unbound in a way diametrically opposed to the daily lives of the Jews at the time, who increasingly encountered spatial barriers.

Michel Foucault's lecture "Of Other Spaces" set off a transdisciplinary discourse on space with its introduction of the term "heterotopia"—from "hetero," meaning "other," and "topos," meaning place.[47] Foucault used this term for spaces that were "other" in any of a variety of senses. Cohn-Beuthen and Wertheimer's depictions of the cemetery cast these Jewish sites as just that: places perceived within their environments as complex and multifarious. They depicted the cemetery as a foothold in the soil and in the homeland, but also as a prospect beyond Jews' limited lives in the here and now. Indeed, Foucault himself considered cemeteries as one example of a heterotopia. He noted that in the modern age they were moved outside the city, so as to express the distance between life and death. In Germany, these two writers turned it into a place beyond time in the positive sense, one that attracted Jews who felt a need for a respite from the noisy city and from the public space that was increasingly rejecting them.

Unlike Marx, for whom the ancient cemetery in the place she grew up denoted the deepening connection between its Jews and the German homeland, and unlike Cohn-Beuthen and Wertheimer, who sought out cemeteries as places of serenity and as broader prospects of memory in advance of emigration, Helene Hanna Thon chose to make a different use of this "other place." Thon was a social activist and Zionist journalist who, having settled in Palestine in 1921, returned to Germany for a visit at the end of 1935. In a piece she wrote for *Jüdische Rundschau* she recounted her visit to the Jewish cemetery in Weissensee, a neighborhood in northeast Berlin, in order to bid farewell to representatives of three generations of her family: two women and a man. The three, she wrote, had seen Berlin as their native soil. They had not known that some of their descendants would settle in the Jewish nation's ancient-new land, but had they known it, they would have been astonished that the members of the next generation would be full of hope as they put down roots there.[48] In Thon's piece, the cemetery serves primarily as a source of legitimacy for leaving Germany to fulfil the Zionist dream.

The great attention that German Jews devoted to their cemeteries, in part because they were visiting these sites more frequently in order to bid farewell to family members buried there, was evidenced by an unusual advertisement that appeared in *Israelitisches Familienblatt* in March 1938. It offered gardening and caretaking services to Jews with loved ones interred in the Weissensee cemetery. By subscribing to the service, the ad noted, Jews would not only fulfill their obligations to the departed but would also provide work for unemployed coreligionists.[49]

The turn to cemeteries as places of Jewish memory and as refuges from Nazifying public spaces is also salient in Willy Cohn's diary. The intensity of Cohn's preoccupation with the subject, which also linked up to his profession as a historian of German Jewry and to lectures he gave, was not typical among Germany's Jews, but does indeed indicate one of the directions in which Jewish attitudes toward their cemeteries developed and intensified. In September 1934, just before the Rosh Hashanah holiday, Cohn noted in his diary that large numbers of Jews were appearing at the "eternal home." He led some acquaintances on a long trip through the cemetery; among other graves they stopped at was that of the nineteenth-century Jewish socialist theorist Ferdinand Lassalle. On the anniversary of the death of the Breslau socialist political activist Hans Alexander, who had been murdered in a concentration camp in September 1933, many Jews arrived at his grave to pay their respects and express their solidarity.[50] The traditional premodern Ashkenazi Jewish practice of visiting graves before the Jewish New Year had apparently gained new popularity under the new circumstances, and now included honoring figures representing German Jewry's political heritage, such as Lassalle, and victims of the Nazi regime like Alexander. The cemetery seems to have felt like a secure place where it was possible, under the guise of paying respects to the dead, to engage in veiled political protest against Nazi terror—another way to use the public space. The perception of the cemetery as a place where Jews were invulnerable to exclusion and harassment would persist even as the circumstances grew more fraught.

Cohen made an explicit connection between Nazification of the German public space and the appeal of cemeteries in March 1936, during Hitler's visit to Breslau. "Today the Führer is coming. The weather is fine . . . so as to evade the whole thing, I am today at a place where Jews are truly wanted—the cemetery on Lohestrasse, so as to have another wordless conversation with my father."[51] His depiction of the cemetery as the place where a quiet dialogue between generations could take place was the polar opposite of the "racket in the streets" that he described later in his account of the Nazi leader's visit to his city.

At the end of the 1930s, in particular after the November pogrom and the subsequent developments that largely put an end to his visits to peripheral communities and his teaching, Cohn began to visit the cemetery even more frequently. And, more so than in the past, he described his time there as an intergenerational conversation: on the one hand with his departed parents and forebears, and on the other with his living daughters, who accompanied him. In December 1938, just before his daughter Ruth left Germany, Cohn took her to the Breslau cemetery "so that she would at least once be in the place in which her ancestors are buried." As they walked among the gravestones, he spoke about her obligation to continue being faithful to the spirit of their home. Susanne, Ruth's younger sister, accompanied Cohn time and again on his visits to the cemetery in 1940 and 1941.[52]

In his book *The Loneliness of Dying*, in which he describes how the shaping of modern civilization placed a distance between the living and the dead and between life and death, Norbert Elias takes stock of the norms of the use of cemetery spaces. The modern cemetery, he writes in this sociological study, is meant to be a place of utter silence, and those present in it are expected to put on serious expressions. While in practical terms it was conceived as a green park within or on the margins of the city, it was unthinkable that it be used for picnics or as a play area for children. Banning any enjoyment on the part of adults and, even more so, the laughter of children, Elias argues, furthered the separation of the dead from the living.[53]

Elias pinpoints something characteristic of some Western societies in the modern age, even if it apparently cannot be generalized to all of them. The conditions faced by the Jews of Germany, especially toward the end of the 1930s, led in fact to a rapid erosion and then collapse of the norms Elias documents. As was the case with synagogues, exclusion from the public space and the constriction of Jewish spaces, especially open ones, led to a shift in the bourgeois spatial worldview, which had designated a specific use for each space, with careful separation between them. Beginning in the late 1930s, cemeteries thus began to serve the needs of the living. So, for example, at the end of 1937 the Jewish community board in Berlin announced that a vocational training course would be held in the Weissensee cemetery as preparation for intensive agricultural studies at other training facilities prior to settlement in Palestine.[54]

The process accelerated in the early 1940s, when cemeteries became the last open space accessible to Jews. Those who remained in Germany thus used them for other purposes. In her account of Jewish life in Berlin in 1941, Elisabeth Freund wrote that Jews needed to spend time in nature, at least on weekends. Her friend Mrs. L and the latter's husband were worn down by their forced labor, but feared that they would be harassed if they went out for walks in parks. But they finally found a safe place to do so: the Weissensee cemetery. "How nice it is there," she told Freund. "Everything is so peaceful, and all the flowers are so wonderful! No one bothered us."[55] Unlike Willy Cohn, Hilda Marx, and others for whom time spent in the cemetery was always charged, by their own account, with memories of and respect for the dead, Mrs. L and her husband made no effort to conceal from Freund that their only motive for going to the cemetery was to use it as a place for a weekend outing. Later in her memoir, Freund recounted the Jewish community's decision to use cemeteries as play and study areas for children:

> We are forbidden to enter parks, Jewish child care centers did not have even yards, not to mention gardens, and if they had them, the children were not allowed to play there because the neighbors complained about the noise. In the end, the Jewish community came up with a solution and turned the open areas in the Jewish cemeteries into playgrounds with sandboxes for young children. Older children and their classmates were required to weed the areas around the graves and to maintain them in good condition. This kept the children busy outside, in the fresh air, and the graves were kept clean. . . . This is what things came to: in Germany, the cemeteries were not just the last resting places of the elderly, but also the only play areas for children.[56]

Cohn's diary also documents acceptance of this process. At first he had reservations about allowing his eight-year-old daughter Susanne to collect chestnuts on their visits to the Breslau cemetery, but as time went by he relaxed. "These days children have so few happy moments," he wrote in October 1940. "It's the only thing that remains to us," he added nine months later, when he described how children had to traverse the entire cemetery to reach their playground.[57]

The first wave of deportations of Jews to the east began in the autumn of 1941. Cohn, his wife, and his two young daughters were sent to Kaunas, where they were murdered. For those Jews who remained in Germany under the threat of deportation, cemeteries continued to serve all the more as places of refuge. The elderly businessman Philipp Manes visited the Weissensee cemetery regularly until he was transported to Theresienstadt in July 1942. He explained his frequent visits as being primarily gestures of devotion to his parents—he made a point of visiting on his father's birthday—but they also offered soothing communion with nature.[58] Among his many activities, Arno Nadel, a multitalented Jewish musician, playwright, and painter in Berlin, led the choir and played the organ for the Jewish community in the Weissensee cemetery until September 1941. But he continued to visit the cemetery thereafter as well, until his deportation to Auschwitz in the spring of 1943. "A look at the cemetery," he wrote in his diary in April 1942. "*Jude* [is emblazoned in the cemetery's] large hall. Also above. Here Jews are wanted. How surprising that the graves are not marked with a piece of white paper bearing the letter J."[59]

The most extreme expression of the changes that took place in the Jewish cemetery space and its transformation, at least to a certain extent, into a secular space can be found in the diary of Victor Klemperer. Klemperer, who had converted to Christianity, had no interest in the cemetery as a Jewish site, neither in a religious nor in a family context. Indeed, he gave it no attention until the deportations began. But at the end of 1942, by which time most of Dresden's Jews had been sent to their deaths and his own life had become much more difficult because of the severe restrictions on his movement and the Gestapo's violent searches of the *Judenhaus* he lived in, Klemperer began to visit the city's Jewish cemetery, where a few of his friends worked. "For Magnus and Steinitz, the cemetery is a refuge," he wrote. "The cemetery administrator has a house out there; he says he does not need to fear a house search; the Gestapo is afraid of the dead (of *their* dead!)."[60] While Cohn and traditional Jews treated visits to cemeteries very seriously, Klemperer evinced a very different tack, for example in October 1942:

> There is something grotesque about my contacts with the Jewish cemetery. Magnus, Steinitz, and Schein . . . have an idyllic refuge there in the gardeners' shed behind the rows of the graves, right beside all those who have been murdered and have committed suicide. They smoke, they fritter their time away, they play cards, they are happy to see visitors. . . . And I myself am no longer in awe of the graves. One soon becomes hardened.[61]

Klemperer, who remained in Dresden until its bombing by the Allies in February 1945, visited his friends in the cemetery again and again. He wrote in his diary that he felt "almost at home" there. It was, he maintained, "the place to get news, where things are always the same."[62] For all Klemperer's implicit and sometimes explicit criticism of the grotesque conduct of the Jews who worked and lived in the Dresden cemetery, in the end it became for him, under the circumstances, a significant and relative safe place—the last Jewish public space in Dresden.

"Jewish Men and Women Work Here Devotedly": Additional Spaces of Jewish Assembly and Refuge

Alongside the expanded use of traditional Jewish places—synagogues and cemeteries—the exclusion of Jews from a wide range of activities in the

German public space led to the emergence of additional Jewish spaces to supply a range of needs. The variety of such spaces was especially notable in the large cities, Berlin in particular. But the phenomenon can be seen elsewhere as well.

Attempts to ban Jews from public spaces already during the Weimar period joined processes of internal Jewish renewal to increase the activity of Jewish organizations and create new communal spaces. Michael Brenner describes Jewish houses of study as part of a Jewish cultural revival during this time, which he sees as part of the development of a distinct Jewish identity within bourgeois German society.[63] Jacob Borut chronicles the establishment and activity of community houses (*Gemeindehäuser*) and youth centers (*Jugendheime*), which hosted social, cultural, and other leisure activities.[64] Rivka Elkin shows how the foundations of the Jewish health care and welfare systems were laid during the republic in response to the increasing needs brought on by social and economic crises.[65]

In the face of the new situation that prevailed during the initial years of Nazi rule, this organizational infrastructure, which operated in a range of Jewish spaces, became a much more important resource for many Jews than it had been in the past. Furthermore, the exclusion of Jews from a swathe of areas in their daily and leisure lives impelled Jewish groups to expand their activities into new areas such as cultural programing, youth activities, and athletics, and these required new spaces to operate in. A detailed discussion of the development of all the types of Jewish community spaces that operated during this period, among them schools, hospitals, and old age homes, goes beyond the scope of this chapter. The focus here is on Jewish lived spaces, and in that regard what is relevant is the nature of common activities, and especially the experience of gathering in such spaces, which operated for several years as Jewish enclaves within the Nazifying German public space. I will offer several examples, with particular attention to Jewish sports spaces.

The Jewish press, which has also been referred to as a sort of Jewish space,[66] devoted much attention to the different aspects of the Jewish public sphere during these years, and the role played by Jewish spaces. The new houses of study that appeared in southern Germany were the subject of a piece in *Jüdische Rundschau* in October 1933. The piece depicted in particular the activities of such institutions in Stuttgart. Because of the new situation, the community centers filled new community roles. Alongside religious studies and Hebrew language lessons, they catered to youth who needed vocational training that would enable them to adapt themselves to new needs.[67] During the years that followed, the houses of study that were established in the large urban communities—where they were distinct from synagogues—served as public platforms for discussions of critical issues and current events. They served as the Jews' town square.[68]

The rapid process of the impoverishment of large swathes of German Jewry, and the German welfare system's increasing refusal to provide services to the Jewish needy,[69] impelled Jewish communities to intensify their social work, which led to the development of Jewish spaces of this sort as well. In 1937 the community and other organizations in Berlin operated fourteen public kitchens that distributed food to needy Jews. Eight of these public kitchens were located in the well-off neighborhoods on the city's west side and catered largely to the middle class and to intellectuals who could no longer support themselves.[70] The community also ran Jewish Winter Relief stations, a project established in the 1930s as a direct response to the exclusion of Jews from the all-German Winter Relief program, which supplied warm clothing and heating devices to the poor. "Everyone is very busy," a *CV-Zeitung* reporter wrote in January 1937 about the Berlin branch of Jewish Winter Relief, which was established as a virtual replica of the German Winterhilfe organization, run by the Nazis, which supplied clothing, food, and heating equipment to the poor but refused to help Jews. "Jewish men and women work here devotedly to help the members of their community who need refuge and security," the article reported.[71]

Another example of Jewish spaces that operated in some of the central communities in Germany was Jewish museums. These had opened their doors before the Nazis came to power, but their activity intensified afterward, and their nature changed. In November 1933 the Jewish Museum in Breslau, which had functioned since 1929 in the framework of the Silesian Museum of Art and Antiquities, moved into the city's Jewish orphanage. The shift from the general German urban space to the internal Jewish community space seems to have changed the nature of the museum, which now aimed to document and preserve Jewish life in Silesia and other eastern areas of Germany.[72] For Willy Cohn, for whom Jewish spaces were of central significance during these years, the museum's reopening in the orphanage was very meaningful.[73] He visited it frequently, and even guided other museumgoers.

The transformation in the kinds of activities these institutions offered and in the role they took upon themselves was on display at the Jewish Museum in Berlin. Ironically, it opened its doors to the public in January 1933, just a few days before Hitler was appointed chancellor. The museum's founders then asked the members of the community to donate family objects of historical value for its collections.[74] Some two and a half years later, when Franz Landsberger became the museum's new director, he issued a similar request to the Jewish public. This time, however, the circumstances were different, and his plea was of a different nature. Landsberger asked the many Jewish families who were leaving the country to donate family heirlooms of Jewish interest. He issued a similar request to the disintegrating communities in the provinces.[75] Recall that in that same year Joachim Prinz had claimed that the emptying of the Jewish communities in these far-flung areas meant that their synagogues were turning into museum spaces. With the same kind of insight, the director of the Jewish museum of Berlin, a city with a vital and functional Jewish community, sought to make his institution a central site in shaping the memory of Jewish life in Germany, by bringing together within it treasures from the vanishing communities.

As they rapidly dwindled, these small Jewish communities in the provinces and the periphery also grew isolated. One way of filling the vacuum was what might be called mobile community spaces. In the dire straits of the early years of the Nazi regime, a network emerged that brought to these places activities especially of a cultural nature, such as lectures and performances. As early as August 1933, as part of a discussion in *Jüdische Rundschau* about the plight of such small communities, Max Reinheimer of Frankfurt noted their desperate isolation and suggested assisting them spiritually and culturally by establishing mobile Jewish libraries and by organizing lectures by rabbis and Jewish educators.[76]

Such activities were pursued in the years that followed by, among others, the Jewish Cultural Federation (Jüdischer Kulturbund), which sent performers on tours of the provinces. In a special issue of *CV-Zeitung* honoring four years of the Cultural Federation's work, Hans Buxman cited the Hamburg Ensemble, which had renamed itself the Traveling Ensemble (Reise-Ensemble). Its members built transportable scenery and lighting, and traveled all over Germany to perform in cities and outlying areas. "The work needed here is not easy, and the burden on each [member of the ensemble] is heavy," Buxman wrote. He stressed that the members of the company did not think of themselves as people from the big city who from time to time visited the provinces. On the contrary, they felt they belonged everywhere they toured. "The ensemble feels an attachment to the audience in each city it performs in," he declared. "Each evening is a new opening night."[77] For the audiences, Martha Wertheimer wrote in February 1937, Cultural Federation performances offered distraction and a temporary refuge from loneliness. For the members of small communities, the shows were sometimes substitutes for their vanishing community lives.[78]

A few months after his dismissal from his high school teaching post, Willy Cohn began working as a lecturer on Jewish history. In addition to giving talks in Breslau, he traveled to outlying communities in Upper Silesia, and sometimes in more distant locations. From the end of 1933 until the end of 1938, he found himself in a variety of Jewish spaces—synagogues, community houses, old age homes, and the like—and took part in the augmentation of the Jewish public sphere in Germany. Cohn's lectures were a piece of the mobile Jewish space. In his diary he frequently wrote about his travels: the usually large size of his audiences, who were packed into crowded places, and his personal encounters with them. He commented again and again on the spiritual isolation of the provincial communities, and sometimes noted the opening of new community centers and synagogues. He also reported about how different Jewish spaces were coming together to occupy the same buildings.[79]

In his personal life, Cohn had experienced spatial exclusion and had coped with the constriction of his personal space, as has been chronicled in the previous chapter. In his travels, he had a different spatial experience. "I am living a strange life now," he wrote at the end of November 1934. "I am on trains a lot, I am now familiar with all the train stations in Silesia, all the waiting rooms, all the posters. I feel at home everywhere."[80] This description might give the impression that he enjoyed freedom of movement and that he experienced open spaces. This might be taken to imply that he had a foothold in space. But further on, Cohn stressed that on his travels he frequently turned in on himself and remained silent, which testifies to constriction. In practice, he did not feel at all at home in these ostensibly open spaces. Rather, he principally went from one point to another, from one Jewish space to another—for the most part isolated and closed places. In January 1935, for example, he gave a lecture next to the Jewish old age home in Würzburg. A Jewish driver drove him from there to a nearby Jewish café, and the next day Cohn went on a tour of ancient Jewish synagogues in Franconia.[81] He generally felt the synagogues and other Jewish spaces he visited and at which he lectured to be places of warmth, security, and Jewish solidarity; but he also sometimes felt crowded and stifled. In certain cases, he reported that these places caused him distress, and that he needed to avoid them or get out in the open to breathe fresh air.[82] Cohn's accounts of his activities in these outlying towns show how Jewish spaces in Germany consolidated as islands of intensive Jewish activity in an alien and hostile environment.

"Living at Gross Breesen Was Like Living on an Island": Youth Movements and Training Farms

Another sort of Jewish space was provided by Jewish youth movements and other youth groups, and by training farms that trained young Jews to be farmers. Jewish youth movements, some of them of Zionist orientation, began to operate in Germany during the years prior to World War I, and were highly critical of the urban bourgeois world from which most of their members came. Centrally, the youth movements took young Jews out of the cities to hike and camp in the countryside, which they saw as a new experiential space.[83] During the Weimar period a new youth movement, Hehalutz, established Zionist training farms, attracting several hundred young Jews a year. These participants experienced rural life and formed close-knit groups that spent extended periods together as they waited to receive immigration permits to Palestine.[84]

In her book on the daily life of Jews under the Nazi regime, Marion Kaplan argues that Jewish children and adolescents suffered much more than adults from their exclusion from public schools and their banishment from the social life of their non-Jewish contemporaries. As the prospects for young people narrowed, Kaplan maintains, they incurred long-term injury to the way they envisioned their future, and endured constant assault on their self-esteem.[85] The wound was especially deep because of the important role the Nazis assigned to non-Jewish youth in their People's Community (*Volksgemeinschaft*). German youth, Rabbi Joachim Prinz argued in *Jüdische Rundschau* in June 1934, enjoyed a special space in the fabric of the new regime, embodied in the Hitler Youth (*Hitlerjugend*), which organized treks and courses and disseminated a new youth literature. In the face of this, young Jews felt isolated and in need of their own space.[86] Indeed, organized Jewish youth activity skyrocketed after the Nazi rise to power. Only a small minority of Jewish teenagers participated in Jewish youth movements and organizations at the end of the Weimar period, but by 1936 about 60 percent of young Jews from the age of twelve into their early twenties were involved. This activity encompassed a wide range of groups, despite their difficulty in operating in German public space, and it responded to young Jews' need for a social framework and a sense of belonging.[87]

Going out into nature, so central to Jewish youth activity prior to the Nazi era, became even more prominent under the Nazi regime. Training farms provided Jewish youth with a new spatial and communal experience. In December 1933, *Jüdische Rundschau*'s youth supplement offered a survey of three training farms in the Brandenburg area, around Berlin. Most residents of the training farms, it reported, were in their early twenties and had previously lived typical urban lives in offices and businesses. The training farms, however, did more than prepare them for new vocations and their move to Palestine. They also offered a more profound experience of community life (*Gemeinschaft*) very much unlike city life.[88] Willy Cohn, who spent several days in August 1934 at the Gross Gaglow training farm, where his son Ernst was living, was astounded by how his son had adapted to the new life. "He looks just like a farmer," Cohn wrote.[89] But he also took account of the many problems involved in the operation of an isolated camp of this sort. Willy Cohn's son, Ernst Abraham Cohn, left Germany for Palestine in December 1934. In 1960 he brought over his father's diary notebooks, and he later translated them into Hebrew.[90]

In 1933 young urban Jews' attempts to maintain a foothold were described in the liberal Jewish newspaper *CV-Zeitung*, although at this point the activities were not all seen as preparation for life outside Germany. Some were attempts to change the lifestyles and vocational structures of Jews living in Germany.[91] For example, the liberal Jewish youth association organized assemblies and activities in the countryside near Lehnitz, north of Berlin. Using language much like that employed by the Zionists, the newspaper wrote that activity in green open spaces encouraged communal solidarity, the opposite of the isolation that afflicted urban Jewish youth.[92] Lehnitz was also the site of a school of home economics organized by the Jüdischer Frauenbund, a Jewish women's organization for teenage girls who had been expelled from German schools, which was also described in the liberal press as an ideal space for the creation of a community.[93]

The important place occupied by youth movement activity and the opportunities it provided for youth to get out of the city is documented in the diary of Ilse Strauss. Born in 1920, she lived in Krefeld. At the age of fifteen she joined the liberal Jewish-German Youth Alliance (Bund deutsch-jüdischer Jugend).[94] She participated in activities such as flag raising, campfires, and organization of ceremonies. Her diary accounts show how the youth group served as a refuge from her everyday difficulties. In June 1935, Strauss participated in a summer camp to mark the Shavuot holiday, during which the youth group visited a number of old synagogues in the rural area. "Some members of the group had set themselves the task of investigating Jewish history in their areas of the homeland [*Heimat*]," she wrote. "The visit was very useful, because the memorial books [*Memorbücher*, complied by these members] include a great deal of useful information."[95] Experiences of this sort helped young people to maintain traction in the German space and form youth communities, symbolized by an oath the members took to continue being loyal to one another even after emigration.

Her Youth Alliance chapter's gradual dissolution as a result of emigration caused Strauss to feel an increasing sense of suffocation and lack of space. This grew ever more evident in her writing in the years that followed, until her own emigration to England in April 1939. "We no longer have synagogues, we don't have children in the high school, we are only a remnant. Last year I was still in Kull," she wrote in her diary in February 1939, apparently referring to Niepkuhlenzug, a region of meanders along the Rhine. "But now," she continued a few lines later, "nothing remains to us. No one comes, everyone is leaving."[96]

For Strauss, like thousands of other young Jews who participated in youth movements at the time, the activities were confined to weekends and overnights of a few days outside the city. In contrast, those who went to training farms, and who were for the most part somewhat older, enjoyed a longer-term spatial experience. Under the conditions in which Jews lived and the pressure to emigrate, Zionism became a mass movement that during the Nazi regime's early years focused primarily on the young. The number of training farms increased significantly as a result. This trend, which began in 1933, reached its peak at the end of 1937, when about thirty of the training arms operated in Germany. Most were sponsored by Zionist organizations—Hehalutz, associated with the labor movement, and the religious Brit Halutzim. Their purpose was to train young Jews for settlement in Palestine. But there were also non-Zionist camps that promoted emigration to other countries, and young Jews also served as trainees at private farms. In 1938 about 5,500 young Jews, comprising between 10 and 15 percent of the total number of Jewish youth in Germany at the time, signed up for training farms.[97]

The training farms gave the youth something to do and a future to look forward to. They opened up the German countryside for young Jews and enabled them to experience open spaces very different from urban Jewish spaces. In practice, they also served as isolated and insulated islands in the German space. Moreover, the Nazi regime intended them to be just that, as seen in a memorandum that the Reich Interior Ministry sent in June 1934 to Minister of Agriculture Richard Walther Darré:

> The Jews envisaged for the retraining farms do not represent a new influx from without but instead already live in Germany, and are currently forcibly unemployed. They therefore have far more opportunity and incentive to act in detrimental ways than if they were in closed camps, tired and distracted by strenuous physical labor, spending their days until emigration with the prospect of having a way out of their existing situation.[98]

The idyllic accounts of life on the training farms also include references to them being remote islands; another metaphor was that of oases in hostile territory. "At Winkel we were like an island," wrote Gerschon (Gerhard) Wolff, born in 1916, in his memoir of the Zionist training farm at which he lived from 1934 until he settled in Palestine in 1936.[99] This experience was not restricted to Zionist youth. Werner Angress, four years younger than Wolff, spent several months as a trainee at the Gross Breesen training farm near Breslau, until he and his family left for Holland in 1937. The camp was founded in 1936 to train young Jews not from Zionist backgrounds in farming in advance of emigration to other countries, and it continued to operate until the Gestapo closed it in 1941.[100] Angress, who later became a historian of Germany in the United States, published a study and documentation of the camp, and later also a personal memoir. "Although we hardly thought about it and didn't talk about it," he wrote in this latter book, "we were aware of the fact that living at Gross Breesen was like living on an island. The Third Reich surrounded us, and when we went to Breslau or home for the very short Christmas vacation, the Nazi state, with its uniforms, flags, and bellowing SA people, was everywhere we looked."[101]

"The Hours We Spent on the Sports Field at Grunewald are the Nicest Memory That Remains to Me": Jewish Athletic Spaces

Physical and athletic activity played an important role in constituting modern Jewish identity in Germany. Jews were active in the exercise and sports associations that were active throughout the country, and this was integral to their transformation into a component of German bourgeois society. Here too the rise of the Nazi regime led to their exclusion, as part of the consolidation of the Nazi-inspired German community (*Volksgemeinschaft*). In his study of Jewish sports in Nazi Germany, Daniel Fraenkel showed that the victims of this were not just famous professional athletes but also, indeed mostly, ordinary German men and women whose banishment from sports clubs, swimming pools, and public exercise facilities "shook the social and psychological foundations on which their daily existence depended."[102] That was the case for Meta Fuß-Opet, who was forced out of the exercise club where she had trained for many years. She wrote of how hard it was for her to leave "the big red house with the high, narrow, and brightly lit windows, through which, in the evening, joyful singing could be heard from young throats."[103]

Thousands of Jewish athletes were, like Fuß-Opet, expelled from German sports clubs during the early months of the new regime. They were taken in by Jewish sports clubs, which quickly expanded their activities. The most important of these Jewish clubs were Maccabi and Schild. The latter was a patriotic German organization that had been founded by the Reich Federation of Jewish Front-Line Soldiers (RjF). Amateurs also joined these organizations. In 1933 Maccabi's national membership grew to 8,000, organized in 25 chapters; by 1935 it had 21,500 members and 136 chapters. Schild had, at the end of 1933, some 7,000 members in 90 chapters; by mid-1936, at its height, it had 21,000 members in 216 chapters.[104] According to contemporary estimates, the year of the Berlin Olympics, 1936, was, not surprisingly, the top year for the Jewish sports clubs, with some 45,000 members—about 12 percent of the Jewish population.[105]

The most urgent problem facing Jews who were banned from German sports facilities was that of finding alternative sites to continue their training. As part of the process of excluding Jews from the German public space, municipal governments and local authorities acted to bar Jewish access to public sports facilities. "We Jews are barred from all sports associations. We have taken note of that," Fritz Wolfes wrote in resignation to the mayor of Hanover in December 1933.

> We are not begging for admission but rather founding a Jewish gymnastics association. But we have no sports hall, no gymnastics apparatus. Why is the city unwilling to lease them to us? . . . If twenty Japanese were to lease a sports hall, nothing would stand in the way of it.[106]

Jewish public activists and young people tried to cope with the situation in creative ways. "The Jewish sports movement in Germany has been through a rough year," noted a *Jüdische Rundschau* correspondent at the beginning of December 1933. "The Jewish sports associations deserve special appreciation for their attempts, despite the lack of exercise halls and playing fields everywhere, to maintain sports activities during hikes, on lawns, and in factory halls."[107]

Here again, from the beginning of the Nazi era, there was a difference between the situation in large cities, Berlin in particular, and the much harsher situation in provincial cities and the periphery. In the big cities, some sort of tolerable Jewish life remained possible for several years. The Grunewald athletic field in the west of Berlin was in many ways an example. A few months before the rise of the Nazi regime, the Jewish community leased the facility and transformed it into a Jewish sports center. "Unemployed young Jews from the big city are discussing where they can engage in sports," *CV-Zeitung* reported in July 1933. They then heard that the community had obtained the field and would also help them get there so as to prepare it for use. "So on a clear morning you can see fifty young people equipped with hoes taking off their shirts to prepare the sports field on their own."[108]

The Jewish press ratcheted up its coverage of Jewish sports events as they became more common. The story about the Grunewald athletic field indicates that it was an attempt to grant young Jews in Berlin, and even in Germany as a whole, a spatial experience that would compensate them, at least to a certain extent and for a time, for their exclusion and alienation from German space. The Reich Committee of Jewish Sports Associations held its first sports day at Grunewald in August 1934, the first such event for Jews throughout Germany. A *CV-Zeitung* reporter wrote that three thousand Jews from all over the Reich attended, including six hundred young men and women who took an active part in the games. Thousands of spectators waved banners, and the organizers declared that the event's principal purpose was to promote the unity of Jewish youth.[109] A great deal of importance was attached to the fact that the games were held outdoors, a fact also underlined by the press. *CV-Zeitung* opened its article on another day of games a week later, this one organized by the Bund Deutsch-Jüdischer Jugend, with the declaration, "This is one of those glorious days of great clarity . . . cloudless skies of deep blue." A thousand people attended, the newspaper reported.[110]

The staging of these Jewish events, with their huge audiences, banners, and rhetoric of unity, was unmistakably modeled on the public rallies the Nazis organized as part of their program of capturing the public space and establishing the People's Community (*Volksgemeinschaft*). Indeed, the stadium was one of the formative spaces of the new Nazi regime. The regime used the events to shape the amorphous masses who assembled in them into a political community and nation. "Given the importance the Nazis assigned to popular rallies," Boaz Neumann argued, "it is easy to understand the legislative intent of forbidding the Jewish population to hold assemblies or rallies of any sort. . . . Legislation of this sort was intended to strip the Jew of his standing in the public space and the public presence required for the solidarity that is a condition of all social and political existence."[111]

The Jewish athletic complex in Grunewald made it possible for Jewish children and teenagers to bypass, at least in part, the spatial restrictions that the Nazi regime inflicted on them. It enabled them to gather together out in the open, a kind of space that was ever more uncommon in Jewish life. Waving banners and marching in parades met a profound need among these young people to feel the exhilaration of solidarity, even if only in an isolated space and for a short period of time. The use of Grunewald by the city's Jewish schools for their sports activities figures in a memoir by Inge Deutschkron, who moved with her family to Berlin in 1927 at the age of five. "The hours we spent on the sports field at Grunewald are the nicest memory that remains to me from my school days," she wrote. "Only there did the depressing atmosphere that weighed on us everywhere dissipate."[112] As a writer in *CV-Zeitung* explained in July in an article about the renovation and redesign of the Grunewald facility so that it could hold five thousand spectators, "These may seem like small things, but the sound made by such small things in these times is of inestimable value, because for Jewish youth sports has ever growing value and meaning, and this awareness must be given concrete expression."[113]

The Jewish press understandably preferred to paint an upbeat picture, but the sense of liberation that young Jews experienced at Grunewald took place within the bounds of the permitted Jewish space and, as Deutschkron wrote, it "vanished the minute we boarded the streetcar on our way home."[114] Furthermore, it was no coincidence that the renovation was completed, with the permission of the authorities, just a few weeks before the start of the Berlin Olympics. The freedom the regime granted the Jews to organize their own athletic activities in cordoned-off spaces reached a height at this time. The complexity of the situation was evident in the fact that the Jewish press, which extensively covered Jewish sports events, almost entirely ignored the Olympics. "There would seem to be nothing more emblematic of the virtual ghetto in which Jewish sports took place in Nazi Germany than the resounding silence of the Jewish sports pages during the Olympics," Fraenkel wrote.[115] For two years following the Olympics, the Jewish sports organizations were able to carry on their activities; the Maccabi Avshalom Petah Tikva handball team from Palestine even played a match at Grunewald in June 1937.[116] But as time went on, this activity dwindled, due to the emigration of young people. In November 1938 the closure of the major Jewish organizations in Germany in the wake of the pogrom meant that Jewish sports activities also came to an end.

The breathing space that Jewish sports enjoyed at Grunewald was limited but exceptional, an expression of the relatively tolerable lives of Berlin's Jews during the regime's early years. Frankfurt's Jewish community, Germany's second-largest, also held Jewish athletic events before large crowds.[117] But, as the contemporary press documents, most of Germany's Jews could hold only modest sports activities in much more constricted spaces.[118]

The challenge involved can be sensed in an article by Erich Sonn, a physical education teacher, titled "School Exercise without Equipment and without Space," which appeared in *Jüdische Rundschau*'s educational supplement. Sonn stressed the importance of physical education in Jewish school, and offered practical advice for coping with the challenge of limited space. Each class session, he argued, should begin with walking or running. "The space difficulties cannot be taken into account," he stressed. "Even in the narrowest schoolyard there is room to gather forty to fifty boys or girls in an open area."[119] Schoolchildren love circle races, he noted, which can easily be conducted in the smallest room by marking out a path. Sonn's message that anything was possible even in less amenable conditions matched the approach taken by the Jewish press, especially when it came to education and children. It is hard to credit his claim that these conditions were in practical terms satisfactory; it seems reasonable to assume that children and adolescents felt closed in. But the article nevertheless says something about the tactics that teachers and sports organizers employed in their efforts, and it fits well with de Certeau's conceptualization of exclusion and the spatial constriction. Not only did these people seek to carry on engaging in physical activity in every available space; they also promoted a way of thinking, that all was possible.

The escalation of spatial exclusion in the second half of the 1930s intensified the need to find other sorts of Jewish sports spaces. These were found outdoors, in other Jewish spaces, and sometimes also in the private sphere.[120] In March 1937, for example, *Israelitisches Familienblatt*'s sports section called on Jewish sports clubs to adapt to the new situation in which they were no longer able to rent sports fields, even of the simplest type. The newspaper proposed that the clubs move as much of their activity as possible out of the city, into woods or farms. It added that "it is possible to exercise without special equipment in every backyard."[121] The ongoing endeavor to use existing spaces to the maximum is reminiscent of the parallel situation with public spaces, and of the change in attitudes toward Jewish places such as cemeteries and synagogues. That can be seen in an assessment that Paul Jogi Mayer, the professional director of the RjF's sports program, wrote in 1937:

> For weeks, even months, athletes have gone from house to house, from one member of the community to another, to locate, for example, community halls that stand empty, for the purpose of group sports. In the end they succeeded, almost throughout the Reich, in finding training sites. So young men and women meet to play on dark winter evenings in synagogue foyers and basements that have been repurposed as sports venues, in unheated factories, and in attics that the wind blows through—men who come to train on their own and women who come for exercise [classes], with and without equipment.[122]

Frequently, Jogi Mayer added, the participants encountered setbacks and were compelled to hand over the new spaces they had prepared for their activities, but that did not stop their enthusiasm for carrying on.

The decline of small communities, which led to the closure of synagogues, meant that those structures were available for reconditioning as new spaces for physical exercise.[123] Given the exigencies, Jewish public figures, rabbis included, realized that the needs of the present outweighed not only the heritage of the Emancipation, during which it had taken form—that is, the view of the synagogue as a sacred space in which only religious activities took place—but also ancient Jewish tradition, which forbade the renovation of a synagogue, even after being abandoned, for another use. The same thing happened with regard to cemeteries. *Israelitisches Familienblatt* reported in September 1938 that the Jewish community in Königsburg had assigned use of the community cemetery to the Bar Kokhba Association and Schild. The two sports clubs, with considerable effort, repurposed the area to serve as an outdoor, fresh-air exercise space for youth. Under the new circumstances, there was no longer any reason to observe the imperative noted by Norbert Elias—that in the modern age, cemeteries had become spaces cut off from life, in which absolute silence prevailed. "No one is concerned that life and death are so close," claimed the author of the essay, "On the contrary—when the youthful voices of our children are heard from over the graves of our dead, it always offers some comfort and raises our hopes."[124]

"The Clear and Historical Imperative . . . to Prepare a New Space for Our Youth": The German Jewish Community Facing Emigration

The children's supplement to the Central Association's newspaper, *CVZ Kinderblatt*, in June 1934 offered Jewish children an educational "journey game" (*Reisespiel*). The game, which required players to advance through sixty different stations by casting dice, was structured in circle form. It began at square one, the Berlin offices of the Central Association, and ended at the same point, after the young players visited various sites of Jewish memory and culture in Germany and Central Europe, among them venerable and new synagogues in cities all over Germany (including Worms, Essen, Düsseldorf, and Breslau) and outside it (Prague, Amsterdam), as well as cemeteries, Jewish museums, teaching and training institutions, and so on (figure 3).[125]

The game, in fact, offered the mental map that the central stream of German Jewry sought to instill in the younger generation at the beginning of the Nazi era, and established its boundaries. It highlighted a variety of ancient and new Jewish places and spaces, like the ones discussed in this chapter.

About three and a half years later, in October 1937, the newspaper offered another journey game (figure 4). But this time, instead of the circular trip to Jewish sites in Central Europe, the young players had to set out on five-stage, one-way trip across continents, beginning at a Berlin train station. The trip took them over land and sea as far as Sydney, Australia.[126] The new game, similar to but different from its predecessor, reflected the changes the mental map—and the imagined space of many German Jews, including children, young people, and adults—had undergone over the intervening years.

The policies of the new regime, and the reality of the lives of Jews living in Nazi Germany, impelled them to consider emigration. There was a surge of immigrants to Palestine in 1933, consisting of veteran Zionists who were carrying out their long-held intent to settle there, as well as others who turned to Zionism because of the situation. There were also political

Figure 3. "Wer reist mit? Eine Reise durch jüdische Kulturstätten in Deutschland und jenseits zur Grenzen" (Who's joining? A trip to Jewish cultural sites in Germany and beyond). *CV-Zeitung* 13, no. 24 (June 14, 1934). Digitized by Johann Christian Senckenberg University Library, Goethe University.

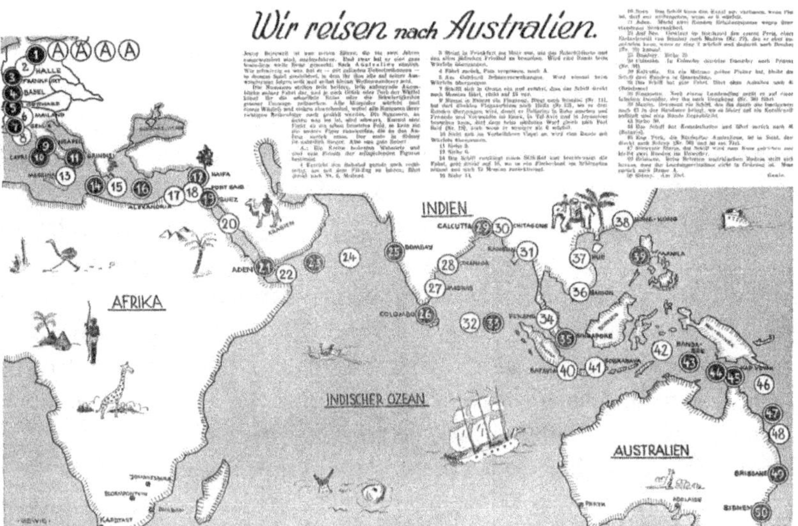

Figure 4. "Wir reisen nach Australien" (We are traveling to Australia). *CV-Zeitung* 16, no. 42 (October 21, 1937). Digitized by Johann Christian Senckenberg University Library, Goethe University.

emigrants who left Germany because they feared the regime would target them. The gradual deterioration of the Jews' position during the years that followed—an accelerating decline in their financial position, and their acceptance that the changes would not be short-lived—impelled many others to consider the possibilities for emigration. In 1933 these emigrants were principally Zionists, who called openly to leave Germany and did so in large numbers. As the situation worsened, and with the promulgation of the Nuremberg Laws, emigration became a central issue on the agenda of the central stream of German Jewry.[127]

As early as 1933, when the question of whether emigration should play a central role in the vision of German Jewry's future was still controversial, a shift in the spatial perceptions of Jews was already evident in their discourse. The constriction of their lived space in their German homeland led to an expansion of their imagined space considerably beyond its previous boundaries. In an article that appeared in September 1933, Hugo Rosenthal, a Zionist educator, sketched the outlines of the space in which Jews could see themselves living. His term for the space was *Lebensraum*, borrowed from the Nazi vocabulary.[128] Even before and during the emancipation, Rosenthal argued, "the spiritual space of our fate" extended well beyond the boundaries of the German nation. Now, he claimed, the invisible but very palpable wall (*Scheidewand*) separating Germans and Jews was intensifying the latter's need for a wider spiritual space. The living space of the generation growing up in Germany was changing, Rosenthal added. The place for young Jews within the German people (*Volkheit*) was narrowing at a rapid pace, but at the same time their place within the Jewish people was expanding. Rosenthal used the term "space" at least partly in a metaphorical sense, but his indication of a Jewish world with a prospect much wider than that of Germany was prophetic. The same idea was expressed in a statement issued by the National Representation of German Jews after it was founded just a few weeks later, in which it referred to "the clear and historical imperative, which stands as a fact impervious to all claims and objections, to prepare a new space for our youth . . . to discover new places and to blaze new trails."[129]

During the second half of the 1930s, in part following the Nuremberg Laws, the subject of emigration became ever more central for German Jews. More and more of them left for a wider variety of destinations. Many others remained in Germany but weighed the possibility of emigration, and even traveled as tourists to check out options for relocation or to visit close family. These changes were clearly evident in Jewish public discourse and in the work of Jewish organizations. A series of atlases were published, full of information about possible places for Jews to move to all over the world, from

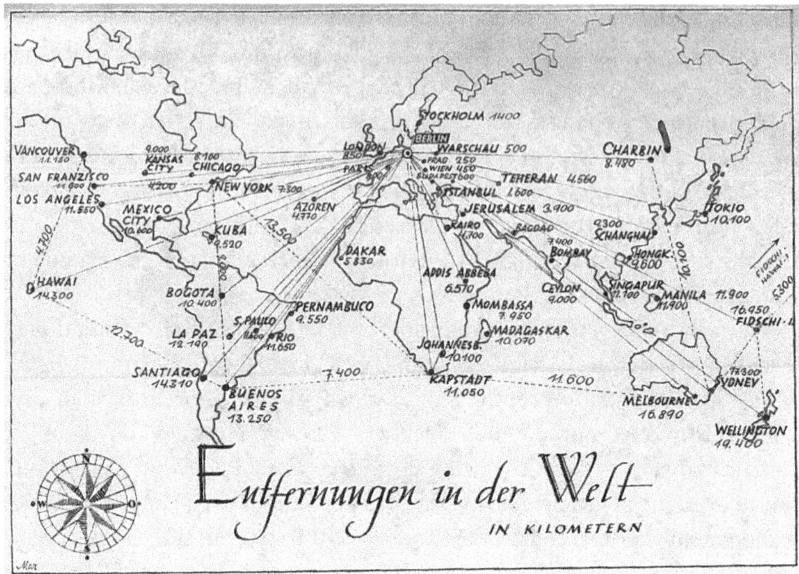

Figure 5. "Distances in the World, in Kilometers." *Philo Atlas: Handbuch für die jüdische Auswanderung* (Berlin: Philo Verlag, 1938).

North and South America to Australia. These culminated with the appearance in October 1938—just a few days before the November pogrom—of *Philo-Atlas*, a handbook for Jewish emigrants with concise information about countries to resettle in.[130] At the back was a map that presented the distance from Berlin to a large number of destinations—a clear manifestation of how German Jews' perception of space had changed (figure 5).[131]

Another notable indication of the change in the Jews' experience of space comes from advertisements in the Jewish press, which focused increasingly on foreign travel and emigration. Many of the ads were taken out by passenger ship companies and a range of travel- and emigration-related businesses such as moving services, foreign-language instruction, furniture and electrical appliances suitable for emigrants, and even heat-resistant prefabricated houses that could be dismantled and reassembled. People also placed personal ads seeking marriage partners with whom to emigrate.[132]

The changes brought on by these circumstances shaped German Jewry as a society experiencing spatial contraction even as, much more than in the past, German Jews were traveling to other countries and preparing for emigration. The manner in which this changed the self-awareness and lived space of German Jews was discussed by Hilde Cohn in an article titled "Going and Coming," which in March 1937 appeared in the liberal Jewish monthly *Der Morgen*.[133] Cohn focused on the transitional moments and "liminal experiences" of these travelers, describing how trips to distant points had become a routine part of the lives of many. The present difficulties, she argued, had made transitional spaces such as train stations, seaports, and airports look very different. Similarly, means of transport such as trains, airplanes, and boats, had become "accessible and banal as means of traversing distances."[134] For example, a trip to South America, which until recently would have been an unimaginable dream for a sixteen-year-old, had now become a common experience for young people. Destinations that had in the past been viewed as exotic and distant were now part of the life plans of many. Jews were now conversing daily about places all over the world, with the result that the mental picture of such places, once fuzzy, had now come into focus. Cohn argued that the emigration fever gripping German Jews had caused world spaces to shrink at this point toward the end of the 1930s. This sense of global spatial contraction, making the most distant places now seem accessible, was another Jewish coping tactic.

In his essay "Non-Places," first published in French in 1992, the anthropologist Marc Augé addresses the constriction of space in our times. Because of the shrinking of global distances, our lives have been inundated with images and impressions from all over the world. Augé argues that these images in our minds are replacing the images and impressions of our immediate physical surroundings.[135] He notes how "non-places" have come into being, these being very different from traditional places, which he calls "anthropological places." Anthropological spaces, Augé asserts, are founded on the spaces in which human beings live in an immediate way, on their geography, and on multigenerational memories of them. The modernism of the nineteenth century, which Augé terms "Baudelairean modernity," gradually shaped new spaces that could still become integrated into traditional anthropological spaces; but what he calls "supermodernity" has accelerated the rise and dominance of nonplaces, a wide variety of abstract spaces that lack all uniqueness, such as hotels, freeways, and airports.[136]

Cohn's analysis of the changing spatial experiences of German Jews clearly has some parallels with Augé's conceptualization of the global situation at the end of the twentieth century. Germany's Jews, whose world was shaped until the Nazi regime as part of Augé's Baudelairean modernity, were forced into this situation. It could be said that the Nazis imposed on them a spatial experience that many others in the West would acquire only half a century later. In that sense, Germany's Jews were ahead of their time. Augé, who writes in a tone that sometimes feels like a nostalgic lament, portrays nonplaces as entirely disconnected from the unique experience of the anthropological space, and associates them with loneliness and alienation. The fact that this pessimism is not apparent in Cohn's piece may be due to the fact that she published her article as part of the Jewish attempt to grapple with conditions that had been forced on them. She may have sought to offer a more positive portrayal of the transitions that these Jews experienced, and of the world opening up before them. But it seems reasonable to presume that many of these emigrating Jews experienced the difficulties of which Augé writes.

A more critical attitude than Cohn's regarding the changes that the growing fervor surrounding emigration caused in the way German Jews viewed the world—one in which there may be a premonition of sorts of what Augé would write in an entirely different context more than fifty years later—can be found in an article by Alfred Hirschberg that appeared in September 1938 in *CV-Zeitung*, to mark Rosh Hashanah. Hirschberg was one of the Central Association's most prominent leaders. He began, "It distresses many of our people to look once every few days at [the map of] the Atlantic [Ocean], at the tables of distances, and at the passenger ship pamphlets."[137] Hirschberg wrote of Jews' growing use of maps as means of coping with their hopes and fears, but he pointed out the problem. "People must know where they might go or where their children already are, and that sometimes increases their bewilderment: [they are but] small souls in a large space." In the face of this perplexity, which could lead to a sense of alienation, Hirschberg called on his readers to adopt an orientation with regard to what he called "the map of the human spirit," which was based, he argued, on profound study of history and sacred texts. Without such a mental map to help focus their Jewish experience, Jews were liable to lose their bearings.

The centrality of transition sites, train stations in particular, in the spatial experience of German Jews during this period could be seen in the literary works they produced. Kerstin Schoor notes that in these literary works, train stations were prominent sites alongside synagogues, cemeteries, and homes.[138] In some of the works, Schoor argues, train stations figure as sites symbolizing hope and the future, while in others they appear as sites of alienation and despair. For example, in Meta Samson's children's story *Spatz macht sich*, the train station appears several times as a place where emotional farewells are bid to family members and close friends before their emigration. A description of the train station from the point of view of one girl reads: "How strange the station seemed today . . . like something dark that could not be fled from."[139] But at the same time, the story also offers the point of view of a friend who is going to settle in Palestine. His encounter with the train station makes him emotional and expectant. Another story, "An Experience in the Central Train Station" by Hertha Rosenfeld, which appeared in *Israelitisches Familienblatt* on November 3, 1938, just a few days before the pogrom, tells of an encounter between the protagonist,

Mrs. Lewin, who is emigrating to Palestine, and the Lowensteins, a couple whose son has done the same just a few weeks previously. The train station provides the backdrop to the tension and uncertainty in the lives of these Jews. Mrs. Lewin loses her suitcase and is treated with hostility by other people at the station, while the Lowensteins are worried because they have not heard from their son for several weeks. On the other hand, the encounter between Mrs. Lewin and the Lowensteins has an optimistic cast. They lend each other support, and at the story's end the Lowensteins receive letters from their son and from Mrs. Lewin, who has arrived in Palestine.[140]

Trains and train stations are also at the center of *The Passenger* (*Der Reisende*), by Ulrich Alexander Boschwitz, who emigrated to England in 1939 at the age of twenty-four. The novel was written immediately following the November pogrom, and was published in 1939 in English under a pseudonym. The German original appeared in print only in 2018. The protagonist, Otto Silbermann, a Jewish merchant from Berlin, has been severely affected by the pogrom. The novel shows him traveling by train all over Germany—first to specific destinations, and then just for the sake of traveling, and to get away. "One can travel to escape serenity," he says in an attempt to explain himself to one of the people he meets. "But one can also travel to find serenity."[141] But the picture painted by the novel is one of a man in constant flight, whose trips without destinations illustrate his detachment from space.

Conclusion: "He Who Knows How to Fly Will Never Bump into Walls"

In November 1935, some two months after the promulgation of the Nuremberg Laws, Alfred Hirschberg published "Spaciousness [*Weite*] within Constrictedness [*Enge*]."[142] Hirschberg spoke to the plight of Germany's Jews in the face of their banishment from the German public space and their retreat into the intra-Jewish sphere. Despite the huge successes scored by this effort, he wrote—pointing to the Cultural Federations and houses of study, as well as to the Jewish press and Jewish literature—there was no avoiding the feeling that they were narrowly hemmed in. Jews had lost their capacity for enjoying art, culture, and intellectual life anonymously, as individuals among thousands, as had been the case during the age of emancipation. Hirschberg quoted a contemporary who took a critical view of these activities: "In narrower circles even the meaning of these things becomes narrower." He acknowledged that there was something to this objection, but countered it by writing of small groups of Jews gathering in small unheated rooms, without electrical lighting, to converse on philosophy and literature. The true spirit, he argued, is always spacious, always expanding, and does not depend on physical spaces. "He who knows how to fly will never bump into walls," he declared. As such, from within this ostensible constrictedness (*scheinbaren Enge*) a Jew could concentrate and achieve a truly broad view of the world. The tension that Hirschberg grappled with, between the plight of the constricted space within which Jewish activities took place and the aspiration for spaciousness, characterizes the entire range of issues discussed in this chapter.

At its center lies the uses for which Jews, as individuals and as a collective, needed Jewish places and spaces of different kinds for a wide variety of activities. They also needed these spaces in order to reshape their public lives under conditions of discrimination and exclusion. As in the previous chapter, here too a central factor was the agency exercised by Jews who strove, with a range of tactics, to preserve and create Jewish spaces for activity. Traditional Jewish sites—synagogues and, later, cemeteries—thus took on a more dominant role in the daily lives of many, and the traditional rules about using these spaces underwent a very real metamorphosis under the new conditions. Furthermore, new spaces emerged for Jewish activity in a wide variety of locations: social assistance centers, cultural centers, sports facilities, and training farms.

The development of Jewish spaces in Nazi Germany reached its height during the second half of the 1930s; but in 1938, even before the November pogrom, Jews began to confine their activities, both as a result of emigration and because of increasingly severe anti-Jewish policies. The dedication of the new Jewish community house in Hamburg, which required a considerable investment of money and effort, in January 1938, can be seen as an expression of confidence in the community's future. According to press reports, on the other hand, the center became the home for a wide range of community activities—education, social assistance, culture—and housed a library and exhibitions, reflecting the process of constriction into limited spaces.[143] The November pogrom dealt a mortal blow to the Jewish public sphere, but did not destroy it utterly. Some such Jewish spaces continued to function under much more difficult conditions, into the early 1940s.

The use and establishment of Jewish spaces was the only way that Jews who remained in Germany could preserve the manifold aspects of their public and intellectual life. But critics within German Jewry charged that it represented the spirit of the ghetto.[144] So, in addition to the tension between spaciousness and constrictedness that Hirschberg addressed, the activity that took place in these spaces exhibited tension between integration and holding on to Germany, and the ever more severe isolation within it. Not only traditional Jewish spaces but also those devoted to more modern activities, such as youth movement hikes and athletics, which in previous eras had symbolized Jewish aspirations to integrate into German spaces, now took place in spaces that became solitary islands within the hostile sea of the German People's Community. These circumstances also led to the development of mobile Jewish spaces, aimed largely at peripheral communities, where Jewish isolation advanced at a much more rapid pace. Moreover, a new mental map of the world emerged in the minds of many Jews. They experienced travel, thought of distances, and imagined the larger world in new ways. Liminal spaces such as train stations took on new significance, reflecting their growing sequestration from the German space, and often their alienation from it.

* CHAPTER THREE *

At Home

When she learned that a new Nazi regulation required the registration of all Jewish property, including homes, Luise Solmitz of Hamburg took out her frustration in her diary. "Only in our house do I feel at home [*Daheim*], " she wrote in April 1938. "I love every stone and every beam. What did we do, for them to want to 'secure it for the requirements of the German economy?' Other people have their homes, too, after all . . . Every day is so full of fear."[1]

Spatial identity is vital for human functioning, argues Marc Fried, an American psychologist, in his study of the consequences of evicting people from their homes in cities. Fried shows that relocations cause profound crises of loss, mourning, and longing.[2] Many German Jews were compelled by Nazi strictures to cope with being forced out of their homes, with their numbers increasing over time. It eventually became a central factor shaping their experience of their lived space. Jews started being forced out of their homes in 1933, first because their declining incomes meant they could not afford the rent, and then because Nazi laws required them to leave. They began to reflect on the significance of their homes, and to fear losing them long before they were actually compelled to leave, as Solmitz's diary shows.

The concept of home, and the experience of being at home, is foundational to the structuring of lived space in the modern age. Home (as opposed to the house) is defined in the *International Encyclopedia of Human Geography* as "a highly fluid and a contested site of human existence that reflects and reifies identities and values."[3] Some see the home principally as a human being's private space. It is also identified as the place where a couple or family lives together. Others characterize it as the sum total of personal possessions and "stuff" bearing memories and emotional value. In the bourgeois world, in normal times, these three elements—private space, family, and personal items imbued with memories—are integrated and taken for granted in the everyday experience of home. In times of crisis, however, that integration is threatened. The rich documentation left by German Jews under Nazi rule offers an opportunity to consider the meaning of each of these components separately when the combination of them is shaken, and to track the changes in the way they are perceived as part of the structuring of the concept of home.

The European bourgeois home of the modern age was typified by a particular division of rooms, in both large houses and smaller apartments. It also exhibited other characteristic features such as its furnishings and interior design. The most fundamental division in the home was between public and private spaces. Walls separated designated spaces—most notably between the living room and the kitchen, and between the bedrooms of adults and those of children.[4] The concept of *Gemütlichkeit*, a term that combines the senses of comfort, gratification, and being in the right place, played an important role in bourgeois German culture. It denotes the warm feeling and sense of belonging that the bourgeois home provided to its tenants.[5] The integration of these Jews into society involved their adoption of and adaptation to the German bourgeois way of life. As part of this process, they fashioned their households in accordance with the domestic ideals of the urban German middle class. This involved instituting a clearer gendered division of labor than had previously been typical in Jewish families. The responsibility for making and maintaining a home was now assigned largely to the family's women.[6]

Contemporary scholars from a range of fields have pondered the close connection between the experience of home and the formation of the bourgeois self. Home, suggests the human geographer Tovi Fenster, can be understood as "an emotional space associated with the self. . . . The order of the home represents internal and emotional balance."[7] This intuition was evident in Germany during the period between the world wars. A house or apartment, claimed the German architect Willy Frank, could be conceived of as an expression of the mindset of the people living in it.[8] For German Jewish men and women in the age of emancipation, the home, with its internal divisions that, to accommodate a growing range of activities, required more space, became the central site of the constitution of the self and of the realization of the bourgeois ideal that "there is a time and place for everything."[9]

The Nazi regime's anti-Jewish policies and the social and economic exclusion they engendered impoverished the Jews, as individuals and as a collective, and led to an ongoing but rapid erosion of the living standards to which the middle class had become accustomed. During the regime's initial years, this compelled many Jewish families to leave their commodious houses and apartments for more cramped quarters. Sometimes this was a temporary measure prior to emigration; in other cases it was meant to serve as a more permanent arrangement. These changes, which palpably challenged the concept of the bourgeois home, escalated in 1938, in particular following the November pogrom, during which many Jewish homes were stormed and vandalized.[10] The situation worsened further on April 30, 1939, with the promulgation of the Law Concerning Jewish Tenants, which provided the legal grounding for expropriating Jewish homes and laid the foundations for concentrating them in designated Jewish houses (*Judenhäuser*).[11]

I will devote the first part of this chapter to the process by which the home space of German Jews contracted, and how they coped with it. Of course, the size of the home space affected its internal division, the entire range of practices performed within it, and the way it was perceived. The second part of the chapter discusses, largely on the basis of the anthropological theories of Mary Douglas, the perception of the home as a "structure in time," and considers the role played by objects and symbols in the shaping of the experience of home. The chapter then proceeds, in its third section, to examine the experience of the home for the community living in it under a single roof—those who belong to the same family, and those outside the family. This, too, underwent significant changes during the period in question. As the previous chapters, here I will use Michel de Certeau's ideas to analyze the way German Jews coped with the challenge of shaping their private spaces through the use of everyday tactics with which they meant to grapple with the impact of Nazi exclusion policies on their home life. I will highlight how Jews exercised agency in fashioning the lived space of their homes.[12]

German Jews extensively addressed the changes in their home lives and in their concept of home both in their personal diaries and in the Jewish press, especially in the women's pages of the community's major periodicals, and in *Blätter des jüdischen Frauenbundes*, published by the League of Jewish Women in Germany. Given that women bore primary responsibility for shaping the bourgeois home in the age of emancipation, it is hardly surprising that most reflection on the rapid changes in the home lives of German Jewry during the Nazi period was done in the framework of a discourse among women.

"Buried Alive": Seclusion, Contraction, Adaptation

"The city," writes Tovi Fenster, "is usually the contrast of home, either positively—city is liberating whereas home is prison, or negatively—'city is dirt,' 'noisy,' 'unsafe.'"[13] The processes that created the *völkisch* space and the exclusion of Jews from the public sphere, as described in chapter 1, made this distinction an especially stark one for German Jews. Many of them tended to avoid public spaces to every extent possible, and turned inward toward Jewish spaces, and even more to the home. The home became, at least for a time, the positive and safe antithesis of the city. For example, Willy Cohn described how the Nazification of Breslau impelled him to spend ever more time in his apartment. "Outside, everything is blooming," he wrote in his diary in early May 1933, "but it is very difficult for us to induce our souls to bloom! I don't notice it so much when I am in my apartment, but when I walk in the streets it infuriates me."[14]

But political events threatened the experience of the home, and sometimes these threats became concrete within a very short period of time. In October 1933, a few months after his dismissal from his high school teaching post, Cohn wrote in his diary that his financial condition meant that his family would not be able to remain for long in the apartment they rented. "The closer I get to the point when we will need to leave this apartment," he wrote, "the more the thought depresses me. I am very reliant on my belongings and my surroundings, in which I have lived for twenty years."[15] Three months later, when their landlord gave them notice, saying that he intended to lease the unit to someone else, Cohn reacted sharply. "It shocked me," he wrote, "because I am very attached to this apartment. I would very much like to remain in it."[16] The family moved into a smaller and less expensive dwelling in March 1934. We can only presume that his reaction to this compulsory change of residence and the challenge of adjusting to a new apartment in a new area was complex, as the section of the diary covering this period has been lost. The subsequent volumes give the impression, however, that Cohn was able fairly quickly to fashion for himself a domestic routine in the new lodgings, where he lived for seven years until his deportation to the east.[17]

Seclusion at home made for major changes in the everyday lives of many Jews. The twenty-two-year-old Berlin journalist Heinrich Marx described such changes in a diary entry of May 9, 1933. "I have a completely different life now," he wrote. "Whereas I used to sit in the library all day and always felt completely at ease there, now I'm increasingly reliant on my room and I'm doubly pleased that it is so cozy [*gemütlich*] here."[18] While such seclusion could sometimes offer a sense of security, it could also lead to depression and despair. These feelings seem to have been particularly harsh for adult men who until 1933 had engaged in public careers. Younger people tended more to seek outside places, and were more likely to emigrate. Women were generally more accustomed to spend time at home, a consequence of the bourgeois division of labor that continued to characterize large swathes of German Jewry.[19]

The difficulty of spending extended time at home is especially notable in Victor Klemperer's diary. During the initial years of Nazi rule, he stayed at home mostly for personal reasons—the poor health from which he and his wife Eva suffered, and the enormous effort they put into renovating their new home. But it certainly also had to do with the increasingly anti-Jewish public atmosphere. As early as March 1933, just a few days after the Reichstag elections, Klemperer was already complaining about the long periods he was spending at home. It made him inactive and constantly preoccupied with the upkeep of his residence. Two and half years later, he described being at home as "an altogether secluded life. Quieter, more enclosed than it ever was before."[20] He also likened the long periods he and Eva spent at home to the time he had spent in the trenches as a soldier during World War I. A trench can provide protection against an external threat, but the metaphor also depicts the Klemperers as living dead. "We are literally digging ourselves in here, as in the trenches," he wrote in the summer of 1935. Three years later his tone was much sharper; he and Eva were "buried alive, buried up to the neck so to speak, and waiting from day to day for the last shovelfuls."[21] Taken as a whole, Klemperer's experience of space during these years is notable for the tension between, on the one hand, seclusion at home, which he connects to withdrawal from the world, entrenchment, and passively waiting for death; and on the other, the experience of driving, which in those same years, as noted in chapter 1, he had linked to life, freedom, and active interest in the world.

Klemperer and his wife moved to their new home in 1934 and, for a few years until their forced removal to a *Judenhaus* in 1940, they enjoyed a larger private space than before. But many German Jews were forced during the early Nazi years to cope with smaller living quarters. Hertha and Erich Nathorff, Berlin physicians dismissed from the positions they had held at hospitals and group practices in 1933, continued their work in a private clinic they set up in a part of their apartment. In the summer of 1934 they reverted some of the rooms to the landlord, and some of the remaining ones doubled both as living quarters and clinic. Hertha described the process in her diary:

> From this point on we will have only one receptionist. I can use one of the rooms I used [to receive patients] as a bedroom. The back part of the apartment will now revert to the use of the landlord, my beautiful living room will pass on to someone else. . . . I sense that, stage by stage, I am being buried here.[22]

At about the same time, Kurt Rosenberg, an attorney in Hamburg who was losing clients, gave up the adjoining unit that had served as his office and moved his business into his family's apartment. Rosenberg described this as "a move that offers no comfort" and as a step backward. It led to difficult feelings of inner desolation.[23]

Nathorff's and Rosenberg's accounts demonstrate the damage done to their spatial stability, which in turn led to a crisis of identity. It was a matter not just of shrinking space but, and perhaps principally, of an increasing convergence of the uses of their private space. The merging of their homes with their work spaces, an inevitable consequence of the reduction of their personal space, can be seen as the abandonment of one of the central tenets of the bourgeois German home: the separation of the different spheres of life. The intermixing of uses, as shown in the previous chapter, was also unavoidable in traditional Jewish spaces such as synagogues and cemeteries, where it also led to many difficulties. Jews like Nathorff and Rosenberg experienced the change as a retreat from the achievements of the age of emancipation and a blow to their bourgeois selves, one that was especially troubling because it impinged on their intimate spaces. In fact, a certain amalgam of uses of private space had been typical of bourgeois Jewish families even before 1933,[24] but this new situation grew increasingly tense for Jews under the Third Reich, and the rapid changes it involved amplified the dissonance between the physical realities of their private spaces and the conceptual world of bourgeois life.

Despite this contraction and exclusion, and the difficulties of the overlapping of uses, the diarists repeatedly evince a profound need for a home in the face of the menaces of the public space. At the beginning of 1938, Nathorff returned home with her husband and son after a visit to friends. The city's empty and alien streets at this first hour of the new year oppressed her. "Where is all the gaiety that the streets were always full of at the time of transition from one year to the next?" she asked. She chose to address this angst in a way that, at least for a moment, enhanced her sense of home. "We turned on all the lights in our home," she wrote. "I want there to again be light in all the rooms, light before the dark."[25]

The centrality of the home as a place of refuge, like the difficulties of adjusting to a smaller home, are expressed in a different way in Meta Samson's children's story *Spatz macht sich*.[26] Spatz is a young teenage girl who, as described in chapter 1, feels helpless and alienated on Berlin's streets. She spends most of her life within a very small space, the private space of her home. Samson recounts how Spatz and her mother move from their own apartment into a rented room in an apartment they share with others. At first Spatz is enthusiastic and curious about the change, but the reduction of her living space soon grows difficult. Spatz's mother, Eva, who has to spend most of her time away from home, forbids Spatz to play in the other rooms or to invite girlfriends over, for fear that they will disturb the other tenants. Spatz, lonely, longs for her old and roomy home: "How Spatz longed for a friend, how much Spatz wanted with all her heart once again to run all over the apartment, as she had done in their old place."[27] Relations with the other tenants quickly become intolerable. Mother and daughter have no choice but to move again, but Spatz's personal living space remains very limited. "The room was too small and too crowded to be able to work and play in it," Samson relates.[28] "What can we do, Spatz?" her mother complains. "We are now surrounded by friendly people, but we don't have a room, we have a thieves' lair. We eat here, sleep here, I work here, you play here, and sometimes, when the kitchen is too crowded, I wash vegetables here, peel potatoes, and iron your dresses."[29] Yet, with all the overcrowding and sense of impermanence, the home lives of the Jewish families and children in the story indicate that they cope with the difficulties. Spatz takes responsibility for shopping and cleaning, which gives her a sense of empowerment. The mother and daughter also forge ties of solidarity with other Jews living in crowded conditions.[30] At this time, Samson was also writing newspaper articles for adults about the challenges of moving into rented rooms, in particular the challenges facing women and mothers.

When the anti-Jewish policy intensified at the end of the 1930s, most saliently after the November pogrom, public space became more dangerous for Jews, who increasingly tended to stay at home. Willy Cohn, who holed up in his apartment after the pogrom for fear that he would be arrested, acceded to his wife's pleas to take a short walk down the street with her. When they returned, he wrote in his diary: "I want to stay home this afternoon and I will remain with my family as much as possible. I feel much more miserable everywhere else."[31] The spatial transformations the pogrom set off for German Jews, and the increasing severity of the anti-Jewish campaign that followed, narrowed the life of fifteen-year-old Elisabeth Block, who lived in the Bavarian town of Niedernburg. When the edict forbidding Jewish children to attend German schools went into effect, she and her brother commenced home schooling, and her daily routine became much more isolated.[32] Walks in the countryside, a major subject in her diary up to that point, suddenly became marginal, and her entries became much more sporadic.[33]

In the years that followed, the Cohn and Block families wrestled with the consequences of their contraction into their home sphere. The Blocks' home was expropriated on October 4, 1939, as part of the regime's Ayranization policy. Elisabeth's family was forced to share it with its new "Aryan" owners.

In what had been their own home, they now became tenants, confined to the upper floor.[34] The Cohns, like many other urban Jews, were compelled in 1939 to take lodgers into their apartment, which distressed Willy no end.[35] A further contraction of their living space was imposed on them when winter came, because of the severe shortage of coal for heating. Unable to keep the entire apartment warm, Cohn had to sleep in his study, while his wife and daughters slept in the bedroom.[36] The nighttime curfew imposed on Germany's Jews when the war began severed them from public space at night. On top of that came the blackout regulations, which limited their freedom within their home as well. "Much time is lost in the evenings because of the permanent blackout," Klemperer wrote in his diary on September 14, 1939. Two weeks later he added: "It's dark at six, and I cannot write downstairs."[37]

As with public spaces, Jews tried to make the best of the constricted space that remained to them. In Berlin in 1941, the musician and teacher Arno Nadel and his wife were ordered to leave their home. They rented a room from another Jewish couple, significantly reducing their home space. Ironically, Nadel's 1942 diary entries frequently and emotionally describe vistas and the outdoors, drawn from memories of walks around lakes outside Berlin.[38] These places were no longer accessible for him, but he found a small-scale surrogate for them in the form of the balcony of the apartment in which he now lived. "Without freedom, without nature, a small piece of balcony has to serve as a substitute for it all," he wrote.[39] The balcony appears repeatedly in his diary as a site of relaxation—a place to drink coffee, where he and his wife could sit together or read to each other, and where he could gaze at the sky or enjoy the little patches of greenery visible from it.[40]

A similar take on the importance a balcony could assume on in the 1940s appears in the diary of the former fur dealer Philipp Manes.[41] As he grappled in July 1942 with the strains of forced labor while awaiting deportation, Manes described his home's balcony as his last refuge. "I took some time to relax on the balcony and read," he wrote in his diary. "My body needs it after standing for so long" in the factory where he worked.[42] About a month later, he added:

> Today it was warm enough and I was finally able to go out to the balcony. The sight of the green leaves outside makes up for all the hours I need to stand and work at the machine. I wait all week for Saturday to bring me freedom after [just] six and a half hours of work.[43]

Under the harsh conditions of the end of the 1930s and early 1940s, the balcony and window thus became the most riveting spaces in the home for writers like Manes and Nadel: sites of comfort, where at least at times they could feel freer and create for themselves a relatively amenable emotional space.

The experience of home, according to the *International Encyclopedia of Human Geography*, involves self-constitutive practices embedded in a spatial context."[44] When he shut himself up at home following the November pogrom, Willy Cohn sought new ways of keeping himself occupied, such as reorganizing his personal library.[45] It was just one example of an entire range of domestic activities that German Jews increasingly turned to under the Nazi persecution that forced them into seclusion. With such practices, Cohn and others, it could be said, sought to preserve some vestige of their bourgeois lives even under the severe isolation imposed on them by the regime. These were ways of continuing to express their emancipated selves. The intermixture of uses that, in earlier years, had been experienced in a negative way by Jews such as Nathorff and Rosenberg, became, in the even more oppressive years that followed, survival tactics with positive connotations.

Under the Nazis, Jewish domestic space, which was designated in accordance with the bourgeois division of labor to serve primarily as a place of consumption, became also a productive and creative space. Cohn taught young people at his home, seeking to carry on to every extent possible the educational work he had previously pursued by traveling to give lectures in Jewish venues and before Jewish audiences. He also continued to write articles on historical and community issues, some of them intended for the Jewish press.[46] Another aspect of everyday domestic culture that preoccupied Cohn, his stamp collection, was representative of a broader phenomenon reflected in German Jewish newspapers, which began publishing philately columns in the mid-1930s.[47] But Cohn's main pursuit in the closed space of his home, as with Klemperer, Manes, and Nadel, was introspection, which included keeping a diary. As I will show in chapter 6, this activity also involved an increasing orientation toward the past—they turned to and thought about it, and sometimes found comfort in doing so.

Victor Klemperer offers the best example of how the home became a creative space. In December 1938, after being barred from the public library, Klemperer decided to write a memoir, his *Curriculum*, a project he continued to labor on after being forced to move into a *Judenhaus* in May 1940. He also devoted as much time as possible to reading, and to a book project, *The Language of the Third Reich: A Philologist's Notebook*, in which he tracked and analyzed the rapid changes in the German language under the Nazi regime. Klemperer carried on this work under ever more difficult conditions throughout the war, which he survived. His physical space shrank, leaving him no choice but to stay at home. His spiritual horizons and even his self also narrowed. At the same time, as he grappled with this menace, Klemperer continued his practices of reading and writing. That is, in adhering to the bourgeois values, he continued to maintain a hold on his self as he knew it.

In June 1942, Klemperer was offered the option of "volunteering" for work in a paper mill. In his diary he recounted how he was tempted to accept the job, as it would have allowed him to leave his home in relative security, expand his space, and pass the time more easily. But in the end, he turned it down. As circumscribed as his life was, he was still able to fill it with things he enjoyed doing. "I am downright happy for many hours of the day," he wrote a few months later, thinking that it might be the final passage that he would write in his diary. "I study, I prepare future work. In years to come I do not need to have any more creative ideas, only the opportunity to work out in detail what I have planned and sketched now."[48]

The Home as a Structure in Time: Memory, Expectation, Redundancy

"Home is not only a space," writes the anthropologist Mary Douglas; "it also has some structure in time."[49] The cycle of daily routine—transitions between day and night, between weekdays and weekends and holidays, and the procession of the seasons—are fundamental characteristics of the home, Douglas maintains, but so are the memory of the past and the expectation of the future. Hotels or other places where people stay transiently have no past or future horizons. In contrast, the feeling of "being at home" is constructed over a deep well of long-term memories from the past, as well as long-range planning and constant investment that looks to the future, in what Douglas refers to as "reallocation, repair, renewal."[50] According to Douglas, the home also has "massive redundancies."[51] Unlike a hotel, a home cannot be measured only by its efficiency and comfort. A sense of home cannot be based only on functional needs. Douglas argues that redundancy—objects and "stuff" lacking any definable use or value—can be charged with significant memories of the home's inhabitants, and even of those of previous generations. These redundant objects are fundamental elements that transform the home into a structure in time. Such memories, designated for preservation for future generations as well, are essential to constituting the home.

As the second part of this book will show, the political, social, and economic crisis that the Nazi regime brought on the Jews changed their "lived time" as it had been shaped in the age of emancipation under the influence of the German bourgeois lifestyle. The slowing of the pace of their everyday lives and their increasing lack of certainty led to a frustrating experience of stationary time and a blocked prospect of the future. These changes made it difficult for many Jews to carry on one of the primary foundations of bourgeois domesticity—making long-range plans for the future—and it damped their motivation to do so. Moreover, the economic and social pressures on Germany's Jews to reduce their private living space, and in some cases even to leave their homes and move into less expensive lodgings or emigrate—later followed by state edicts compelling them to do so—necessarily meant that they had to part with many of their domestic belongings.

The social psychologists Mihaly Csikszentmihalyi and Eugene Halton maintain that "one of the most important psychological purposes of the home is that those objects that have shaped one's personality and which are needed to express concretely those aspects of the self that one values are kept in it."[52] According to the cultural theorist Bill Brown, "Human subjects and material objects constitute one another."[53] In other words, having to part with domestic objects, including those handed down from previous generations, further exacerbated the pain and loss felt by German Jews when they had to leave their homes. The "structure in time" that German Jews had experienced in their homes until 1933 faced a real threat, both from the perspective of their link to the past in memory, and from that of their view of the future, in expectation and long-term planning.

The public discourse that grappled with these issues for the most part addressed Jewish women, as they were the ones who were expected to keep their homes and families up and running even in times of crisis.[54] In an article that appeared in May 1934 in *Der Morgen*, a monthly magazine read by liberal German Jewish intellectuals, Meta Samson considered the challenges involved in moving from a large apartment into a furnished room. The changes this involved, she argued, had had a severe impact on the bourgeois Jewish family:

> Many Jewish families are now giving up their apartments so as to rent a "furnished room," at least for a short time, until finding new work, or indefinitely. It is much more than an outward change. The relinquishment of property that comes with this decision shatters ways of thinking and feeling, the inner kernel around which the husk of external life is woven.[55]

Samson anticipated what Marc Fried has written about the sense of loss and grief involved in being uprooted from home.[56] "The Jewish woman and mother preoccupied with her everyday household duties," she maintained, was losing not only her home but also her position and the prestige it gave her. After such moves, Jewish women felt that they had been cast into a void in which they could no longer fulfill their roles as wives and mothers. It was as if they had lost their standing in their families and in society.

> Furnished rooms, full of an alien life and an alien fate—threads that do not intertwine—can never replace the sense of home [*Zuhause*]. . . . The ominous dissolution of the family, their expulsion from home [*Heim*], and the loss of the familial sense of belonging can be expected to have unforeseen consequences.[57]

What had been lost, Samson now told her readers, both male and female, was the bourgeois apartment which "with all its decorated and furnished spaces, organized life almost automatically." They needed to prepare for this new situation.

> Property has lost its meaning. . . . What the man brought in as the breadwinner and the woman created as the maintainer [of the home] has now been sold at a ridiculous price or is rotting in the attic. There is no longer anything to "represent." There are no more elegant rooms; a person must now stand on his own.[58]

Samson rebuked housewives who proved unable to adjust to these new circumstances. She told them they had to give up all the things that Mary Douglas called redundancies. "Everything that takes up too much space and time should be avoided," she maintained. But despite her demand to come to terms with reality and relinquish central elements of material culture and the bourgeois way of life, Samson did not dismiss the importance of the home as an idea, or the Jewish woman's central role in constituting it. Indeed, she assigned her a new responsibility:

> The Jewish woman who has lost her home and her status . . . must recover her personality. . . . The Jewish woman must, in her heart and mind, find new ways of creating a home and of holding the family together—not with comfortable rooms, but with a common purpose in life. . . . The new Jewish home must be created from within the experience of life in a furnished room.[59]

Samson, in other words, proposed a transformation of the concept of the home, and asserted that women must adapt to the new circumstances. Home (which she usually referred to as *Heim*, but sometimes as *Zuhause*) now related primarily to emotional space, and had to do more with belonging than with comfort. Notably, these are the same concepts the architectural historian Joseph Rykwert uses when he distinguishes between a house, which is a *place* of refuge with walls, doors, a roof, and other such physical elements, and a home, which is primarily a *state* of emotional well-being, stability, and family.[60] When life is stable, the physical house enables an ongoing emotional sense of comfort and well-being, and the distinction between house and home can be disregarded. But the crisis that German Jews faced decoupled the two. Samson needed the distinction to explain to her female audience the complexity of the situation they faced, and most importantly to encourage them to gird their loins and work to preserve the more substantive concept of home.

While Samson called on her readers to leave behind everything that took up a lot of space, she did not address the question of what to do with objects imbued with memories. The question of "the migration of belongings," meaning reevaluating them in advance of the move so as to decide what to take and what to leave behind, was discussed at length by other writers in the Jewish press.[61] In her article "Before the Move," published in *CV-Zeitung*'s women's supplement in March 1934, Hetta Bamberger condemned the common wisdom that only "useful" objects should be taken when moving. Bamberger described a drawer in her grandmother's old desk that was full of personal objects, ostensibly useless but permeated with memory. The drawer and its contents had aroused her and her brother's curiosity when they were children. Her depiction of the drawer fits Douglas's concept of redundancy as a key feature of the home:

> The drawer contained many things, and it will continue to contain them, even though we must be very cautious in calculating the space [we will have] in the new, much smaller apartment. We must part with so many things! We cannot allow ourselves to make the parting even harder than it already is for us. [People say that] "everything that is not useful is a burden." But this "utility" should not be defined only according to practical matters. . . . Our times certainly demand changing direction, being more sensible, having a clear understanding of our new tasks. We must give up many things, set aside things we loved—and that means emotions as well. But we must not give up all mementoes [*Raritäten*, rare or unusual personal objects], those which are more than just curiosities [*Kuriositäten*], to oblivion. We must give ourselves and future generations the possibility of enjoying this luxury, which in practice is not really a luxury in the sense of superfluous things. So much vitality, potent emotions of connection, which stand beyond time and space, burst forth from these objects. . . . We do not want to serve a fetish, but we do want to ensure that the vital emotional values contained in these objects will be preserved for us and for those who come after us.[62]

Bamberger's attitude toward these objects corresponds with Walter Benjamin's discussion of the nature of collecting in his article "Unpacking My Library." Collecting, according to Benjamin, is a human activity characterized by "a relationship to objects that does not emphasize their utilitarian value, but studies and loves them as the scene, the stage of their [owners'] fate."[63]

The drawer in Bamberger's home, full of memories of the family's past, represents another aspect of Benjamin's view of collecting. "Inheritance is the soundest way of acquiring a collection," he argues. "Collectors' attitudes toward their possessions stems from their feelings of responsibility toward their property."[64] For Bamberger, the home, to the extent that it serves as a means of transmitting family memories from one generation to another (as represented by the drawer), relates more to time and redundancy than to space. In fact, she not only considers the utilitarian value of these objects but also proposes different meanings for the terms "useful" and "luxury" than those common in German Jewish discourse. In doing so, she points to the kind of action she wants to promote when her readers grapple with the challenge of preserving the experience of home.

A somewhat different view of the incongruence of the bourgeois dometicity of the age of emancipation and the conditions Jews faced under the Nazis was voiced a few years later, in March 1938, in an article by Frieda Vallentin in *Blätter des jüdischen Frauenbundes*.[65] The symbols of the bourgeois life of abundance, such as crystal glasses, chandeliers, and fine sets of dishes, need to be left behind, she argued, because they "are no longer appropriate for our time." Nevertheless, alongside stressing the importance of constructing a simpler life, Vallentin recognized the need to create a homey atmosphere in the new surroundings, and to maintain what environmental psychologists call the environmental past.[66] "The atmosphere we create in our new home lives (*Häuslichkeit*) is vital for our lives just as fertile soil is vital for a plant," Vallentin wrote. "After being removed from our familiar surroundings, we feel—as they say—uprooted."

Vallentin took a more pragmatic view than Bamberger, perhaps because of the changing circumstances of the intervening years between their essays. "Not only have spatial conditions changed," she noted, "but also our views of what constitutes utility in a household."[67] She acknowledged the difficulty of "parting from objects that once symbolized happiness," but at the same time she reminded her readers that "all these items are only things, lifeless objects." Instead of being so connected to symbols of the past, she encouraged her readers to construct and design a home in a different style, one more appropriate to the new circumstances. "When it comes to the new apartment," she wrote, "we must husband our courage so that we can reshape our lives, and thus the decoration of our living space, in bright and heartening colors and colorful materials." Vallentin thus did not advocate giving up the home, but rather proposed to her readers a new sort of home—one that, as it happens, was consistent with Douglas's theoretical framework. Unlike the concepts of home presented above, in which the private space serves to preserve and create memories of the past, Vallentin presented the home as organized in accordance with expectations of the future.

A different emphasis can be found in an article by Lise Lewinneck that appeared in July 1938 in the women's section of *Israelitisches Familienblatt*. Addressing the issue of moving and her readers' uncertainties about what to pack and how to decide what to take and what to leave behind, Lewinneck stressed the need to forget the past so as to enable the construction of new lives in the future. She called on Jewish women to take with them only useful items. Her justification for this was not merely practical. Something more fundamental was involved. The old furniture, she maintained, was "too heavy and not useful for anyone." Such things were essentially "ballast of memory that needs to be cast off bravely into the sea of oblivion."[68] Lewinneck also adduced the metaphor of the old drawer full of memories that Bamberger used. But Lewinneck used it for opposite purpose. "We must throw away the old letters with the drawer," she asserted, advising the reader to refrain from any attempt to shape a new life in the constricted private space that remained as a home similar to the home of the past, as an emotional space and as a structure in time. There was no place for memories or redundancies of any kind. It should be kept in mind that at the time Lewinneck wrote, in the summer of 1938, increasing numbers of Jewish families were bidding farewell to loved ones, especially members of the younger generation who were emigrating. This made it difficult for them to design the new and smaller living quarters as a home in the family sense. Unlike Samson, Bamberger, and Vallentin, Lewinneck thus advocated giving up any attempt to foster a feeling of home in Germany, with regard not only to memories of the past but to the view of the future. Her position concerning the home space was inexorably connected to an awareness of living in a waiting period, which will be examined in chapter 5.

Alongside the different positions on these issues that appeared in the press, there are personal writings by Jews who emigrated and moved into smaller living spaces or into *Judenhäuser* at the end of the 1930s and the beginning of the 1940s. These offer an entire range of attitudes about the importance of domestic objects and keepsakes, attitudes molded by rapidly changing family and personal circumstances.

In March 1939, as he packed his belongings and prepared himself for emigration to the United States, Erich Seligmann, a fifty-nine-year-old Jewish physician from Berlin, wrote in his diary about the rapid dismantling of his home. Surrounded by boxes, he felt as if "we ourselves are choking from the belongings that we are taking down from the attic and from the pieces of furniture that can't be sold. The large bookcase, which was my pride and joy, will apparently be cut up into small pieces for firewood."[69] On top of his painful parting from his bookcase, he was compelled about two months later to burn personal and family documents. "For the past few days, I have been tearing into shreds hundred-year-old documents (letters, poems, and more) belonging to my grandfathers and from my parents' social circle. They do not need to emigrate with us. No one is staying here, who can still have any interest in them?"[70] In deciding to leave these documents behind, Seligmann deliberately parted ways both with Germany, his birthplace, and with his home. He liquidated the latter's most salient symbols. In other words, he carried out Lewinneck's approach in a concrete way.

Unlike Seligmann, who described his decision to destroy these documents in a rational tone, Klemperer was much more emotional when he wrote of dismantling his home in Dresden in May 1940, prior to his compulsory move into a *Judenhaus*: "The chaos of the move . . . it's a matter of getting rid of all ballast. . . . I should like to extend the concept of ballast to almost everything I own and [am] virtually ravaging my past."[71] Klemperer's practical need to pack up his belongings caused him to rail against his property. As Amos Goldberg put it, he responded "to the eradication of his future by the Nazis in an analogous fashion—with his own destruction of his past."[72] In the tempest of the external chaos of the move and the harsh emotional trauma it brought with it, nearly all the redundancies that up until then had constituted Klemperer's experience of home turned into ballast. He experienced this erasure, of both the past and the future, as the destruction of his home in the most profound sense of the term. But that was not the whole picture. As seen above, Klemperer nevertheless tried to get a grip on the experience of home in the *Judenhaus*, turning it, despite the difficult conditions, into a productive space.

Liquidating domestic belongings charged with personal memories was not, of course, the only response exhibited by German Jews to the crisis they faced. Philipp Manes, who began his diary when war broke out in September 1939, made frequent reference to the disposal of the many belongings in his apartment—letters, books, furniture, and many items that had belonged to his parents. "I began to arrange and get rid of things," he wrote in November 1939, while readying for moving from his home into a furnished room in Berlin. When a neighbor advised him to burn all his letters, diaries, documents, and pictures without thinking twice, Manes took a different approach:

> I can't do it. . . . I wanted to get old with all these documents and letters around me. They were meant to comfort me and accompany me later, when I left my home. But as it now appears that it is possible to take only the most essential items, I need to part, as hard as it is, with objects that have meaning for me alone—and which for another are only a burden.[73]

Manes accepted the fact that parting with some of his memory-infused belongings was necessary; but despite that, he had difficulty coping with the process of choosing among them. His perception of the home, which he clearly identified with the transmission of memory between generations, is evident in a passage in his diary from October 1941:

> I packed all my books and stamps with the rest of my keepsakes. In the wonderful leather suitcase that our children gave me I have kept old letters, including the original parting letters from my parents, letters from my great-grandmother, and other old documents. All this will be for Eva and Rudolf [and his children] when they establish a home [*Heim*] and make use of these memories [*Andenken*], as a cornerstone for the family museum.[74]

So, in contrast with Seligmann, who imagined his home after his emigration as a new beginning in which all the memories of his previous life would only be a burden ("Who can still have any interest in them?"), and with Klemperer, who furiously attacked the symbols of his past, Manes felt a need to preserve, to every extent possible, objects charged with memory for the next generation, "when they establish a home." When Manes began keeping his diary in September 1939 when the war began, he dedicated it to his four children, all of whom had managed to get out of Germany. He and his wife were deported from Berlin to Theresienstadt in July 1942, and more than two years later, in October 1944, they were transported from there to Auschwitz, where they were murdered.

Another approach to the challenge of moving into a cramped home space, one that evinces an interesting aspect of spatial resistance, emerges in the letters of Kati Moses, a widow living in Berlin. In the summer of 1939, the fifty-three-year-old Moses moved from her home to a rented room in an apartment she shared with others. In a letter to her son, who had settled in Palestine, she wrote of her efforts to maintain the comforts of home (*Gemütlichkeit*) despite the deteriorating situation and her insecurity about what the future held for her. "Sometimes a person might think: What purpose does it serve to build something over and over again?" she pondered. "Yet—even in this situation we don't want to lose the warmth of home. There are enough examples of losing it all around us. So I have decorated the room nicely, as small as it is."[75]

She then detailed how she had tastefully furnished her room—less than 140 square feet (13 square meters): hanging curtains, and arranging books and porcelain in her sideboard. In this regard, she accorded perfectly with the pattern described by the French cultural historian Daniel Roche. Items of furniture, he showed in a different context, can express and signify a person's life path.[76] The widow from Berlin showed that Roche's thesis serves not only under conditions of stability and prosperity, but also in times of crisis and distress. In seeking to keep as much of her old furniture as she could, even to the point of paying for repairs to items damaged in the move, Moses maintained her grip on her previous life. She divided her single room into spaces that she treated as being no less distinct than they had been in her previous home—her work room, constituting her desk; her bedroom; her dining room, where she ate; her pantry, where she stored food; and her living room, where she received guests. In doing so, she maintained, at least in her mind, a map of the different functions defining the rooms in a bourgeois home. Filling her room with objects that for the most part had no immediate use—redundancies that made her past a felt presence in her new location—as well as storing food and repairing her furniture, indicated that her gaze was set on the future. In other words, in addition to maintaining the lived space of her bourgeois background, she maintained its lived time, in Douglas's sense.

In August 1941, a few months after being forced out of her house in Bamberg and into a *Judenhaus*, Karoline (Lina) Löbl, the widow of a well-off businessman, marked her eightieth birthday. She insisted on celebrating even though the rest of her family had already emigrated. The birthday picture (figure 6), most likely taken by one of the other residents in the *Judenhaus* and sent to her son in Ecuador, shows how she adhered to the values of German *Gemütlichkeit*.[77] It shows bottles of what seems to be liquor arranged on a sideboard, and a floral arrangement, as well as pieces of furniture that no doubt bore family memories. A few months later, Löbl was deported to the Theresienstadt ghetto.

The resolve of Moses and Löbl to shape the tiny living space that remained to them in the spirit of the urban bourgeois mores to which they had become accustomed, and to invest that space with meaningful memories, demonstrated their refusal to accept an empty life of unfathomable waiting that lacked both past and future. Their need for continuity in the spatial experience of home helped them cope with loneliness, difficult living conditions, and the uncertainty that surrounded them. In preserving and, to a certain extent, even fashioning for themselves a new home against all odds, these two widows rejected the advice of Samson and Lewinneck and chose

Figure 6. Karoline (Lina) Löbl's eightieth birthday. Private photograph, courtesy of Werner Löbl.

differently than did Klemperer and Seligman. In doing so, they fought to maintain their human dignity.

"Strangers . . . Have Taken Over My Things": The Division of Private Space

The development of the home and the domestic ideal of the modern European middle class was closely bound up with the rise of the nuclear family. In the early modern age, upper-class families had shared their household spaces with servants, apprentices, and other members of the lower classes.[78] But the marriage patterns of the later modern age created a new sort of household: the home. In contrast with the early modern household, based largely on common economic activity, integrating manufacturing and consumption in the same space, the home was fashioned as an intimate emotional space aimed first and foremost at providing the growing need for privacy, which was a central element in the development of the bourgeois self.[79] Home life was thus increasingly separated from production, which was moved into other spaces. A new concept emerged, that of "being at home," which meant feeling fully comfortable with the close family members sharing that same private space. Scholars have noted that for many, the home space constituted "an expanded boundary of the self, one that includes a number of past and present relationships."[80] As the need for privacy grew, the permanent presence of strangers from outside the family in the home space came to constitute a hazard in the way of domestic warmth and calm.

For German Jews, fostering family life at home had become central to their process of integration into the German bourgeois world.[81] The living conditions they found themselves facing under the Nazi regime menaced from multiple directions this ideal, which had become so central a shaper of their identities. Emigration, first that of young adults and then of adolescents and even children, not only broke up the bourgeois family unit but devastated the experience of home for those who remained. Parting from close family members earlier than dictated by bourgeois conventions tested the expanded selves that were a product of the age of emancipation. The breakup of the family was accelerated by the mass arrests at the end of 1938, when the detainees—most of whom were men—were told that the only way they could avoid being sent to concentration camps was to emigrate and leave their wives, children, and parents behind.[82] Parting from close family members, the natural partners in the emotional unit that was the home, came along with another problem. Increasing economic pressures, along with government edicts restricting the housing available to Jews, forced many families to share their private living spaces with other Jews from outside their families, and sometimes even with total strangers. The need to live in close quarters with others eroded, and sometimes completely upended, the comforting experience of home.

The decision that many German Jewish parents made to send their children out of the country was, according to Marion Kaplan, "the most excruciating moment of their lives." Political developments quickly proved that the decision had been the right one, but that did not change the fact that the parents "suffered intensely from the loss of daily intimacy."[83] The severe impact it had on the experience of home was clearly attested to by Willy Cohn when he wrote in his diary about the emigration of his daughter Ruth in June 1939. "Ruth left home today and took part of my heart with her," he lamented. "It will be lonelier now at home, but it is important to think of what is best for the children."[84] The departure of other family members was also difficult. Erich Seligmann's mother-in-law, who had lived for many years with him and his wife, went in February 1939 to join her son in Portugal. "We will miss our devoted mother," he wrote. "The rooms, which were full of her unassuming tranquility, have turned empty and cold. . . . For the first time since 1905 we are alone in our apartment."[85]

Faced with social isolation, increasing exclusion from public spaces, and restriction to Jewish spaces at the end of the 1930s, Jews sometimes tried to turn their private homes into sites of social and cultural life. In September 1937, *Israelitisches Familienblatt* called on its readers to bolster social

Figure 7. Wedding celebration of Sally and Ruth Stiefel, Duisburg, July 10, 1938. Jewish Museum Berlin, inv. no. 2012/63/151. Donated by Irene Starr and Richard Stiefel in memory of their parents and family.

connections (*Geselligkeit*) among Jews by inviting neighbors over and organizing private social events, home concerts, and evenings of communal reading.[86] Given the pressures they faced, Jewish families now increasingly held wedding receptions in private homes. One such celebration was caught in a photograph taken at the wedding of Sally and Ruth Stiefel in Duisberg on July 10, 1938 (figure 7).[87]

The move of social and cultural life into the private sphere is also documented in diaries. Philipp Manes recounted how groups of Jews gathered from time to time in private homes for musical evenings and reading groups. Manes, who took part in such events between 1939 and 1941, described them as "true joy for the soul" and "comfort for our so heavy mood."[88] Sometimes he even recounted how such events were able to take him out of the constricted world of the here and now and into the free space of the imagination. "We are [spiritually] disconnected from the here and now, led into other lands and sailing through higher realms. 'O, blessed art' [*Du holde Kunst*]."[89]

The concept of *Geselligkeit*, which refers to small social groups and cultural activities held largely in private spaces, was in fact a familiar practice among the German bourgeoisie.[90] Such activities in the home could not, of course, replace the warmth and intimacy of the home atmosphere, the

Gemütlichkeit; but at least to some extent they could help preserve particular elements of the Jewish bourgeois home and prevent them from becoming "cold and empty," as Seligmann put it.

Nevertheless, most cases in which Jews shared their private spaces with other Jews not of their families were compelled by much more prosaic circumstances. The phenomenon of individuals and families sharing their private spaces with strangers is not, of course, unique to Jews under the Nazi regime. Between the world wars, many of the inhabitants of the Soviet Union's cities shared their apartments with strangers, a result of the fact that the Bolshevik revolution accelerated the process of urbanization without commensurate construction of new dwellings.[91] In countries of immigration, such as the United States, Canada, and Palestine under the British Mandate, complex relationships developed between tenants who shared private spaces. Homeowners and tenants shared "intimate neighborly relations" because there was no other choice.[92] Nevertheless, the case of the German Jews differed from these others. Only under the Nazis was an entire social stratum that had previously been part of the urban middle class (and in some cases the upper middle class) forced, within the space of a few short years, from living in spacious houses and apartments into sharing intimate spaces. Unlike in those other cases, the process that German Jews underwent was a result not of accelerated modernization or internal or external migration, but of a deliberate policy of exclusion.

Writers in the Jewish press tried to help their readers adjust to and cope with their new and complicated living circumstances. In an article of July 1938, Frieda Vallentin addressed the challenge of intimate neighborliness among strangers. She indicated the need to balance the needs of all parties: new boarders who had had to leave the privacy of their homes for a rented room, and homeowners who were compelled to sacrifice the quality of life to which they had become accustomed by taking in tenants. The only way of addressing this complex challenge of excessive daily proximity among families that were not a single emotional units, she argued, was to find the way to respect others and, to every extent possible, provide them with both physical and emotional privacy:

> The subdivision of an apartment or the bringing in of a lodger—this requires much tact and delicacy, to obtain tolerable life together. . . . One must be fair to *both sides*. Toward the side that reached the point of bringing strange people into one's home, and toward the side that was compelled to seek a home among strangers. One must give up many habits and perhaps even convenience, while the other must move one's habits and comfort into the property of a strange person. . . . The strangers seek a "home"

> [*Zuhause*], they seek warmth and hominess [*Gemütlichkeit*], to be at home [*Heimischsein*], a fulcrum of serenity [*Ruhepol*].[93]

The very fact that Vallentin used four different words in a single sentence to describe the experience of home reflects the difficulty that Jews of her time encountered precisely in this matter. In her essay, published in *Blätter des jüdischen Frauenbundes*, the League of Jewish Women periodical, she adhered to the gendered roles that were accepted bourgeois mores. As such, ignoring the fact that many wives now worked outside the home for the first time and many men had lost their jobs, she stressed that men, as heads of their families who returned home tired from their day of work, needed a private space even in the new circumstances. To be at home, she argued, meant having the right to a personal space, even if it was a very small one. "Everyone needs to have in the home a space that he can consider *his own*—a small and peaceful place for himself, with no disturbances."[94]

The dissolution of many Jewish families, largely as the result of emigration, challenged the unquestioned link between family and home. Could the experience of home and shared domesticity develop among strangers in the absence of the family unit? In her work about patterns of domesticity among prisoners of war during World War I, Iris Rachamimov argues that the men she studied displayed a profound emotional need to create a significant experience of home during the long period they spent as prisoners in conditions of uncertainty. The result was that they "created versions of domesticity in which 'home' was enacted and performed."[95] While this experience was temporary and ambivalent, she claims, it nevertheless challenged the accepted concept of home and the unquestioned connection between it and the family.

An article that appeared in *Israelitisches Familienblatt* in January 1937 described the shared lives of several Jewish widows who moved in together in the Berlin suburb of Grunewald. The article posed a challenge similar to that experienced by the prisoners of war, in that it showed how domesticity could be created among a group of people sharing no family ties. The widows, whose close family members had emigrated or died, had to cope with the dissolution of their homes, in which "every object was charged with added value inasmuch as they bore with them a stratum of memory," wrote the author, Doris Wittner.[96] Following their painful departure from their homes, they moved into rented rooms in which they had the status of "permanent tenants" (*Dauermieterinnen*), a formal and impersonal term that Wittner chose precisely to express the desolation of the move. She also described life in the shared home as that of a "surrogate home" (*Heimersatz*), very different from her description of the widows' previous lives in their family homes, which contained many objects full of memories for them. Nevertheless, Wittner reported the displays of solidarity and community among these widows living "in an impressive house in the heart of a green park," far from the noisy and hostile city. While the shared home could not feel like their original homes, Wittner described it as a green island, and likened the widows living there to the survivors of a sunken ship:

> Even the survivors of a boat that has gone down at sea can build a human community that will be felt as beneficent, and with tenderness and affection it can replace the little and valuable things that a person had with their family and in their home. A person who enters the garden of this home, with its tall trees, and sees this harmonious group of women occupied with their reading, sewing, and frequently coming together to play a game of soothing bridge, cannot imagine that behind this pleasant façade hides a burden of harsh fates.[97]

Even after losing their original homes and the dispersion of their families, these widows could, as Wittner reported, build for themselves a community of solidarity in their private living space. In doing so, they consummated a central element in the concept of home as proposed by Mary Douglas.[98] Like the prisoners of war, although under completely different conditions, the shared intimacy they developed among themselves could answer, at least partially and for a time, their profound need for the homes and families they had lost.

While newspaper articles sought to encourage their readers to adapt to the intimate neighborly relations that had become unavoidable, private documents reveal just how complicated the challenge was in practice. At the end of May 1940, Victor Klemperer and his wife Eva were forced out of their home in Dresden into a small detached house that had been turned into a *Judenhaus*. The first diary entry he wrote after the move shows just how enormously difficult this forced intimacy with strangers was. "The greatest loss of time is caused by the constant fussing interference of strangers," he fretted. He added that his new surroundings were characterized by a "very great promiscuity." Nevertheless, in the very same passage in which he voiced his disgust with his new intimate neighbors, he recognized that the residents of the *Judenhaus* would become his community. "This house is really a community, all of whose members truly share the same fate [*Schicksalsgemeinschaft*]."[99]

Unlike the Klemperers, who were moved from their homes into the *Judenhaus*, Jeanette Schocken, the widow of the department store proprietor

Joseph Schocken, continued to live in her villa in Wesermünde, which is today part of Bremerhaven in northwest Germany. Schocken, in her late fifties, remained there until she was deported to the east in November 1941. In 1939 she began to take in boarders, including entire families. The way she coped with this difficult challenge is documented in letters she sent to her children Heinz and Hilda, who emigrated to Seattle in November 1938.

Schocken's letters indicate that she faced a very fluid situation that required constant change in the functions of each room in her house, change that eroded the home's bourgeois configuration. In June 1939, just before some new families moved in, she even considered leaving herself and moving, at least for a time, into a guest house or rented room, so as to evade the inconvenience and discomfort of her own home.[100] In the end, she resolved to remain and to cope with the challenges. When the Goldmann family arrived, Schocken began referring to one of the rooms as a *Wohnküche*, a kitchen/living unit—an expression that until then had not been used in bourgeois homes. When the Pinthus family—Jeanette's brother, his wife, and their son—moved in, she designated the room into which they moved as a *Eß-Wohn-Schreibzimmer*, a study-dining-living room.[101] The coining of such new terms was an attempt to continue to demarcate, to the extent possible, distinct spaces within the home and, in doing so, to maintain at least a symbolic hold on the bourgeois habitus of the division of the home space into rooms with distinct purposes. The letters document a process by which this widow adapted to her new circumstances. She even voiced satisfaction with the daily presence of other people in her home, as the residents became a community. "Life with G [the Goldmann family] is rather pleasant and cozy [*gemütlich*]," she wrote a few months after they moved in.[102]

The adjustments Jews had to make when other people moved into their houses are documented in the copious letters that Dr. Hans Schmoller, a Berlin pediatrician, and his wife Marie Elisabeth wrote to their son Hans Peter. Hans Peter left the capital in 1937 and in 1938 moved to Morija, a city in the British crown colony of Basutoland (today's Lesotho) in southern Africa. The letters contain detailed accounts of the family apartment and the changes it underwent after Marie's mother and sister, whose family name was Brenner, moved in on December 31, 1938. The family's living room was divided in two by cupboards and curtains, with one half becoming a room for the two new residents and the other ironically called "Neutralien," a name perhaps inspired by the German silent comedy *Die Prinzessin von Neutralien* (The Princess of Neutralia). Even though the apartment was more cramped, Neutralien preserved something of bourgeois domesticity and the separation between private and public spaces, and thus made it possible for its inhabitants to maintain their bourgeois selves. Over the course of the weeks that followed, the letters repeatedly describe Neutralien as a refuge or haven, a space shared by all, marked, more than the apartment's other spaces, by a cozy and serene domesticity (*Gemütlichkeit*) or comfort (*Behaglichkeit*).[103] Neutralien also sustained redundancy by serving as a repository for family mementoes and knickknacks with no practical utility, reminders of the family's bourgeois standing and domesticity. In the summer of 1941, when the Schmollers reported to their son that they had been compelled to rent out another room in their apartment, they stressed, "Neutralien is still there."[104] Beyond shaping the domestic space, the name "Neutralien," like "study-dining-living room," was a term with a whiff of ironic self-disparagement that, under the circumstances, can be seen as a sign of self-awareness and agency.

Holidays and birthdays play a key role in constituting the bourgeois family and domesticity in the Western world, according to Elizabeth Pleck.[105] The letters of the Schmollers and of Janet Schocken tell of the efforts they made to maintain domesticity and create a family atmosphere under new circumstances. The Schmollers and Brenners celebrated birthdays and holidays in their shared home, and held musical evenings as well.[106] Schocken regaled her children with depictions of the evenings in which all denizens of the house sat together, sewing, playing cards, and drinking tea.[107] They also all celebrated Hanukah together, she told her children: Mrs. Goldmann playing the piano, the children drinking hot chocolate while listening to fairy tales on the gramophone and playing hit the pot.[108] Schocken's battle to keep up a homey atmosphere reached its height in the autumn of 1941, as they waited helplessly to be deported to the east. "I am expecting a move into a new home and location in the near future," she wrote to her children, hinting at the impending deportation. But she made a point of adding: "Yesterday was Erich's birthday, we sat together and relaxed and drank (ersatz) coffee, despite the hard times. Edith baked a very nice apple cake."[109]

The effort to sustain a sense of shared experiences and solidarity in the home space with relatives and even strangers who were compelled to live together can thus be understood as a type of resilience in the face of the pressures created by the exclusion of Jews. It was an attempt to find a surrogate for the nuclear family that had dispersed all over the globe. Much like Kati Moses, Janet Schocken and the Schmollers were aware that their situation was a transient one and their lives unstable, but they nevertheless acted to preserve significant elements of their domestic atmosphere.

In Gertrud Kolmar's case, intimate neighborly relations were detrimental to more than the experience of home. At the beginning of 1939, when she was forty-four—soon after the November pogrom—her father, whom she lived with, was compelled to sell the commodious family home in

Finkenkrug, a town west of Berlin replete with parks. The two moved into a five-room apartment in the city. "There is so much to unpack, to repack, to move!" she wrote to her sister in February of that year, as they were in the midst of the process. "I am not sure whether you know that we were unable to move all the things we planned into the three rooms that we intend to use for ourselves (we want to rent out the other two unfurnished), even though we have already gotten rid of many things."[110] From this point, and until 1943, Kolmar's letters, mostly sent to her sister in Switzerland, recount an ongoing contraction of her private space, continually eroding her sense of home.

Kolmar was never able to develop a feeling of home in her city apartment. In June 1941 she wrote, "One of my acquaintances remarked during a visit last year that I use the word 'at home' [*zuhause*] only when I speak about Finkenkrug, as if the place in Berlin is not my home."[111] Her sense of alienation from the apartment in Berlin connected with similar feelings she had about the city itself; it was far from the countryside she was accustomed to. The urban milieu was, she wrote, "impersonal" (*Unpersönlich*) and "insubstantial" (*Wesenlos*).[112]

The need to share her home with boarders from outside her family was difficult for Kolmar from the start, and her frustration simply increased as her personal space shrank. "In Finkenkrug we lived at a clear and fine distance from all this," she wrote in February 1940, with regard to the gossip her flatmates liked to engage in regarding matters that were none of their business. "Here," she added, "people are packed so closely, like hens."[113] The word she used here was *zusammenglucken*, from *glucke*, hen; the verb *glucken* means "cluck." She thus depicted the women in her apartment as a clutch of squawkers whose constant cacophony she could not escape.

The overcrowding and lack of privacy forced Kolmar to revise her daily routine. It came to the point where she could write poetry only at night.

> Right now this activity [writing] happens at night through several stages: I go to sleep early, and when the boarders on the top floor come home with a great ruckus in the middle of the night, between 1 and 3 a.m., and wake me up, then I have already slept a few hours, and then my "spiritual work" can begin. And when I have pushed the "child" [her poem] a few more centimeters forward, it's already past 5 in the morning, and I can allow myself to drift off again for a bit.[114]

This way of managing her sleep was a tactic Kolmar adopted, to put it in de Certeau's terms, to enable herself to continue with what she saw as her constitutive activity—writing poetry—against all odds in the circumstances in which she found herself. Regarding her creative work, she wrote two years later, "I think that all this must be real, true art if it isn't dependent on long hours of leisure, on the peace and quiet of a study, on external tranquility and comfort, but is able to overcome every insufficiency of time and space."[115]

Kolmar and her father were obliged in May 1941 to rent her room out as well, and she had to restrict herself and her belongings to an even smaller space. "We experienced a move and we put it past us with the slogan 'moving apartments within her home,'" she wrote to her sister. "We began by renting out the two back rooms (one of which was mine) at the beginning of May," she explained. "Furnished. That means we had to move again, reorganize our furniture and take the things out of the closets and move them elsewhere. That took a long time and required a lot of thought, because we do not suffer from any excess space in the apartment."[116]

From this point onward, she no longer had a room of her own. She slept in the dining room, which simply served to bolster her sense of homelessness. "Ever since my bed has been in the dining room," she wrote a few months later, "I in essence do not have any place to stay in, I have no space for myself, and the feeling of homelessness [*Heimlosigkeit*] that I have always felt here has grown much stronger."[117] Beginning in March 1942, she shared a room and a half with her father, a change that had a very concrete effect on her routine. "I can no longer write at night—those were my most productive hours."[118]

It was not only her physical space that contracted. Her unavoidable interaction with the other residents produced in Kolmar feelings of disgust and alienation from life in the apartment. "It is wonderful that the tenants here feel entirely at home," she wrote sarcastically in September 1941, "but that means that they come and go in our rooms."[119] More than a year later, she wrote to her sister to explain her revulsion for the apartment:

> It's because my boarders live there. Strangers who have taken over my things, mine and ours. Nothing belongs to me anymore. Maybe my room. But only when everyone else is out. Because if they are there, they generally gather in the kitchen, and they will certainly not forego animated conversation. . . . All this penetrates the closed door to my room, driving out the silence, the tranquility, the gravity and the quiet energy that I have collected there within myself and which I wanted to preserve.[120]

For many German Jews, home was a refuge, the polar opposite of the Nazified public space, and thus they preferred to spend as much time there as possible. Kolmar was different; at this point she chose the opposite tactic.

"I try to spend my day outside the house if it is at all possible," she wrote in August 1942, "and I frequently have arguments, necessary or unnecessary, with father, who says that these long walks outside exhaust me and that it would be better if I stayed quietly at home. At home! As if there still is such a thing."[121]

The alienation Kolmar felt in her apartment in Berlin led her to develop, paradoxically, positive feelings about the armaments factory where she spent most of her day, engaged in forced labor. It reached the point where, in the summer of 1942, she began relating to the factory as her home, and in her letters it gradually took the place previously occupied by her country home in Finkenkrug.

> I quickly began to perceive the work at the factory not only as a necessity, as compulsory, but as a sort of lesson. . . . I slowly came to understand that I was forming [at the factory] feelings of home [*Heimatgefühle*] that I do not have here [in the apartment, where she was writing] and know that I will enter those somewhat gray walls with a sense of "home again" when I return there on Monday.[122]

Kolmar addressed this subject in more detail in December 1942, when she remarked on the absurdity of the fact that, despite the monotony and arduous nature of her work, she felt that each time she went through the gate that she was at home again. "The noise of the machines at the factory debilitates me less than the prattling of the people in the apartment," she explained.[123]

Conclusion: "Everything Is So Empty"

On April 7, 1939, a few weeks before she and her husband emigrated to the United States, and a short time after her son reached England as part of the *Kindertransport*, Hertha Nathorff used the verb *hausen*, meaning roughly "inhabit," to refer to how she lived in her apartment as it emptied of its contents: "I inhabit our empty apartment. The empty rooms depress me. Everything is so empty."[124] Her choice of this particular verb, which generally refers to temporary shelter such as a tent, shack, or cave, was clearly deliberate. The more common choice would have been *wohnen* (reside) or *leben* (live in). She apparently used *hausen* to denote her dissolving sense of home. Her parting with her son, the clearing out of her belongings that bore memories of the past, and her lack of any future horizon had drained the concept of home of its substance. Nathorff, it will be recalled, had clung to domesticity even as it changed and contracted. She could allow herself to let go only when she was on the verge of beginning a new life overseas.

In his essay "Building Dwelling Thinking," Martin Heidegger expanded the meaning of the word *Wohnen*—dwelling or lodgings. Adducing the ancient German word *Baun*, Heidegger argued that "dwelling" was not simply an activity that human beings carried out. It meant something much more profound about human existence. "The way in which you are and I am, the manner in which we humans *are* on the earth, is *Baun*, dwelling," he wrote. "The old word *bauen*, which suggests that man *is* insofar as he dwells, *also* means, at the same time, to cherish and protect, to preserve and care for."[125] Heidegger's essay, based on a lecture he gave in 1951, gave voice to the longing for a home that many Germans felt after the war. But on a deeper level it invoked the need for domesticity and the practices that constitute it, which define human existence. This idea seems to take hold in particular at moments of crisis, which require rethinking one's perception of oneself, the past, and the future. In this sense, the intensity and extent to which Jews grappled with this question under the Nazi regime reveal just how profound an existential crisis they were undergoing.

In this chapter I have presented the range of ways in which German Jews coped with the concept of home and the experience of "being at home," with all its constituent elements. Home was, I maintain, primarily an emotional space, a site charged with environmental past and a focal point for broadening the boundaries of the self, and much less simply a place of comfort and convenience. It played a central role in German Jews' struggle to enable themselves, even in their darkest hour, to maintain a human existence that would provide for their most profound emotional needs. I have recounted a broad and varied range of tactics used by Jews to adapt the concept of home to the new reality. Some Jews attempted to spend as much time as possible at a place that gave them refuge and tranquility within the home, such as a balcony. Others—women in particular—tried to maintain something of the internal division of the bourgeois house, the redundant objects that characterized it, and its variety of functions, even when their space became extremely constricted. There were also some who fashioned within their four walls a new range of domestic activities, even turning their homes into creative spaces. In contrast with those who employed these tactics, which involved a display of agency on the part of women and men of nearly all ages, there were others who were rapidly worn down, sometimes to the point of despair and grief for the loss of their experience of home. The bottom line, however, is that, at least for as long as they remained in Germany, the vast majority of these German Jews who put their feelings into writing continued, in one way or another, to hold on to the sense of home against all odds.

This chapter is based in part on the insights of Mary Douglas and Joseph Rykwert, who proposed that the home must be understood not just as a place in a spatial perspective, but as a state in a temporal perspective. The concept of home is linked with the cyclical nature of daily life in the private space, with objects, and with memories, which lend a depth of connection to the personal and intergenerational past. The home is also imbued with hopes, expectations, and arrangements for continuing to live in it in the future. The reverse of this is that when the experience of home erodes, the threat of its dissolution also has a temporal aspect, in that it means losing an active link to and interest in the past, and losing belief in the future. A sterile transience takes over in which time stands still. These issues will be examined in the second part of this book.

PART 2

Time

* CHAPTER FOUR *

The Circle of Time

The Nazi Party celebrated Hitler's birthday on April 20, 1933, in the midst of its rapid takeover of the German state and civil society. Three days later, Walter Tausk wrote in his diary: "The only thing the government has done for the people so far is to manufacture holidays in great quantities—national holidays with bombastic colorful rostrums and grandiloquent speeches about the nation." Tausk lived in Breslau and in January 1933 began to devote the greater part of his diary to documenting how political changes under the new regime were affecting his life and surroundings. Subsequently he addressed the Nazi plan for marking May Day. "This same plan will be in operation on May 1, 'the international holiday of labor.' Just as the Catholic Church once appropriated pagan holidays for its own purposes, so as to galvanize the masses, so Hitler is acting with May 1, which was the day of the Socialist International."[1] A few days later, Tausk described the regime's preparations, which included appropriating the public space by hanging masses of swastika flags on trees all over Breslau without any regard for the esthetics of the city's streets and squares. He also recounted the personal protest he intended to make against the new holiday. "For May 1 I am preparing—in protest against the Nazi idiots [*Nazioten*] all around me—a large Prussian flag," he related. "I want to hang the flag from my living room window, because I was a Prussian and took part in the war at the front, and because I will not allow them to dictate my convictions."[2]

Norbert Elias asserts that the measurement of time is a social institution meant to regulate human lives. Humans' incessant efforts to control the flow of time, to restrain it, and to harness it to their needs in the context of the time regimes that organize human life are, he maintains, an inseparable part of the civilizing process.[3] Elias considers the various aspects of this fundamental activity, which he calls "timing," and sees it as founded on a synthesis between the cyclical nature of natural phenomena (such as the movement of the heavens and the procession of the seasons) and the social need for temporal regulation. He presents calendars, which have appeared in and become emblematic of different cultures, as recognizable products of this synthesis of nature and society. Modern industrial societies, he adds, are characterized by more intensive synchronization processes among the individuals and groups that constitute them, in what he calls processes of active timing.[4] In such societies, which are characterized by high-intensity regulation of time, the regulated and precise experience of time becomes part of the very fabric of its members' selfhood.[5]

The measurement of time and the design of calendars have been discussed in recent decades by sociologists, anthropologists, and other social scientists in a variety of contexts. Eviatar Zerubavel, one of the founders of the new field of the sociology of time, analyzes the processes that impel human beings to mark synchronously, at given times each year, events in their shared past. This communal invocation of such a memory often has a spatial aspect, such as the making of a pilgrimage to the location where the recalled event took place. Sometimes it involves ceremonies that symbolically reenact the event, a common element of many religious and national holidays. According to Zerubavel, these practices are fundamental to the establishment of a collective identity.[6]

Calendars and ways of measuring time have emerged in cultures throughout history. The shaping of the annual cycle on the axis of time engenders constant tension between sensing time as a straight line and sensing it as a circle, giving rise, over epochs and cultures, of different perceptions of the world and human existence.[7] Historians have used case studies to show how the reshaping of holidays, located at specific points on the yearly cycle, along with the creation of new commemorations and the elimination of old ones, has reflected profound political and cultural changes. David Cressy has demonstrated how the calendar played a role in shaping a Protestant English national culture in the seventeenth century. Cressy argues that initiatives such as the elimination of many saints' days with roots in Catholic tradition, rearrangement of some of the remaining principal holidays to synchronize them with the agricultural cycle, and the declaration of the king's coronation day as a holiday created a new map of time meant to disconnect England from Rome.[8] Mona Ozouf notes the important role that holidays and days of national commemoration played in shaping the collective experience in revolutionary France at the end of the eighteenth century. The republican calendar, she demonstrates, was meant not only to embed the memory of the revolution in the annual cycle, but to purge the French calendar of a dense web of customs coming from the previous era and to make it more rational, efficient, and unified. Ozouf offers a detailed analysis of the connection between the reshaping of time by the revolutionaries and their practices of seizing control of and reshaping the public space.[9]

A rapid process of temporal standardization ensued during and especially toward the end of the nineteenth century. It could be seen all over the world, but was most evident in Europe. Standardizing the precise measurement of time played a decisive role in the transport revolution that Europe underwent during this period, in which trains enabled the movement of people and goods all over the continent and beyond. The unitary calendar and then the clock were fundamental to progress.[10] The process was also evident in the consolidation of the rising bourgeois European way of life, which for all intents and purposes designed a new calendar that replaced that of rural life and the agricultural seasons, and imbued holidays with new significance in family life.[11] The Gregorian calendar, rooted in Christianity, underwent a process of secularization, even if incomplete, as its holidays took on other meanings. In some parts of German society, for example, Christmas metamorphosed into a national civic holiday. It became a family and consumerist celebration, subordinating its religious significance.[12]

In everyday life in the public sphere, the standardization of time led to a rise in synchronization, which played a decisive role in the consolidation of the nation-state. The publication of newspapers at fixed times, Benedict Anderson argues, was a major factor in creating imagined communities in the modern era. The regularly distributed newspaper, read by people spread over a large area who did not know each other personally, became a principal means of producing a sense of solidarity that transformed them into a national community. This could happen because they shared a point of view and a set of experiences at fixed times. The press both illustrates and embodies Anderson's claim about "how important to that imagined community is the idea of steady, solid simultaneity through time."[13] The simultaneous experience of the present by means of the daily perusal of newspapers whose day of publication appeared prominently under their mastheads played a critical role in constituting public time and fashioning modern collective identities.[14] The annual cycle, as shaped by the national calendar, thus became a central factor in affiliation with the national culture, work routines, the community, and family life, particularly in the middle class.

The integration of the Jews into modern German society was first and foremost an integration into the German bourgeoisie. According to Jacob Katz, writing in the 1930s, most Jews became, during the emancipation era, a subgroup of the German middle class. Subsequent historians address factors such as education, professional profile, and the bourgeois way of life as fundamental characteristics of German Jews' integration into their surroundings.[15]

The entry of Germany's Jews in the new middle class quite naturally found expression in a change in their attitude toward time. The freedom of movement, employment, and residence that they gained as a result of political change and their exposure to the daily press was supplemented by the transport revolution brought on by trains and the accelerated urbanization and industrialization of the late nineteenth century. All these inculcated in the Jews a more modern mentality of time, in the spirit of the values of the rising bourgeoisie. The distinctiveness of Jewish life alongside Central European Christian society in the premodern age had been based in part on their different annual cycle and temporal regime.[16] The Jews' rapid assimilation into German society at the end of the nineteenth century and the beginning of the twentieth inevitably involved synchronizing themselves with the dominant time regime surrounding them, in particular the annual cycle as manifested in the civil calendar.

Even so, a place remained for the Jewish cycle in the world of emancipated Jews, particularly in the private family and the communal spheres. "Our year was replete with the imprint of the rhythm of Jewish life, within Jewish circles, with our Jewish friends," Rahel Straus wrote in her memoir. In this passage, Straus, an Orthodox Jew born in Karlsruhe in 1880, referred to her childhood and youth in the imperial period. She added that "in parallel, there was the civil calendar with its celebrations, school, vacations, and holidays."[17] Along with appropriating the new civil calendar and its social time regime, and the faith in progress it involved, many Central European Jews thus also preserved a more traditional Jewish perception of time.

In this chapter I will address the Nazification of time as it was manifested in the reshaping of the German national calendar. I will then consider the variety of Jewish responses. The annulment of the legal emancipation that German Jews had enjoyed and their exclusion from German society under the Nazi regime meant that they were also excluded from the German calendar. As I have shown in the preceding chapters with regard to space, in the context of time these Jews also had to cope with exclusion and find new ways to shape the calendar by which they lived. In the first part of the chapter I will present reactions like that of Tausk, who sought to protest the exclusion of the Jews from the German cycle of time by holding onto German national symbols. Such responses were notable mostly during the Nazi regime's early years. As time went by, other attitudes seem to have moved to the fore. Another way of coping with the challenge of shaping the cycle of time under escalating conditions of exclusion can be seen in the way

German Jews remade the traditional Jewish calendar. That is the subject of the chapter's second part.

"Today Is National Labor Day. . . . With Us It Is the Opposite": The Jews and the Nazi Calendar

When the Nazi Party rose to power in Germany and merged into the state, it established a new temporal regime in which time itself was Nazified. It did not take long for the Nazis to put in place their own calendar, replacing that of the Weimar Republic. They appropriated existing commemorative dates, such as Mother's Day, infusing them with racial doctrine. May Day, a socialist holiday, was renamed National Labor Day and became a day off with pay. Memorial Day for Germany's fallen soldiers, which the republic had instituted, was remade as Heroes' Memorial Day, commemorating fallen Nazis. Christmas was also Nazified. The Nazi cycle began with the commemoration of the party's rise to power on January 30, continuing with the Führer's birthday on April 20, National Labor Day on May 1, Midsummer's Day on June 21, the harvest Thanksgiving at the beginning of October, Heroes' Memorial Day on November 9, the winter solstice on December 21, and Christmas. Heroes' Memorial Day was in many ways the climax of the Nazi year. It was designed along the lines of Easter, including a new version of the Passion Play, staged in the streets of Munich as a dramatic reenactment of the death of the martyred perpetrators of the Nazi putsch in 1923. In fact, the regime tried to replace the Christian calendar with a completely overhauled year.[18] There were also days, such as *Parteitag*, to mark the opening of Nazi Party rallies, and the days of the plebiscites the regime held from time to time and treated as holidays.

The Nazification of time was the obverse of the Nazification of space, two processes that were the focal points of the establishment of the *Volksgemeinschaft*, the People's Community. On Nazi holidays and other dates of political significance, like plebiscite days, the Nazi conquest of the street was even more apparent than on weekdays. The public space filled up with symbols such as flags, uniforms, and torchlight parades. These days made vast impressions on ordinary Germans and helped legitimize the regime in their eyes. That can be seen in the way they wrote about them in their diaries.[19] These events were characterized by a violent and exclusionary atmosphere, directed principally at the Jews.

How did Jews react to the Nazification of time? Diarists such as Walter Tausk made frequent reference to how the German calendar was being reshaped by the addition of new holidays. Willy Cohn, like Tausk a resident of Breslau, wrote in a typical entry on April 20, 1933: "Today is Hitler's birthday.

Throughout the city the streetcars are festooned with swastika flags alongside flags of black and white and red." Cohn was referring to the imperial flag, which the Nazis restored as the national flag until in the mid-1930s the Nazi flag itself was adopted as the national flag. "The Horst Wessel song [the Nazi anthem] can be heard from the windows of the houses," he wrote. "It is reminiscent of the kaiser's birthday."[20]

Cohn's account is a good illustration of the transition from the pre-Nazi calendar to the new one. Visual and audio space was taken over by Nazi symbols, but the imperial flag flew alongside them, reminding Cohn of the birthday of Kaiser Wilhelm II, a memory from another era. Indeed, such commemorations from the imperial age would be recalled by some Jewish writers in the years that followed, in the paradoxical context of the new Nazi holidays.

For Kurt Rosenberg of Hamburg, May Day 1933, of which he wrote twice in his diary, served as an opportunity to take stock of the state of Germany and its Jews:

> Today is National Labor Day. Flags upon flags, even on children in strollers. The train conductors wear swastika armbands. We remain at home, with us it is the opposite. . . . At the time that I write, crowds of Brown Shirts are passing under my window, heading for the municipal park. . . . We face the dissolution of our lives' work and are full of powerless bitterness and anger. But I am not helpless. I am seeing to it that the mental spinal cord of my thinking will not be stunned.[21]

Rosenberg was clearly trying to maintain his mental fortitude, but beyond that, the Nazi takeover of space and time on this day seems to have accelerated his process of disconnecting himself from his surroundings. "Is this the nation of poets and thinkers?" he wrote later in the day. "We were proud to belong to it, to give it the best of our strength and our will. We must lament the fate of Germany more than our own fate, which has left us without a roof over our heads."[22] Like Tausk, Rosenberg quickly grasped that the Nazi capture of the public space and the calendar was a deliberate policy. As he wrote on May 19, "The holidays grow ever longer. Labor Day, the day welcoming the Reich governor [*Reichsstatthalter*] in Hamburg."[23]

Jewish children who attended German schools also experienced the new Nazi holidays. Elisabeth Block of Niedernburg, who almost never mentioned political events in her diary, described Labor Day—May 1, 1934, when she was eleven years old—as a festive day free of conflict. She made note of the many flags hung in her school in honor of the holiday, and described how she listened to the speeches of "Dr. Goebbels and our Führer," delivered in Berlin and broadcast on the radio.[24] But presumably this account, which reflects this young writer's innocent predisposition until the end of the 1930s to maintain her grasp on her surroundings, is the exception that proves the rule. For Margot Littauer, a high school student in Breslau who was five years older than Block, the commemoration of this day was an experience of exclusion and a watershed in the way she felt in her surroundings. The assignment her teacher gave her class—to write an essay on May Day's significance in the Nazi state—prompted several of her classmates to bring up for discussion the issue of whether it was even proper for the Jewish students to address the holiday. In her memoir, Littauer recounted how the teacher tried to display a certain measure of tolerance, but in the end, because of pressure from most of the students, she brought the discussion to an end by saying, "I am thus in favor of opposing the Jews dispassionately and removing them from among us. They are indeed foreign to us, and they obstruct our nationhood."[25]

Jewish children and teenagers in different places experienced the Nazi holidays as exclusionary, but not only because of the way their teachers and "Aryan" classmates behaved.[26] Even when they attended Jewish schools, they were denied, at least in some places, the option of evading the Nazi cycle of holidays and what it symbolized. In his memoirs, the Jewish educator Heinemann Stern portrayed Jewish schools as places of refuge from the wretchedness these young people experienced in the public space. The authorities, he remarked, forced Jewish schools to observe the national holidays, such as Hitler's birthday, and as part of that, teachers and students were required to listen to speeches on the radio, which included vitriol against the Jews.[27]

In his diary, Victor Klemperer offered a perceptive view of the new holidays, as part of his scholarly scrutiny of the symbolic and linguistic aspects of the Nazi phenomenon. He analyzed the Nazis' use of the calendar in comparison with that of other regimes and in other eras. On August 11, 1934, the date on which the Weimar Republic had marked Constitution Day (*Verfassungstag*), he noted that the holiday, canceled under the Nazi regime, had never made an impact. He explained that the republic had principally valued reason and condemned the corporeal, and had played down the importance of the nation. In this sense, the Republic had been, he maintained, too "Protestant" in character. "With the present government," he wrote, "the opposite is the case, and it exaggerates this opposition to the point of absurdity [*Unsinnige*]."[28] The modern Protestant mentality that characterized the Republic had led to the secularization and disenchantment of the traditional calendar. The number of holidays was reduced and the number of regular weekdays rose as a result. This rationalized public time and lent it a more linear flow. The Nazis, Klemperer suggested, once again imbued the year with enchantment by infusing it with irrationality. Over the years that followed, Klemperer wrote in his diary of the regime's unsuccessful attempt to change the names of the German months, just as the French Revolution had done. Furthermore, he observed, Hitler's birthday was marked in quasireligious ways.[29] The atmosphere that the Nazi regime instituted was, as Klemperer put it, that of one long holiday. It found expression not only in the national calendar but in local calendars. "It is noticeable, everywhere and always—we have passed through so many places in the last few months," he wrote in his diary in June 1938, meaning the drives he and his wife had made through Germany. "Again and again, and not only on Sundays: festivals and flags. Fairs . . . sports meeting of an SA unit, united, 600th, 625th, 650th, etc., etc., anniversary of a town . . . always festivals, the People's Community, Third Reich, flags, flags, flags."[30]

The Nazification of the German calendar was also discussed in the Jewish press in Germany, especially during the regime's initial years. The writers could not, of course, speak freely in public about the significance of the Nazi holidays, but many opinion pieces addressed the way Jews experienced and construed them, and at times even sought to imbue them with meanings. In a piece that appeared in *CV-Zeitung* on February 1, 1934, Alfred Hirschberg, one of the leaders of the Central Association, addressed what had happened on January 30, the anniversary of the Nazi rise to power. The first anniversary of the establishment of the Third Reich, he wrote, had been celebrated as a holiday in Germany, but the voice of Germany's Jews had not been heard then. They could not find themselves within this new situation, whose victims they had become. Hirschberg addressed the Nazi holiday largely by calling for a profound and long-range examination of Jewish history in Germany, and for self-criticism regarding the difficulties that had emerged during the age of emancipation and the possibility that Jews might at some point find a formula for their future integration into the Nazi new order.[31] The disparity between the consciousness of time that the Nazis wished to inculcate and that of liberal Jews, as expressed by Hirschberg, is evident in the fact that, precisely on the day that for the Nazis symbolized a look to the future, the dawn of the thousand-year Reich, Hirschberg called on his readers to look a thousand years back into the history of German Jewry. He again addressed the January 30 holiday in another article he wrote a year later, in which he stressed the need for "general responsibility," which was necessary for carrying on Jewish life in Germany.[32] *Jüdische Rundschau* offered a different assessment of January 30. According to this Zionist newspaper, it was a day of mass celebrations by the German people that should bring home to Germany's non-Zionist Jews, who had lived until 1933 in the illusion that they were Germans, that they needed to break free of the "spiritual ghetto" of the age of assimilation and foster their Jewish identities.[33] In contrast, the members of the Central Association would not easily give up their German national affiliation. These ideological polemics about how to understand the liberal heritage of the emancipation and the future of German Jewry were evident in their differing attitudes toward the holiday marking the inception of the Nazi regime.

January 30, April 20, and November 9 were manifestly Nazi holidays, bound up with anti-Jewish polemics that could not be explained away. Other days marked on the Nazi calendar were portrayed by some writers in the Jewish press as "softer" in their attitude toward the Jews. Some writers, during the regime's early period, sought to maintain a hold on the holidays so as to preserve a certain measure of synchronization with the new German year. This, for example, was the attitude toward Memorial Day, which the Weimar Republic had instituted to honor the German soldiers who had fallen in World War I (*Volkstrauertag*). It was observed on the fifth Sunday after Easter.[34] In March 1933, when German politics was undergoing rapid change in the transition from democracy to Nazi rule, *CV-Zeitung* cited this day as proof that Germany's Jews were patriotic Germans. The people's day of mourning, the newspaper declared, should serve as an opportunity for examining history and remembering the Jews who had given their lives for Germany. The Jews, it argued, were duty-bound to maintain their honor even in this time of changes. Only in this way could they maintain the possibility that they would be allowed to contribute to the construction of the homeland's future.[35] This attitude, if in a somewhat more skeptical form, was apparent a year later in an article by Alfred Hirschberg, in which he called the graves of fallen soldiers, including those of Jewish soldiers, the "foundations of the new Germany," thus intimating that Memorial Day expressed the Jews' connection to the German homeland.[36] In fact, the character of the day had begun to change already in March 1933; a year later it had undergone an utter transformation. A new law passed in February 1934 changed its name to Heroes' Memorial Day (*Heldengedenktag*). Furthermore, instead of being observed as a day of mourning on which flags were lowered to half mast, it became a day sanctifying heroism, and flags were flown at full height. Under the encouragement of Nazi Propaganda Minister Joseph Goebbels, the day was used to promote the reinstatement of military conscription, to underline the connection between the Wehrmacht and the Nazi Party, and to hallow the cult of war.[37] The Jewish press did not mark the day in subsequent years.

The attempt to maintain a connection to Memorial Day was an extension of the direction Jewish discourse had taken during the Weimar period. In contrast, Jewish writers addressed National Labor Day not as a new version of May Day but as an entirely new holiday, integral to the Nazified German national calendar. In an article in *CV-Zeitung* on April 27, the day Goebbels declared the day's new name, Hirschberg did not deny that Germany's Jews were becoming increasingly isolated. He invoked the metaphor of walls that divided the lives of most Germans from those of German Jews.[38] Nevertheless, while maintaining that the Jews needed to build a separate living space for themselves, he stuck to an inclusive interpretation of the Nazi propaganda minister's statement about the relevance of National Labor Day, attempting to show that it indicated that the Jews were also part of the German people in their commitment to labor. In this spirit he tried to connect the new holiday to the Jewish world, to their duty to work and bear responsibility behind the walls that isolated them.

A few days later, an editorial in *Jüdische Rundschau* described what it called the "Day of German Labor" as representative of the new Germany uniting under the banner of peaceful labor. The Jews, it declared, should not delude themselves into believing that the talk about German labor and German goods included them, when these same terms had been used in an antisemitic context on April 1, the day of the boycott of Jewish businesses. Nevertheless, the new Nazi May Day was not bound up with antisemitic propaganda. As such, and given that labor was a fundamental Zionist value, and that the Nazis had stressed the distinction between the labor of those of Jewish extraction and those of German extraction, the editorial said that "we aspire to integration into the new and powerful German state" based on German labor.[39] In other words, in this Zionist view, Jews could connect with the holiday not by marking the day as Germans but by celebrating Jewish labor, complementing what the Nazi government was doing. This position was consistent with the attitude German Zionists had taken toward the Weimar Republic. They had called then for Jewish citizens to act as German citizens while nevertheless maintaining a distance between themselves and Germans.[40] In practical terms, this option, like the continuation of the emancipation of the liberal age, quickly proved to be without any foundation in reality.

While the writers in the Zionist newspaper made no mention of National Labor Day in 1934 and thereafter, Hirschberg continued to address it in *CV-Zeitung* in 1934 and even in 1935, when the liberal leader called on the excluded German Jews who were forced to stand on the sidelines anxiously watching the day's parades to find their own way to live the values of labor and community.[41] But from that point onward the major German Jewish newspapers ceased to make any reference, good or bad, to the holidays on the German national calendar.

Even as the Jewish press went silent on this subject, diarists continued to write of the impact of Nazi holidays on their everyday lives. As these holidays served as a major tool of the Nazis in the establishment of the People's Community, they were observed with mass rallies in urban public spaces. Jewish diarists evinced an opposite reaction, an inclination to go into isolation and to seek silence far from the city streets. Kurt Rosenberg wrote of how he and his wife went for walks in the country to escape the mass events of May Day, the crowds and noise of the Nazified city square.[42] Willy Cohn shut himself up at home on Nazi holidays. On May 1, 1935, for example, he wrote that his wife had canceled travel plans because of National Labor Day.[43] On Nazi holidays, he wrote a few months later, Jews had a duty to act with "simplicity and discretion."[44] The contrast between the German street with its holiday spirit and the experience of the excluded Jews stands out especially in Klemperer's account of the atmosphere on April 10, 1938, the day of the plebiscite that endorsed the Anschluss of Austria into the Greater Reich. "Yesterday evening pealing bells for a whole hour," he wrote. "On top of that, the red smoke of the torchlight processions over the city, windows were lit up, even up here in our lonely place."[45]

Alongside the isolation and seclusion the diarists described on Nazi holidays, they also depict a different experience of time: a slow, passive wait until the danger passed, and real fears about what the future would bring. So Rosenberg retrospectively described the atmosphere in his home on the night of September 15, 1935, the day of the Nazi Party rally at which the anti-Jewish Nuremberg Laws were proclaimed. He wrote of the helplessness, apprehension, and slowness with which time passed each time a party rally (*Parteitag*) was held: "There was tension everywhere, rumors flew."[46] In advance of the next annual party rally, in September 1936, all the Jews waited in fear, he wrote, "for the new measures and laws against them, for weeks and months. The days were full of foreboding and worry." On the day of the rally itself, "throughout the day—we waited hour by hour, read newspapers, listened to the radio, waited for new trouble. How deep has it sunk into the soul."[47] These feelings were also accompanied by real physical distress and a hammering heartbeat. Unlike its predecessor, the September 1936 rally did not produce a new escalation against the Jews; but the experience of helpless waiting, which will be discussed in more detail in the next chapter, made them observe the date in the Nazi calendar despite themselves.

November 9, the Nazi Memorial Day for the so-called martyrs of the 1923 putsch, was described by Willy Cohn in his diary in 1937 as an especially grim and menacing day, even prior to its violent culmination in the pogrom of the following year.[48] A year later, on the morning of November 9, 1938, just a few hours before the pogrom broke out, Cohn noted in his diary that it was a fateful day in history, marking the twentieth anniversary of the Berlin revolution of 1918 and the fifteenth of the attempted Nazi putsch in Munich. "There is again a November atmosphere on the street," he added.[49] In the years after the pogrom, this date was charged with further traumatic memories, and as it approached, diarists gave voice to even more dread than usual. "At the beginning of November," Walter Tausk wrote in his diary in November 1939, "a question arose among the people: 'What will happen this time on November 9?' Something must happen again, after all. The day can't pass without some sort of spectacle." Religious Jews mourned their burned synagogues, he added, while the liberals were overcome with anxiety and fear. In the end, "on November 9 nothing happened."[50]

From the end of the 1930s, after the pogrom, the voluntary isolation of Jews on Nazi holidays was sometimes exacerbated by something new—restrictions on Jewish movement on these days. On December 3, 1938, the regime declared a day of solidarity and imposed a curfew (*Ausgehverbot*) on Breslau's Jews, forbidding them to leave home during most hours of the day. The justification was that "they do not take part in German solidarity." After quoting this, Tausk added that "it's not so bad as long as they leave you alone. Even in good bourgeois Aryan circles . . . [they] stay off the streets today, because we are under mob rule, which is even worse that in the era of the French Revolution."[51] The imposition of such restrictions by the government was the ultimate expression of exclusion from the national calendar along with exclusion from the street. Willy Cohn, who reported on this stricture in Breslau, placed it in a broader historical context. "Such measures are being opposed now for the first time since the Lateran Council,"[52] he wrote in his diary, meaning the conclave that had convened in Rome in 1215 to make a series of decisions about furthering the segregation of Jews from Christians. The recognition of this reversion to medieval precedents led Cohn to lose his faith in the principle of progress and to replace it with a cyclical view of history. "World history is a cycle," he wrote.

"Still a Bit under the Influence of Christmas": Christmas and the Gregorian New Year

Jews were also excluded from synchronization with the German People's Community on Christian holidays, most notably Christmas. During the nineteenth century and at the beginning of the twentieth, Christmas was refashioned as a modern holiday of bourgeois character, appropriate for the middle class's family and consumption values. It was also supplemented with national traditions and characteristics. This was part of the consolidation of nation-states in the West.[53] In Germany, the Christmas atmosphere

(*Weihnachtsstimmung*) during this period was shaped largely in keeping with the values of the Protestant urban bourgeoisie, with the use of practices and sentiments taken from the bourgeois home. It became part of German national culture in a process that reached its acme at around the turn of the century. As Joe Perry has shown, different cultural and political groups produced different versions of Christmas at this time.[54] The Jews' synchronization with German time during the age of emancipation was evident in this context as well. Starting in the last third of the nineteenth century, some Jews, especially those of the urban middle and upper middle classes, began celebrating Christmas in united Germany as an expression of their affiliation with German culture. Others did not celebrate Christmas but refashioned Hanukah, which occurs at around the same time of year, under the influence of the new German Christmas. For example, they exchanged gifts under a tree (a combination sometimes referred to as *Weihnukka*, an amalgamation of Christmas and Hanukah). It is important to stress, however, that conservative and pious Jews, as well as some Zionists, voiced sharp criticism of such practices.[55]

The Nazi regime, well aware of Christmas's symbolic potency, commenced already in 1933 to appropriate Christmas and turn it into a part of the Nazi calendar, and to use it in its process of consolidating the People's Community. The holiday was infused with racial myths of blood and soil, and renamed the "People's Christmas" (*Volksweihnachten*). In this new spirit, it was observed with street festivals, at Nazi Party branches, within the SA, by the Hitler Youth (*Hitlerjugend*), and by other Nazi organizations. The charitable activities traditionally associated with the holiday, in particular the Winter Relief of the German People project (*Winterhilfe*, which the Nazis renamed *Winterhilfswerk*), promoted a racist and exclusionary character. Christian theologians, principally Protestant ones, who were in tune with the regime, sought to produce a new version of Christmas that would be free of its Jewish roots, as part of a broader effort to Germanize Christianity.[56]

Jews responded vehemently to these developments, which led inexorably to them being pushed even further out of synchronization with their German surroundings. "Christmas Eve will be marked this year in Germany by fewer Jews than in the past," predicted a *Jüdische Rundschau* editorial on December 22, 1933. The author criticized the prevailing attitude of viewing the celebration of Christmas in Jewish homes as a mark of high culture, adding, "If the new era that began for Germany's Jews in 1933 is not evident only in their external fate, but sets off an inner awakening as well—it will be reflected in a change in the approach to Christmas."[57] The setting aside of Christmas, on the basis of the German Zionist principle of maintaining a distance from German culture, was described in this article as a statement of not belonging (*nichtdazugehören*) in the German surroundings. The editorial thus proposed that its readers bolster their connections to Judaism and to Hanukah, with an understanding of its significance for Zionism.[58] Significantly, it was at just this time that the Zionist movement in Germany and around the world was nationalizing traditional Jewish holidays, and this was especially notable when it came to Hanukah.

Similar voices could also be heard in the liberal Jewish press. Many young people who had up to this point experienced Christmas as a holiday with a tree, presents, and all the other trappings, so explained a counselor in the *CV-Zeitung* youth supplement at the beginning of December 1934, now felt clueless and had no desire to celebrate it. They sought a new holiday to mark the beginning of the winter, and this liberal Jewish counselor offered Hanukah.[59] The proposal of the radically assimilationist Association of German National Jews (Verband nationaldeutscher Juden) to hold a festive evening to celebrate Christmas as a German holiday prompted the Liberal Rabbi Ignaz Maybaum to condemn, in *CV-Zeitung*, what he termed a tiny and marginal group, and to stress the religious Christian nature of the holiday, which made it utterly alien to Judaism. Perhaps it might have been possible to think otherwise in the past, he acknowledged, but now, under the new political circumstances, it was clear to all that it was God's command to distance the Jews from this Christian holiday.[60]

In conservative Jewish circles, which even prior to 1933 had much decried the Jewish turn toward Christmas, the call to set Christmas aside in favor of Hanukah came along with a more general critique of the path taken by Liberal Judaism in the age of emancipation. "Less Light—but Ours!" an article that appeared in the Orthodox weekly *Der Israelit* in November 1934, told the story of a boy from a Liberal Jewish family who asked his parents to buy him a Hanukah menorah as a Christmas gift, which he wanted to light joyfully under the tree on the Christmas table. "In times past," the writer added, clearly hinting at recent political developments and the exclusion of the Jews from the German People's Community, "it was presented to us so many times and in such a clear way where we belong, that we might hope that in the meantime the Christmas lights have gone out even in Liberal homes, where they believed that the ancient and familiar happiness of the Jewish family needed the support of foreign rites and customs."[61]

Writers in the newspapers of all Jewish tendencies presented a clear and unambiguous message of cutting free from Christmas. The more personal perspective provided by diaries reveals a much wider range of both emotional and intellectual reactions, as well as, in some cases, misgivings and difficulties. The attitude these writers evinced with regard to Christmas, which they often addressed in the context of the tension between it and Hanukah, very personally and most profoundly reflected the way they coped with their exclusion from the German community, and the question of whether they could really reconnect with their own Jewish roots.

"Christmas Eve 1933. My wife is in her room with white wine," the journalist Max Reiner wrote in his memoir. "She has suffered a great deal from the political, economic, and social changes. This evening her nerves betrayed her. . . . It always used to be that we would travel on Christmas, or celebrate it at home with the family, as many Germans of the Jewish faith did. This time we are alone in our large apartment."[62] In this passage, Christmas reveals a profound crisis in the Reiner family, and the loosening of the connection to it is emblematic of the profound isolation in which the couple found themselves. The holiday also brought home the incongruence of life before and after Nazi rule.

The diary of Dr. Erich Seligmann of Berlin, fifty-four years old at the time, portrays the tension surrounding Christmas in a different way. In the spirit of Jewish public discourse as seen in the press, the Seligmanns chose to celebrate Hanukah instead of Christmas. But his personal reflections indicate how difficult this was. On Christmas Eve 1934, he wrote, his son Rolf, who lived and worked in Spain, returned for a brief family visit after more than a year abroad. "And so," Seligmann wrote, "Christmas became a joyous holiday for us." But he did not leave it at that.

> Who can deny that, even though it was justly rejected by the Jews, the ideas and thoughts associated with this holiday belong to the finest aspects of German Christian thinking? We celebrate Hanukah with complete introspection, full of pride about the return to our history, full of "in spite of it all [*Trotz*]," but nevertheless we—don't listen to the Zionists!—are still a bit under the influence of Christmas.[63]

The word *Trotz* alludes to the expression *Trotzjudentum*, which had been in use since the appearance of modern antisemitism in Germany. It meant deciding, proudly, to adhere to one's Jewish identity despite, and perhaps even because of, anti-Jewish pressures. This feeling provided Seligmann with the impetus necessary to induce his family to set aside their observance of Christmas in favor of Hanukah. But it was not enough to stop them from feeling an intimate connection to the non-Jewish holiday. The complexity of the transition from Christmas to Hanukah observance is evident differently in a passage from the diary of Lisbeth Schmidt, a Frankfurt housewife and mother of four daughters. Schmidt, whose family lived an Orthodox Jewish lifestyle, related that a Jewish girl from Berlin had come to visit a neighbor of hers in June 1936. Schmidt's daughter Margrit spoke to the visiting girl and learned that in recent years her family had stopped observing Christmas and now celebrated Hanukah instead. "Margrit told me this in astonishment because she [the girl from Berlin] eats pork."[64] For the Orthodox girl, eating pork was emblematic of rejecting a Jewish life, yet here the girl had given up Christmas for Hanukah. It was a textbook example of *Trotzjudentum.*

Kurt Rosenberg wrestled with Christmas in a more complex personal and intellectual way, as evidenced by a 1935 passage from his diary. Rosenberg from time to time included in his diary essay-like passages expressing his thoughts. He addressed the tension between the holiday's nature as a Christian religious holiday unconnected to the Jews, and its transformation into a part of German culture, indeed central to affiliation with it; he used the German word *Kulturzugehörigkeit*, cultural affiliation. "In my childhood I experienced Christmas and the Christmas tree as a winter holiday, devoid of religious content . . . as a German holiday, celebrated at home, knowing that thousands of German neighbors were celebrating like me, in the same way." But now that the holiday had become charged with nationalist and even *völkisch* ideas, Jews could no longer accept it. As a result, the synchronization with their neighbors that Rosenberg had remarked on was disappearing. Having to grapple with this strain, as well as with how to differentiate Hanukah from Christmas, was, he maintained, emblematic of his time (*Zeittypisch*). Under the prevailing circumstances, he added, "we can no longer navigate within the boundaries of German thinking of the present, because we cannot find within it a place for our way of thinking."[65]

It was not only assimilated Jews with little connection to Jewish observance who felt the pain of parting from Christmas. More traditional Jews also sometimes felt a connection to the holiday because it was part of the calendar of the society within which they lived and which they felt part of. Many Jews, observant ones included, had in the past taken part in the shopping spree that preceded the holiday.[66] Now, with their financial position worsening and their social exclusion increasing, they had to do without this aspect of the holiday as well. According to a diary entry from 1933, Willy Cohn, who came from a religious background and spent much time writing and lecturing on Jewish holidays, seems to have seen no contradiction between that and the many memories Christmas evoked of his parents' home.[67] In the years that followed, Cohn underwent an experience of taking leave of Christmas. "It is pretty to see the homes where trees are lit up," he wrote in 1935, a few months after the promulgation of the Nuremberg Laws. "It is a nice holiday, but we the Jews must try not to imitate it, because there is no point in doing so."[68] In 1935 he wrote, "It's nice to look from the street at the houses where the trees are lit," adding that "only a few of them know they are celebrating the birthday of a Jew."[69] Three years later, a few weeks after the harrowing experiences of the November pogrom and its aftermath, Cohn voiced even more potently his rupture from his surroundings in recounting a trip to downtown Breslau on Christmas Eve. "On the visit to the inner city," he wrote, "I felt like a stranger. People are making their final purchases before Christmas. We live outside that."[70]

Cohn's leave-taking from Christmas is also evidenced by his memories of how he had experienced the holidays in previous years. On Christmas in 1937, for example, he recalled the four Christmases he had spent at the front during World War I and the many people he had known then, "some of them no longer living, some scattered all over the world and all trace of them lost."[71] These memories portrayed a world that no longer existed, and underlined Cohn's alienation from the Nazi Christmas. It is symbolic that on the last Christmas on which he wrote in his diary before being deported to the east, which occurred on the first day of Hanukah 1940, Cohn chose to mention only the Jewish holiday, completely disregarding the Christian one.[72]

Along with the diarists who chose to disengage from Christmas in whatever way, there were others who continued to hang on to it despite, and perhaps precisely because, of their social isolation. Elisabeth Block frequently wrote in her diary about the Christmases of her childhood and adolescence. She set down an enthusiastic account of her family's celebration in December 1933, when she was eleven. It included a tree piled with presents and emblazoned with lights. Her positive Christmas experience may not have been connected to political events,[73] but when she wrote again as an older girl, at the end of the 1930s and the beginning of the 1940s, it was hard to keep politics at bay. In November 1938, a few days after the pogrom, Elisabeth and her sister Trude were expelled from their school and parted sadly from their girlfriends. They continued their studies at home, mostly under their mother's direction, and preparations for the approaching Christmas became a central part of their home schooling. "I am now very busy with dividing my time [between the different subjects she was studying at home] and preparing for Christmas," she wrote in her diary, "and feel quite as satisfied as before, when I went to school."[74] The sixteen-year-old Block described the holiday as an exciting family event that everyone eagerly anticipated after so much planning; everyone dressed in their holiday finest, exchanged gifts, and sang Christmas songs.[75] The holiday also occupied a central place in her diary in the years that followed. In 1939 Block stressed that despite the war, the gifts were just as special as they had been in the past. In 1940, just a few weeks after her father Fritz was released after long months of arduous forced labor, she wrote that the family gathering, and the songs they sang together, were "almost just like in other years." Similar descriptions appeared even in 1941.[76] For the Blocks, Christmas seems to have continued to anchor the family and its cultural identity and affiliation, and the family members hung onto it even more tightly, the deeper their isolation grew.

Holding onto Christmas was not always a family decision—for example, not in the case of the Schmollers of Berlin. The father of the family, the pediatrician Hans Schmoller, chose in 1941 to shut himself in his room in the family apartment and mark Christmas by decorating a tree branch, putting lights on it, and arranging a table with photographs of members of the family who had left Germany. His wife and his sister-in-law, who lived with them, refused to celebrate the holiday.[77] It was the last Christmas the Schmollers and the Blocks would enjoy in their homes in Germany. The Blocks were expelled from their home in Niedernberg in the spring of 1942 and transported to the area of Lublin in Poland, where they were apparently murdered in the Belzec death camp. Hans Schmoller and his wife were deported to Theresienstadt in October 1942, and he died there a short time after.

Victor Klemperer, the convert to Christianity who was married to an "Aryan" woman, marked Christmas each year in his diary without any of the angst exhibited by many other Jewish writers, and without any reference to Hanukah. "Eva cut a few branches from a fir in our garden and arranged them into a tree," he wrote on the first Christmas after the November pogrom. "Christmas Eve passed more pleasantly than I had dared hope."[78] Klemperer did his best to mark the holiday, at least symbolically, in every year that followed until 1944.[79] It may be that precisely for that reason he discerned the profound changes that the holiday underwent during the Nazi era. Christmas, he commented in his diary in December 1938, "was completely dechristianized," and was portrayed in the Nazi press as a Greater German Christmas (*Grossdeutsche Weihnacht*), with no trace of Jesus or the Jews.[80] Two years later, as part of his project on the language of the Third Reich, he addressed the transformation that the German term *Sippe*—clan—had undergone. It had had a negative connotation in the modern era, he noted, but had been glorified under Nazi rule, as a term that implied that all Germans belonged to one extended family and shared a common descent. One manifestation of this was the practice of referring to Christmas as the Clan Feast (*Fest der Sippe*), another expression that excluded Jews.[81]

If the process of integrating Jews into German society had involved the synchronization of their time with that of the Germans, including some sort of marking of Christmas or at least reference to it, the process of forcing them out can be characterized as a desynchronization. The exclusion of Jews from the holiday, which no longer represented liberal German national values and even shed its Christian foundations in favor of Nazi ones, did not cause it to become just a routine day for them. Like the new Nazi holidays, Christmas in its Nazi guise became a day on which their exclusion from the German environment grew more severe. This reached its height during the war. Klemperer related that the Jews of Dresden were almost completely forbidden to leave their homes during the entire week between December 24, 1941, and January 1, 1942, except for a "shopping hour" they were allowed on four of those eight days.[82] This desynchronization process, in which Jews were confined to their private spaces on days devoted to the majority community—had been common practice in Central Europe prior to the emancipation.[83] The revocation of the emancipation thus included a reinstatement of these strictures.

The celebration of New Year's Eve was also addressed by Jewish diarists, many of whom referred to it as *Silvester*, short for Saint Sylvester's Day, as was common in Germany—or by the more neutral term *Jahreswende*, the turn of the year. On this holiday the emphasis was less on the emotions surrounding family gatherings or religious ceremonies, and more on taking stock of oneself and one's actions over the course of the past year, and intentions for the year to come. Such self-evaluation often extended further into the past and future. Silvester, Alfred Hirschberg wrote in *CV-Zeitung* toward the end of December 1933, marked the passing of another year. "What we German Jews felt often painfully on the new German's holidays—being excluded from the general festivity—is something we will again become sharply aware of over Silvester."[84] The passage into 1934 served Hirschberg as an opportunity for a broader discussion of what the Jews had undergone during the eleven preceding months, and of the experience of Jewish time. "Eleven fateful months are an eternity in the life of the individual," he wrote, but "eleven fateful months are but a short instant in the history of the community." German Jews, facing the turn of the year wounded and traumatized, should take the long historical perspective to help them weather these difficult times. The end of the year reawakened the sense of being excluded from the cycle of the German calendar, because "when the Silvester bells sound at the end of this year, we will no longer have any shared history with Germany." He urged his readers to look back on the long generations of Jewish life in Germany, and to seek there the right template for shaping their future. The turn of the year thus elicited from Hirschberg thoughts about the pace of time, the relationship to the past, and a long-range generational perspective, all of which will be central issues in the chapters that follow in this book. Time and memory continued to preoccupy Hirschberg in various ways in articles he published in *CV-Zeitung* over the next three years. The impression is that, as the years passed and Germany's Jews grew more isolated, he increasingly pondered the meaning of the passage of time, and looked to the past.[85]

Jewish diarists also sometimes addressed New Year's Eve as a time for self-examination and introspection. This was particularly evident among older writers who had an awareness of history. The end of the German calendar year was a good time to sum up, wrote Willy Cohn in his diary on December 31, 1933. "The German press . . . is full of how this year was a year of fulfilment. I will offer no opinion of that. For us, the Jews of Germany, it was not a year of fulfilment." Cohn hoped that under the new circumstances, young Jews would turn toward "healthier development," but in the final analysis he summed up 1933 as a year that "took our homeland from us." He added, "We will not celebrate Silvester tonight, German Jewry is in mourning."[86]

In marking the New Years that followed, Cohn sometimes took up the subject of the tension between the Jewish and civil calendars. "In a few hours the year 1936 will come to an end," he wrote on December 31. "It is naturally the time that a Jew also takes stock of where he stands. Of course, we have for thousands of years had our own count of the years, but when a person writes down the calendar date day after day, those days inevitably become part of their thinking." Like Christmas, New Year's led Cohn to bring up memories, in this case a memory of the year 1900, the turn of the century. He recalled that most of the people whose company he had enjoyed then were no longer alive. At the end of a diary entry in which he can be understood as distancing himself from the general calendar, and thus by implication from his German surroundings as a whole, he wrote, "As Jews, we have no reason to celebrate this day in any raucous way."[87] Three years later, Cohn "involuntarily" sent off the year 1939 with "an existential soul-searching." The year, he said, had marked "a unique concurrence of calendars." It was "a transition into a new century of Jewish years [the year 5700] and the beginning of a new decade of the common era." He offered a grim assessment of the world's future, with "half of it going up in the flames of war."[88] On the last New Year of his life, Cohn's thoughts darted back and forth between memories of better times and worries about the future."[89]

Victor Klemperer also liked to sum up the horrors of the past year as December came to an end, sometimes going into more detail than Cohn did. On New Year's Eve 1938, he wrote of having some "scraps of freedom and life" that he had still enjoyed during most of the year, but which had been taken away toward its end: using the library, driving his car, or going to the movies. All of these activities had provided him, as described in chapter 1, with liberating spatial experiences. At the same time, he stressed that he did not want to be too hasty in stating that "we have already reached the last circle of hell."[90] Four years later, writing on December 31 from the *Judenhaus* in much more dire circumstances, Klemperer observed, "Everyone with whom we spent last New Year's Eve has been blotted out by murder, suicide, and evacuation. . . . Out of ten Nazi years thus far, this year, 1942, was the worst." Despite his use of a euphemism, Klemperer probably understood by that time that the Jews were being not simply evacuated but murdered. The day was also an opportunity for an annual inventory of his writing and research work. The year 1942, during which his living conditions had deteriorated drastically, had not been a good one. "I was unable to produce anything all year," he lamented. "Everything has been snatched from my hand."[91]

"The More Shocked Our Souls Are, the Deeper the Holidays Speak to Us": The Jewish Calendar

In her book *Palaces of Time*, about the Jewish calendar in Central Europe during the early modern period, Elisheva Carlebach argues that Ashkenazi Jews held fastest to traditions connected to the Jewish year at times when they felt besieged, isolated, and insecure about their future.[92] Carlebach shows that the traditional calendar nevertheless continued to play a role in Jewish society even in better times. She also notes that, unlike many aspects of traditional Judaism, which underwent significant changes and restructuring among German-speaking Jews in the nineteenth and twentieth centuries, the calendar remained almost unmodified. Many Jews may have curtailed their relationship with the calendar and disregarded traditions associated with it, but no modern Jewish ideology of any significance ever supported its abolition or replacement with the Christian calendar.[93] Moreover, she adds, during the final decades of the nineteenth century, Jewish almanacs and calendars became very popular among German Jews of all camps.[94] The traditional Jewish calendar in fact served German Jews, in the age of emancipation as well, as a means of maintaining and constituting identity. Alongside the assimilation and secularization processes they underwent, the great majority of them continued to encounter, each year during holidays, fundamental experiences from the Jewish collective past.[95] To use the words of Eviatar Zerubavel, it could be said that emancipation-era Jews continued to be a mnemonic community; and the Jewish calendar served them as a central means of mnemonic socialization, in which they continually synchronized the events of their collective Jewish past with the present realities of their lives.[96]

The gradual exclusion of Germany's Jews from synchronization with the German cycle of time under Nazi rule quite naturally tightened their hold on the Jewish cycle of time. This process was evident both in the communal discourse, as manifested in the Jewish press of the time, and in the lives of families and individuals. The first expression of this can be found in what Jewish writers wrote about the Pesach (Passover) holiday that fell in April 1933, a few days after the institution of the regime's initial anti-Jewish measures—the boycott of Jewish businesses on April 1, and the Law for the Restoration of the Professional Civil Service, promulgated on April 7.

An editorial that appeared in *Jüdische Rundschau* on April 7, marking the approaching Pesach holiday, addressed the increasing importance of Jewish holidays in the lives of German Jews.

> The more shocked our souls are, the deeper the holidays speak to us. In thought-free times, when life goes on, we disregard the ancient truths of our Jewishness. But in times of crisis, when we are subject to confusion, their glow lights up the dark for us. All the Jewish holidays are holidays of comfort. Of comfort and memory.[97]

According to this writer, the Jewish holidays had become more relevant to Jewish life in the current crisis. They induced deeper thought and longer memories. Especially interesting is the claim that associated the growing need for these holidays with the interruption of the simple forward flow of time. The sharp break in the linear and uniform flow of time, the lived time that was identified with the bourgeois habitus and concept of progress, led Jews, in this account, to need the traditional cycle of the Jewish calendar. Unlike the linear time that typifies progress but, at the same time, is devoid of contemplation, Jewish holidays, laden with long historical memory, encourage reflection. Our holidays, the editorial stated, are not simply days of celebration without reason. They are days of introspection and self-awareness. "The Haggadah has never said so much in any year as it says in this one. It is all right for our times," Willy Cohn wrote in his diary on April 11, 1933, the day after the Seder night, clearly referring to the evils he was living through.[98]

Other writers also made a connection between Pesach, a holiday to which intergenerational Jewish memory is central, and this sort of reflection on deep history. The Liberal Rabbi Max Wiener told his readers in *CV-Zeitung* to remember the way that Jews in previous generations had battled their fate and sought to maintain their honor. He added that they must keep in mind that future generations would look back on the way they—the German Jews of the twentieth century—had coped with the difficult challenges they had faced.[99] From another perspective, the Zionist leader Kurt Blumenfeld wrote in *Jüdische Rundschau*, prior to Pesach in 1933, that the Haggadah's dictum that "in each generation a person must see himself as if he himself came out of Egypt" should be read in light of the four generations of Jewish emancipation and assimilation who had removed themselves from the Jewish community of destiny and were now being compelled to return to it.[100] The transition from measuring time by years to measuring it by generations was one of the signs of those times, as will be shown in chapter 6.

The celebration of Pesach, and the Seder night that opens it in particular, became much more meaningful for German Jews in the years that followed, as Jacob Borut has shown. Starting in 1934, the Jewish newspapers published many items about how the Seder was conducted, both by families and by organizations and charitable associations. A reporter from Berlin remarked in April 1934 that "never before have so many participated" in Seder ceremonies "which there have never been anything like."[101] Some communities also conducted courses to teach families who had never observed the ceremony to do so. The Prussian Association of Jewish Communities (Preußischer Landesverband jüdischer Gemeinden), which was not religious in character, called in 1934 for all communities to promote the organization of Pesach Seders. In advance of Pesach two years later, it declared that "to every extent possible, efforts should be made to ensure that no Jew remains without a Seder on this Pesach."[102]

The Pesach holiday continued to serve writers in the Jewish press as an opportunity to convey to their readers ideas on fundamental issues of concern during that period. For example, in an article of April 1935, when Pesach was approaching, Rabbi Schiff of Karlsruhe wrote that when the Children of Israel left Egypt, from slavery to freedom, they had turned from a rabble into a people's community (*Volksgemeinschaft*). He stressed the contemporary connection to this ancient community (*Urgemeinschaft*) by means of a chain of generations stretching back thousands of years. Using language somewhat reminiscent of that used by the Germans around him, Schiff proposed that Jewish history resembled a wave line (*Wellelinie*), an oscillation from high to low points and back again over history. This was a comforting narrative of Jewish history promoted by liberal Jewish spokesmen at the time.[103]

In the second half of the 1930s, when emigration became a major subject on the public agenda of German Jews, many likened it to Pesach and the Exodus. The Exodus, Rabbi Ignaz Maybaum wrote in April 1936 before Pesach, was not simply a historical event in the Jewish people's past. Its story must be told in each generation in a manner that will fit its contemporary context. Jewish emigration from Germany and the expansion of the German Jewish diaspora, in Palestine and throughout the world, thus had to be seen as "the carrying out of God's command."[104]

A year later, April 1 occurred in the middle of the week-long Pesach holiday. It was the day on which German Jews marked the fourth anniversary of the economic boycott against them. Alfred Hirschberg likened the process of emigration that many German Jews were undergoing to the forty years of wandering in the wilderness. The ancient story could imbue them with new strength in the "narrow space" of Jewish life that remained to them.[105] Rabbi Leo Baerwald of Munich went even further, presenting the holiday as an exemplar. Jews, he said, had throughout history always been in passage. "We, as we know, are always wandering [*Wanderschaft*], people crossing from one place to another [*Übergang*]. Pesach reminds us of that over and over, anew." He did not mean the terrifying figure of the Eternal Jew, he claimed. The situation could depress only a person who constantly looks backward. One who looks forward is aware that every human being dwells on earth for only a short time.[106]

Sukkot was also celebrated more prominently than in the past, and was used to consolidate the Jewish community, and to explain current events in general and the insecurity of Jewish existence in particular. The construction of the temporary huts or booths that are one of the holiday's major observances became more widespread, especially in Jewish public spaces and the yards of synagogues. Numerous communities, for the first time in many years, observed the custom of spending the last night of the holiday, called Hoshana Rabbah, studying Jewish texts.[107] In an article he wrote in October 1933, the Liberal Rabbi Caesar Seligmann proposed seeing the move into these temporary dwellings as a metaphor for the state of Germany's Jews. The permanent home they had built over 150 years of emancipation had collapsed, and now they found themselves among its ruins. Seligmann portrayed the holiday as a call from the depths of Jewish memory to leave this rickety home and move into the eternal home of their forefathers, their Jewish identity.[108] As with Pesach, German Jewish opinion leaders of the 1930s, especially from the liberal camp, used Sukkot to promote Jewish emigration,[109] as they did also with Shavuot, the third of the three holidays connected to the Exodus and the forty years in the wilderness.[110]

As with these three festivals, more Jews began to observe the two high holidays that fell in September or October, and in ways that made those holidays much more salient in the Jewish milieu and more a subject of public discussion. They, too, were refashioned and enlisted as usable pasts for contemporary needs.[111] Jewish communities offered classes to help their members prepare for Rosh Hashanah, the Jewish New Year, and Yom Kippur, the Day of Atonement. Jews attended synagogue in record numbers.[112] "For the first time in many years, all businesses were closed on Yom Kippur, including those in the secondary communities [those outside the large cities]," *Israelitischen Familienblatt* reported from the Jewish Koblenz community in October 1934.[113]

Newspaper articles portrayed Rosh Hashanah as a holiday stressing the profound need for soul-searching, accompanied by both gazing deep into the past and looking to what lay in the future, in light of present events.[114] Like the secular New Year, but much more forcefully, the passing of the Hebrew year provided an opportunity to take stock on both personal and communal levels, and to reflect on the circle of time. "For us, the Jews of the Exile, whose daily life is conducted in a non-Jewish world . . . these holidays are the most Jewish part of the year," a *Jüdische Rundschau* editorial proclaimed in September 1934. "It is not enough to look only at the religious aspect. . . . In all parts of the world synagogues are packed, and in all of them the same 'we' is pronounced in the same language." The piece considered at length, from a Zionist perspective, the reconnection of many Jews with their collective identity. Another traditional name for Rosh Hashanah—the Day of Remembrance—was especially appropriate under the circumstances, the editorial noted.[115]

This same season a year later, a short time after the Nuremberg Laws went into effect, elicited a contemplative Rosh Hashanah piece from Rabbi Manfred Swarensky, a Liberal Jewish leader. Many Jews felt, he noted, that their "sense of life" had faded, and reasoned that there was no point in planning and preparing for the future. They despaired of both humanity and God, and were overcome with "a pagan belief in blind fate." In the face of this burgeoning sense of futility, which can be seen in terms of the collapse of the bourgeois perception of time, Swarensky offered Rosh Hashanah. As a holiday that embodied the Jewish faith that all is in God's hands, it was an invitation to adopt an experience of time flowing at a slower but surer pace, more cyclical than linear, more directed toward the past and less manifestly goal-directed with regard to the future. People unnerved by the shock of current events, Swarensky proposed, might find that what seemed inexplicable from their narrow perspective could take on profound meaning in a longer view. Only with such belief, he argued, was a person capable of seeing events from the outside, from a distance, and imbuing them with meaning.[116]

The arrival of Yom Kippur, the Jewish holiday most associated with soul-searching, prompted calls for a historical accounting. An editorial in *Jüdische Rundschau* marking Yom Kippur in 1933, began, typically for that publication, with a critique of the age of assimilation. While stressing that *Jüdische Rundschau* was not a religious newspaper, the editorial asserted that "many of our readers will welcome our publication today of a religious consideration of Yom Kippur." The word "atonement" (*Versöhnung*), the article maintained, was one of many internal contradictions, but fundamentally it implied the possibility of a new start in the wake of overcoming a crisis.[117]

The Liberal Rabbi Max Eschelbacher referred in 1934 to Yom Kippur as "Responsibility Day." It required the Jews, whom the German people saw as convicted criminals, to seek to understand the meaning of the changes that had occurred in their world.[118] This attitude only grew stronger in the years that followed. The worse their plight, the more Jewish writers addressing Yom Kippur called on their readers to accept their fate, as they sat down "on the ruins, the ruins of our ideals and hopes, on the ruins of the concepts and views that we loved, and on the ruins of our bourgeois economic existence." It was time to look inward and try to make a new start.[119]

Willy Cohn, a Jew who observed many religious and national traditions, offered a telling view of the turn of the Jewish year and the High Holidays. "So the year 5693 comes to an end," he wrote in his diary on September 20, 1933. "A difficult year for the Jews of Germany, perhaps the most difficult one for hundreds of years. But also a year of internal unification and connection."[120] A *longue durée* approach to Jewish history, long with the generational flow of time that will be discussed in chapter 6, can be seen in Cohn's reports of the following years. The Jewish custom of visiting the graves of loved ones toward the end of the month of Elul, just prior to Rosh Hashanah, turned in 1934 into a mass pilgrimage by Breslau's Jews. "I went with Trude to the cemetery. Crowds of people were there on the last day of the month of Elul."[121] Cemeteries took on an ever larger role in the Jewish world in the years that followed. Cohen wrote of wandering for a long time among the graves of all the people he had known who were buried there. Three years later, welcoming the year 5698 in 1937, he voiced his fears that the year's Hebrew designation was a bad omen: the letters signifying the year spelled out the word for murder. Writing again about the graves of his acquaintances, he remarked, "There will soon be more friends underground than above it, at least in Germany." He added, "The time spent in the cemetery on the eve of Rosh Hashanah is always a great need of mine."[122]

The multigenerational *longue durée* of Jewish history from the perspective of the holidays can also be seen in Cohn's passages on Yom Kippur. In October 1935 he wrote of his expectation that the day would offer him some serenity, "as it has granted its powers to uncounted generations."[123] Four years later, in 1939, he noted that it was the first Yom Kippur in centuries in which Jewish prayer services were not being held in Breslau.[124]

Another date on the Jewish calendar that received new meaning was Tisha B'Av, the ninth day of the month of Av, a fast day that marked the destruction of Jerusalem and other tragedies in Jewish history. In his memoir of his family's life as part of a rural community in northwestern Germany, Eric Lucas wrote,

> Until this time [1933], a dam had separated the Sovereigns [the name by which his wealthy rural Jewish family had come to be known] from the Middle Ages. Old dark legends still lingered in their minds, but they scarcely thought about them. They would speak about these legends only around the time of the fast in commemoration of the destruction of the holy Temple of Jerusalem, in midsummer, when the days were hot and long, and one could sit in the twilight and talk softly, and think about the whole long story of the innumerable sufferings of the Jewish people and their lost homeland.[125]

Lucas's memory of the way this day was marked, and the symbolism it involved, was connected to events in Germany after January 1933.

Most German Jews disregarded Tisha B'Av until the Nazis came to power, with the exception of the more observant of them and the Zionists. The reason was the belief that the emancipation had put an end to the era of destruction in Jewish history. But history took another turn in 1933, causing Jewish writers to reexamine this traditional day of mourning. Zionists and liberals took different views, in keeping with their outlooks. The hopes of more than a century of Jewish life within German culture had collapsed, wrote Max Wiener in an article on Tisha B'Av in *Jüdische Rundschau*, the Zionist newspaper. It was now imperative to transform the pain into a constructive force. He called for the advancement of the Zionist vision in Palestine.[126] The Ninth of Av, which commemorated the worst days in Jewish history, Alfred Hirschberg maintained in an article in *CV-Zeitung* in July 1934, demanded historical awareness and a chain of memory passed from generation to generation. It was not meant to cause Jews to lose themselves in their painful memories. Even on such a day, Hirschberg argued in an attempt to hold onto what remained of the liberal view of history, Jews needed to recognize in the midst of their suffering that history was making progress.[127] But Willy Cohn's diary evinces mostly melancholy in connection with the day, with traces of an analogy between past catastrophes and the calamities of the current era. "Today is the eve of Tisha B'Av," he wrote in his diary in July 1936. "Each year Jerusalem is destroyed again for us."[128] Four years later, when he reported in his diary on an especially rabid anti-Jewish polemic that appeared in the SS newspaper *Das Schwarze Korps*, he observed, "It seems symbolic that I read this article on the Ninth of Av—when the great persecutions always happen."[129]

Hanukah and Purim, two holidays celebrating the victories of Jews over their enemies, also played an important role in the Jewish year. Hanukah, which during the Weimar Republic had already been presented as a counterweight to Christmas, took a prominent role and gained great popularity under the Nazi regime. It evoked a memory of the heroism of the Maccabees and the liberation of the Jews from foreign oppression that contrasted sharply with the day-to-day humiliation Jews were experiencing.[130] Jewish communities, synagogues, youth movements, and other Jewish organizations held Hanukah parties, and teenagers held discussions about how best to celebrate it.[131] The editors of the children's sections of German Jewish newspapers also frequently addressed Hanukah. "The light of the candles is capable of banishing darkness and warming frightened children who shiver from the cold," ran a Hanukah tale in *Kinderblatt*, the children's supplement to *CV-Zeitung*. While these special powers were connected in the story to the holiday's customs, they could be seen as an allusion to the plight of contemporary Jews.[132] The Jewish press, no matter its political and religious ideology, devoted space to the significance of Hanukah. Zionist writers tended to tie it to the Jewish national revival, while the Orthodox *Der Israelit* largely stressed the theme of religious faith.[133] After the Nuremberg Laws went into effect, liberal Jewish writers displayed an interesting inclination to appropriate the Hanukah story and apply it to the decline of emancipation, making it not a commemoration of victory, but one that evoked the ability of a powerless minority to survive in the face of stronger forces.[134]

Purim commemorated a Jewish victory over Haman, an adversary who sought to slaughter the Jews living in the Persian Empire. Haman was a descendent of Amalek, and the holiday was thus also connected to the commandment to symbolically blot out the memory of that ancient nation, depicted in Jewish sources as the archetypical enemy of the Jews. Another theme of Purim was the reversal of fortune, with the seemingly weak Jews triumphing over their enemies. All these elements were used to read current events.[135] Also notable was the revival of the custom of stamping the feet when, during the reading of the Purim story in the book of Esther, Haman's name was pronounced. The custom had fallen by the wayside in modern Germany. Now it was reinstated, and everyone knew who the current nemesis was, even if it was never made explicit.[136]

The increasing adherence to the Jewish calendar was also evident in the attention given to relatively marginal dates in the Jewish year that had almost never been observed previously by the vast majority of German Jews. One of these was Tu Bishvat, the new year of the trees. In 1933 it was observed almost exclusively in Zionist circles. But thereafter, its celebration

Figure 8. CV Jewish calendar. *CV Zeitung* 14, no. 41 (October 10, 1935). Digitized by Johann Christian Senckenberg University Library, Goethe University.

spread to liberal schools and synagogues. The same thing happened to some extent with Lag Ba'omer, which evoked the Bar Kokhba revolt against the Romans.[137]

The remaking of the Jewish cycle of holidays was also evident in the printing of Jewish calendars by the central political movements among Germany's Jews. In October 1935 the Central Association's *CV-Zeitung* published a Jewish calendar for the year 5696 (figure 8).[138] Alongside the traditional holidays, it also noted a number of anniversaries connected to the Central Association's ethos and to central figures in the history of liberal Judaism in Germany. These included January 4, 1936, the 150th anniversary of Moses Mendelssohn's death; February 17, the 80th anniversary of Heinrich Heine's death; March 17, the 50th anniversary of the death of Leopold Zunz, the founder of Judaic studies; and April 2, the 130th birthday of Gabriel Riesser, the German-Jewish jurist and politician who fought for the legal emancipation of the Jews. Illustrations of these and other figures adorned the calendar, Mendelssohn most prominently. On the other hand, Christmas, German national anniversaries, and of course Nazi holidays were not noted at all.

The Central Association's 5696 calendar was in a sense the temporal complement to the spatial picture of Jewish Berlin provided by the map that the Central Association issued in January 1937 (discussed in chapter 2). The map sought to reflect the lived space of Berlin's Jews, and almost exclusively marked Jewish places while ignoring both the larger German city and the Nazification it had undergone. The calendar offered a similar template of the Jews' lived time. It attempted to recreate the annual cycle of Germany's Jews in the face of their growing alienation and the Nazification of the German year. It sought to fill the year with meaningful dates and to codify a pantheon of heroes for liberal German Jewry.[139] In the years that followed, the Central Association continued to issue calendars, pocket-sized booklets of Jewish everyday life, which oriented their users in the German Jewish public sphere and included a range of Jewish historical anniversaries and commemorations, including some relating to late leaders of the Central Association.[140]

The Zionist Federation of Germany issued its *Palestina Kalender*, a calendar for the Jewish years 5696 and 5697 (fall 1935 to fall 1937).[141] Edited by Rabbi Joachim Prinz, it provided considerable information about Zionist activities sponsored by different groups. Prinz claimed that the calendar's purpose was to bring photographs of Palestine into the daily lives of Germany's Jews. It integrated days of Zionist significance as part of the Jewish cycle of time. Five of these dates appeared in the calendar for the first of these years, some of them anniversaries observed on their Hebrew dates rather than on the Gregorian ones that the Central Association's calendar used. Among them were the anniversaries of the deaths of Joseph Trumpeldor on 11 Adar and of Herzl on 20 Tammuz. The establishment of the Hebrew University of Jerusalem was, however, observed on its Gregorian anniversary, April 1. The following year's calendar added more anniversaries, including those of the deaths of Zionist leaders like Leo Pinsker, Ahad Ha'am (Asher Zvi Hirsch Ginsberg), and Max Nordau, for a total of nine such commemorations. Other Jewish calendars were issued by Jewish welfare organizations and by the Schocken publishing house.[142] The Jewish press also addressed other aspects of the Jewish calendar. In its Rosh Hashanah issue of 1937, *CV-Zeitung* included an article that portrayed the world of "our forefathers" through an analysis of Jewish calendars from the eighteenth and nineteenth centuries.[143]

The Nazi regime, it should be noted, paid little heed to the Jewish calendar, and seems not to have attributed much importance to it. But there were cases in which the regime deliberately ratcheted up its attacks on Jews on holidays. Berlin's police commander issued a directive in July 1938 instructing that Jews should be summoned for interrogation "predominantly on Saturdays and Jewish holidays."[144]

Conclusion: Returning Enchantment to the World

In September 1944, Victor Klemperer was residing in the third *Judenhaus* he had been compelled to move into by the authorities in Dresden. The vast majority of the city's Jews, as in Germany as a whole, had by this time been deported and murdered. Klemperer recorded in his diary how he had learned from the Cohns, a mixed couple living in the same residence, that it was Rosh Hashanah.

> Frau Cohn (the Aryan half) told me at a quarter to five in the morning, "Today is your high holy day, today is New Year. My husband has worked it out." There was sometimes talk at Thiemig & Möbius [apparently the place where Herr Cohn was at forced labor] that no one here knew the dates of the Jewish holy days—a calendar has not appeared, there is no longer any religious practice. The Jews left here are only those in mixed marriages, those who have more or less broken away, therefore.[145]

In other words, Herr Cohn took action to hold onto the Jewish calendar by reconstructing it and calculating the day of the Jewish New Year—this at a time when no Jewish public sphere remained in Germany. Klemperer, it seems from his account, had no interest at all in this fact, but something he appended to this passage shows that Jewish time, at least as it might affect other Jews, meant something in the context of the struggle against Nazism. "I pictured myself with what rejoicing this Jewish New Year will be celebrated in Italy, in France, in all the countries from which the Germans have had to retreat," he wrote. "It has truly become 'the Jewish War'; abolition of the Jewish laws is everywhere one of the Allies' first acts."[146]

Klemperer's diary in fact evinces a measure of internalization of the Nazi cycle of time as imbued with meaning, at least during the regime's final period. He mentions Nazi holidays a number of times, not just as an onlooker analyzing the emergence of the phenomenon, but as a person who attributes meaning to them, even if it is negative meaning.[147] This reached its climax a short time before the collapse of the regime, about two months after Klemperer fled Dresden under an assumed identity. "Today is the nineteenth," he wrote the day before Hitler's birthday. "Russians and Anglo-Americans are simultaneously closing in on Berlin; I, too, am almost superstitiously on edge, awaiting what this April 20 will bring, on the German and on the enemy side."[148]

The modernization of European societies was bound up with secularization and rationalization of the calendar. Many traditional holidays and holy days were done away with, so as to allow a homogeneous, linear, and continuous flow of time that was consistent with capitalist values and the bourgeois lifestyle. This process may be seen as one aspect of what Max Weber termed "the disenchantment of the world." In that light, the Nazification of time can be seen as an oppositional process of returning enchantment to the world. The new cycle of time created by the Nazis sought to replace the uniformity, homogeneity, and flatness of time that they associated with the bourgeois world and the Weimar Republic with nonuniform time. This found expression in a crowded and intensive calendar full of highly meaningful excitement.[149] The Jews were compelled against their will to experience the Nazi year not as participants, but as people exposed to ever more isolation, anxiety, and exclusion on the climactic days of the Nazi year. It was another aspect of their spatial disconnection and their confinement to Jewish and private spaces. Being cut off from synchronization with the cycle of time of their German surroundings heightened their need to turn to their own tradition in search of an alternative timeline based on Jewish memory. The potency of these two processes is evident even in the diary of Victor Klemperer, an apostate Jew alienated from his Jewish origins yet intensely hostile to Nazism. He nevertheless attributed significance to dates of the Jewish year as well as the Nazi year, against the background of the final stage of the war.

The way that Jews experienced the year was an important part of their lived time as it was shaped during this period. It was closely tied to the rate of time's flow, which became much less uniform than it had been in the past. The Jewish year was also characterized by a turn to the past, as Jewish holidays and commemorations connected the members of the community to the gain of intergenerational memory. These issues will be the focus of the next two chapters.

* CHAPTER FIVE *

The Flow of Time

Kurt Rosenberg, an attorney living in Hamburg, was closely tracking political developments in his country and worldwide in April 1934, and pondering whether he and his family should emigrate. "The days follow one upon the other, full of unremitting anxiety," he reported in his diary. In his account, time was a rapid and menacing succession of moments in which he was trapped, frightened and helpless. The experience of time itself weighed heavily on him. It was not just political developments and the bleakness of everyday life; the very sequence of one day after another increasingly alienated him from Germany, which progressively ceased to be his homeland. The passing days "march toward a future that promises nothing but the same anxieties," he wrote.[1] In the same vein, Rosenberg's diary entries from this period contain descriptions of creeping time, and of time spent waiting in frustration. A few weeks later, he wrote that many people were arguing that one needed to wait for the political situation in Germany to clarify. He added that unlike them, "I 'can' not wait, but in the current situation I must wait; I under no circumstances want to move my family into the unknown."[2] Powerlessness and the inability to know what the future held in store were thus connected to the menacing sense of time accelerating out of control, as well as to the sense of creeping time. "Everything flows," he wrote in June 1934 in reference to Germany's rapid rearmament. But a few sentences later, he wrote of his work: "There is a deathly silence in the office, waiting for nothing."[3]

How does time flow in the modern world? The sociologist Alberto Melucci describes time flowing in one direction, at a uniform and precise pace, as a central component of bourgeois and capitalist culture. Such time is possible thanks to advanced measuring devices developed in the modern age. This sense of time, Melucci shows, is exemplified by a constant striving to achieve goals. It provides a basic frame of reference for practices of accumulation and saving, and encourages values such as self-control, deferral of gratification, and self-discipline.[4]

In his anthropological-historical work on the European bourgeoisie, Orvar Löfgren shows that from the individual's point of view, the perception of linear and goal-directed time fits in with the fundamental message of the "vision of life as a career." According to this idea, people are obliged to take full advantage of the time at their disposal and the possibilities on offer to them, in order to actualize all their potential, focus on personal development, and broaden their horizons.[5] Presumably this was the principal way in which Rosenberg and many other bourgeois Jews experienced time in the generations prior to the Nazi regime.

Nevertheless, the sense of the uniform and linear flow of time was not absolute even during the bourgeoisie's golden age. Alongside social or public time, which flowed uniformly and could be efficiently divided in a quantitative way, members of European bourgeois society continued to experience and speak of time in qualitative and subjective ways. A variety of thinkers and investigators sought to depict this experience of time using concepts such as *durée*, psychological time, experienced time, or inner time. Such time, unlike public time, did not flow uniformly and could not be quantified simply. It was more emotional and personal.[6]

The pace at which time flows as it is experienced in the present is closely tied to the way a person views the future. In his book *Lived Time*, the psychiatrist and phenomenologist Eugène Minkowski distinguishes between two kinds of experience of the near future: activity and anticipation. While in a state of activity, individuals turn to the future and set circumstances in motion so as to control events; when they find themselves in a position in which most of their relationship to the future is based on more passive anticipation, they are compelled to wait for a future shaped by environmental forces that are stronger than they are.[7] Stephen Kern, who analyzes Minkowski's distinction in its historical context, argues that the tension between the consciousness of activity and the consciousness of anticipation with regard to the future was especially typical of the World War I generation.[8] The helpless waiting that was characteristic of trench warfare at the front, and the passive anticipation experienced by civilians as they waited for news of the war's progress, were both polar opposites of the planned, measurable, and foreseeable future typical of the bourgeois way of life.

The Nazification of time, which, as the previous chapter has shown, refashioned the annual cycle, involved both a defiance of the bourgeois pace of time and a reaction to the passive experience of "trench time." Nazism rejected "system time" (*Systemzeit*), which it identified with the political heritage of the Weimar Republic, with the idea of gradual political and parliamentary processes in the political arena, and with negotiation and international relations. Instead, the young Nazi movement proposed immediate action as the correct way to make sweeping and long-lasting historical changes.[9] Ian Kershaw wrote of "the rapidity of the transformation that swept over Germany between Hitler's takeover of power on 30 January 1933 and its crucial consolidation and extension and the beginning of August 1934. . . . This rapidity was astounding for contemporaries and is scarcely less astonishing in retrospect."[10] Kershaw attributes the acceleration of the pace of events under the Nazi regime not only to political circumstances, but first and foremost to Hitler's attitude toward time. The Führer's fundamental perception of time gradually became an overwhelming obsession, a sense that time was running out for Germany and for himself as a leader seeking to leave an imprint on history. He thus needed, again and again, to act immediately, with full force, and without restraint.[11] "The bold forward move [*Flucht nach vorne*], Hitler's trademark, was, therefore, intrinsic to Nazism itself," Kershaw argues.[12] It also offers a context for understanding the Nazi doctrine of the *Blitzkrieg*, the absolute opposite of trench warfare, as a Nazification of time on the battlefield.

In this chapter I will consider the way in which German Jews experienced and interpreted the flow of time. Changes in the flow—the feeling that time was slowing down to the point of standing still, as well as the experience of time surging forward at an uncontrollable rate—are phenomena familiar to all human beings. They were thus not foreign to the Jews of Germany, many of whom had experienced them during World War I, on the front and in the rear. They had also lived through the political and economic crises of the Weimar Republic prior to 1933. But following the Nazi rise to power and the experience of the high velocity of Nazi time, of which they were to a large measure victims, the Jews of Germany displayed a rich discourse about the flow of time.

This chapter will open by presenting and analyzing the discourse on waiting in the German Jewish press. As I will show, the question of whether to wait or to take early action of one sort or another was an issue of debate in the two major Jewish political organizations of the time, the Central Association and the Zionist Federation of Germany (Zionistische Vereinigung für Deutschland). The discussions addressed fundamental questions regarding the identity and political culture of German Jews. I will then discuss the issue of creeping or halted time from the point of view of the individual, based primarily on diaries. These were, for the most part, written by adult men who had a difficult time coping during the early years of the

Nazi regime because of the slowdown in time and the helplessness they felt. But this slowdown was not the only thing that characterized the lived time of Jews during this period, especially in the late 1930s, when many German Jews displayed the symptoms of what was termed "emigration fever." I will show that, throughout these years, these writers, both those who wrote in the press and those who wrote in their personal diaries, also reported the opposite phenomenon, of time accelerating, sometimes to the point of actual loss of control. Both creeping and accelerated time, I will argue, were in many ways two aspects of the same larger phenomenon. In the last part of the chapter I will comment on how time was experienced by those Jews who remained in Germany during the war years, in escalating conditions of exclusion, in forced labor, and finally under constant threat of deportation and death.

"Inner Tranquility" or "Fervent Action": The Liberal and Zionist Discourse Confronting the New Regime

The dizzying pace of change in Germany during the early months of 1933 had its roots in the Nazi ethos of immediate action. The initial reactions of the two most important German Jewish political organizations, the Central Association and the Zionist Federation, were cautious. Their instinct was to wait to see how the situation developed, an approach that accorded with the traditional Jewish reaction to the outbreak of anti-Jewish sentiments and actions, for example during the pogroms of 1881 in Russia.[13] An editorial published in the Central Association's periodical *CV-Zeitung* at the beginning of March addressed the anti-Jewish hate campaign. It argued that the Jews, thanks to their history, knew how to cope with suffering. The publication called on its readers to act responsibly, quietly, and with self-discipline. "The person who gets through this time with good sense, who maintains, now and always, inner tranquility, truly serves the homeland."[14] It told its readers to keep a level head and to wait, to get through the difficult period without causing needless tremors, at least implicitly hoping for an improvement in circumstances.

The *Jüdische Rundschau*, the semiweekly newspaper of the Zionist Federation, also evinced an inclination to wait and see. For example, on March 21—the day the newly elected Reichstag convened in Potsdam for an event, the *Tag von Potsdam* (Potsdam Day), that would later be seen as the symbolic transfer of power from the traditional German elites to the Nazi Party—an editorial in this newspaper argued that Jews needed to understand the overall significance of such events. "Jewish public opinion is tense, its eyes directed with expectation [*Erwartung*] and trepidation toward

Berlin to see if the German Reich will be the *sole* power in the Western world to actually make anti-Jewish practice . . . an official policy."[15]

In April 1933 the new government rapidly began instituting a systematic anti-Jewish policy, by legislative and other means. At this point the difference between the attitudes toward time displayed by Jewish liberals and by Zionists began to diverge. The former continued to advocate waiting patiently, while the latter began stressing more and more the need for immediate action. On April 6, a few days after the regime's one-day economic boycott of Jewish businesses and professionals, the *CV-Zeitung* published a short article by Rabbi Ismar Elbogen, headlined "Haltung." It called for German Jews to persevere and display solidarity, fraternity, and mutual aid.[16] The word *Haltung* has a range of meanings, but can be translated as "standing erect" or "keeping a stiff upper lip." It was soon appearing frequently in the liberal Jewish periodical, in opinion pieces that called for grit and stability. One such piece also evinced a critical tone toward the regime for its new anti-Jewish policy. Its principles, according to Elbogen's response to the economic boycott of April 1, did not meet the standard of responsible and discreet conduct.[17]

Some three months later, German Jews began to grasp the significance of the events of the spring of 1933, which had completely changed their lives. At this point the Central Association laid out its ethic of time in a more systematic way, in an editorial titled "Responsibility" (*Verantwortung*). At the core of the article was an insight about how uncertain the future was:

> The person who is aware of the responsibility that the situation requires and is not blinded by the belief that he has prophetic abilities cannot err with an excess of self-confidence and say, so it will be, so we see it, so see the forces that control our future. While we act and aspire, *we still do not have a clear view of the end of the difficult road that we walk on*. It is the imperative of honesty and responsibility to declare that.[18]

The paradigm of taking action with regard to the future is based on faith in the ability to anticipate it, or at least its general contours, and to influence it. The author of this editorial was aware that at this moment, Germany's Jews lacked a clear view of what their future held in store. He attacked those who made themselves out to be prophets and proposed plans of action based on their forecasts of the future. The writer argued that the community required "a long period of confidence under tense conditions." Refraining from action (*Unterlassung*) could also be a form of action, he argued, especially in a situation in which doing something (*Tun*) could cause damage. It was an eloquent and explicit call for German Jews to adopt, under the circumstances in which they found themselves, a passive attitude toward the future: to hold fast to what they had, in recognition that in a state of uncertainty any more activist policy might be detrimental.

The ethic of waiting retained a prominent place in the Central Association later on, as well. Some of its spokesmen adduced long-term insights from Jewish history.[19] In October 1934, for example, a Liberal rabbi, Felix Goldmann, called on his readers to adopt "resilience" (*seelische Haltung*).[20] In a historical survey of calamities that had befallen the Jews, Goldmann made a distinction between the Jews' "fate" and their tenacity. He quoted Ecclesiastes 3:1, "To every thing there is a season, and a time to every purpose under the heaven," to describe the tactic of perseverance that he maintained Jews should follow when faced with the Nazi acceleration of time and the unknown threat it represented. This call to preserve what there was, which inevitably meant waiting until the worst was over, included a distinction between the age of emancipation, during which Germany's Jews conducted an active campaign for their political rights, and the current era. "The active era [the age of emancipation] in Germany has passed," he wrote. "It is no longer the time to attack [*Angriff*] but to reinforce self-endurance." Goldmann also wrote that the future of German Jewry depended first and foremost on perseverance and preservation (*Beharren*), another central concept in the semantic field of the waiting ethic.[21] In April 1935, Hans Reichmann, another prominent spokesman for the Central Association, argued in an article marking the second anniversary of the economic boycott, "A person who has a sense of responsibility for his community knows that it would be wrong to make emotional judgments, and will not trust leaders who today rejoice to the heavens and tomorrow plunge deep into deathly melancholy."[22] According to Reichmann, this sense of responsibility, which required a temperate evaluation based on historical perspective, thus stood in opposition to hasty and frantic decision making. Only such a state of mind, he maintained, could enable Germany's Jews to bear their fate honorably (*würdig*).

Opposed to the sit-and-wait ethic of those who spoke for liberal Jewry, the Zionist speakers and writers during the events of spring 1933 called for a more accelerated experience of time, what might be called "action time." They declared that Jews should quickly comprehend the fundamental change in their circumstances. Rapid action was vital, they argued, as they attacked the inclination of liberals, like many German Jews, to wait passively. A *Jüdische Rundschau* editorial at the end of April 1933, published in response to legislation limiting the number of Jewish students in German educational institutions (the Law against the Overcrowding of German Schools and Universities), maintained that people needed to accept that most Jewish children would not be able to attend German schools anymore. It was thus necessary to rebuild the Jewish school system throughout Germany, after decades of neglect. "What are German Jews waiting for?" the author asked, adding that the need for new thinking in education had been obvious even before the law was promulgated. "If the historical meaning of the turning point [*Wende*] is before our eyes, and we know the goal we need to strive for or lead to after the collapse of the [liberal] age, then we must act on this subject with *fervor*."[23] This Zionist writer opposed the waiting ethic of the liberals, which advocated slow adjustment to the new circumstances and a sense of an unclear future. The historical significance of the change was clear to him and required immediate action. That, not passively waiting, was the correct way to take responsibility.

This perception of time stands out in an article that the leader of the German Zionist Federation, Kurt Blumenfeld, published in May 1933. "We live in a changing world," he claimed, contending that the country's Jews needed to grasp the significance of the new developments and to try to influence them. Doing so, he wrote, "is our most urgent duty." Blumenfeld criticized the inclination of some groups of Jews to view the policies of the Nazi regime as a transitory phenomenon, and their belief that the old political system would slowly return. This way of thinking, the Zionist leader argued, grew out of the psychological motivations of assimilating Jews who were seeking to continue along that same path. Blumenfeld launched a direct offensive against this mindset and the waiting ethic of liberal Jews:

> Maybe we can wait, maybe we are really proscribed from trying to bring about an accelerated change in the way we think about our positions and actions? We must not allow such considerations any place today. The pace of developments in Germany is rapid. We Jews stand within it . . . and this needs to be our duty, in the name of the Jewish interest and at the same time in the interest of Germany, to be able to stand as *partners in deliberating* on these processes.[24]

The rapid pace of Zionist activity in Germany at this stage was very much evident its rapid growth. In only a few months, the pressure created by events transformed German Zionism from a small avant-garde into a mass movement.[25] Its willingness to make decisions quickly could also be seen in the rise in emigration of German Zionists to Palestine already in 1933, Blumenfeld himself among them.

In a series of articles on traditional Jewish holidays published in *Jüdische Rundschau*, Rabbi Max Wiener discussed the issue of waiting from a more theoretical perspective, touching on Jewish memory. One example was a

Hanukah piece, "Waiting and Acting," from December 1933.[26] Alongside their struggle against the assimilating Hellenists, Wiener argued, the Maccabees also fought against the traditional Jewish approach characterized by passive martyrdom. Throughout Jewish history, he wrote, there had been a conservative and submissive approach that had encouraged a "contemplative theoretical mental attitude." It was coupled with waiting for the arrival of the Messiah and, he maintained, it was characterized by escapism. Against this static theoretical approach, which did not see historical processes as having actual meaning, there emerged during the period of emancipation a practical way of life characterized by the activism of the modern Jew. Now, he argued, with the end of the age of individualism of the nineteenth century, Jews had once more to shoulder responsibility for their people as a whole, but the tendency of their forefathers from pre-emancipation times to engage in "theorization and waiting" could not and should no longer be the focal point of Jewish experience. "We believe not only in our fate, but *first and foremost in our history*. We believe that new things will happen to us and by our own hands, that not *waiting* [*Warten*] but *action* [*Wirken*] must be our lot."[27]

An original and balanced theoretical treatment of the question of waiting can be found in an article by Rabbi Leo Baeck, which appeared on September 29, 1933, at the time of the Rosh Hashanah holiday. It preceded by just a few days the declaration of the establishment of the New National Representation of German Jews (Reichsvertretung der deutschen Juden), which Baeck headed. The Jews of Germany, he wrote, were welcoming the new Jewish year even as they recognized that they had lost something. But, he argued, for the younger generation the new year was one of hope.[28] To be young, Baeck maintained, meant to be able to face the future expectantly. The biblical concept of hope indicated anticipation (*Erwarten*), a concept that differed from simple waiting (*Warten*). Waiting was typified by a short time frame, looking to the next day only, whereas anticipation looks to time that bears the new on its wings. Baeck criticized those of his contemporaries who had for too long acted as a "generation of waiters" (*ein Geschlecht von Wartenden*), and called on his readers to change their attitude to the future from one of waiting to one of anticipation. A person who only waits, he declared, remains in his routine. The one who expects has hope and true faith, having at its foundation the anticipation of God. Unlike most of the others adduced in this section, Baeck, in his attitude toward waiting, did not express a clear political position, but his distinction between waiting and anticipation brings home the gap between the waiter's prospects, which are closed, or at most are open only for the short term, and the much more open horizon of the person who lives in anticipation.

In the years that followed, the subject of waiting was addressed less in the German Jewish press. Political developments and the question of the regime's stability grew less relevant, and the freedom of expression allowed to writers on these questions narrowed significantly at the end of 1935.[29] In the late 1930s waiting, to the extent that it was discussed, was tied to the most important issue for the Jewish press at the time: emigration. "The Jews in Germany are still waiting for the results of these welcome efforts," a piece in *CV-Zeitung* declared at the beginning of September 1938, following the ambiguous results of the Evian conference on Jewish refugees who sought to flee from Germany and Austria. Indeed, the author maintained, "the pace of history, and the treatment of historical problems, always moves slowly . . . but the fact that we are fundamentally only the objects of this situation makes the waiting especially difficult for us."[30] The difficulty in waiting was thus the passivity imposed on the Jews because of their weakness in the international power system and their inability to affect their fate.

"We Are Not Alive, Only Existing Like Plants": The Creeping Time of the Early Years of the Nazi Regime

In addressing the flow of time, Alberto Melucci distinguishes between the linear flow of social time, which makes it possible to speak of "before," "after," and causal chains, and the inner time of the individual. The two may flow at very different rates, with both emotional and somatic manifestations.[31] In a similar vein, Eviatar Zerubavel demonstrates that human beings experience different flows of time in differing life circumstances. One example is the different experience of time on weekdays and weekends, or between periods of intensity (in personal life or in history) and other periods that seem less hectic.[32]

Waiting, which is often felt as "empty time" between more significant periods, is a fundamental experience of human existence and of the way people sense the flow of time. The increasing attentiveness to the issue of time on the part of social scientists, especially sociologists and anthropologists, has in recent decades produced a range of studies on waiting. Scholars distinguish between short-range periods of waiting (traffic jams and lines, for example), which are generally experienced as trivial and part of daily life, and long-term waiting, a social and historical phenomenon that is imposed on some groups, especially those subjugated to the regime in a hierarchy of power relations. It is this latter form of waiting that requires thorough analysis.[33]

The pace at which time flows in the private lives of individuals in general, and the issue of waiting specifically, are also of interest to historians. Stephen

Kern has shown that the idea that time is composed of uniform segments, "boxed days on a calendar," was popular at the beginning of the twentieth century with regard to public time, but people of that era were very much aware of the much more fluid nature of personal time.[34] Iris Rachamimov and Ronit Or have recently written about life in POW and detention camps during World War I, a classic test case of long-term waiting.[35] They base themselves in part on the memoir of Paul Cohen-Portheim, *Time Stood Still*, which uses those words to describe his experience of time and that of others who spent World War I in an internment camp for prisoners of foreign citizenship. "Days, weeks, months, years, all these artificial divisions follow each other in endless monotony, time has ceased to have any signification; where there is no aim, no object, no sense, there *is* no time. One gives in, one surrenders, one's will is broken."[36] The time experienced by these prisoners, Rachamimov argues, was totally severed from their past lives, and was typified by a sense of disconnection and a lack of any prospect and anticipation of the future. Some said they were trapped in an "agonizing endless loop." Using this analysis of the consciousness of time, she comments on the range of strategies the prisoners used to cope with their time in the camp.

Applying this perspective to the diaries of German Jews in the 1930s reveals a complex and multifaceted attitude toward the experience of the slowdown of private time and of waiting. Notably, waiting and creeping time were documented in the early years of the Nazi regime primarily by adult men, the principal sector of people who left detailed diaries. This fact is worth mentioning because of the conventional view that links the passive experience of time to middle-class European women, in contrast with men who supposedly have a career mentality involving a more active relationship with the future, and thus a different experience of the flow of time.[37] The circumstances inflicted on German Jews after the Nazi rise to power led to a gender reversal in this regard. The daily routines of many men were seriously disrupted in the regime's early years, and they were pushed out of the public space; many of them had no work to do and spent much time idle, according to Marion Kaplan. At the same time, many women carried on with much of their routines in the sphere of their families and their needs, or actually had to earn a living.[38] On top of this, writing was for many the most important means of coping with the challenge of waiting and creeping time. As such, women, who experienced less of a break in their daily routines in the regime's early years, spent less time documenting their changing experience of time. Indeed, women who did not have to work outside the home may not have experienced as much of a change as men did.

The writers of these diaries offer a range of accounts of and insights about waiting, a variety that reflects the fluid character of private time.

Uncertainty, about both the situation in Germany and their personal lives, is the main reason they are waiting—or, as they sometimes call it, "passing time"—until things become clearer. "The Nazis act like victors, the streets are full of brown and black uniforms," Willy Cohn wrote on January 31, 1933. "We need to grit our teeth and try to get through this period."[39] Ambiguity about the political situation, which continued even after the Nazi regime had ensconced itself in power, blended in the case of Cohn and many others with uncertainty about the professional and economic future, and led Cohn to choose to wait. On May 2, 1933, he reacted in his diary to the installation of a portrait of Hitler in the teachers' room of the Johannesgymnasium high school, where he taught in Breslau. The school was considered a liberal bastion in the city, and many of its faculty and students were Jews.[40] For Cohn, this event, which demonstrated the extent of the new regime's penetration into society, went hand-in-hand with the question hovering in the air about the future of his job there. Here, too, he maintained that waiting was the most rational choice in the face of the ongoing lack of certainty. "The most important thing now is to wait," he wrote. "Everything, after all, might change."[41] A few weeks later, Cohn learned that he would be suspended from his position, and he again addressed the issue of waiting, which he now saw as intertwined with the idea of the efficient use of time:

> The school janitor arrived to give me a letter on my being put on leave forthwith. I thought that this would happen soon. . . . Every look into the future is at this moment pointless [*müssig*], because I must first wait to see what the amount of my pension will be. . . . Of course, I have different plans, but first I need to wait so as not to ruin anything. . . . I am not one of those people who does not know what to do with their free time. My time will always be full.[42]

Uncertainty, and the sense that everything was still reversible, was the main reason why Cohn chose to wait and not immediately take steps to emigrate. This led to tension with his wife, whose predilection was for active time. "Trudy is always pushing on the subject of emigration," he wrote on June 27, 1933. "I am of the opinion that we must first wait."[43] According to Marion Kaplan, these differing views were characteristic; Jewish women in Germany tended to push more for emigration, even as men were reluctant.[44] Cohn himself became even more adamant about it after consulting with a friend. "He is definitely of my opinion," he wrote the next day, "not to emigrate under any circumstances, but to wait and see how things develop . . . and in the meantime I can wait quietly and take advantage of my time for creative activity. He also thinks, as I do, that it would be a mistake to make plans for months ahead, when they can change daily because of events."[45]

The tension between the sense of time accelerating because of the pace of events in Germany, and the experience of waiting that was imposed on one personally, stands out in the diary of Kurt Rosenberg of Hamburg. "One day follows another," he wrote on June 25, 1933, in response to the new regime's continued attack on what remained of the Social Democratic Party. "My body temperature, which goes up all the time, very much bothers me. The doctor says there are many cases like this—without a diagnosis."[46] The anxiety produced by the rapid pace of time of Nazi policy caused Rosenberg real physical distress; his inner experience of time took on a physical dimension. Cohn, more than a decade his senior, portrayed waiting for developments in 1933 as a rational choice, one he tried to take advantage of. Rosenberg, at this point, largely stresed the aspect of powerlessness. On April 7, after insinuating that other lawyers—those classified by the Nazis as "Aryans"—were trying to "acquire" his clients, Rosenberg raised the idea of emigration. But he remarked, "It will be necessary to wait to see if necessity will impel me to that."[47] He depicted the lack of a clear decision regarding his status as a lawyer and the postponement of that decision for a few months as part of "the prolonged and galling lack of clarity" in which he found himself.[48]

In contrast with the bourgeois time regime of the age of emancipation, which was typified by systematic dynamism and planning that looked to the future, Rosenberg linked his experience of waiting and of creeping time, on the one hand, to a passive state of decline and paralysis and, on the other, to frantic and pointless activity. In fact, these were two sides of the same phenomenon. "Waiting, waiting for the unknown—with no possibility of expanding activity, but with new difficulties," he wrote in August 1933 on life in Germany, after returning from several weeks of vacation in Czechoslovakia. "Like a slow death . . . all that remains is flaccid, passionless, and hopeless, more anxious by the day, and ever more wailing."[49] "Day by day, we are buffeted to and fro," he wrote a month later; "at one time we want to establish a guest house and children's home on the Riviera, at another to represent a German firm overseas, and a third time to wait. No decision has yet been made. We live constantly on the brink of a leap [*auf dem Sprung*]."[50] By this time, Rosenberg had lost control over shaping his time, his ability to plan in any real way or carry out plans for his personal and professional future on a linear temporal scale. To a large extent he had become powerless in the face of the vicissitudes of time.

Victor Klemperer, whose insights about Nazi time I discussed in the previous chapter, also frequently addressed in his diary changes in the flow of time and their effect on his consciousness. The rapid rate at which the new regime implemented its exclusionary policies elicited, as early as April 1933, a state of mind of passive waiting accompanied by anxiety. "And every day new abominations," he wrote a few days after the economic boycott, as anti-Jewish legislation was promulgated. He added: "A Jewish lawyer in Chemnitz kidnapped and shot. . . . Provision of the Civil Service Law. Anyone who has one Jewish grandparent is a Jew. . . . For the moment I am still safe, but as someone on the gallows, who has the rope around his neck, is safe. At any moment a new 'law' can kick away the steps on which I'm standing, and then I'm hanging."[51] At this point Klemperer understood that he had escaped the immediate impact of the Law for the Restoration of the Professional Civil Service, thanks to his service as a soldier on the front in World War I; but the ominous wait for the regime's next moves gave him no respite. "The calamitous berserk policy continues to gallop ahead," he wrote a month later, a few days after the book burning, while new restrictions were being imposed on Jews. "I am waiting," he added.[52] Later in this passage, he presented the lives of the Jews under the pall of this waiting as a social phenomenon that ought to be documented: "The *mood* of the present time, the waiting, the visiting one another, the counting of days, the inhibited telephone conversations and correspondence—all that could be recorded in memoirs one day."[53] Waiting, in Klemperer's account, did not always express itself in passivity and a blunting of the senses. Sometimes it involved intensive if erratic activity, and rapid mood swings. In June, for example, he described an acquaintance who was "waiting feverishly [*fieberhaft wartent*] between hope and despair. This jitteriness was a manifestation, Klemperer thought, of "emigrant mentality."[54] The loss of control over the time of Klemperer's daily life was evident in the change in his power relationship with the authorities, which he experienced as humiliation. "I am waiting like a junior clerk to find out whether I am given notice on October 1," he wrote in July 1934.[55]

Another notable aspect of Klemperer's attitude toward the flow of time and his expectations for the future was his hope, repeated again and again in his diary, that Hitler's rash foreign policy would lead to the regime's collapse. But time after time, he voiced doubt that this would happen. In January 1935, when he learned that in the plebiscite in the Saarland, a decisive majority had voted for annexation to Germany, he said of himself, "I said: let's wait and see, but I do not believe my own words."[56] At the end of 1937, some hope welled up when Hjalmar Schacht left his post as Reich minister of economics; but Klemperer also had major doubts. "It is nevertheless possible that future historians will describe this little point as the beginning of the end," he speculated. "Only: how many years separate this beginning from the final end? I cannot wait much longer."[57] Klemperer's inclination to count the days until the regime's end only became more pronounced during the war years, along with his frustration at not knowing whether he would live to see that day.

These writers connected the closing off of prospects for the future and the creeping time they experienced to the narrowing of their vistas and the emptying of their space, leading to intensifying loneliness. Already in April 1933, Cohn linked the need to wait and the slow pace of time to being shut up in his house and the loneliness it brought: "I sink into a depressive state, am not always able to flee into books. Activity outside the house is out of the question. It is impossible to think about the future—one simply has to wait."[58] For Klemperer, the blocked prospects and confinement evoked experiences from the world war. "Worries are increasing to such a degree that I no longer can or should allow myself to think about them; it is just like being in the dugout: if one is forever thinking about the next shell, then one goes mad. . . . We are literally digging ourselves in here, as in the trenches [*Schützengraben*]."[59] In addition to spatial confinement in his apartment and its immediate environs, Klemperer wrote of the emptying of his social world, which he linked to the experience of frozen time. "The loneliness weighs ever more heavily," he wrote in his final entry for 1937. He described the accelerated attenuation of his social environment as more and more people he knew emigrated, and he added a comment on "the terrible standstill of time."[60] The disintegration of his social environment, his affiliation with which was a point of reference for the flow of time, inevitably affected his experience of time. Unlike those who emigrated, whose very decision to leave restored their access to the flow of time, Klemperer remained behind in isolation, experiencing time as standing still.

The confinement and loneliness of many German Jews, which grew even more severe at the end of the 1930s as their social environment emptied and their daily routines were disrupted, was addressed by the contemporary Jewish press. The author of an article headlined "The Lonely Man," appearing in *Israelitisches Familienblatt* in June 1938, offered the portrait of a Jewish man who had not yet reached retirement age, but who had lost his job because of the regime's anti-Jewish measures. After long years of intensive work, he found it difficult to fill his time. His children, according to the article, had already left Germany; his circle of acquaintances and friends was contracting. His plight was all the worse because he was still in the prime of his life and required work and human companionship. From time to time he found a social outlet in attending synagogue or community events; these briefly ameliorated his loneliness. But most of the time he was closed off from the world, as if he were on a desert island. One aspect of his loneliness was that time crept. His years of work, when he had contact with many other people, the article related, "are behind him, and now, when he wakes up in the morning, he sees before him a day without commitments. Each hour passes at its full length, the minutes on the clock pass slowly, because they are not filled with work."[61]

The pain and loneliness caused by being forced out of a job, the linear flow of time, and the open prospects for the future were sometimes brought on by contact with others whose time seemingly continued to flow in a straight line. In June 1935, about two years after his dismissal from his post at the Johannesgymnasium, Willy Cohn ran into a non-Jewish acquaintance. The man related what was going on at Cohn's old school, which had been renamed the Horst Wessel High School. Almost no Jewish students remained. "These matters touched me only a bit," Cohn wrote in his diary. "Two years have gone since my *Rausschmiss* [being sacked, literally being kicked out], and I have built myself another world." Nevertheless, it hurt, even if he tried to dismiss the memories as "but some phantoms" of his former life. Cohn had indeed built himself a rich professional and personal world, as recounted in chapter 2. He was involved in cultural activity and became a sought-after lecturer in Jewish communities throughout Silesia. Nevertheless, the encounter with his former colleague pained him. That night he wrote in his diary: "We are not alive, only vegetating [*vegetieren*]."[62] The lives of "Aryan" teachers continued to flow along the continuum of time, but Cohn's life had shriveled, cut off from that career path, and had lost something of its fullness. This moment of painful candor, it seems, revealed that even in the case of such a central figure in Jewish public and cultural life at the time, the life of a Jew in Germany, living on waiting time, had ceased to be a fully human life.

Did Cohn, Klemperer, and Rosenberg see any way out of the creep of time and the blocked horizon? Immediately after his painful admission that Jewish life under Nazi rule was not truly alive, Cohn added, "Luckily, the future of our youth is tied to the Land of Israel, and they will build a free life there in the future."[63] This was principally a manifestation of Cohn's Zionism, and it was directed at his adult children, one of whom, Ernst Avraham, had gone to Palestine under the aegis of the Youth Aliyah program a few months previously. Two of his other children would later also make their way there. But, more profoundly, this statement can be seen as an acknowledgement that only emigration could save Jews from the slowdown of time and open new horizons for them. "The number of emigrating Jews, the largest part of whom are traveling to an unknown fate, is rising all the time," Rosenberg wrote in September 1936. "Ever more familiar faces from our circle, people we love, are leaving us. Again and again the question arises among us whether to follow in their footsteps, and we feel how tied we are to the soil [*Boden*]. We also ask ourselves if we are not missing something by waiting."[64] Some two years later, Klemperer arrived at a similar insight. He wrote of several acquaintances who had left Germany, contrasting them with himself, who had remained. "All these people have made new lives for themselves," he wrote in July 1938, marking the birthday of his wife, Eva. "We have been left behind in disgrace and penury, in some degree buried alive, buried up to the neck so to speak and waiting from day to day for the last shovelfuls."[65] The difficulty of celebrating a birthday that in different circumstances would have expressed the progress of life by one more year, was thus tied up with the experience of confinement, which in this passage is extended by the metaphor of burial.

The very act of writing a diary, and the restless intensity of raising the same subjects over and over again from different points of view, were manifestations of the limbo in which these writers found themselves and the way they coped with it. In October 1937, Kurt Rosenberg traveled to the United States, where he spent two months. Despite his distaste for American culture, he decided in the end, in the face of the deterioration of life in Germany, that he could live in the US with his family. When he returned to Germany he devoted all his energies to preparing his family for emigration, vigorous activity directed at the future, until they left in September 1938. Notably, Rosenberg stopped writing his diary when he made his trip to the United States, and did not resume it when he rejoined his family. Moreover, when he finally extricated himself from the void in which he had been living and the creeping time he had experienced by settling in the United States with his family, he never again took up his diary.[66] The older Cohn and Klemperer, however, who were unable to get out of Germany and away from the creeping time of their lives, descended after the November pogrom into a life that was ever more shut in. And they continued writing their diaries even more intensively once the war started. Later, as I will chronicle in the next chapter, they turned to writing their memoirs.

"Hours Like Days and Weeks Like Years": The Acceleration of Time and Emigration Fever

Waiting and creeping time were only one side of the lived time of Germany's Jews. The segregation of Jews in the 1930s and the pressure to emigrate that it caused could also speed up the experience of time. This was more than just the fast pace of the imposition of Nazi policies and of international political events. It was also an experience of the acceleration of Jewish history and of communal and individual human life, a phenomenon that had several aspects. Many Jews, including some who also had the experience of waiting and described the slow creep of time, expressed feelings of extreme pressure and urgency, feelings that became more salient in the late 1930s. Some of them also tied this experience to their inability to make long-range plans.

In September 1933, Rabbi Max Wiener remarked on the speeding up of Jewish life in the age of emancipation. From the point of view of the rupture in Jewish history that he and his countrymen were facing, Wiener claimed, Jewish conduct in the age of emancipation stood out principally for its "unique *acceleration* [*eigenartige Beschleunigung*] of historical events."[67] The Europeanization of the Jews—their transition from life in the ghetto at the margins of society to the comfortable feeling of liberal Europe—had taken "just five generations." Today, in retrospect, we can begin to fathom the price paid by Jews on the excessive velocity of the process. The speed, Wiener maintained, prevented Jews from discerning the way the world around them was changing—until emancipation imploded before their eyes. Wiener's use of a scale of generations to gauge past events was part of the tendency, which I will address in more detail in the next chapter, to "compress" historical periods—in this case, that of the emancipation of the Jews. What is important here is his treatment of the acceleration of time, which he argued expressed the loss of control and misunderstanding of surrounding events. Note that this came from a person who just a short time earlier, as related above, had disapproved of the tendency of Jews prior to the emancipation to engage in a "contemplative theoretical mental attitude," and had called on them to prefer action to waiting.

About a year later, at the beginning of November 1934, Kurt Rosenberg wrote in his diary about the way he experienced the acceleration of time, considering the past while thinking of the present. "We learned to divide internal struggles and historical upheavals over the span of a century or at least decades," he wrote, "and what is now seeping into this understanding is the thought that our [sense of] time has adjusted to a speedier way of living. . . . Sometimes one can stand at a distance, but a person caught in a burning house doesn't have the option of thinking about a summery, placid vista."[68] It is interesting to note that Rosenberg, who, as shown above, frequently wrote about the experiences of waiting and of creeping time, rejected the logic behind the ethos of waiting advocated by the liberal Jewish leadership. The acceleration of the pace of events and, implicitly, the transformation of time itself into a central player, made it impossible to look at time from a distance or to consider it calmly. If creeping time was likened to the trenches of World War I, accelerated time was equated with a burning house from which people need to flee immediately. A few months later, when he failed in his attempt to extend the validity of his license to practice law, Rosenberg again began to express a sense that "time is running quickly." To this he added that "life is dissipating. You work but it is impossible to build anything."[69] Rosenberg's depiction of time as both creeping and passing rapidly testifies to his sense of having lost control of the flow of time, as well as that of having lost his autonomy. Either way, he lost his ability to plan his life.

Nazi intimidation and restrictions imposed directly on Jews were not the only sources of the sense of rapid change in their daily lives. Even more important was the external and internal pressure to move, especially in the case of Jews who moved from provincial towns into the large urban communities. These pressures made Jewish life feel provisional, and affected the way interpersonal relations were constructed, friendships and romances in particular. This issue was treated in depth in an article entitled "Friendship—Now" by the journalist, writer, and human rights activist Martha Wertheimer, published in July 1937 in the Leipzig Jewish community's newspaper.[70] Wertheimer, who was also involved in the education of Jewish teenagers in programs preparing them for emigration, addressed the way relationships were made in the context of the "Jewish situation" of her time, as she called it. She wrote about the experience of accelerated time. In the past, she claimed, social relations could develop and mature. People's friendships could develop "slowly and surely, on the basis of their internal lives." Under these circumstances, friends could also bear periods of separation. They had waited with confidence for letters, and this had fostered positive expectations of reuniting in the future. Furthermore, this waiting for the renewal of ties had made the relationships more interesting and profound. Wertheimer described the now bygone age as one of certitude (*Gewissheit*) and security (*Sicherheit*), two signature characteristics of the bourgeois experience of time, which proceeded at a constant pace and lent itself to control and planning. This experience of sequential time, she implied, could engender relations that developed at a moderate pace, in keeping with the bourgeois way of life.

Wertheimer contrasted the way social relations had developed in this earlier period to what she called the new "Jewish situation," a liminal time in which people lived in a constant state of rupture, parting, and separation (*im Aufbruch*). Life in these circumstances was founded on a sense of ongoing uncertainty regarding the length of time each person could remain in place and when they would leave. In this situation, the time needed for relations to mature and become well-founded was simply not available to Jews. "Two people who could wait confidently one for the other in other times, who could allow themselves to meet and then meet again, today face each other knowing from the first moment of fondness between them that they have no time to wait for each other." The loss of security and certainty, the heritage of the past age, was evident in every leavetaking and greeting, and even in letters, which were now experienced as menacing, as the last human contact prior to an unpredictable parting. "The sense of restlessness shadows all social relations . . . among Jews, and the question always smolders—When will you go away again? . . . The wonderful innocence of waiting for one another has been lost."

Nevertheless, Wertheimer also offered her readers a positive take on this new situation. These friendships, created on the fly, she argued, have an "incomparable charm" growing out of the willingness to connect quickly and, inevitably, to part quickly as well. "Our friendships, fashioned so rapidly, burn with a different fire," she wrote. In her time, people could not allow themselves to be passive. When they spotted an opportunity for a meaningful tie, they did not have the luxury of waiting patiently for the relationship to develop according to its "internal rules."

> It is as if we have arrived on a different planet, a young one, closer to the sun, which orbits it much more quickly. Its days are like our hours, its years are like our weeks. So we spend hours together as if they were days, and what is given to us in days expands into months in our concentrated existence.

Under these volatile circumstances, Wertheimer argued, people were impelled to speed up the pace of establishing new relationships, sometimes beginning with their initial encounter, and to reveal their feelings quickly so as to make the most of every moment left to them. Wertheimer took the metaphor of "borrowed time" to an extreme when she connected it to living with a constant awareness of the approach of death. A person living in such a state of mind, she claimed, realizes that every parting may be the last, and this helps overcome hesitations and shyness and enriches interpersonal life in whatever time remains. "It will be of great value if our hours are like days and our weeks like years," she wrote. In the face of this sense of borrowed time and of an obstructed future, she called on her readers to focus on what the present moment offered, as her title, "Friendship—Now," suggested. Every now, she proclaimed, must be turned into a long and meaningful stretch of time.[71]

Other writers did not accept Wertheimer's upbeat assessment of the possibility, in times of uncertainty and accelerated time, of fashioning meaningful friendships and, by implication, romantic relationships as well. Such a pessimistic and critical assessment can be seen in Günter Friedländer's booklet *Jewish Youth between Yesterday and Tomorrow*, which came out in July 1938.[72] Friedländer was an educator and a central figure in the Jewish youth movement Ring-Bund jüdischer Jugend, affiliated with the Central Association; in the late 1930s he was helping children and teenagers prepare for emigration. In this book he portrayed the mental state of young Jews in Berlin. Many Jewish parents, he claimed, had stopped putting effort into cultivating their homes and even the cultural education of their children, instead seeking to steer them only in practical directions. The result was that young people were coming to feel less connected to their homes and surroundings, and were experiencing what he called a sense of "spacelessness" (*Raumlosigkeit*), which brought with it a profound confusion about their orientation in time. By this he meant a loss of rootedness in the past, along with an experience of fragmented time that prevented them from developing in the present and building themselves for the future. Young Jews, he said, "know only today, live from one day to the next, and do not try to raise their gaze beyond that."[73] This also led, he argued, to superficiality in social and romantic interactions among young people. They were influenced to a great extent by the cinema, trying to imitate the shallow and unstable relationships they saw on the screen. "They try to dance, flirt, and pretend they are in a film," he wrote.[74] In fact, he argued, more meaningful relations could be developed under the prevailing circumstances. It may well be that his desire to encourage his readers to do so led him to offer a more pessimistic analysis of the situation, one very different from Wertheimer's.

As Germany ratcheted up its persecution of the Jews during 1938, especially toward the end of that year, the sense of insecurity among the country's Jews worsened. Time felt increasingly pressured for them. The sense of accelerating time reached its height in the months that followed the November pogrom, which produced emigration fever.[75] Hans Reichmann, a leading figure in the Central Association, was arrested following the pogrom and incarcerated for seven weeks in the Sachsenhausen concentration camp before being released on the condition that he leave Germany. He described the feeling of the time in an account he wrote in London the following summer. Jews rushed to liquidate their property, he said. "Magicians offer their services . . . asking a fee of several hundred marks to expedite the process," he wrote ironically. "Their assistance would be worthwhile for the Jews, they said, because time was money, and who knew if tomorrow a new directive would appear that would forbid taking goods out of the country, property that as of today could still be salvaged."[76] The frantic search for a haven to emigrate to also speeded up time, creating what Reichmann described as a whirlwind. "Jews do not sleep," he wrote; "their thoughts fly to all ends of the earth as they try to find a country that will deign to receive them. . . . The whirlwind of emigration grips us, and we hobble through a welter of regulations on taxes and duties, from one formal process to the next, and each day I must present myself at new offices and authorities. . . . Our home is in the midst of a whirlwind of liquidation."[77]

Alongside this panic, Jews who wanted to emigrate had to spend long periods waiting, both to receive a visa to their country of refuge and for the bureaucratic process in Germany to play out. These other countries put German Jews on waiting lists; a high number meant virtually no chance of being able to flee the Reich, where life was becoming intolerable. Klemperer wrote in March 1939,

> Everyone is making enormous efforts to get out, but it is getting ever harder. We personally do not appear to be having any success. Silence all around. From the American consulate in Berlin we received Waiting List Registration Numbers 56429 and 56430. And so everything remains unchanged for us. . . . I [am] gloomily fatalistic. Endless reading aloud by day and night, lately all kinds of visitors, a great deal of household stuff, a little work, now English, now memoirs, and endless waiting.[78]

The tension between enforced waiting and the pressure of accelerated time during the period of emigration fever is documented in the letters that Sigmund and Gertrud Hirschberg of Berlin exchanged with their son Hans, who had settled in Palestine not long before. In the weeks following their son's departure, they had tried to arrange for themselves and their daughter to leave for somewhere. The couple's entire world, like that of many other German Jews of the time, revolved around trying to find a place to go, and arranging their emigration. Again and again, they had to wait, as their letter of March 19 detailed:

> Each preparation for emigration is organized entirely from the start. . . . You receive a place in line—after ten days. You report at the assigned time, and despite this you are sent back, only to return four or five hours later. . . . After a long wait and thorough interrogation you receive the document. With the forms filled out (nineteen forms), some of which you have to fill out by hand, others on a typewriter and still others in print letters, you need to return to 31 Oranienburger Straße. Here you again receive a number in line, and return a few days later, and again wait a long time. After that . . . you need to go through three Jewish offices and ten Aryan offices. At the end comes the Gestapo, whose people must also make their stamp. If you get through all the obstacles, which is never possible without being sent home several times, then you receive, three weeks later, an invitation to take your emigration papers. Now you must picture those pitiful people, who must at each of these agonizing stations sit crowded together and wait for

> many hours in packed, stifling rooms, and then you can understand that they descend into despair.[79]

Waiting and uncertainty seem to reach a new height here, where they are coupled with spatial crowdedness in the form of "packed, stifling rooms." The dimension of uncertainty and passive anticipation of the future is evident in the Hirschbergs' inability to have any real effect on their own emigration. In March and April 1939, the parents told their son about their attempts to explore possibilities of leaving for the Philippines, Bolivia, Chile, and Harbin, China.[80] In the end, at the beginning of May, they suddenly managed to get tickets to sail for Shanghai. "That is how time stretched out for us," Gertrud wrote her son from Berlin on April 20, 1939. "We live only in anticipation."[81]

The couple's time not only stretched out but became more intense. The time they spent waiting to emigrate was very different from the empty time Jews had experienced at home in the early years of the regime, when they could not make any decisions about their future. Then, when Sigmund and Gertrud finally grabbed an opportunity to emigrate to Shanghai, it came suddenly and unexpectedly, casting them into accelerated time. They had to respond quickly, Sigmund wrote Hans: "Sunday, May 7, we will leave for Trieste and from there on a boat to Shanghai. . . . You can picture how excited we are. I thus can't write to you today, because everything has happened so quickly." Gertrud added: "In haste and excitement."[82] A few days later, already on their ship, the couple offered more detail on "how everything happened so quickly" and involved "great anxiety" and turmoil.[83]

Emigration fever thus brought the tension between two ostensibly contradictory senses of time—passive waiting and accelerated time—to a new height. In practice, these seem to be two faces of the same coin: creeping and stopping time and accelerated time both express the collapse of linear time, which flows at a unified pace and allows rational planning of the course of life and a measure of control over it.

"How Much Longer? But When?" Personal Writing during the War Years

When World War II broke out in September 1939, a sixty-four-year-old Berlin businessman, Philipp Manes, began a war journal. In his diary he portrayed his life with his wife, Trude, after their four children managed to leave Germany before the war began, until they were deported to the Theresienstadt concentration camp in the summer of 1942. Through the end of 1941, Manes continued to be employed at the fur business that he had owned until it was Aryanized at the end of the 1930s; but when more severe restrictions were imposed, he was put into forced labor at a factory near Kreuzberg. Other than going to work, and attempting from time to time to go for walks in the Tiergarten, a park near their home, to calm down, when that was still possible, the couple lived their lives increasingly shut up at home.

From the perspective of his life in Berlin, Manes wrote from time to time in his diary about his experience of time as his life, and those of all Jews in Germany, changed radically. Time oscillated constantly between slow and fast, he reported. During the war's initial year, when it looked as if he and his wife would manage to emigrate to Shanghai in the footsteps of their younger son, Manes described time as creeping along as they waited to receive the emigration permit that would finalize their move. "The first day of spring," he wrote in March 1940. "There is no anticipation in my heart. The days plod along laboriously—each one brings us closer to the decision that must fall—one way or the other."[84] Looking forward, to the days passing before a decision about emigrating, his experience was one of slow time. On the other hand, when he looked back on the time that had passed, he largely sensed the opposite. At the beginning of May 1940, when he began the second volume of his journal, Manes wrote that "eight months have passed quickly. Their substance does not change. Waiting week by week for letters from our children, and since March for the permit."[85]

The tension between these two depictions of time—seen first as plodding, but then in retrospect as a monotonous period having passed quickly—can be understood with the help of insights provided by Thomas Mann in the "Excursus on the Sense of Time" segment of his novel *The Magic Mountain*.

> It is generally believed that . . . monotony and emptiness . . . weigh down and hinder its [time's] passage. This is not true under all conditions. Emptiness and monotony may stretch a moment or even an hour and make it "boring," but they can likewise abbreviate and dissolve large, indeed the largest units of time, until they seem nothing at all. Conversely, rich and interesting events are capable of filling time, until hours, even days, are shortened and speed past on wings; whereas on a larger scale, interest lends the passage of time breadth, solidity, and weight, so that years, rich in events, pass much more slowly than do paltry, bare, featherweight years that are blown before the wind and are gone. . . . When one day is like every other, then all days are like one, and perfect homogeneity would make the longest life seem very short, as if it had flown by in a twinkling.[86]

Mann's description captures the feeling of the confined, drab, and monotonous life that Manes and the other Jews who remained in Germany during the war had imposed on them as an experience of empty time. In retrospect, the time was experienced as accelerated but largely meaningless. This is consistent with the claim, made by Moritz Föllmer in his historical study of Berlin, that the exclusion under which Jews lived in the Nazi era, which forced them to focus ever more on the daily grind of survival, seriously impinged on their capacity for experiencing personal agency and inflicted on them a state of what he calls "reduced individuality."[87]

One salient cause of the sense of waiting and creeping time was the anticipation of letters from family and spouses, and the longing for them. The difficulty was exacerbated not only by the increasing social and spatial isolation that followed the November pogrom, and especially the outbreak of war, but also the disruption of the mails and, even more, the closing off of the emigration option. "Of all the things fate has foisted on us," wrote Willy Cohn, whose adult children had already left the country, "waiting for the mail is one of the hardest."[88] The creep of time in the face of longing for loved ones is expressed even more graphically in a letter written on June 7, 1940, by a young physician in Berlin, Valerie Scheftel, to her close friend and apparent lover Karl Wildmann, who had emigrated to the United States in September 1938:

> "You will be with me in this world!" This one sentence from your last letter is with me all the time, wherever I am. I hear it, see it, feel it . . . for when will I be with you, tell me, I beg you, darling, when? I have no answer to that question, and the consulate just says something about 1 to 2 years, so that is infinite, unimaginable, inconceivable, the same as 100 years for me. I must be with you in the shortest time possible, immediately now.[89]

The events of the war themselves, which awakened in some Jews who remained in Germany a hope that the Nazi regime would come to an end, also shaped their experience of time. This is especially notable in Klemperer's diary. He devoted much space to relating the progress of the war to the extent that he knew it, and to coping with the tension between, on the one hand, the state of the war and his expectations of how long it would go on, and on the other hand his own personal time. "This Christmas and New Year's Eve," he wrote at the end of 1939, "we are decidedly worse off than last year, we are threatened with the confiscation of the house—despite that, I feel better than I did then; there is a movement now, and then everything was stagnating. I am now convinced that National Socialism will collapse in the coming year."[90] About three weeks later, he wrote of the conflict between his hope for a Western invasion of Germany and his personal difficulty in waiting for such an event: "So we daily expect the invasion. . . . The sooner the battle begins, the sooner the outcome will be decided. Perhaps still in time for us after all. We talk about it day after day. But the waiting gets harder every day."[91] When the war carried on far longer than he had hoped, and his expectations were dashed, Klemperer again in the summer of 1940 experienced time standing still. "We have no sense of time anymore," he wrote at the height of the air war with Britain. "Everything is an undifferentiated viscous endlessness."[92] The tension between the "big time" of the war and his personal feeling that he was living on borrowed time frequently caused Klemperer to feel pessimistic. "In the *long term* Hitler cannot remain victorious," he wrote in April 1941. "All world conquests fall apart at some point. All I am interested in now is our temporally very limited particular fate. And I am fatalistic about that."[93]

In the following years of the war, Klemperer's perception of time continued to shift. Sometimes he made pessimistic predictions that the war was liable to continue for many more years, and described time as frozen, or as creeping "at a snail's pace." At other times he had hope that the end of the war was near.[94] It became increasingly difficult to cope with the expectation that the regime would collapse in the face of military defeat or a popular uprising, an expectation that became ever more excruciating. Again and again he wrote in his diary "How much longer? [*Wie lange noch?*]" and "But when? [*Aber wann?*]"[95] Sometimes, however, he portrayed his waiting for the unknown as serene. "We live from day to day for as long as we are allowed to live," he wrote. "One thing *must* happen in the course of the coming months: Either Hitler perishes or we do. At all events the end is near. We intend to await it calmly."[96]

The increasing severity of the strictures on how these Jews conducted their daily lives had a more concrete impact on their experience of time. For example, the hours during which Jews were permitted to buy food were restricted, requiring them, housewives in particular, to spend hours waiting in long and wearying lines.[97] On top of such restrictions came arbitrary harassment. Klemperer, who was especially jealous of his time, described in May 1942 how he had stood in line at a shop to buy potatoes; when his turn came and he had given his ration coupon to the proprietor, "a young female, dyed-blond hair, dangerously narrowminded-looking face, perhaps a shopkeeper's wife, stepped up from behind [and said] 'I was here first—the Jew has to wait.' Jentsch served her obediently and the Jew waited." He connected this incident to another delay he experienced. He feared that the Gestapo would burst in to search the house. "Now it is almost seven o'clock, and for the next two hours the Jew is again waiting for the house search."[98] A wait that took place in public was, for Klemperer, more humiliating. "This waiting in front of shops, which is often my lot, is particularly horrible," he wrote a few weeks later. "There are prams; children and dogs are playing, blathering females are coming and going . . . and the whole world eyes my [yellow] star. Torture—I can resolve a hundred times to pay no attention, it remains torture."[99]

After the war began, and especially starting in 1940, the German authorities conscripted Jews for forced labor. The policy was aimed at ameliorating the shortage of manpower needed by the German economy, while further intensifying anti-Jewish persecution. The Jews were often employed in harsh conditions, though in other cases they enjoyed reasonable circumstances. Most Jews who remained in Germany at this point had to work at least ten hours a day, making their lives more pressured.[100] Inevitably, it also shaped their experience of time.

Elisabeth Freund, an economist born in 1898, was conscripted in April 1941 for forced labor in a laundry, and afterward at an arms factory in Berlin. In the account she wrote at the end of 1941 immediately after emigrating, she made frequent reference to how she had experienced time while working. "The heat that pervaded the hall," she wrote about her first day at the laundry. "It was horrible during the final shift. The final hours crept by. We were exhausted. In the end it was over."[101] In her account, the flow of time changed depending on the nature of the work. The more monotonous the work, the more slowly time passed. "The right screw—screw it in, the wrong screw—set aside, right, wrong," she wrote of her work in the arms factory. "There are people who might be right for this monotonous work, but I certainly am not. Even though I manage to do it quickly, the time creeps by while I am doing it. I decided to work for half an hour without looking at the clock. A long time afterward I glanced at the clock again. Only fifteen minutes had passed."[102] A short time thereafter, when she was temporarily moved into a different department where she manufactured gun magazines, she felt a real sense of emancipation thanks to the relative variety of the work, which in turn changed her experience of time:

> While I must overcome physical exhaustion, I prefer the soldering work to sorting screws. Each magazine requires ten different movements. Between them I also need to get up from my chair to bring new magazines or to go [as part of her work] to another worker in the next hall . . . and when I do that, I can take a little breather and rest. The time passes more quickly, although I tire more.[103]

Arno Nadel, a teacher and musician from Berlin born in 1878, was conscripted for an entirely different sort of labor. His rich and varied Jewish background landed him a position at the central library of the Reich Main

Security Office (*Reichssicherheitshauptamt*), where he was responsible for cataloging the Jewish books that the Nazis looted from communities all over Europe. His work, largely with Yiddish books, also provided the foundation for an exhibition organized by the Security Office. In June 1942, while sitting on the balcony of his home—one of his last refuges—during one of the short rest periods he received, he described the natural wonders of the summer. Then he drifted into melancholy nostalgia for the hikes he had used to take in the forests with his wife. He had already forgotten those sights, he wrote, "in the fields of my misery . . . in my eternal daily sorrow." His forlorn thoughts of those landscapes led him to turn directly to the subject of time. "O dearest time, sweet time, my friend, where have you gone? How wonderful it was that I divided you, took advantage of you, before I became a slave at God's will. Don [the name Nadel used for himself in his diary], the slave prince, with a wagon and dust, a load and backaches, and even worse, aches of the soul."[104] Nadel experienced the division and exploitation of time in the past as an expression of his freedom, and described his loss of control over it, which reached its height at his forced labor, as slavery. Time continued to preoccupy Nadel in the weeks that followed, and at times he recorded new insights in his diary, some of them comforting, that he derived from the old books he worked with.[105] In March 1943 Nadel and his wife were deported to Auschwitz, where both were murdered.

Minkowski offers the experience of the passengers on the sinking *Titanic* as an extreme example of the mode of expectation characterized by a passive attitude toward the future. "Expectation penetrates the individual to his core, fills him with terror," he wrote.[106] This certainly applies to the experience of the diarists quoted here, who toward the end of 1941 gradually learned of the Nazi program to deport Jews to the east. "Every day news from many cities, departure of large transports, postponements, then departures again, with sixty-year-olds, without sixty-year-olds—everything seems arbitrary," Klemperer wrote at the end of November 1941. "Everyone . . . waits from day to day."[107]

Philipp Manes, who in early 1940 still expected that he and his wife would be able to join their son in Shanghai, continued to experience the tension between creeping and accelerated time even after their prospects for emigration came to nothing. The tension became more severe with the constant fear of receiving a deportation notice to an unknown destination. "How the weeks fly by," he wrote in January 1942. "I would like to stop the days, or alternatively give wings to the months so as to bring the final resolution closer. Not knowing is worse than knowing what will happen in the end. Waiting for mail—will we receive a notice or not—and then a sigh of relief because we have gained another day and we can be secure in it."[108]

While Manes, like most other writers quoted here, was in the end sent to his death in the east, Klemperer, a Protestant convert married to a non-Jewish woman, remained in the *Judenhaus* for couples in mixed marriages in Dresden. It was a long period during which he experienced nerve-wracking anxiety because of the constant threat of deportation to the east, the fate of the great majority of the families of other Jewish residents at the house. In the end, as a result of the chaos that ensued in the city after the Allied bombing of February 13, 1945, Klemperer was able to flee the *Judenhaus* and avoid deportation and death. Some two weeks later, when he found temporary refuge in the countryside, where he hid under a false identity, he was still writing in his diary about passively waiting for death. "Tomorrow the hog will or was to be slaughtered; a big event," he wrote of the village in which he found himself. He added that the slaughter was delayed because the butcher was conscripted into the army. The story became his own. "I feel I am like the hog," he wrote. "A brief stay of execution, no more, and the deliverance on February 13 will have been for nothing."[109] In seeing himself as the pig, he underlined the helplessness and terror he felt in the face of what he experienced as the inevitable death that awaited him, a state of mind he could not shake off even after he took his fate into his own hands by fleeing. His reduced individuality, to use Föllmer's term, had reached the point of erasing the distinction between himself and a beast.

Conclusion: "The Awareness of the Heavy Hours . . . Became the Real Torment"

The sociologist Hartmut Rosa, who argues that the acceleration of time is the most fundamental characteristic of the modern experience, expands on the phenomenon in the context of sociohistorical processes as well as individual lives.[110] Rosa shows how acceleration has in the modern era become a cultural value in its own right, a code of social success. More and more people, in particular members of the upper classes and elites, have internalized it and conduct their lives accordingly. This process, Rosa argues, came together with the rising consciousness of a more open future. It is evident in the daily lives of individuals, as well as in the way they plan and shape the entire course of their lives. In addition, it can be seen in historical time itself. Rosa also points to situations in which individuals and societies experience a deceleration—sometimes as a matter of choice, and at other times out of necessity. Sometimes people find themselves in situations—some of them personal, like illness or accident, some of a broader historical nature, such as practices of discrimination and exclusion—in which they are compelled against their will to slow down the pace of their lives and experience time standing still. These people must cope constantly with the desynchronization of their time from the faster pace of time in the society in which they live. When faced with the impossibility of living up to the expectation of an accelerated pace of life, an expectation born of the internalization of the ethos of modern society, they are liable, Rosa argues, to descend into depression and to see no way out of their plight.[111]

The Jews who lived in Germany under Nazi rule experienced a double desynchronization. German society became the community of the *Volk* (*Volksgemeinschaft*), and was conducted according to the new Nazi politics of time. The Jews were also barred from the accelerated social, economic, and mental developments that German society underwent. The transition into slow time and the experience of its creeping pace were palpable both in their daily lives and the in blocked prospects of their long-range plans. In the end, only emigration could extricate them from this experience of time.

The sense of creeping time was often tied up with being socially and spatially isolated. On June 23, 1941, Victor Klemperer was arrested and held for eight days for violating the wartime blackout. His experience of his prison conditions, which he set down a short time after his release, offers a further, particularly extreme example of the link between spatial isolation and creeping time. "[I] left the house on Monday after a late breakfast and a heartfelt leavetaking in a very reasonable state of mind," he wrote. "[I told myself that] eight days are not an eternity, I would send greetings, a greeting, perhaps even be able to receive a visit. . . . Only at the second that the door fell shut . . . the eight days turned into 192 hours, empty caged hours. And from then on the awareness of the heavy hours did not leave me again and became the real torment of these days."[112] In his depiction of his time in jail, Klemperer referred to "slow-moving time" that could not be compressed (*Die zähe Zeit*). Further on, he described his time in a solitary cell as "true endlessness" (*wirkliche Endlosigkeit*), and broke the days and nights remaining to him into "endlessnesses," in the plural (*Endlosigkeiten*).[113] This extreme isolation from the rest of the world brings to a climax his experience of time as unending, creeping time, as time standing in place.[114]

Alongside the slowdown of time to the point of it stopping entirely, German Jews also described the opposite experience, of time accelerating and even galloping at high speed. As shown in this chapter, it was not just a reflection of the dominant time of the Nazi regime. Rather, in certain situations, especially at times of transition, it also expressed a personal experience of an uncontrolled speedup of time. The process of acceleration is a fundamental characteristic of modernity and an expression of its values, according to Hartmut Rosa; those it leaves behind are compelled to shift to a slower pace, as oppressed losers. Rosa notes that the faster pace of time has also led to a pathology of acceleration that causes real injury to individual autonomy.[115] The historical context he addresses, that of late modernity, is manifestly different from that which caused the dizzying acceleration of the pace of life experienced by German Jews in certain situations. But there is something common in the profound threat to individual autonomy that is the result of this situation. Both the extreme slowdown and extreme acceleration of time and the sometimes sudden and uncontrollable oscillations between those states pulverized the modern bourgeois way of living once been so dominant in the personal consciousness of these Jews, to the point of looming as a real danger that could dissolve the human subject.

* CHAPTER SIX *

Turning toward the Past

The first wave of antisemitic measures instituted by the new regime arrived in the spring of 1933. In response, writers in the Jewish press evoked Jewish history more and more frequently. Looking to the past, rabbis, social activists, and pundits looked for ways to understand and cope with their plight, and sought solace for their suffering. The return to history was a fundamental need for the Jews, wrote Fabius Schach in *Israelitisches Familienblatt* in March 1933: "The past speaks to us today, proposes that we join it. It is not dead, it has much more to give. . . . At a time when the zeitgeist is to draw strength from ancient times, we Jews should not be ashamed to return as well to history."[1]

Schach's article focused on the heritage of the nineteenth century, the age of emancipation and Jewish integration into German culture. Other writers maintained that Jews needed to look to earlier periods of Jewish history, those in which Jews had turned inward while living in foreign and even hostile surroundings. In this way they could find comfort amid the vicissitudes of the present. "At this time of crisis, when fate turns its iron fist against us," Rabbi Caesar Seligmann, a leading liberal-minded Frankfurt rabbi, argued in June 1933, Germany's Jews needed to return to their sources and reexamine their history and heritage. "We need once again to be cognizant that we did not come into European culture as beggars," he stressed.[2]

In his book on the reshaping of space and time at the turn of the twentieth century, Stephen Kern notes that, desperately seeking stability in the face of rapid technological and political change, many Westerners of this era looked to history. While, on the verge of the new century, some argued that adhering overmuch to the past would lead to enslavement to tradition, there were many others for whom the past served as a source of identity and meaning.[3] This grip on the past, the sociologist Alberto Melucci argues, can serve as a place of refuge in the face of an unknown future. But, he adds, holing up within that refuge is liable to turn it into a prison.[4]

During the early years of the Nazi regime, Jews were pushed out of and excluded from the German calendar's cycle of seasons and special days. This unbalanced the steady flow of time in their daily lives, and blocked their prospects for the future. Under these circumstances, and in the face of the severe blow to their bourgeois customs, which had been founded on planned activity that looked to the future, more and more of them turned to the past.

This chapter focuses on Jews' turn toward the past—be it the Weimar Republic, the nineteenth century's age of emancipation, or earlier periods in both German and Jewish history—and its role as an important factor in the shaping of their lived time. Jewish writers also increasingly looked back into their family and personal pasts. The chapter begins by considering the rapid increase in evocation of the past in Jewish public spaces, and the need of commentators and opinion shapers to draw insights from the "usable past" when faced with the barrier that stood between themselves and their futures. It will then show how individuals, diarists among them, addressed the past. This process, which began in the 1930s, grew even more pronounced as those who remained in Germany during the war years became ever more captivated by the past—by historical events and processes and by chronicles of their communities, but even more by personal memories. The last part of the chapter will look at another aspect of this orientation: the tendency among Jews, both in their communal discourse and on a personal level, to see and interpret the past in generational terms. This trend was also evident in the preoccupation with genealogy and the crafting of family trees during this time.

"History Teaches about the Present": Usable Past in Community Discourse

From the dawn of Jewish studies in Germany, with the establishment of the Society for Jewish Culture and Jewish Studies (Verein für Kultur und Wissenschaft der Juden) in Berlin in 1819, the field was characterized by tension between the objective evaluation of the Jewish past and the use of the knowledge produced by this field for social, political, and educational purposes. Intellectuals, rabbis, and scholars of Jewish history also participated in the public arena and wrote in the press. They sought to present their work, and their view of the world of the past, to a broad public while highlighting its implications for their own times. During the age of emancipation, they labored to create a usable past for German Jews—a historical narrative that would provide a basis for their integration into the German national movement and German bourgeois society.[5] This usable past, in a range of variations, was also disseminated among Jews by means of historical novels and popular articles in the Jewish press. Prominent Jewish leaders and writers also delved into the histories of the communities in which they lived.[6] Later, during the final years of the Weimar Republic, Jewish historians and pundits offered popular histories as an integral part of their battle against the rising Nazi tide. They also devoted considerable attention to the German past, expressly aimed at a general German audience, not just the Jewish community.[7]

After the Nazis came to power, the nature of the political discourse about history and current events in the Jewish public had to change. Jewish activists and writers could no longer use the past as a political instrument for battling Nazism and antisemitism. That did not, however, put an end to the Jewish public preoccupation with the past, which indeed increased. German Jews continued to study and teach history, and the discussions they engaged in about Jewish history played out in Jewish publications. The number of popular books on historical subjects that appeared under these new conditions surged, and prompted a lively public discourse that crossed political and ideological boundaries.[8]

When Jewish historians, intellectuals, and public figures looked back in time, they did not do so in a vacuum. The Nazi regime that operated around them also evoked the past, seeking to craft from it a historical memory that would serve its purposes. The Nazis did not succeed in achieving full accord among academic historians, nor were they able to inculcate the Nazi view of history as the only view, but many of the conservative spokesmen for the historians' guild who managed to retain their university positions were inclined toward political support for the regime, and promoted national-*völkisch* and antisemitic views of the German past.[9]

Jewish writers were explicit about the parallel between their use of history within the Jewish community and Nazi Germany's use of it to draw lessons from the past to be applied to the present and used to build what it saw as a better future. The difficulty, wrote Stefan Fraenkel in an article titled "History Teaches about the Present," which appeared in *CV-Zeitung* in April 1934, concerned how much objectivity a historian could display in such circumstances.[10] As a member of the liberal camp who sought to reassure the Jewish public and to prevent what its leaders saw as unjustified panic and overreaction, Fraenkel stressed the need to use the past to provide a correct perspective on current events. He acknowledged that recent developments evoked memories of traumatic events in the history of German Jewry—injustices, expulsions, and even massacres—and there was unquestionably a long history of Jewish suffering in the country. Nevertheless, perhaps even precisely for that reason, it was important to keep in mind the more tranquil periods in that history, and the development of centuries-old bonds between Jews and the German nation. In an attempt to present history as a framework that could put different proportions on the current crisis, another writer, this one from the Orthodox camp, argued that not all current events and troubles qualified as history, which comprised significant events of long-range impact.[11] Such calls to develop a sense of historical proportion with relation to current events grew out of a fundamentally conservative approach that sought to maintain the stability of life in former times. The claim that Jewish suffering under the Nazis was simply a reversion to the norm of Jewish history, these conservative voices worried, was overhasty and liable to obliterate, in one fell swoop, the magnificent legacy of Jewish integration into Germany.

The turn to history and the use of the past were also discussed in the context of the Jewish educational system. Because of the growing exclusion of Jewish children and teachers from German schools, the Jewish school system expanded rapidly during the regime's early years.[12] In May 1934, the liberal educator and Central Association activist Fritz Friedländer addressed the challenge of teaching history in Jewish schools. The conflict that had arisen from the fact that Nazi educational directives applied also to the Jewish system, he wrote, was especially acute in the teaching of history. Nazi Interior Minister Wilhelm Frick's order to prepare new history textbooks that would center on the concept of race made it all the more problematic. The National Representation of German Jews, Friedländer maintained, would have to find a way to combine patriotic national (*Heimat*) studies with the history of the German Jewish community.[13] A few months later, Friedländer, who in subsequent years would remain a prominent voice on issues relating to the turn to the past and the writing of history in times of crisis, wrote about the need to change the emphasis in Jewish historical activity in Germany. He called on Jewish historians to tackle burning issues like emigration, and the professional structure of German Jewry.[14] The need of children and adolescents to craft for themselves a picture of the Jewish past in the face of the changing needs of the present and the challenge of Jewish historical education would continue being discussed in the Jewish press in the years that followed.[15]

The escalation of Jewish exclusion made it increasingly difficult for the community's historians to adhere to their scholarly ethos in the writing of history, an ethos that was a component of the bourgeois heritage of the age of emancipation. An interesting attempt to maintain that approach in the face of the current crisis can be found in an article Willy Cohn wrote for the

Frankfurt Jewish community's newspaper a short time after the promulgation of the Nuremberg Laws. He distinguished between the tradition of objective historical writing in Germany associated with the school of Leopold von Ranke, which sought to recreate history "as it actually happened" (*wie es eigentlich gewesen ist*), and the fervent patriotic way of writing that he identified with Heinrich von Treitschke, who made no pretense of detached objectivity. According to Cohn, Jewish historiography was typified by a clear tendency to write with passion, as evidenced by the work of Heinrich Tzvi Graetz and Simon Dubnow, and more recently in popular history by Joseph Kastein, who had no pretentions of being a scholar.[16] Cohn advocated the detached Rankean source-based approach, which he claimed was more accepted at universities in the United States and Western Europe. He criticized Jewish historiography for not taking sufficient account of the role the Jews had played in world history. But given the grave situation German Jews were now facing, it was not reasonable to expect that historians would compose systematic studies according to such rigorous scholarly standards. All that could be demanded was education that would conserve that ethos to be used at a future time. The older generation was seeking to maintain something of the scientific tradition and ambition that had characterized the attitude to the past that prevailed before 1933, Cohn noted. At the end of his article, he argued that apologetics and indictments were not part of the historian's toolbox.

Cohn's attitude, stressing the importance of impartial scholarly inquiry into the Jewish past, seems to have been very much a minority position at the time. There was a notable tilt toward value judgments and attempts to draw practical conclusions from the past that could be applied in the present.[17] Historians, pundits, and public figures adduced history during this period in response to a profound need felt by many Jews to understand their past and to use it to imbue the tragic reversal of Jewish fortunes in Germany with meaning. The turn to history was also a way of reconstituting a Jewish identity that would be meaningful for those Jews who were coping with a crisis of identity now that the German state and society had turned their backs on them.[18] This was evident, for example, in the public debate that followed the publication in 1935 of a history of German Jewry by Ismar Elbogen, the rector of the College for Jewish Studies (Hochschule für die Wissenschaft des Judentums) in Berlin and one of the country's leading Jewish historians.[19] Some praised Elbogen for his "stoic restraint" in interpreting history, but others, disappointed, criticized him for not more explicitly linking the past to the horrific present. Either way, Elbogen, like other prominent historians such as Selma Stern and Ismar Freund, did not remain indifferent to the public's need for a fresh look at the past. They took part in the public lectures organized by the German Jewish community, and published in the Jewish press historical surveys about a range of subjects.[20]

The attempt in the early years of the Nazi regime to hang onto the age of emancipation was also evident in the organization of a range of events marking important jubilees, such as the centennial of the emancipation of the Jews of the province of Posen in Prussia (1933), and the 125th anniversary of the grant of civil rights to the Jews and the establishment of the Jewish council in Baden (1934). No less notable were events with a much more integral Jewish character, such as the 900th anniversary of the establishment of the old Jewish synagogue in Worms, marked with a ceremony in that city in which Jewish leaders from all over Germany participated; the 800th anniversary of the birth of Maimonides (1935); and the 150th anniversary of Moses Mendelssohn's death (1936).[21] Jews, cut off from the German cycle of time (as discussed in chapter 4), began to mark a variety of holidays and memorial days on their new calendars. Such jubilees were another way of imbuing the past with meaning and breaking free of total dependence on the sorry perspective of the present.

"People Are Increasingly Turning Their Gaze to the Past": The Turn to the Past in the World of the Individual

The turn to history is also evident in the personal worlds of the diarists, especially those of intellectual bent. At the end of March 1933, as indications that a boycott of Jewish businesses was impending, Kurt Rosenberg wrote of the imperative of thinking about current events in a historical and detached way. Doing so, he argued, could make it easier to cope with the crisis.[22] About three months later, after a series of new government measures that had begun to affect his daily life, Rosenberg set down in his diary a more substantial discussion of this issue. "I have been thinking a lot about the nature of National Socialism," he began. "It must be seen as a single event in a long series of developments going all the way back to the French Revolution."[23] Rosenberg fleshed out the subject in a long essay, quite different in nature from most of his diary entries up to this point. He sought to explain the rise of the Nazis from a long-range historical and sociological perspective while at the same time addressing questions such as the role played by the masses in history, and the principle of the leader.[24]

Rosenberg's turn to history when he devoted many pages of his diary to these issues was part of the way he grappled with his social and spatial isolation. The historical past, it seems, served him both as a source for finding meaning in his difficult present circumstances, and a way of interpreting events to create detachment from his plight. It was a project that seemed to make his loneliness easier to bear. Indeed, his efforts to interpret events by taking a *longue durée* approach can be seen as another aspect of his response to the experience of accelerated time at precisely this juncture, as shown in the previous chapter. It was a phenomenon especially notable in his case.

Rosenberg's turn toward history did not always grow out of a need to find meaning in current events. He sometimes presented it in his diary simply as a way of diverting his mind from his troubles, and specifically as a way of coping with creeping time. "Waiting, waiting, and again waiting in a way that has no chance. It is so disabling," he wrote in February 1934. A few lines later he commented, "I am reading Charles Diehl's *Venice*, a history of Venice. Everything pulls in the direction of history because it creates detachment, reassuring detachment."[25] The calming respite of the turn to the past to some extent paralleled the "breathing breaks" he had experienced on his brief trips out of Germany during the regime's early years.[26] The temporary reprieve in another space was reflected in the respite offered by another time.

Willy Cohn took a different tack. In contrast to Rosenberg, who turned to European history as a whole, Cohn looked to Jewish history. Ousted from his teaching position in 1933, he devoted much of his time to researching and teaching Jewish history in a number of Jewish frameworks. As we have seen, he also published pieces on the subject in the Jewish press. "People are increasingly turning their gaze to the past," he wrote on October 14, 1933, and a week later reported in his diary on a lecture he gave before a packed house in Beuthen titled "The Pulse of Two Thousand Years of Jewish History."[27] As noted in previous chapters, Cohn frequently referred to the creeping flow of time and the closing of his time horizon, as well as to being closed up in a shrinking space. For him, lecturing and writing on the past was the opposite sort of experience. "This morning I worked mostly in the field of Jewish history," he wrote in September 1935. "It brings me great joy to fill up my empty spaces." Cohn's encounter with Jewish history filled not only gaps in his knowledge but, in a more profound sense, the inner voids caused by his exclusion from German society.[28]

Cohn's finely honed historical consciousness led him, as he wrote, to make note of the national memorial days that dated from the time of the German Empire and how they contrasted with the very different circumstances and temporal regime of the present. For example, he recalled the birthday of Kaiser Wilhelm II, January 27, not on that date but on April 20, 1933, the day Hitler's birthday was first observed as a national holiday.[29] Another anniversary from times past that Cohn kept in mind was Coronation Day, which was also the date the Reichstag was founded. It was January 18, the date on which Wilhelm I had been crowned in 1871, celebrated on that date under the empire. When he recalled it in 1939, Cohn remarked in his diary: "Now we live alongside history, in which we once played an active role."[30] Cohn also thought of August 11, the day the constitution of the Weimar Republic was declared, and mentioned it in his diary. "Another historical era that has come to an end," he wrote in 1940.[31]

Beyond engagement with history and the effort to use it to get a more detached perspective on the events they were living through, or at least some solace and distraction, Jewish diarists increasingly wrote about their own personal stories and pasts. In his study of diary writing during the Holocaust era, Amos Goldberg asserts that keeping a diary became particularly popular during periods of major change. The experiences Jews underwent during the Nazi era, he argues, prompted many of them to try to reorganize their life stories and fashion a "narrative identity" in the face of the changes they were experiencing.[32] Not only did the amount of journal writing increase sharply, but the nature of the diaries changed as well, as is documented in Janosch Steuwer's work on diary writing among different groups of Germans during the early Nazi years. Steuwer shows how political and historical processes that until then had remained at the margins of the private lives of most of these writers, if they mentioned them at all, became dominant when they sat down to write in their diaries, and impelled them to develop a broader view of their own life stories.[33] Writers became more reflective in their diaries, addressing their pasts more than they had used to do, and sometimes composing memoirs. In the case of German Jewish diarists, the experience of increasing exclusion from public space, as future prospects were blocked and time creeped, also caused them to turn toward the past.

Victor Klemperer's life also changed drastically under the Nazi regime, the rise of which marked a turning point in his diary. He had begun to keep a journal at the age of sixteen. In 1932 he considered stopping because of a severe personal crisis, but he returned to the diary with redoubled zeal when the Nazis came to power. Finding the time to write became a daily struggle. In July 1933 he wrote that his lack of mental composure was making writing difficult. In the midst of this, Klemperer mentioned that the idea of writing a memoir attracted him. "The thought of the memoirs excites me ever more strongly," he wrote, waxing nostalgic about his experiences as a young man at the beginning of the twentieth century, the first piece of theater criticism he published, and his first involvement with politics.[34] In the years that followed, even before he sat down to actually write his memoirs, his attempts to hold onto the past became one of the ways he and his wife, Eva, coped with the ever more secluded lives that the political situation imposed on them. So, for example, in February 1935 he wrote about Eva's habit of sometimes playing old records, songs one no longer heard on the gramophone in the new Germany. Tangoes, jazz, and other exotic music that had been popular under the republic both moved and maddened him. "There is freedom in them, a sense of the world [*Weltsinn*]," he wrote. "In those days we were free and European and decent."[35]

The past was sometimes a presence during Klemperer's travels. As noted in chapter 1, he frequently drove around Germany in his car between 1936 and 1938. On one such trip, in May 1936, he and Eva went to the mountain vacation spot of Kipsdorf, in the heart of a forested area, a place they had not visited for many years. There they reconnected with pleasant memories from years past.[36] Those memories sharply contrasted with their very different present circumstances. In February 1935, Klemperer remarked that he very much missed the music of the Weimar period, in these days in which he could not hear it in public. In 1936 he discovered that Kipsdorf's beautiful main street had been renamed in honor of Hitler. *Der Stürmer* was prominently displayed at the train station.

But Klemperer did not always portray the past as the binary opposite of the present and a consolation for the menace of current times. The past could sometimes exacerbate the dread. In August 1937, Klemperer reported in his diary about a photograph in *Der Stürmer* that he had seen at every street corner. It showed two German girls in swimsuits at the beach who declared, with reference to a "Jews Prohibited" sign also seen in the photo: "How nice that it's just us now!" The expression "just us now" triggered a memory from far back in Klemperer's life, when he had been a high school student in Landsberg in 1900 or 1901. On Yom Kippur, when all the Jewish students except Klemperer were absent from school, the teacher opened the lesson by joking, "It's just us today!" The remark may well have been entirely innocent; it could be that the teacher had no intention of using the word "us" to exclude the Jewish students. Indeed, he had also used the remark in entirely different circumstances in which, at least according to Klemperer, there were few traces of antisemitism. But now the memory came back to him, and "these words took on a quite horrible significance." They sounded like testimony confirming that the Nazi perception of the Jews as others reflected the way Germans saw the world.[37] This incident from the past had not itself been traumatic, and the young Klemperer had not attributed it to antisemitism when it happened. But in 1937 he could not help connecting it with the photograph in *Der Stürmer*. The recurrence of the phrase he had first heard in school brought about what Goldberg describes, in his interpretation of this diary entry, as a spasm of the past within Klemperer's present mind. "Thus, the normal order of time between present and past—crucial to the course of the life story—-collapses," Goldberg maintains. "The present tarnishes the past, which returns to the present to demolish Klemperer's place as a Jew within the social order."[38]

The turn to the past as a source of comfort, in the face of time standing still and a blocked future, is linked by some writers to their family memories as well as their personal pasts. "The Jews are engaging in self-reflection," Rosenberg wrote in June 1934, following a long discussion on the "insensible waiting" and fatigue that it caused. "The happy home is the only counterweight for this, harmony with the wife and children," he wrote. "I am working a lot on my writing, addressing the past, which is again alive for me."[39] A few months later, when he celebrated his thirty-fifth birthday, Rosenberg made reference to a family party his wife and children had made as the best bulwark against "this time." The circle of personal time, as experienced on his birthday, and the family support group around him were presented as the antithesis of "this time"—the developments in Nazi Germany.

But, as with Klemperer, Rosenberg's contact with the past was not just a source of solace and calm; it could also confront him with the difficulties of the present. "[This] time not only produced new concepts, but also did away with the contours of existing concepts," he wrote. "The solution will not be an easy one for us, because we are situated on the boundary between two eras, and we therefore have not the objectivity of cool judgment, but only the sense of being imprisoned and in despair between yesterday and tomorrow."[40] Memories of the past, which sometimes provide solace, could bring the tension and disharmony between past and present to the fore, and thus could make life all the more difficult. "The processing of past time works together with current suffering to produce a draining and constantly recurring melancholy," wrote Rosenberg a year later, articulating the insight more sharply.[41]

Using the past as a bulwark and a solace requires drawing a clear boundary between it and the present. If the boundary dissolves, the present is liable to inundate the past. That dynamic would seem to explain the fact that visits to cemeteries and the graves of ancestors—from which many Jews derived empowerment and an intergenerational connection that helped them withstand the horrors of the present, as detailed in chapter 2—made Rosenberg feel that his world had been lost. That was his experience when he stood among the headstones: "Yesterday is sinking, today is arbitrary, and tomorrow is uncertain and terrifying."[42]

Rosenberg saved himself from the collapse of the past and the experience of creeping time by leaving Germany, after which he ceased writing his diary. Klemperer, in contrast, like other diarists, wrote all the more intensively about himself and, in particular, about his own personal past. On December 6, 1938, just three days after he was barred from the Dresden library,

Klemperer decided to devote himself to writing the story of his life.[43] This project lay at the center of his world for more than three years, until he had to put it aside in March 1942 out of fear that the Gestapo would find the manuscript during its periodic searches of his room. Klemperer's devotion to documenting his past in the midst of the vast changes in his everyday life, including his move into a *Judenhaus* in May 1940, was one of his ways of coping with his increasingly severe spatial isolation and the adversity of creeping time. "I am sticking to the *Curriculum*," he wrote in April 1941, with regard to his immersion in the memoir. "I shall bury myself in it, as often as [the] household and Eva's illness leave me time."[44]

The turn to the past grew more dominant for Willy Cohn as well. He began writing his memoirs in the mid-1930s.[45] But it was only during the final years of his life, when he was no longer permitted to lecture before Jewish communities and the opportunity to write for the Jewish press had almost entirely vanished, that he devoted himself intensively to writing his autobiography, which would serve as documentation of the greatest age of German Jewry.[46] From time to time, Cohn addressed this project in his diary, as part of the fact that his daily routine was coming to focus ever more on the past. He wrote in the summer of 1941, "Yesterday before noon I had several good hours. I dictated a fairly large passage of my memoirs. . . . Today, after all, many live in their memories of times past."[47] But Cohn, whose autobiographical writing was also a genealogical project for which he made many visits to cemeteries, often felt that his focus on the past was nothing more than an inescapable consequence of his blocked future—perhaps even a comfortable prison. "We already live so much in the past," he wrote. "For me personally, there is no future in sight."[48]

Philipp Manes of Berlin, who in September 1939 began keeping what he called a war diary, also spent the first year of the war documenting his own personal and family past. In September 1940, when he completed this chronicle, he wrote in his diary about the importance of conveying his memories to future generations. Moreover, Manes also compared the experience of completing his composition of this work to the traditional celebration held by observant Jews to mark the completion of the writing of a Torah scroll. It was an experience he remembered well from his younger days, and the comparison is indicative of the sacred or spiritual aspect of the project.[49]

Manes looked to the past also during his walks around Berlin and its environs with his wife. On a visit to Potsdam in May 1940, for example, the two of them evoked their four children, who had grown up and emigrated before the war, and were now scattered all over the world. "Everywhere we go, memories of the time when we went there with our children well up," he wrote. "We walked in their footsteps and frequently asked [each other] whether we still remember."[50] These walks, which read like a mental map of Manes's childhood and life in Berlin, grew less frequent as the regime's anti-Jewish exclusion policies became more draconian.[51] The vitality and tangibility of the past for Manes can also be seen in an entry from early 1942 referring to his mother's birthday. Her image, and that of other family members, had risen before him just when he was closing his eyes at night:

> Mother's birthday. It was so cold that I could not visit her grave, but I thought of her all the time, with her living image before my eyes; for me she is not dead—only distant. What a joyous day January 13 was in her home, how happy Mother was when we celebrated her birthday just in our small circle.... Those were colorful days, when the entire family celebrated together in joy. There is much to remember and much to relate. . . . The present has brought only sorrow and anxiety. The disquiet about our terrible future never ceases. . . .[52]

As the present grew ever more grim, the more the past accompanied Manes wherever he went—when he lay down to sleep, when he rose, and when he walked along the road. In May 1942, when he was conscripted into compulsory labor in the area of the Kreuzberg district of Berlin, memories and scenes from his childhood welled up within him, as he had grown up not far from the factory where he was working, and had taken walks in the area with his parents during his childhood and teenage years. These memories, he maintained, made it easier for him each morning when he reported for his monotonous work in the screw-making plant. "Each morning I gaze at the little balcony of the house on Brandenburg Street, and my mother waves hello," he wrote. "The memories go with me everywhere, and despite all the burden, they cast a bit of light on the darkness of our time."[53]

This attitude toward the past appears in an original way in the writings of the poet Gertrud Kolmar. In September 1941 she recounted the long conversations that her father and the Jewish boarders they were compelled to house in their Berlin home had had about "the good old times," including those of their childhood and youth. "It is pleasant for Father to spend hours telling stories about his teenage years and his professional life; they [the boarders] enjoy listening, and he forgets his pains while he speaks."[54] Kolmar absented herself from these conversations, which included everyone "except me." This was a clear expression of the profound alienation she felt during these years from her home environment, and in particular from the tenants, whose presence in her home had been forced upon her. Yet other passages in her diary show that she also underwent an internal process of turning toward the past, which even reached depths more profound than the boarders' talk of the good old days.

"I feel close only to what has passed," Kolmar wrote to her sister in June 1941. "What is happening to me now seems to me unreal, distant. Even when I am not dreaming, I am not really awake; I walk through an area between worlds [*Zwischenwelt*] that does not touch me and which I do not touch.[55] Kolmar retreated into an imaginary realm that she sometimes described as beyond time and eternal,[56] and which she also tended to identify with her past and her memories. Her life with memories of her past, as she put it in December 1942 about three months before her deportation to Auschwitz, had the ability to warm her even on a cold winter day. "Must I regret that only memories now remain to me?" she asked. "On the contrary, I am happy that I have them; and even if they are not like the warmth of summer, they nevertheless warm me like a good stove on cold days."[57]

"A Foothold on German Soil for Hundreds of Years": Generational Time and the Turn to Genealogy

In his book *Time Maps*, Eviatar Zerubavel addresses the use of the generation as a unit of historical distance. Measuring ages by generations means converting the accepted units of measuring time that are based on the physical cycles of the heavens into the cycles of biological life, as does Ecclesiastes: "Generations come and generations go." Doing so, Zerubavel argues, shrinks historical distances in the mind. For example, saying that Christopher Columbus lived and sailed twenty generations ago means that only twenty people separate us today in time from him. That makes him sound much closer than saying that he lived five hundred years ago. Genealogical contacts, Zerubavel argues, create a consciousness of continuity and close the gap between past and present.[58]

In the same spirit, making the past—historical, family, and personal—more accessible and relevant to the lives of German Jews increasingly involved measuring past time in terms of generations, and using the term "our ancestors" (*Ahnen*). In the context of a debate over the future of the German leadership, a writer in the Zionist newspaper *Jüdische Rundschau* attacked, in July 1933, what he argued was a lack of Jewish leadership in Germany. He maintained that the new historical era required fashioning a new form of Judaism based on inner strength and fortitude: "Only Judaism, only awareness of being connected to a succession of generations that have suffered similarly, can provide [German Jewry] with the ability to endure."[59] The collapse of emancipation and the belief in progress, which the Zionists recognized earlier than most other writers, thus prompted this Zionist writer to turn to past generations—meaning to Jewish historical memory—as a source of strength and resilience. A bit more than a year later, in an article that appeared in *CV-Zeitung* in advance of Rosh Hashanah, Julius Brodnitz challenged his readers to prove themselves "worthy of our forefathers," who knew how to preserve their self-respect in times of travails and suffering.[60] Brodnitz, a liberal, called on his readers to look back on a thousand years of Jewish history in Germany and, with their help, to recognize the ethical mission that the current crisis had imposed on German Jews.

The measure of time by generations complemented the increasing use of the Hebrew calendar by Jewish commentators in the Jewish press in the late 1930s, and intensified as it became increasingly clear that the future of German Jews depended on the emigration of the younger generation. The emancipation era—that is, the 125 years that had begun with the Prussian edict of 1812—had lasted "from our perspective, five generations," wrote Alfred Hirschberg, one of the leading spokesmen for the Central Association, in "Tradition," an article from March 1937. Eulogizing an age that had already ended, Hirschberg used the generational yardstick to telescope it into a period with a definite beginning and end, but more importantly to underline the need to pass the heritage of emancipated Jewry to the young generation leaving Germany. "Our aspiration is that from them [the younger generation] will emerge cohorts that maintain the best tradition of Jewish fortitude that developed over [these] five generations."[61]

The generational measure of time stood out as Germany's Jews increasingly engaged in genealogical research to construct family trees. The connection between this trend and the wider preoccupation in Nazifying Germany with questions of family origin and racial purity is undeniable. The goal for the larger German population was to obtain an Aryan racial pass (*Ahnenpass*).[62] Nevertheless, the Jewish phenomenon seems to predate the Nazi rise to power, and it served specifically Jewish needs.

In 1931, Martin Hirsch presented his family with a detailed chronicle of its past two centuries, including a family tree. The occasion that set him off on this project was his mother's seventy-fifth birthday, as he related in a detailed introduction. The idea had come to him long before, he wrote; but he had decided to embark on it in view of the plight of German Jewry at the beginning of the 1930s.

> If I have decided to write at this juncture, for the first time, a chronicle of the Hirsch family, it is the execution of a plan that I have anticipated for many years already. . . . For twenty years . . . they have frequently been accusing us, the Jews, of having no right to live in Germany because we are "of alien origin" [*Fremdstämmige*]! . . . This after a war in which 12,000

> Jews gave their lives for the German homeland. . . . These accusations must be addressed not only through the study of Jewish culture, but also by the study of the Jewish family. Our claim to the German homeland cannot be better documented than by proof that our forefathers have lived on German soil for hundreds of years.[63]

Hirsch's object of using his research into his family's history in the battle against antisemitism was typical of this time of political battles and cultural warfare at the end of the Weimar period. The Nazi rise to power quickly put an end to those struggles, at least on the surface. Political language changed rapidly, but the Jewish interest in genealogy burgeoned. Jacob Jacobson, director of the central archives of Germany's Jews (Gesamtarchiv der deutschen Juden), wrote in an article of March 1934 about the way the archive, which until recently had mostly served scholars, had now become a resource for large numbers of Jews who wanted to reconstruct their family histories and sketch out family trees.[64] Jacobson attributed the change not only to the reinforcement of the family as an institution, but to what he called "practical reasons." The archive's staff were having trouble processing all the requests coming in, he wrote. The Society for the Study of the Jewish Family, the press reported in July 1934, was now receiving inquiries from a wider public and had considerably increased the scale of its activity.[65] In January 1936, a few months after the promulgation of the Nuremberg Laws, *CV-Zeitung* reported that the study of the family and the construction of family trees had now become a popular hobby. Albert Piehbig of the Society for the Study of the Jewish Family suggested that Jews who wanted to pursue such research could avail themselves of a range of sources and ways of conducting it: interviews of family members, trips to cemeteries, and the use of community and national archives. Unlike Martin Hirsch, who five years earlier had attributed his work on a family tree to the Jewish struggle to maintain a foothold in Germany, Piehbig maintained that genealogy had become a leisure activity, an alternative to sports or stamp collecting. Also, he said, Jews preparing to leave Germany wanted to take their family histories and heritage with them to their new homes.[66]

Contemporary diaries and memoirs demonstrate how the experience of generational time intensified in times of crisis. The telescoping of time achieved by measuring it in generations created a foundation for intergenerational discourse, even if it was only imagined, and expressed the need to conduct a historical accounting. The representation of time from the generational perspective was in some cases tied to pilgrimages to cemeteries, which naturally lent themselves to conducting imagined conversations with previous generations. As noted in chapter 2, Willy Cohn made frequent trips to cemeteries, during which he sometimes "conversed" with his forebears. His trips to Breslau's Jewish cemetery also served his construction of his family tree. Cohn described how he walked among the headstones recording the birth and death dates of all the people to whom he was related. This project of delving into his family's roots, in which he engaged for several years, also impelled him to visit other cemeteries in the region.[67] Philipp Manes, who made frequent trips to the Weissensee cemetery in Berlin, experienced it as a "time bubble" that encompassed both the past and the future but not the troubling present. "I stood there a long time," he wrote of a visit to his parents' grave. "My thoughts turned to the past. I saw my parents and remembered their blessings, the blessings they gave me each day . . . and I also look to the future, which has not revealed its secrets to any of us. I became serene and calm on that hill."[68]

Some at the time saw their visits to cemeteries and encounters with previous generations as part of their process of leaving Germany. David Grünspecht, a livestock dealer, wrote in his memoirs of his need to have one last look at his homeland and its vistas. It was, he observed, the place where his family had lived for generations. Before emigrating, he visited the graves of his parents and other relatives.[69] Hans Reichmann made a final trip to the graves of his mother's family in Polish Silesia before he received a special passport that was valid for emigration only. In his memoir, which he wrote in 1939, he described how "five straight generations of the Sachs and Knopf families" were buried there. "I envied them," he added, "because they have indeed been gathered to their fathers."[70] The impending break in this generational continuity as a result of his emigration seems to have been what impelled him to make this final trip.

The experience of time and intergenerational memory also appear in the younger generation's view of the future, especially among those who left early. The phenomenon stands out in Willy Cohn's writings. Three of his five children emigrated in the 1930s. "Wölfl just departed," he wrote in April 1933 of his eldest son. "It was a very difficult farewell . . . we are left behind. So our ancestors were compelled to take their bundles. Today maybe you take a metal-plated suitcase. But it is the same Jewish fate."[71] In the years that followed, Cohn remarked any number of times on the need to convey intergenerational memory to his children. In June 1933 he recounted taking his daughter Ruth to synagogue, to the seats where he and his father had once sat. During the service, he pointed out to her the things his own father had shown him thirty years earlier. "So generations come and go," he wrote.[72] More than five years later, just before Ruth left Germany, he took her to the local cemetery and showed her the graves of her ancestors. "I told her about the recurring fate of the Jewish people," he related.[73] Cohn's use of the word "fate" in both farewells can be connected to a cyclical experience of time. In the years that followed—until he, his wife, and his two young daughters were deported to the east—Cohn visited the cemetery more and more frequently, and described the trips more and more in terms of an intergenerational dialogue, both with his parents and forefathers and with his daughters, who accompanied him.[74] The work on his family tree also preoccupied him, right up to the moment when he was sent to his death.[75]

Conclusion

In his book *On Aging: Revolt and Resignation*, the essayist Jean Améry discusses the relationship between aging and time. As people age, he argued, the past becomes more salient in their lives, becoming an inseparable part of their lived present. According to Améry, the difference between the way a young person and an old person experience the world grows out of the distinction between space and time. The young person's future horizons are, in fact, the world he or she experiences as a space open before them—space, and not time. In contrast, the aging person increasingly experiences passing time as a negation of the space that had once been open. The aging person's experience of the world thus shifts from space into time.[76] As the years go by, Améry maintains, old people amass time within themselves. As they become more excluded from space, which the aging process takes away from them, they increasingly experience themselves through the act of remembering the past.[77]

In this spirit, it is unsurprising that Victor Klemperer addressed his own aging several times in his diary. "How old have I become," he wrote on September 16, 1935, a day after the Nuremburg laws were promulgated. "Apart from going shopping or to the library, I sit at my work all day—apart from the large amount of time spent on the cat boxes and making tea and coffee . . . an altogether secluded life, quieter, more enclosed that it ever was before."[78] His aging, as described in this passage, was due not to his chronological age or his physical condition, but to a way of life forced on him because he had been excluded from German society and pushed into isolation. His closed spatial horizons were exacerbated by the experience of a blocked future, as can be seen in an entry from a few months earlier, cited above, in which he wrote of how much he missed the music of the Weimar Republic. "These must be the saddest days of my life," he recounted. "In the past, when I felt bad, I had the future to look forward to. Now I often think I am unable to go on."[79] Klemperer did not give up his space easily. He fought for it, as related in chapter 1, at the beginning of 1936, when he began taking road trips in the automobile he had purchased, and again in the early 1940s, when he took walks with his wife. Yet, even at the height of his automobile trips, he continued to contemplate his aging; and his relationship to his past took on an increasingly large role in his world.[80]

Améry's novel take on aging does a good job of explaining why German Jews increasingly looked to their communal past, and all the more to their family and personal pasts. The Nazi exclusion policy that led to the closing in of space on them—in the original understanding of the term "space," as discussed in the first part of this book, and also in the sense of their horizon of future time, as Améry proposes—impelled them to turn ever more to the past, to delve into it, and sometimes to actually live within it. They generally described the turn to the past as a source of comfort, distraction, and tranquility, and it sometimes enabled them to give meaning to the events they were living through, and to place them in context. In other cases, however, the memories could be very troubling, amplifying their present plight.

Conclusion

"The fundamental deprivation of human rights," Hannah Arendt contends in *The Origins of Totalitarianism*, "is manifested first and above all in the deprivation of a place in the world which makes opinions significant and actions effective."[1] The spatial segregation of Germany's Jews under Nazi rule illustrates Arendt's claim. Their exclusion from public spaces, already during the regime's early years, increasingly pushed them into spaces and places that were by definition Jewish. The rules governing the use of such spaces, as they were shaped in the social discourse and implemented by individuals and families during the age of emancipation, quickly eroded under the pressure of circumstances. At the end of the 1930s the German government intensified its persecution, restricting Jews ever more to their homes. Many Jews, including some of those whose voices are heard in this book, chose to leave Germany while that was still possible. Those who remained were in the end doomed to their deaths—in Arendt's terms, the ultimate and utter deprivation of their spatial rights.

In his book *Being-in-the-World*, Boaz Neumann shows that Arendt's claim about "the deprivation of a place in the world" was influenced by the thinking of Martin Heidegger. Neumann counters Arendt with another view, which he maintains is also based on Heidegger: "A human being, as a political creature, can lose their political place in the world. As a social creature, they can lose their social place in the world. As an economic creature, they can lose their economic place in the world. But as a being-in-his-world they cannot lose anything, including their being-in-the-world. A person is always somewhere in the world."[2] Neumann's argument can be used to explain how, until their deportation and mass murder, Jews coped with the Nazi attempt to deprive them of a place in the world and their spatial identity. Those ways of coping were the subject of the first part of this book. The struggle to maintain a foothold of some sort in the public space and in the German natural setting was evident, for example, in Victor Klemperer's drives through the countryside and, when he was no longer permitted to drive, the long evening walks he took with his wife. The redefinition of the uses of traditional Jewish public spaces, such as synagogues and cemeteries—as reflected in Jewish public discourse and, in particular, in Willy Cohn's diary—was another way of dealing with the challenge of maintaining a claim on space. The same was true of the establishment of new Jewish spaces, such as training farms and athletic spaces, and the increasing Jewish preoccupation with the question of home. The Jews' foothold in space also played out in their minds—a phenomenon that grew more salient as their hold on political, social, and economic places weakened. This could be seen in their development of new practices suitable for the changing situation, new ways of describing and imagining global spaces, and new modes of sustaining the images of spaces and places in their memories, imaginations, and dreams. Especially notable in this regard were the pregnant insights that Gertrud Kolmar included in her letters.

Alfred Hirschberg, one of the most articulate representatives of German Jewry's liberal camp, addressed the issue of space in an article he published in the Central Association's newspaper on the occasion of the New Year in January 1936. Just a few months had gone by since the promulgation of the Nuremberg Laws, which stripped German Jews of their equal citizenship, Hirschberg adduced the concept of the ghetto. "We have not turned into ghetto Jews and we do not want to turn into ghetto Jews," he declared. While the autonomous way of life that German Jews were adapting to under the circumstances put them at a certain remove from the world around them, he argued, it did not sever them from it entirely. Unlike the sealed walls of the ghetto, he asserted, "the walls around us have apertures [*Zinnen*] in them, through which one can look out without obstruction to spaciousness [*Weite*] and the future."[3]

Hirschberg also probed the issue of the measure of time—for example, in his article "Between Pesach and Easter," of April 1935. The movements of the stars and planets, which we understand by means of the theories of Copernicus and Newton, he argued, are unfamiliar to us, and we get lost in their cold harmony. They are insufficient to imbue time with order and meaning. The solution to this dilemma, Hirschberg maintained, could be found in the Jews' cultural history and festivals, especially the Seder ("order," in Hebrew) ceremony with which Pesach began. The Seder was the most appropriate source with which to impose order (*Ordnung*) on the lives and thinking of the Jews in the face of Easter (*Ostern*) and what it represented.[4] By Easter, Hirschberg seems to have meant not only Christianity, but more generally the German calendar cycle, which had been enlisted in the service of the Nazi *Volk* community and infused with antisemitism. Alongside the physical movements in the skies, which for thousands of years had been the fundamental reference frame for measuring movement and time in human society, he pointed to the cultural traditions of the majority society, from which Jews had been excluded, and to Jewish tradition.

Exclusion from time, like exclusion from space, can also alienate human beings from their surroundings. Exclusion from the annual calendar cycle, and from control of time, is one of the most fundamental forms of any sort of persecution. During the age of emancipation, the German Jews became integrated into the German national cycle of time and the pace of modern time. As this integration became part of their bourgeois values and lifestyle, it was also especially vulnerable to this aspect of Nazi persecution. Jews, especially middle-class men who were accustomed to being the masters of their schedules, could no longer identify with the German calendar once it was Nazified. The pace of their lives thus decelerated and sometimes reached a full halt. Their lived time transformed from a linear progression that could be controlled and planned into a series of ever more frequent pauses. And yet they sometimes encountered situations in which they needed to make life-or-death decisions and carry them out rapidly, in an instant—another manifestation of being denied control of their time.

In the conventional historical narrative, time ostensibly flows in synchronization with the indifferent monotone of the clock. But even as Jews grappled with being stripped of their control of time, time played an active role in constituting their experience of the world, and of the activity of "timing," or what Hirschfeld called "order," which becomes more overt in such situations.[5] The Jews' increasing alienation from the German calendar impelled them to imbue the traditional Jewish calendar with new meanings, enriching it with holidays and memorial days as their exclusion from their surroundings deepened. Especially challenging and frustrating was their need to cope with the sense that time was creeping ever more slowly—as expressed, for example, by Kurt Rosenberg in his diary. In Rosenberg's case it led in the end to emigration to the United States and a return to the linear flow of time. But those who remained in Germany continued to experience this anguish, which became even more pronounced during the war. It found its most excruciating expression in Klemperer's account of his imprisonment in the summer of 1941, and in Elisabeth Freund's and Arno Nadal's experience of forced labor.

This book has almost not touched on the spatial and temporal experience of German Jews imprisoned in concentration camps or deported to the east, or of those who emigrated from Germany. I will briefly address them here, leaving them for future inquiry.

Hundreds of Jews were incarcerated in camps in Germany betweeen 1933 and 1938, this at a time when there was not yet a systematic Nazi policy of interning Jews, as Jews, in concentration camps. Rather, the individuals in question were arrested for a range of reasons and were treated particularly harshly. Their numbers grew to tens of thousands over the course of 1938, beginning with the wave of arrests in Vienna that followed Austria's annexation to Germany in March of that year, through the arrest of more than two thousand Jews in the so-called June action directed against "asocials," and culminating in the massive roundup of twenty-seven thousand Jewish men following the November pogrom and their incarceration in Dachau, Buchenwald, and Sachenhausen.[6] Their experience of space in the concentration camps exacerbated the sense that there was no way out and that the world was closing in on them. But most of the people detained during this period were held for a short time—a few weeks or months—and then released. The arrests were explicitly aimed at impelling emigration. Presumably, the sense of desperately waiting for help from outside in obtaining their release was at the center of the prisoners' experience, as is indeed evident in the writings of Hans Reichmann.[7]

The systematic deportation of Jews from the Reich to the east began in October 1941. Some were sent directly to sites where they were murdered. Others were placed in ghettos, such as in Theresienstadt, Lodz, Riga, and Minsk, where they generally remained for brief periods in horrific conditions (except, in some cases, in Theresienstadt), before the great majority of them were sent on to their deaths.[8] The process of being uprooted, and the physical conditions Jews suffered, led to hopelessness and a passive waiting for death. It shaped the way they experienced space and time in their last months of life.

There are different estimates of the number of Jews who emigrated from Germany between January 1933 and the official ban on Jewish emigration imposed in October 1941. But there is general agreement that more than half of the members of the Jewish community left the country. The first wave of almost 40,000 Jews chose this route in 1933. Emigration continued thereafter at a slower pace, reaching 130,000 by the beginning of 1938. In the two years that followed, as conditions worsened, a similar number left. A few thousand more managed to leave the country in 1940 and 1941. As the situation worsed, emigration turned into the massive flight of refugees who were forced out of the country.[9]

These emigrants experienced space in widely divergent ways, depending in large measure on their specific circumstances and destinations, as well as their age and the ways of life to which they were accustomed. They found themselves in different situations and viewed themselves differently. For many of those who ended up in the United States, Mandatory Palestine, and to a large extent in Britain, emigration was an opportunity to start over. For young people in particular, but also for some older ones, it provided a new space in which to establish themselves—a new beginning in time. Some of them were part of new collective enterprises, Zionism in particular, while others found themselves new families, communities, and careers. Nevertheless, some of the emigrants, especially older ones, found integration into these new spaces difficult and remained in a state of mourning for their past experiences and the homeland they had lost.[10] Other destinations, such as Shanghai, where thousands of German Jews found themselves between 1938 and 1940, served as much less amenable temporary shelters. Most of the Jews in Shanghai were concentrated in a restricted sector referred to as the Shanghai ghetto, where they struggled for survival, waiting to move on to a permanent location where they could rebuild their lives.[11] Even worse off were those approximately thirty thousand Jews who moved to countries that were later occupied by the Nazis during the war.

*

The connection between the shaping of lived space and that of lived time has been a theme of this book. Often the two phenomena cannot be separated. The Russian-American sociologist Pitirim Sorokin has noted the intimate connection between what he calls sociocultural space and sociocultural time. These differ from physical space and time in that they are shaped by subjective human experience. Sociocultural space, he adds, cannot be measured and is not continuous as physical space is, while sociocultural time does not flow at a uniform pace but exists in the consciousness of human beings, where it runs in different cycles and at different tempos. According to Sorokin, it is impossible to imagine a human consciousness based on homogeneous and neutral physical space and time. Sociocultural space and time, not their physical correlates, lend meaning to human consciousness. They are vital to human awareness; without them people cannot orient themselves in the world.[12] Boaz Neumann's insights would indicate that sociocultural space and time are not states in which humans exist, but products of their ongoing activity.[13] The German Jews portrayed in this book left a wealth of documentation that shows the complexity of this activity in increasingly extreme circumstances.

The exclusion and alienation of German Jews from the German public space was especially intense at special places on the Nazi calendar. On Nazi holidays and memorial days, Jews were even more excluded from German time than usual. Under the pressure of circumstances, this included the retreat of the Jews from German spaces, under the open sky, into Jewish spaces, the great majority of which were closed spaces. It was bound up with the blockage of their prospects for the future, and with the Jewish turn toward their communal and personal pasts, which reached its height in the latter years of the Nazi regime. Synagogues and cemeteries, two manifestly Jewish spaces that opened up to a wide variety of uses they had previously not had, played an important role in the formation of the Jewish experience of past-directed time and the centrality of intergenerational memory. The changes that German Jews' private spaces underwent during this period also affected their experience of time. Being shut up at home intensified their isolation from the cycle of time in the surrounding culture, and it made their lived time even more interrupted and non-uniform in its flow.[14] At the same time, German Jews had to cope with major changes in the character of the home space. They were forced to move into smaller spaces, and consequently to give up many personal and family objects that bore memories. In these smaller homes, the internal spatial divisions that were part and parcel of the bourgeois way of life could be maintained only with great effort, as the home space was shared on the most intimate level with neighbors, whether boarders or fellow tenants in an apartment or home, or the other residents of the *Judenhäuser* into which some Jews were forced to move. All these harsh developments wore away at the experience of the home as a "structure in time," a place that connected its inhabitants both to their personal and family pasts and to their futures. The increasing transience of the experience of the home space, and the erosion of the security that homes usually provide, were thus bound up with the experience of crumbling time and the inability to look to the future.

The articles in the Jewish press, and the egodocuments that have served as the principal source for the reconstruction of the world that Jews experienced, were produced as Jews grappled with the challenge of reconstituting meaningful space and time. The readership of Jewish newspapers and periodicals rose considerably during the Nazi regime's early years, and more and more writers published their thoughts there. The Jewish press served to a large measure as the most important means of creating an imagined Jewish community and consolidating a Jewish public sphere. The debates and discussions that appeared in its pages—in opinion pieces, but also in the sports, children's, and women's supplements—not only reflected the refashioning of the Jewish spatial experience but served as a force impelling that process. The press also served as a primary tool for restructuring Jewish time. Appearing more or less regularly until the end of 1938, the Jewish press brought home and redefined the Jewish calendar and created, among Jews all over Germany, a certain measure of synchronization with their German surroundings and the world as a whole. It served as a partial and provisional remedy for the lack of synchronization with their German surroundings.

Keeping personal diaries and writing long, detailed letters to distant family members can also be seen as a way of creating a mental space that could in some ways compensate for contracting public and personal spaces. Victor Klemperer, Willy Cohn, Kurt Rosenberg, and Hertha Nathorff, among others, wrote more extensively and profoundly in their diaries as they were pushed into the margins of the Jewish space. In doing so, they created alternative personal spaces. In Rosenberg and Nathorff's cases, the process ended when they left Germany for the United States. For Cohn, it ended when he was deported from Breslau and murdered in Kaunas. In Klemperer's case, the climax came during the five years in which he lived in three different *Judenhäuser* in Dresden. Family correspondence, spurred largely by the tragic breakup of families caused by emigration, particularly of children, and the desire of those who remained in Germany to maintain close contact with those who had left, also served as a writing space that offered some compensation to people like Kati Moses, Gertrud Kolmar, Hans and Marie Schmoller, and Sigmund and Gertrud Hirschberg. It was a way for them to paint a picture of their world for their loved ones. Diaries, letters, and other sorts of writing, whether pursued regularly or intermittently, also filled up time and imbued it with meaning.

German Jews had to cope with being pushed out of German society's space and time in a situation in which the Nazi regime had great power and they had nearly none. The Jews, as a community and all the more as individuals, had no effective way of opposing, challenging, or modifying Nazi policy. All they could do in the face of the exclusion strategy imposed from above was to find and foster coping tactics from below, to use Michel de Certeau's terms. In this way they could exert agency that could shape their experience of time and space in their minds and daily lives under the regime's constraints. A wide range of such coping strategies are described in this book. They show that, even under the most extreme persecution, German Jews had some room to maneuver and shape their lives.

Jews sought to maintain a hold on German public spaces and the countryside through the shrinking windows that the Nazi exclusion policy left them, to use Hirschberg's image. These efforts need not be understood as manifestations of political shortsightedness or misunderstanding of Nazi repression. They were, rather, a means of communal or individual self-expression, and sometimes of defiance of the regime. Jews developed a variety of spaces of refuge, such as training farms and sports facilities, and in a more general sense they reshaped the German urban and rural areas that remained open to them. They did this again and again as the possibilities open to them contracted. Such was Kati Moses's project of creating, in her small room, something akin to the functional divisions of the spacious bourgeois home in which she had once lived. The Schmoller family's Neutralien—a small piece of a once larger room, maintained as a common space where the many residents of their cramped living quarters could meet—was another such attempt. The same was true of time. The Jewish calendar was refashioned, in part by imbuing traditional holidays with new meanings. There was also a conscious attempt to address the slow pace and emptiness of time by turning to the past and to the world of the imagination, as Philipp Manes did in retreating into childhood memories during his compulsory labor.

The story of the Jews under the Nazi regime is first and foremost a chapter in Jewish and European history. But the issues addressed in this book, combining use of the wealth of historical sources with the insights of social and cultural studies, have broader human significance. Today, too, members of political, ethnic, or religious groups are persecuted by being pushed out of public spaces and denied control of their time, even if that takes place in contexts very different from those discussed here. The refugees of the current era not only are uprooted from the spaces they once knew, but find themselves subject to a harsh time regime involving long periods of waiting, uncertainty, and empty time, as well as frantic flights in search of refuge. Under the extreme conditions of the Nazi regime, German Jews availed themselves of the cultural capital and means of expression available to them to discuss questions such as the meaning of home under conditions of spatial instability, the difficulties presented by the extreme slowing down or speeding up of time, and the connection between aging and the experience of space and time. All these are issues that, in an entirely different context, touch on the lives of many people today.

Acknowledgments

Everyone, everywhere, ponders the experience of space and time in all its complexity. During my years of researching and writing this book about the experiences and thoughts of German Jewish men and women who lived under Nazi rule, I sometimes found myself grappling with the issue intensively in my personal life as well. For example, I paid close attention to the way I experience and use public spaces, and examined how transitions between different spaces shape my consciousness. I sought to understand the role played by different sorts of community spaces in my daily life, and I wrestled with the experiences that constitute my sense of home under changing circumstances. At times, in my personal and professional lives, I also found myself facing states of waiting for the unknown, and I sought to discern under what circumstances I experienced time as creeping or even standing still, and why it other times it seemed to speed past.

When the covid-19 crisis broke out at the beginning of 2020, these questions became much more salient in the lives of many people in Israel and throughout the world, and were widely discussed in the media and public forums. Compulsory distancing from public spaces and severe restrictions on mobility, even if temporary and accepted as unavoidable, along with home isolation, became at least for a historical instant the lot of many. The way people experienced time also changed. Waiting for the unknown became much more concrete, and the regular flow of time around which many Westerners had arranged the fabric of their lives was severely shaken. While I completed writing this book before the crisis broke out, I continued to be preoccupied with it as it was edited and translated into English.

The challenge I set myself when I set out on this research project was to examine the rich, complex, and tragic world of German Jews under the Nazi regime, but from a new point of view. My goal was to understand these lives in contexts that would arouse interest beyond the community of scholars of the history of German Jewry, and those who study the Holocaust. I hope, therefore, that this book not only reveals new aspects of an important period in Jewish history, but also brings its readers closer to the world of the Jews it presents by conveying the way they coped—in entirely different historical circumstances, of course—with problems and challenges that we all wrestle with, especially in this current period in which we live.

The research on which this book is based had its inception in 2012, when I served on the faculty of the Schechter Institute of Jewish studies in Jerusalem. That same year, the Center for Research on the Holocaust in Germany, which I have headed since then, was established at Yad Vashem. During my initial years of work on this project, I also served as the director of research at the Leo Baeck Institute for the Study of German-Jewish History and Culture in Jerusalem. I am grateful to all three of these institutions, each one of which, in its own fashion, provided me with a base and support for this study.

The inspiration to address the theoretic issues of space and time, and to apply them to the world of German Jews under the Nazi regime, came largely from my long tenure as a fellow of the Van Leer Jerusalem Institute library. Working there daily, and especially engaging in ongoing dialogue there with researchers in a broad range of social and cultural sciences, provided me with an intellectual base for examining the world of German Jews from a new point of view.

In October 2014 I commenced my work in the faculty of the Department of History, Philosophy, and Judaic Studies at the Open University of Israel, which has been my academic home ever since. The university's Research Authority, under the direction of Daphna Tisch Idelson, was of great assistance in helping me submit a request for the Israel Science Foundation grant that I benefited from in the years 2015 to 2018 (grant 372/15). This generous award enabled me to move my research forward during the hectic years in which I served as department chair. The Open University served then as, and continues today to be, a place of lively and supportive academic dialogue. My conversations with my colleagues, historians and social and cultural scientists from various departments, have enriched my knowledge daily.

During my research work I was assisted by colleagues and friends who gave of their time and wisdom. I first want to thank Judith Siepmann, my research assistant, who worked with me in collecting and analyzing my sources. For close to three years, Judith invested her best energy and time in poring over press clippings, diaries, and documents. It is thanks to her keen eye for important material and her precise understanding of my research needs that I was able to include such a wide range of voices in this book and analyze them in depth.

Nomi Halpern, my colleague at Yad Vashem's Center for Research on the Holocaust in Germany, was of great assistance in collecting sources, and at times also in deciphering them. Ofer Ashkenazi, director of the Richard Koebner Minerva Center for German History at the Hebrew University of Jerusalem, read my manuscript more than once and helped me improve it. He also furthered its publication in Hebrew as part of the Koebner Center's series at the Hebrew University's Magnes Press, in cooperation with Yad Vashem. Another reader of the entire manuscript was Maya Lahat-Kerman, whose sensitive suggestions and corrections aided me considerably in producing the final version. The encouragement and support I received from Maya during the writing itself was instrumental in enabling me to complete the manuscript before I took up the post of vice president for academic affairs of the Open University in October 2019.

I also want to thank, in alphabetical order, other colleagues and friends from whose support and attention I benefited, whether from their critical eye, from conversations that gave me inspiration, or in any other way: Doron Avraham, Jay R. Berkovitz, Yaakov Borut, Tami Chapnik, Havi Dreifuss, Birgit R. Erdle, Tovi Fenster, Daniel Fraenkel, Wolf Gruner, Dana Kaplan, Adam Klin-Oron, Christoph Kerutzmüller, Ishay Landa, Rachel Livne Freudenthal, Shira Miron, the late Boaz Neumann, Inbal Ofer, Orr Scharf, David Silberklang, and Varda Wasserman.

Parts of this study were presented at research workshops and conferences in Israel and elsewhere. In each case I benefited from discussion, which helped me extend my examination and give it a firm foundation in my research questions and findings. The International Institute for Holocaust Research at Yad Vashem made it possible several times for me to lecture on aspects of my work; for this I am grateful to its head, Dan Michman, and to its director, Iael Nidam-Orvieto. Other parts of this work were presented in the History, Philosophy, and Judaic Studies Department of the Open University of Israel. I also want to thank my translator, Haim Watzman, for his careful and professional work, which has enabled me to present my research findings in English in the best possible way. His precision was also led me to a better understanding of some of the passages I quote in the book, and to more careful formulation of my arguments. Further thanks go to the professional team at the University of Chicago Press: Kyle Wagner, Kristin Rawlings, and Renaldo Migaldi.

Finally, I need to thank my beloved family: my four children, Shira, Noa, Itamar, and Neta, and my sons-in-law, Udi and Amir, as well as my partner, Shoshana, and her children, Yotam and Miryam, who were at my side throughout my research and writing. Each one of them helped in their own way to imbue my life with meaning outside this study. I am also lucky that my beloved parents, Yaakov and Carmela, have continued to guide and support me in my studies over the years. I dedicate this book to them.

Notes

Introduction

1. "Rosch-Haschana-Wünsche der Reichsvertretung der Juden in Deutschland," *Israelitisches Familienblatt*, September 2, 1937.

2. Boaz Neumann, *Being-in-the-World: German Worlds at the Turn of the 20th Century* [in Hebrew] (Tel Aviv: Am Oved, 2014). A similar claim has recently been made by A. R. P. Fryxell, "Time and the Modern: Current Trends in the History of Modern Temporalities," *Past and Present* 243, no. 1 (May 2019): 296.

3. Examples of this literature: Abraham Barkai and Paul Mendes-Flohr, *Renewal and Destruction: 1918–1945*, vol. 4 in Michael Meyer, ed., *German-Jewish History in Modern Times* (New York: Columbia University Press, 1998); Abraham Margaliot and Yehoyakim Cochavi, eds., *History of the Holocaust: Germany* [in Hebrew, 2 volumes] (Jerusalem: Yad Vashen, 1998); Arnold Paucker, ed., *The Jews in Nazi Germany 1933–1943* (Tübingen, Germany: J. C. B. Mohr, 1986); Wolfgang Benz, *Die Juden in Deutschland, 1933–1945: Leben unter nationalsozialistischer Herrschaft* (Munich: C. H. Beck, 1988); Otto Dov Kulka, ed., *Deutsches Judentum unter dem Nationalsozalismus*, vol. 1 (Tübingen, Germany: Mohr Siebeck, 1997); Rivka Elkin, *The Heart Beats On: Continuity and Change in Social Work and Welfare Activities of German Jews under the Nazi Regime, 1933–1945* [in Hebrew] (Jerusalem: Yad Vashem, 2004); Moshe Zimmermann, *Die deutschen Juden 1914–1945* (Berlin: Oldenbourg Wissenschaftsverlag, 2010).

4. Marion A. Kaplan, *Between Dignity and Despair: Jewish Life in Nazi Germany* (New York: Oxford University Press, 1998); Saul Friedländer, *Nazi Germany and the Jews, Vol. 1: The Years of Persecution 1933–1939* (New York: Harper & Collins, 1997).

5. Trude Maurer, "From Everyday Life to a State of Emergency: Jews in Weimar and Nazi Germany," in Marion Kaplan, ed., *Jewish Daily Life in Germany 1618–1945* (New York: Oxford University Press, 2005), pp. 271–373; Wolf Gruner, "Defiance and Protest: A Comparative Micro-Historical Re-Evaluation of Individual Jewish Responses towards Nazi Persecution," in Claire Zalc and Tal Bruttmann, eds., *Microhistories of the Holocaust* (New York: Berghahn, 2017), pp. 209–26.

6. Alon Confino, *A World without Jews: Nazi Imagination from Persecution to Genocide* (New Haven, CT: Yale University Press, 2014). For further examples of cultural his-

tory in the field, see Leora Auslander, "'Jewish Taste'? Jews and the Aesthetics of Everyday Life in Paris and Berlin, 1933–1942," in Rudy Koshar, ed., *Histories of Leisure* (Oxford, UK, and New York: Berg, 2002), pp. 299–318; Joachim Schlör, "'Take Down Mezuzahs, Remove Name-Plates': The Emigration of Objects from Germany to Palestine," in Simone J. Bronner, ed., *Jewish Cultural Studies, Vol. 1, Jewishness: Expression, Identity, and Representation* (Oxford, UK, and Portland, OR: Littman Library of Jewish Civilization, 2008), pp. 133–50.

7. Henri Lefebvre, *The Production of Space* (Oxford, UK: Blackwell, 1991).

8. Edward W. Soja, *Postmodern Geographies: The Reassertion of Space in Critical Social Theory* (London and New York: Verso, 1989) was his essential work on the subject. See also his reflective discussion of his professional identity, his research enterprise, and the range of his influence on the Spatial Turn, including in the field of Jewish history: Edward W. Soja, "Taking Space Personally," in Barney Warf and Santa Arias, eds., *The Spatial Turn: Interdisciplinary Perspectives* (London and New York: Routledge, 2009), pp. 11–35.

9. Anna Lipphardt, Julia Brauch and Alexandra Nocke, "Exploring Jewish Space: An Approach," in Lipphardt, Brauch, and Nocke, eds., *Jewish Topographies: Visions of Space, Traditions of Place* (Aldershot, UK, and Burlington, VT: Ashgate, 2008); Simone Lässig and Miriam Rürup, eds., *Space and Spatiality in Modern German Jewish History* (New York and Oxford, UK: Berghahn, 2017).

10. Norbert Elias, *Time: An Essay* (Oxford, UK, and Cambridge, MA: B. Blackwell, 1992); Eviatar Zerubavel, *Time Maps: Collective Memory and the Social Shape of the Past* (Chicago: University of Chicago Press, 2003).

11. Gabrielle M. Spiegel, "Memory and History: Liturgical Time and Historical Time," *History and Theory* 41, no. 2 (2002), pp. 149–62; Alon Confino, "Memory as Historical Narrative and Method," in *Germany as a Culture of Remembrance: Promises and Limits of Writing History* (Chapel Hill: University of North Carolina Press, 2006), pp. 153–58.

12. See, for example, Stephen Kern, *The Culture of Time and Space, 1880–1918* (Cambridge, MA: Harvard University Press, 1983), pp. 65–88.

13. This statement follows the analysis of Jacob Katz, one of the great twentieth-century historians of the Jewish people, in his doctoral dissertation. The dissertation was approved in 1935 in Frankfurt am Main, under the Nazi regime. See Jacob Katz, *Die Entstehung der Judenassimilation in Deutschland und deren ideologie* (Darmstadt, Germany: Wissenschaftliche Buchgesellschaft, 1982). For more current studies that address this issue, see David Sorkin, *The Transformation of German Jewry 1780–1840* (New York: Oxford University Press, 1987); Simone Lässig, *Jüdische Wege ins Bürgertum: Kulturelles Kapital und sozialer Aufstieg im 19. Jahrhundert* (Göttingen, Germany: Vandenhoeck & Ruprecht, 2004); Shulamit Volkov, *Germans, Jews, and Antisemites: Trials in Emancipation* (Cambridge, UK: Cambridge University Press, 2006).

14. Steven M. Lowenstein, "The Beginning of Integration, 1780–1870," in Marion Kaplan, ed., *Jewish Daily Life in Germany 1618–1945* (New York: Oxford University Press, 2005), pp. 93–171; Marion A. Kaplan, *The Making of the Jewish Middle Class, Women, Family and Identity in Imperial Germany* (New York: Oxford University Press, 1991).

15. Wolfgang Schivelbusch, *The Railway Journey: The Industrialization of Time and Space in the 19th Century* (Berkeley: University of California Press, 1986).

16. Monika Richarz, "Demographic Developments," in Michael A. Meyer, ed., *German-Jewish History in Modern Times, Volume 3: Integration in Dispute 1871–1918* (New York: Columbia University Press, 1997), pp. 7–34.

17. On the German cultures of travel during this period, see Rudy Koshar, *German Travel Cultures* (New York: Berg, 2000); On Jewish vacations, see Kaplan, *The Making of the Jewish Middle Class*, pp. 123–26.

18. For a discussion of this in the context of cafés, see Sarah Wobick-Segev, *Homes Away from Home, Jewish Belonging in Twentieth-Century Paris, Berlin, and St. Petersburg* (Stanford, CA: Stanford University Press, 2018). In her book on Jews at spas in Germany, Mirjam Zadoff proposes the term "bourgeois experiential spaces." See Mirjam Zadoff, *Next Year in Marienbad: The Lost World of Jewish Spa Culture* (Philadelphia: University of Pennsylvania Press, 2012).

19. Kaplan, *The Making of the Jewish Middle Class*, pp. 30–35, citation p. 33. And see also Nancy R. Reagin, *Sweeping the German Nation, Domesticity and National Identity in Germany, 1870–1945* (New York: Cambridge University Press, 2007), pp. 1–109.

20. Martina Steber and Bernhard Gotto, eds., *Visions of Community in Nazi Germany: Social Engineering and Private Lives* (New York: Oxford University Press, 2014); Paolo Giaccaria and Claudio Minca, eds., *Hitler's Geographies: The Spatialities of the Third Reich* (Chicago: University of Chicago Press, 2016); Teresa Walch, "Degenerate Spaces: The Coordination of Space in Nazi Germany" (PhD diss., University of California, San Diego, 2018); Joshua Hagen and Robert C. Ostergen, *Nazi Germany: Place, Space, Architecture and Ideology* (Lanham, MD: Rowman & Littlefield, 2020).

21. Joe Perry, *Christmas in Germany: A Cultural History* (Chapel Hill: University of North Carolina Press, 2010), pp. 65–92, 139–88.

22. Ismar Schorsch, *From Text to Context: The Turn to History in Modern Judaism* (Hanover, NH: University Press of New England, 1994).

23. Lothar Kroll, *Utopie als Ideologie: Geschichtsdenken und politisches Handeln im Dritten Reich* (Paderborn, Germany: Schöningh, 1999); Christopher Clark, *Time and Power: Visions of History in German Politics, from the Thirty Years' War to the Third Reich* (Princeton, NJ: Princeton University Press, 2019), pp. 171–210.

24. Peter Fritzsche, *Life and Death in the Third Reich* (Cambridge, MA: Harvard University Press, 2008), p. 9.

25. Janosch Steuwer, *"Ein Drittes Reich, wie ich es auffasse": Politik, Gesellschaft and privates Leben in Tagebüchern 1933–1939* (Göttingen, Germany: Wallstein Verlag, 2017), pp. 82–132.

26. Amos Goldberg, *Trauma in First Person: Diary Writing during the Holocaust* (Bloomington: University of Indiana Press, 2017); See also Alexandra Garbarini, *Numbered Days: Diaries and the Holocaust* (New Haven, CT: Yale University Press, 2006).

27. For a discussion of the concept of egodocuments, see Rudolf Dekker, ed., *Egodocuments and History: Autobiographical Writing in Its Social Context since the Middle Ages* (Hilversum, Netherlands: Verloren, 2002).

28. For a survey of the Jewish press in Nazi Germany, see Herbert Freeden, *The Jewish Press in the Third Reich* (Providence, RI: Berg, 1993); Katrin Diehl, *Die jüdische Presse im Dritten Reich: Zwischen Selbstbehauptung und Fremdbestimmung* (Tübingen, Germany: M. Niemeyer, 1997).

29. Michael Nagel, *1933 as a Watershed? Form and Function of the German-Jewish Press before and after the Nazi Takeover* [in Hebrew] (Jerusalem: Yad Vashem, 2015), p. 37.

30. On the increasingly severe restrictions imposed on the Jewish press from the summer of 1935 and the intensification of the regime's linguistic violence, see Thomas Pegelow Kaplan, *The Language of Nazi Genocide: Linguistic Violence and the Struggle of Germans of Jewish Ancestry* (New York: Cambridge University Press, 2009), pp. 102–59.

Chapter 1

1. Willy Cohn, *Kein Recht, Nirgends: Tagebuch vom Untergang des Breslauer Judentums, 1933–1941*, ed. Norbert Conrads (Cologne: Böhlau, 2006), pp. 259 (entry for August 14, 1935) and 452 (entry for July 23, 1937).

2. Michael Burleigh, *The Third Reich: A New History* (New York: Hill & Wang, 2000), pp. 239–41; Boaz Neumann, *Nazi Weltanschauung: Space, Body, Language* [in Hebrew] (Haifa and Tel Aviv: University of Haifa Press, 2002), p. 142; For a comprehensive treatment of highways during the Nazi period, see Thomas Zeller, *Driving Germany: The Landscape of the German Autobahn 1930–1970* (New York: Berghahn, 2007), pp. 47–126.

3. Cohn, *Kein Recht*, p. 359 (September 27, 1936).

4. For Lefebvre's pioneering discussion of space, see Henri Lefebvre, *The Production of Space* (Oxford, UK: Blackwell, 1991).

5. Michel de Certeau, *The Practice of Everyday Life* (Berkeley: University of California Press, 1984).

6. Boaz Neumann, *Nazi Weltanschauung*, p. 138. On the Nazification of space see, for example: Hans-Jochen Gamm, *Der Braune Kult: Das Dritte Reich und seine Ersatzreligion* (Hamburg: Rütten & Loening, 1962), pp. 43–56. For an account from the Jewish perspective, see, for example, the diary of Walter Tausk of Breslau. Walter Tausk, *Breslauer Tagebuch 1933–1940*, Ryszard Kincel ed. (Berlin: Aufbau Taschenbuch, 2000), pp. 28 (February 24, 1933), 32 (March 7, 1933), and 68 (April 29, 1933).

7. Peter Fritzsche, *Life and Death in the Third Reich*, (Cambridge, MA: Harvard University Press, 2008), pp. 65–75; Janosch Steuwer, "*Ein Drittes Reich, wie ich es auffasse*": *Politik, Gesellschaft und privates Leben in Tagebüchern 1933–1939* (Göttingen, Germany: Wallstein Verlag, 2017), pp. 43–47.

8. Cohn, *Kein Recht*, pp. 149 (August 18, 1934) and 262 (August 17, 1935). For an extensive discussion of the way in which Cohn depicted the Nazification of public space in Breslau, see Anja Schnabel, *Bleiben in Breslau: Jüdische Selbstbehauptung und Sinnsuche in den Tagebüchern Willy Cohns 1933 bis 1941* (Berlin: Be.bra Wissenschaft Verlag, 2018), pp. 99–112.

9. Daniel Siemens, *Stormtroopers: A New History of Hitler's Brownshirts* (New Haven, CT: Yale University Press, 2017), pp. 123–34.

10. Jan Petersen, *Unsere Strasse: Eine Chronik, Geschrieben im Herzen des faschistischen Deutschland 1933/34* (Berlin: Dietz, 1947); Steuwer, "*Ein Drittes Reich, wie ich es auffasse*," pp. 50–52.

11. Martina Steber and Bernhard Gotto, eds., *Visions of Community in Nazi Germany: Social Engineering and Private Lives* (New York: Oxford University Press, 2014).

12. Michael Wildt, *Volksgemeinschaft als Selbstermächtigung: Gewalt gegen Juden in der deutschen Provinz 1919 bis 1939* (Hamburg: Hamburger Edition, 2007), pp. 12–13, 68. See also Teresa Walch, "With an Iron Broom: Cleansing Berlin's Bülowplatz of 'Judeo-Bolshevism,' 1933–1936," *German History* 40 (2022): 61–87.

13. Alon Confino, *A World without Jews: Nazi Imagination from Persecution to Genocide* (New Haven, CT: Yale University Press, 2014), pp. 76–87.

14. Marion A. Kaplan, *Between Dignity and Despair: Jewish Life in Nazi Germany* (New York: Oxford University Press, 1998), p. 21.

15. Siegfried Neumann, *Nacht über Deutschland: Vom Leben und Sterben einer Republik; Ein Tatsachenbericht* (Munich: List Verlag, 1978), pp. 86–87. On the practical imple-

mentation of the dejudaization of the law, see, for example, Abraham Ascher, *A Community under Siege: The Jews of Breslau under Nazism* (Stanford, CA: Stanford University Press, 2007), p. 80. On the universities of Dresden and Munich, see Victor Klemperer, *I Will Bear Witness: A Diary of the Nazi Years, 1933–1941* (New York: Modern Library, 1999), p. 10 (March 31, 1933).

16. On the theater, see Heinemann Stern, "Die Suche nach der jüdischen Kultur," in Margarete Limberg and Hubert Rübsaat, eds., *Sie Durften nicht mehr Deutsche Sein: Jüdischer Alltag in Selbstzeugnissen 1933–1938* (Frankfurt: Campus Verlag, 1990), p. 256. On the café-bakery, see Tausk, *Breslauer Tagebuch*, p. 57 (April 3, 1933); Kaplan, *Between Dignity and Despair*, p. 45.

17. On the *Kinderfest*, see Hans Winterfeldt, "Ein Kind erlebt die Ausgrenzung," in *Sie Durften nicht mehr Deutsche Sein*, p. 212. On the pharmacy, see Shlomo Wahrman, *Lest We Forget: Growing Up in Nazi Leipzig 1933–1939* (New York: Mesorah Publications, 1991), p. 62.

18. On the importance of the local nature of anti-Jewish policy, see Wolf Gruner, "Die NS-Judenverfolgung und die Kommunen: Zur wechselseitigen Dynamisierung von zentraler und lokaler Politik 1933–1941," *Vierteljahrshefte für Zeitgeschichte* 48, no. 1 (2000): 75–126.

19. Wildt, *Volksgemeinschaft als Selbstermächtigung*, pp. 138–47.

20. Christoph Kreutzmüller, Ingo Loose, and Benno Nietzel, "Nazi Persecution and Strategies for Survival: Jewish Businesses in Berlin, Frankfurt am Main, and Breslau, 1933–1942," *Yad Vashem Studies* 39, no. 1 (2011): 31–34.

21. Hans Winterfeldt, "Ein Kind erlebt die Ausgrenzung," in *Sie Durften nicht mehr Deutsche Sein*, pp. 213–15. The profound social isolation of rural Jews, who "left their homes only when absolutely necessary," was depicted in the memoirs of the Jewish educator Heinemann Stern, who contrasted it with the much more secure status of Berlin's Jews. See Heinemann Stern, "Einsam in vertrauter Umwelt," in *Sie Durften nicht mehr Deutsche Sein*, p. 173.

22. "Kleinstadt und Dorf, Wir vergessen sie nicht," *CV-Zeitung*, June 22, 1933; Q. E., "Die wichtigen zweidrittel," *CV-Zeitung*, July 12, 1934; "Die Not der Kleingemeinden," *Jüdische Rundschau*, August 25, 1933.

23. G. N., "Fahrt in die Provinz, Zur Situation der kleinen Gemeinden," *Jüdische Rundschau*, May 29, 1934.

24. Q. E., "Die wichtigen Zweidrittel," *CV-Zeitung*, July 12, 1934.

25. Cohn, *Kein Recht*, p. 290 (October 21 and 24, 1935). For a comprehensive discussion of the range of representations of space in Silesia in Cohn's diary in the 1930s, see Anja Schnabel, *Bleiben in Breslau*, pp. 125–53.

26. Victor Klemperer, *I Will Bear Witness: A Diary of the Nazi Years 1942–1945* (New York: Modern Library, 2001), p. 300 (February 28, 1944). The passages quoted from this published English translation of Klemperer's diary have been edited for accuracy and clarity.

27. Tausk, *Breslauer Tagebuch*, pp. 143–44 (March 22, 1936). Hans Reichman described in much the same way how at the end of the 1930s, Jews in Berlin were forbidden to approach any area where Hitler or Goebbels might possibly appear, out of concern that the Jews might glance at these leaders for an instant, even through a window. See Hans Reichmann, *Deutscher Bürger und verfolgter Jude: Novemberpogrom und KZ Sachsenhausen 1937–1939* (Munich: R. Oldenburg Verlag, 1998), p. 256.

28. Cohn, *Kein Recht*, p. 315 (March 22, 1936).

29. Johann Wolfgang von Goethe, *Autobiography of Goethe: Truth and Poetry Relating to My Life*, trans. John Oxenford (Auckland, New Zealand: Floating Press, 2008), p. 322.

30. Trude Maurer, "From Everyday Life to a State of Emergency: Jews in Weimar and Nazi Germany," in Marion Kaplan, ed., *Jewish Daily Life in Germany 1618–1945* (New York and Oxford, UK: Oxford University Press, 2005), p. 337; Moshe Zimmermann, *Deutsche gegen Deutsche: Das Schicksal der Juden, 1938–1945* (Berlin: Aufbau, 2008), pp. 23–55. About the concentration camps, see Kim Wünschmann, *Before Auschwitz: Jewish Prisoners in the Prewar Concentration Camps* (Cambridge, MA: Harvard University Press, 2015), pp. 196–210.

31. Alfred Wiener, "Zwischen Himmel und Erde," *CV-Zeitung*, June 1, 1933.

32. On Wiener's life, see Ben Barkow, *Alfred Wiener and the Making of the Holocaust Library* (London: Vallentine, Mitchell, 1997).

33. Julie Meyer, "Ueber dem Alltag," *CV-Zeitung*, January 25, 1934.

34. Cohn, *Kein Recht*, p. 21 (March 21, 1933).

35. Hermann Klugmann, "Wiesenbronn wird antijüdisch," in *Sie Durften nicht mehr Deutsche Sein*, pp. 150–51.

36. Marta Appel, née Insel, in Monika Richarz, ed., *Jewish Life in Germany: Memoirs from Three Centuries*, trans. Stella P. Rosenfeld and Sidney Rosenfeld (Bloomington: Indiana University Press 1991), p. 352.

37. Frieda Hirsch, *Mein Weg von Karlsruhe über Heidelberg nach Haifa 1890–1965* (Israel: n.p., 1965), p. 135. On this, see Guy Miron, *German Jews in Israel: Memories and Past Images* [In Hebrew] (Jerusalem: Hebrew University Magnes Press, 2004), p. 102.

38. *Das Tagebuch der Hertha Nathorff*, ed. Wolfgang Benz (Munich: R. Oldenbourg, 1987), p. 46 (July 6, 1933).

39. Benedict Anderson, *Imagined Communities: Reflections on the Origin and Spread of Nationalism* (London and New York: Verso, 1991), p. 62.

40. Klemperer, *I Will Bear Witness, 1933–1941*, pp. 126 (June 11, 1935) and 131–32 (September 16, 1935). Citation from September 1935.

41. Reichmann, *Deutscher Bürger und verfolgter Jude*, p. 261.

42. Kurt F. Rosenberg, *"Einer, der nicht mehr dazugehört": Tagebücher 1933–1937*, ed. Beate Meyer and Björn Siegel (Göttingen, Germany: Wallstein Verlag, 2012), p. 144 (September 6, 1933).

43. Klemperer, *I Will Bear Witness, 1933–1941*, p. 52 (January 27, 1934).

44. Cohn, *Kein Recht*, p. 134 (July 5, 1934).

45. Victor Klemperer, *Ich will Zeugnis ablegen bis zum letzten: Tagebücher 1933–1941* (Berlin: Aufbau-Verlag, 1995), p. 73 (December 15, 1933). This citation does not appear in the English translation.

46. See for example: Klemperer, *I Will Bear Witness, 1933–1941*, p. 352 (August 11, 1940: "closely confined"); *Klemperer, I Will Bear Witness, 1942–1945*, p. 213 (April 16, 1943: "more and more constraining"). On the experience of contracting living space (*Lebensraum*), see also Ernst Marcus, "Der Spielraum wird immer kleiner," in *Sie Durften nicht mehr Deutsche Sein*, p. 192.

47. Rosenberg, *Einer*, p. 293 (May 17, 1935).

48. Cohn, *Kein Recht*, p. 175 (November 6, 1934).

49. Cohn, *Kein Recht*, p. 259 (August 14, 1935); see also p. 452 (July 23, 1937).

50. Georg Simmel, "Metropolis and Mental Life," in David Frisby and Mike Featherstone, eds., *Simmel on Culture: Selected Writings* (London and Thousand Oaks, CA: Sage Publications, 1997), pp. 174–86.

51. Cohn, *Kein Recht,* p. 274 (September 12, 1935).

52. *Das Tagebuch der Hertha Nathorff,* p. 72 (August 30, 1935).

53. *Das Tagebuch der Hertha Nathorff,* p. 86 (August 8, 1936).

54. *Das Tagebuch der Hertha Nathorff,* pp. 89 (November 10, 1936) and 91 (Christmas, 1936).

55. *Das Tagebuch der Hertha Nathorff,* p. 117 (October 13, 1938).

56. *Das Tagebuch der Hertha Nathorff,* pp. 84 (June 12, 1936) and 140 (December 17, 1938). On the experience of the Berlin space in Nathorff's diary, see also Moritz Föllmer, *Individuality and Modernity in Berlin: Self and Society from Weimar to the Wall* (Cambridge, UK: Cambridge University Press, 2013), p. 136.

57. Kerstin Schoor, "Die Stadt als Un-Ort: Literarische Bilder Berlins als Paradigma literarischer Entwicklungen nach 1933," in *Vom literarischen Zentrum zum literarischen Ghetto* (Göttingen, Germany: Wallstein Verlag, 2010), pp. 299–366.

58. Meta Samson, *Spatz macht sich,* 2nd ed. (Berlin: Altberliner Verlag, 1990) [1st ed.: 1938].

59. Jana Mikota, "Jüdische Schriftstellerinnen—wieder entdeckt: 'Sollte sich Spatz nun freuen oder traurig sein, daß die großen Geschwister so weit fort waren?' Die Schriftstellerin, Journalistin und Pädagogin Meta Samson," *Medaon* 6 (2010): 1–7.

60. The quote is from Cohn, *Kein Recht,* p. 538 (November 11, 1938); the concept "*Stubenarrest*" appears there on p. 541 (November 13, 1938). For a description of taking in air by a window, see p. 544 (November 14, 1938).

61. Cohn, *Kein Recht,* p. 571 (December 22, 1938).

62. Reichmann, *Deutscher Bürger und verfolgter Jude,* p. 279.

63. On the curfew, see Maurer, "From Everyday Life to a State of Emergency," p. 360; Kaplan, *Between Dignity and Despair,* p. 150.

64. Klemperer, *I Will Bear Witness, 1933–1941,* p. 361 (November 11, 1940).

65. Klemperer, *I Will Bear Witness, 1933–1941,* pp. 432–34 (September 17, 18, and 19, 1941). See also in this context Zimmermann, *Deutsche gegen Deutsche,* pp. 97–98. A *Judenhaus* was a Jewish-owned dwelling, exclusively for Jewish tenants and subletters.

66. Klemperer, *I Will Bear Witness, 1933–1941,* p. 456 (December 31, 1941).

67. Klemperer, *I Will Bear Witness, 1942–1945,* p. 5 (January 12, 1942).

68. "War Diary, 1939–1942" of Philipp Manes, WL (Wiener Library, London), doc. 1346, box 10 4.5a, pp. 168 (September 19, 1941) and 168–69 (September 21, 1941).

69. Elisabeth Block, *Erinnerungszeichen: Die Tagebücher der Elisabeth Block* (Augsburg, Germany: Bayerische Staatskanzlei, 1993), p. 253 (September 21, 1941).

70. Block, *Erinnerungszeichen,* p. 256 (October 26, 1941).

71. For a description of his removal of the yellow star, see Klemperer, *I Will Bear Witness, 1942–1945,* p. 415 (February 19, 1945).

72. On *amidah* and defiance, see Yehuda Bauer, *Rethinking the Holocaust* (New Haven, CT, and London: Yale University Press, 2001), pp. 119–66; Wolf Gruner, "Defiance and Protest. A Comparative Micro-Historical Re-evaluation of Individual Jewish Responses towards Nazi Persecution," in *Microhistories of the Holocaust,* ed. Claire Zalc and Tal Bruttmann (New York: Berghahn, 2017), pp. 209–26.

73. S. N., "Alltag und Epoche, Eine tröstliche Erscheinung," *Jüdische Rundschau,* February 24, 1933.

74. Tausk, *Breslauer Tagebuch,* p. 38 (March 13, 1933). And see also his similar account of entering Jewish businesses that had been blockaded during the economic boycott of April 1933: Tausk, *Breslauer Tagebuch,* pp. 52–56 (April 1, 1933). For another account of a

struggle to the courts during this period, see Karl Friedländer, "Ich galt nicht mehr als Frontkämpfer," (pp. 69–74), in *Sie Durften nicht mehr Deutsche Sein.*

75. Tausk, *Breslauer Tagebuch*, pp. 68–70 (April 29, 1933).

76. Gerta Pfeffer, "Ich hätte gerne mitgetanzt" (pp. 140–42), in *Sie Durften nicht mehr Deutsche Sein.*

77. Mirjam Zadoff, *Next Year in Marienbad, The Lost World of Jewish Spa Culture* (Philadelphia: University of Pennsylvania Press, 2012).

78. In this context, with regard to cafés, see Sarah Wobick-Segev, "Buying, Selling, Being, Drinking; or, How the Coffeehouse Became a Site for the Consumption of New Jewish Modalities of Belonging," in Gideon Reuveni and Sarah Wobick-Segev, eds., *The Economy in Jewish History: New Perspectives on the Interrelationship between Ethnicity and Economic Life* (New York: Berghahn Books, 2011), pp. 115–18.

79. Klemperer, *I Will Bear Witness, 1933–1941*, p. 8 (March 20, 1933).

80. Klemperer, *I Will Bear Witness, 1933–1941*, pp. 230 (July 19, 1937) and 238–39 (October 9, 1937).

81. *Das Tagebuch der Hertha Nathorff*, p. 70 (March 12, 1935).

82. Cäcilie Lewissohn, "Ich könnte immerzu heulen über die Aussichtlosigkeit, hier je wegzukommen," in Angela Martin, Claudia Schoppmann, eds., *"Ich fürchte die Menschen mehr als die Bomben": Aus den Tagebüchern von drei Berliner Frauen 1938–1946* (Berlin: Metropol, 1996), pp. 78–79 (November 1, 1943), 82 (November 15, 1943), 90 (January 1, 1944), 91 (January 25, 1944), and 94 (February 6, 1944).

83. Klemperer, *I Will Bear Witness, 1933–1941*, pp. 230 (July 19, 1937) and 238–39 (October 9, 1937).

84. Marion A. Kaplan, *The Making of the Jewish Middle Class, Women, Family and Identity in Imperial Germany* (New York: Oxford University Press, 1991), pp. 123–26. On the German bourgeois culture of travel which was developed during the nineteenth century, see Rudy Koshar, *German Travel Cultures* (Oxford, UK, and New York: Berg, 2000), pp. 19–64.

85. Marion A. Kaplan, *Between Dignity and Despair*, p. 52.

86. Siegfried Neumann, *Nacht über Deutschland: Vom Leben und Sterben einer Republik; ein Tatsachenbericht* (Munich: Paul List Verlag, 1978), pp. 95–96.

87. See, for example, Rosenberg, *Einer*, pp. 126 (June 25, 1933) and 128 (August 7, 1933).

88. Erich Seligmann, entry for August 23, 1937, in Diary II of Erich Seligmann (1908–38), Erich Seligmann Collection, AR 4104, box 1, folder 1, Leo Baeck Institute.

89. The subject comes up a number of times in Seligmann's diary. See, for example, entries for August 4, 1936 (the rope tightening); April 26, 1937; May 24, 1937; December 24, 1937; and February 4,1938, in Diary II of Erich Seligmann (1908–38), Erich Seligmann Collection, AR 4104, box 1, folder 1, Leo Baeck Institute.

90. "On 9 September 1935 the Gestapo Central Office Outlines to Reich Minister Walter Darré Its Own Proposals for the 'Solution of the Jewish Question," in Wolf Gruner, ed., *The Persecution and Murder of the European Jews by Nazi Germany* (hereafter *PMJ*), *Vol. 1, German Reich 1933–1937* (Berlin and Boston: Walter de Gruyter, 2019) doc. 195, pp. 515–16.

91. On Jewish resorts in Germany, see "Wohnt in jüdischen Hotels!" *Gemeindeblatt der israelitischen Religionsgemeinde zu Leipzig*, July 7, 1933; Joseph Carlebach, "Besucht jüdische Gaststätten!" *Israelitisches Familienblat*, June 21, 1934; W., "Der jüdische Hotelier," *Israelitisches Familienblat*, November 18, 1937.

92. Arno Herzberg: "Urlaub vom Alltag," in "Ferien! Beilage des Israelitischen Familienblattes für die Reisezeit," *Israelitisches Familienblatt*, June 25, 1936.

93. Eduard Schreiber, "Ferienreisen einst und jetzt," *Frankfurter israelitisches Gemeindeblatt* 11 (August 1936): 414–15.

94. For a more comprehensive discussion of vacations in the world of German Jews during this period, see Ofer Ashkenazi and Guy Miron, "Jewish Vacations in Nazi Germany: Reflections on Time and Space amid an Unlikely Respite," *Jewish Quarterly Review* 110, no. 3 (Summer 2020): 523–52.

95. Klemperer, *I Will Bear Witness, 1933–1941*, pp. 142–43 (December 31, 1935).

96. Klemperer, *I Will Bear Witness, 1933–1941*, p. 149 (January 24, 1936).

97. Klemperer, *I Will Bear Witness, 1933–1941*, p. 141 (December 31, 1935).

98. Koshar, *German Travel Cultures*, pp. 116–21. For an account of the different characterization of the automobile culture in different European cultures, see Rudy Koshar, "Cars and Nations: Anglo-German Perspectives on Automobility between the World Wars," *Theory, Culture & Society* 21, no. 4/5 (August-October 2004): 121–44.

99. Such advertisements were especially prominent in the Zionist newspaper, *Jüdische Rundschau*. See, for example, April 17, 1935 (p. 57); May 10, 1935 (p. 14); December 6, 1935 (p. 25).

100. Vera Craener, "Schofföre für die Welt, Internationaler Führerschein—stark gefragt," *Israelitisches Familienblatt*, February 18, 1937.

101. Friedrich Solon, "Ein 'jüdischer' Auffahrunfall," in *Sie Durften nicht mehr Deutsche Sein*, p. 175.

102. Alexnader Szanto, in Monika Richarz, ed., *Jewish Life in Germany: Memoirs from Three Centuries*, trans. Stella P. Rosenfeld and Sidney Rosenfeld (Bloomington: Indiana University Press, 1991), p. 347.

103. "On 27 December 1934 the Gestapo Central Office dissolves the Association of German Motor Car Owners for having Jewish members," *PMJ*, vol. 1, doc. 148, p. 419, note 4. On Auto-Club 1927, see also Landesarchiv Berlin, rep. 342, no. 26806. A copy of this file is in the Yad Vashem Archives, M.55/JM.16908.

104. Klemperer, *I Will Bear Witness, 1933–1941*, p. 166 (May 21, 1936). The English version's translation of the second phrase misses the mark; see Klemperer, *Ich will Zeugnis*, p. 266.

105. On his driving experiences, see *I Will Bear Witness, 1933–1941*, pp. 161–62 (April 28, 1936) and 164 (May 16, 1936). On refraining from trips in order to save fuel, see p. 193 (October 4, 1936). On the trip to Berlin, see pp. 218–23 (May 22, 1937).

106. Tim Dant, "The Driver-Car," *Theory, Culture & Society* 21, no. 4/5 (August-October 2004): 61–79. See also Mimi Sheller, "Automotive Emotions: Feeling the Car," *Theory, Culture & Society* 21, no. 4/5 (August-October 2004): 221–42.

107. On the trip to Kipsdorf, see Klemperer, *I Will Bear Witness, 1933–1941*, p. 166 (May 24, 1936). On the trip on the Autobahn, see pp. 193–94 (October 4, 1936). For Klemperer's account of the roadside restaurant (Long Distance Lorry Drivers' Restaurant), see p. 267 (September 11, 1938).

108. Klemperer, *I Will Bear Witness, 1933–1941*, p. 158 (March 31, 1936).

109. "The wine exporter Frederick Weil from Frankfurt travels through Germany in the early summer of 1938," document 54, in Susanne Heim, ed., *The Persecution and Murder of the European Jews by Nazi Germany (PMJ), 1933–1945, vol. 2, German Reich 1938–August 1939* (Berlin and Boston: Walter de Gruyter, 2019), pp. 202–7; here p. 203.

110. Marion A. Kaplan, *Between Dignity and Despair*, p. 120.

111. "On 20 July 1938 Berlin's chief of police issues guidelines for the discrimination against Jews," *PMJ*, vol. 2, doc. 68, pp. 237–46; here p. 242.

112. "On 25 August 1938 the situation of Jews in Germany is summed up in a report to the American Jewish Joint Distribution Committee," *PMJ* vol. 2, doc. 88, pp. 277–81; here p. 280.

113. For these two incidents, see Friedrich Solon, "Ein 'jüdischer' Auffahrunfall,'" in *Sie Durften nicht mehr Deutsche Sein*, pp. 175–76; Arthur Samuel, "Weiteres Unheil nach der Entlassung," in *Sie Durften nicht mehr Deutsche Sein*, pp. 318–19.

114. The Jüdischer Auto-Club was disbanded on the orders of the regime a few days following the November pogrom. See: "The Times, 15 November 1938: Article on the Situation of the Jews in the Reich," *PMJ* vol. 2, doc. 155, p. 458.

115. Klemperer, *I Will Bear Witness, 1933–1941*, pp. 279 (December 6, 1938) and 284 (New Year's Eve, 1938).

116. Klemperer, *I Will Bear Witness, 1942–1945*, pp. 14 (February 15, 1942), 49 (May 8, 1942), and 213 (April 16, 1943).

117. Peter Gay, *The Bourgeois Experience: Victoria to Freud*, vol. 2, *The Tender Passion*, (New York and Oxford, UK: Oxford University Press, 1986), pp. 145–46.

118. See, for example, Cohn, *Kein Recht*, pp. 41 (May 7, 1933), 108–9 (November 30, 1933), 266 (August 26, 1935), and 461 (August 24, 1937); Klemperer, *I Will Bear Witness, 1933–1941*, p. 133 (September 16, 1935). Others, during the early years of the regime, experienced museums as neutral spaces immune from Nazification, and as islands of sanity. Kurt Rosenberg of Hamburg recounted in his diary how, during his visit to the Kaiser Friedrich (today Bode) Museum in Berlin, he experienced a sense of "inner completeness" notably different from the increasing alienation he felt in the city's streets. See Rosenberg, *Einer*, p. 196 (May 21, 1934).

119. Klemperer, *I Will Bear Witness, 1933–1941*, pp. 194 (October 9, 1936) and 199 (October 18, 1936).

120. Klemperer, *I Will Bear Witness, 1933–1941*, pp. 277–78 (December 3, 1938); Cohn, *Kein Recht*, p. 586 (January 15, 1939); Reichmann, *Deutscher Bürger und verfolgter Jude*, p. 83.

121. On labor and work in Arendt's thinking, see Hannah Arendt, *The Human Condition*, (Chicago: University of Chicago Press, 1998), chapters 3 and 4 (pp. 79–174).

122. Cohn, *Kein Recht*, pp. 601 (February 7, 1939) and 604 (February 14, 1939).

123. Cohn, *Kein Recht*, pp. 650 (June 1, 1939) and 657 (June 18, 1939).

124. For these quotes, see Cohn, *Kein Recht*, pp. 652 (June 5, 1939) and 653 (June 6, 1939).

125. Cohn, *Kein Recht*, p. 918 (March 21, 1941).

126. For the quote, see Cohn, *Kein Recht*, p. 883 (December 23, 1940). See also pp. 707 (October 19, 1939) and 856 (October 7, 1940). For Cohn's characterization of the "sleepy institution," see p. 739 (January 4, 1940). Cohn's daily visit to his barber also provided an opportunity for human contact with "Aryans" and exposure to current information and the mood of non-Jewish society. See, for example, pp. 743 (January 18, 1940), 766–67 (March 16, 1940), and 787 (April 30, 1940).

127. On the lending library, see Cohn, *Kein Recht*, p. 874 (November 28, 1940). On his use of others to check books out of the university library, see p. 754 (February 13, 1940).

128. Klemperer, *I Will Bear Witness, 1933–1941*, p. 280 (December 6, 1938).

129. Klemperer, *I Will Bear Witness, 1933–1941*, p. 442 (October 31, 1941).

130. Klemperer, *I Will Bear Witness, 1942–1945*, p. 30 (March 17, 1942).

131. For the quote on Klemperer's dependency on books, see Klemperer, *I Will Bear Witness, 1942–1945*, p. 33 (March 24, 1942). On his anxiety about the sense of emptiness, see p. 75 (June 12, 1942). On his attempt to access the Jewish community's library, see p. 54

(May 18, 1942). On the Lending Library, see pp. 72–73 (June 11, 1942) and 126 (August 19, 1942). On libraries of deportees, see p. 120 (10 and 11 August, 1942).

132. Cohn, *Kein Recht*, pp. 812 (June 23, 1940), 813 (June 27, 1940), and 817 (July 9, 1940). On nature walks as a response to an inner need for space and the search for sights not marked "prohibited to Jews," see also Martin Andermann, "Das Schreckliche war auch faszinierend," in *Sie Durften nicht mehr Deutsche Sein*, p. 167.

133. Klemperer, *I Will Bear Witness, 1933–1941*, p. 354 (August 30, 1940).

134. Klemperer, *I Will Bear Witness, 1933–1941*, p. 366 (December 31, 1940). See also p. 358 (October 14, 1940), where he describes how Eva felt that these long walks were "the only thing she has left."

135. Franz Hessel, *Walking in Berlin: A Flaneur in the Capital* (Cambridge, MA: MIT Press, 2017); Walter Benjamin, "The Flaneur's Return," in *Selected Writings, Vol. 2* (Cambridge, MA: Harvard University Press, 2005), pp. 262–67.

136. Elisabeth Freund, *Als Zwangsarbeiterin 1941 in Berlin: Die Aufzeichnungen der Volkswirtin Elisabeth Freund*, ed. and annotated Carola Sachse (Berlin: Akademie Verlag, 1996).

137. Freund, *Als Zwangsarbeiterin 1941 in Berlin*, p. 81.

138. Freund, *Als Zwangsarbeiterin 1941 in Berlin*, p. 95. And see a more comprehensive account of Freund's writing in Moritz Föllmer, *Individuality and Modernity in Berlin*, pp. 148–51.

139. On the tension between these trends, see Philipp Nielsen, *Between Heimat and Hatred: Jews and the Right in Germany 1871–1935* (New York: Oxford University Press, 2019).

140. Thomas Lekan, *Imagining the Nation in Nature: Landscape Preservation and German Identity 1885–1945* (Cambridge, MA: Harvard University Press, 2004), pp. 153–203.

141. Michael Imort, " 'Eternal Forest—Eternal Volk': The Rhetoric and Reality of National Socialist Forest Policy," in Thomas Zeller, Franz-Josef Brüggemeier, and Mark Cioc, eds., *How Green Were the Nazis? Nature, Environment, and Nation in the Third Reich*, (Athens: Ohio University Press, 2005), pp. 43–72.

142. Thomas Zeller, *Driving Germany*, pp. 79–179.

143. "Helft der Jugend wandern!" *CV-Zeitung*, June 15, 1933.

144. Joachim Michael Meyer, stud. jura. The comment appeared without a headline as one of the responses to the article "Helft der Jugend wandern!" *CV-Zeitung*, June 15, 1933.

145. Hans Lamm, "Schafft jüdische Jugendherbergen!" *Israelitisches Familienblatt*, September 14, 1933.

146. Andreas Paetz and Karin Weiss, eds., *"Hachschara": Die Vorbereitung junger Juden auf die Auswanderung nach Palästina* (Potsdam, Germany: Verlag für Berlin-Brandenburg, 1999).

147. Rosenberg, *Einer*, p. 110 (May 27, 1933).

148. Rosenberg, *Einer*, p. 189 (May 1, 1934).

149. Cohn, *Kein Recht*, pp. 59 (July 10, 1933) and 62 (July 22, 1933); Klemperer, *I Will Bear Witness, 1933–1941*, p. 264 (August 24, 1938).

150. Rosenberg, *Einer*, pp. 293–94 (July 23, 1935).

151. See, for example, Rosenberg, *Einer*, p. 372 (November 6, 1936). Similar feelings of alienation and distance from beloved landscapes and natural sites appear also in the diaries of Willy Cohn and Victor Klemperer. See, for example, Cohn, *Kein Recht*, pp. 154 (September 5, 1934), 219 (April 28, 1935), and 287 (October 10, 1935); Klemperer, *I Will Bear Witness, 1933–1941*, p. 264 (August 24, 1938).

152. Joachim Prinz, *Wir Juden* (Berlin: E. Reiss, 1934). On Prinz's book and the controversy it aroused, see Guy Miron, *The Waning of the Emancipation: Jewish History, Memory, and the Rise of Fascism in Germany, France, and Hungary* (Detroit: Wayne State University Press, 2011), pp. 34–45.

153. Joachim Prinz, "Das Leben ohne Nachbarn: Versuch einer ersten Analyse," *Jüdische Rundschau*, April 17, 1935. English translation in *PMJ*, vol. 1, doc 161, pp. 451–54 (citation from p. 452).

154. Prinz, "Das Leben ohne Nachbarn," *PMJ*, vol. 1, p. 453.

155. Letter from July 23, 1939 in Martha Wertheimer, *In mich ist die große dunkle Ruhe gekommen, Briefe an Siegfried Guggenheim* (Frankfurt am Main: Arbeitsstelle zur Vorbereitung des Frankfurter Lern- und Dokumentationszentrum des Holocaust, 1993), p. 9.

156. Peter Miesbeck, "Einführung," in Elisabeth Block, *Erinnerungszeichen*, pp. 42–46.

157. See, for example, Gertrud Kolmar: *Briefe*, ed. Johanna Woltmann (Göttingen, Germany: Wallstein Verlag, 2014), pp. 127 (November 9, 1941), 154 (April 27 1942), and 161 (May 19, 1942).

158. Gertrud Kolmar: *Briefe*, pp. 196 (January 10, 1943) and 203 (February 20/21, 1943).

159. Harold M. Proshansky, Abbe K. Fabian, and Robert Kaminoff, "Place-Identity: Physical World Socialization of the Self," *Journal of Environmental Psychology* 3 (1983): 57–83.

160. Moritz Föllmer, *Individuality and Modernity in Berlin*, p. 136.

161. Moritz Föllmer, *Individuality and Modernity in Berlin*, pp. 7, 145, 150.

Chapter 2

1. *C. V. Wegweiser durch Berlin: Stadtplan mit Abbildungen jüdischer Einrichtungen und Gebäude aus der jüdischen Geschichte der Stadt Berlin* (Berlin: C. V., 1937). The Central Association of German Citizens of the Jewish Faith, established in 1893, was compelled, in the wake of the Nuremberg Laws and pressure from the regime, to change its name to the Central Association of Jews in Germany.

2. Heinz Berggrün: "C.V. Wegweiser durch Berlin," *CV-Zeitung*, January 28, 1937.

3. Karl Schlögel, *In Space We Read Time: On the History of Civilization and Geopolitics* (New York: Bard Graduate Center, 2016), pp. 56–79.

4. Jacob Borut, "Struggles for Spaces: Where Could Jews Spend Free Time in Nazi Germany?" *Leo Baeck Institute Year Book* 56 (2011): 307–50. On the authorities' demand that Jewish activity in the German space be unseen, see p. 340.

5. Yi-Fu Tuan, *Space and Place: The Perspective of Experience* (Minneapolis: University of Minnesota Press, 2001).

6. Borut, "Struggles for Spaces," p. 309.

7. Simone Lässig and Miriam Rürup, "Introduction: What Made a Space 'Jewish'? Reconsidering a Category of Modern German History," in Lässig and Rürup, eds., *Space and Spatiality in Modern German Jewish History* (New York and Oxford, UK: Berghahn, 2017), pp. 1–20.

8. Mordechai Breuer and Michael Graetz, *Tradition and Enlightenment: 1600–1780*, vol. 1, Michael Meyer, ed., *German-Jewish History in Modern Times* (New York: Columbia University Press, 1996), pp. 172–73; Jacob Katz, *Tradition and Crisis: Jewish Society at the End of the Middle Ages* (New York: Schoken Books, 1971), pp. 179–80; Samuel Krauss, *History of Jewish Houses of Prayer* [in Hebrew] (New York: Ogen, 1955), pp. 302–16.

9. Michael Meyer, "'How Awesome Is This Place!' The Reconceptualization of the Synagogue in Nineteenth-Century Germany," *Leo Baeck Institute Year Book* 41 (1996): 51–63, esp. 59.

10. On the difficulty that synagogues, especially liberal ones, had in creating an active community experience and attracting worshippers, which reached its height during the Weimar Republic, see Paul Mendes-Flohr, "Jewish Cultural and Spiritual Life," in Abraham Barkai and Paul Mendes-Flohr, *Renewal and Destruction: 1918–1945*, vol. 4 in Michael Meyer, ed., *German-Jewish History in Modern Times* (New York: Columbia University Press 1998), pp. 152–53.

11. Andreas Gotzmann, "Out of the Ghetto, into the Middle Class: Changing Perspectives on Jewish Spaces in Nineteenth-Century Germany; The Case of Synagogues and Jewish Burial Grounds," in Lässig and Rürup, eds., *Space and Spatiality in Modern German Jewish History*, pp. 44–149. See also Saskia Coenen Snyder, *Building a Public Judaism: Synagogues and Jewish Identity in Nineteenth-Century Europe* (Cambridge, MA: Harvard University Press, 2013).

12. Citation from Willy Cohn, *Kein Recht, Nirgends: Tagebuch vom Untergang des Breslauer Judentums, 1933–1941*, ed. Norbert Conrads, (Cologne: Böhlau, 2006), p. 75 (September 9, 1933). See also p. 55 (June 24, 1933).

13. Cohn, *Kein Recht*, p. 55 (June 24, 1933).

14. Cohn, *Kein Recht*, pp. 75 (September 9, 1933) and 20 (March 20, 1933)

15. Suzanne Auerbach, "Konzert in der Synagoge," poem in *Blätter des Jüdischen Frauenbundes*, 11 (November 1933). A similar feeling of escaping from everyday tribulations into the warm intimacy of the synagogue can be found in Hilde Marx's depiction of a small synagogue in Frankfurt, her city of birth. See Hilde Marx, "Liebe zur kleinen Synagoge," *Israelitisches Familienblatt*, July 6, 1933.

16. Oskar Guttmann, "Vorträge und Konzerte," *Berliner Rundschau, Jüdische Rundschau*, February 23, 1934.

17. "Aktuelle Fragen," *Israelitisches Familienblatt*, April 29, 1937.

18. Mona Ozouf, *Festivals and the French Revolution* (Cambridge, MA: Harvard University Press, 1991), pp. 128–29.

19. On flag marches and torchlight processions, see Boaz Neumann, *Nazi Weltanschauung: Space, Body, Language* [in Hebrew] (Haifa and Tel-Aviv: University of Haifa Press, 2002), pp. 138–42. On stadiums as mass open-air spaces in the service of Nazism, see pp. 100–21; also Hans-Jochen Gamm, *Der Braune Kult*, pp. 43–56, 90–126.

20. "Synagogen-Konzerte in Oberschlesien," *Jüdische Rundschau*, September 15, 1933; and see also a similar sentiment stated by the liberal public activist Margarete Goldstein, quoted in Michael Meyer, "Liberal Judaism in Nazi Germany," in Moshe Zimmermann, ed., *On Germans and Jews under the Nazi Regime: Essays by Three Generations of Historians; A Festschrift in Honor of Otto Dov Kulka* (Jerusalem: Hebrew University Magnes Press, 2006), p. 291. See also Jacob Borut, "Struggles for Spaces," p. 342.

21. Marta Appel, née Insel, in Monika Richarz, ed., *Jewish Life in Germany: Memoirs from Three Centuries*, trans. Stella P. Rosenfeld and Sidney Rosenfeld (Bloomington: Indiana University Press 1991), p. 358.

22. "Die Synagoge: Unser Beth-Am," *Israelitisches Familienblatt*, August 1, 1935. On the opening of synagogues for the entire day, see "Anregunegn, die verwirklicht werden sollten," *Israelitisches Familienblatt*, July 19, 1934. On the participation of schoolchildren in events at synagogues, see "Die Gestaltung des Oneg Sabbat: Ein Wort zu den Feiern in der Synagogen," *Jüdische Rundschau*, September 10, 1935.

23. "Der Zwischenfall in der neuen Synagoge," *Israelitisches Familienblatt*, September 14, 1933.

24. See, for example, "Konzerte und Vorträge," *CV-Zeitung*, February 4, 1937; "Kassel: Lernvorträge und Weihestunden," *Israelitisches Familienblatt*, September 23, 1937. For a more comprehensive treatment, see "Zur jüdischen Situation der Zeit: Gemeindeabend in Berlin," *Israelitisches Familienblatt*, February 3, 1938.

25. Martha Wertheimer, Siddy Goldschmidt, and Paul Jogi Mayer, *Das Jüdische Sportbuch: Weg, Kampf und Sieg* (Berlin: Verlag Atid, 1937), p. 43.

26. Alfred Karger, "Äußerlichkeiten oder mehr?" *Israelitisches Familienblatt*, March 25, 1937.

27. "Der einsame Mensch," *Israelitisches Familienblatt*, June 30, 1938.

28. Joachim Prinz, "Zur Analyse der Zeit," *Jüdische Rundschau*, November 5, 1935.

29. Cohn, *Kein Recht*, pp. 533 (November 5, 1938) and 534 (November 7, 1938).

30. Abraham Barkai, "Exclusion and Persecution: 1933–1938," in Abraham Barkai and Paul Mendes-Flohr, *Renewal and Destruction: 1918–1945*, vol. 4 in Michael Meyer, ed., *German-Jewish History in Modern Times* (New York: Columbia University Press 1998), p. 221.

31. Hans Reichmann, *Deutscher Bürger und verfolgter Jude: Novemberpogrom und KZ Sachsenhausen 1937–1939* (Munich: R. Oldenburg Verlag, 1998), p. 82.

32. Reichmann, *Deutscher Bürger und verfolgter Jude*, p. 254. There is extensive scholarship on the November pogrom. See, for example, Saul Friedländer, *Nazi Germany and the Jews, Vol. 1: The Years of Persecution 1933–1939* (New York: Harper & Collins, 1997), pp. 269–98; Alon Confino, *A World without Jews: Nazi Imagination from Persecution to Genocide* (New Haven, CT: Yale University Press, 2014), pp. 115–41.

33. On the burning of the New Synagogue and the pogrom in Breslau, see Abraham Ascher, *A Community under Siege: The Jews of Breslau under Nazism* (Stanford, CA: Stanford University Press, 2007), pp. 166–74.

34. On Rosh Hashanah, see Cohn, *Kein Recht*, p. 693 (September 14–15, 1939). On Yom Kippur, see p. 696 (September 22, 1939).

35. Cohn, *Kein Recht*, p. 875 (November 30, 1940).

36. On praying on his last Yom Kippur, see Cohn, *Kein Recht*, p. 987 (September 30 and October 2, 1941). On the last Jewish public buildings remaining in Breslau, see Tamar Cohen Gazit, ed., *In the Talons of the Third Reich: Willy Cohn's diary 1933–1941* [in Hebrew] (Jerusalem: Hebrew University Magnes Press, 2014), p. 963 n174.

37. Avriel Bar-Levav, "Another Place: The Cemetery in Jewish Culture" [in Hebrew], *Pe'amim* 98–99 (2003): 5–38.

38. Lucia Raspe, "Die Lebensbedingungen des Ghettos in der jüdischen Brauchtumliteraur der frühen Neuzeit," in Fritz Backhaus et al., eds., *Frühneuzeitliche Ghettos in Europa im Vergleich* (Berlin: Trafo, 2012), pp. 303–31.

39. Sylvie-Anne Goldberg, *Crossing the Jabbok: Illness and Death in Ashkenazi Judaism in Sixteenth- through Nineteenth-Century Prague* (Berkeley: University of California Press, 1996), p. 205.

40. Andreas Gotzmann, "Out of the Ghetto," pp. 149–51.

41. Nils Roemer, *German City, Jewish Memory: The Story of Worms* (Waltham, MA: Brandeis University Press, 2010), p. 108.

42. Edwin Landau, in Monika Richarz, *Jewish Life in Germany*, pp. 312–13.

43. On acts of vandalism against Jewish cemeteries, which escalated during the final years of the Weimar Republic, see, for example, "125 Friedhofsschändunden in Deutsch-

land," *CV-Zeitung*, July 8, 1932; "Gegen Friedhofsschänder," *Jüdische Rundschau*, August 30, 1935. On the limitations placed on Jewish funerals and the harassment of those who attended them, especially in rural areas, see, for example, Marta Appel, née Insel, in Monika Richarz, ed., *Jewish Life in Nazi Germany*, p. 358.

44. Hilde Marx, "Alter jüdischer Friedhof in Franken," *CV-Zeitung*, January 10, 1935. For another piece from the press about the cemetery as an expression of Jewish presence over many generations in Germany, see Ludwig Mayer, "Der jüdische Friedhof in Kriegshaber," *Jüdische Rundschau*, October 25, 1935.

45. Erich Cohn-Beuthen, "Sonne auf Gräbern," *Israelitisches Familienblatt*, July 2, 1936.

46. M. W. [Martha Wertheimer], "Schnee auf Gräbern," *Israelitisches Familienblatt*, January 21, 1937.

47. Michel Foucault, "Of Other Spaces," *Diacritics* 16, no. 1 (Spring, 1986): 22–27.

48. Helene Hanna Thon, "Abschied von drei Gräbern," *Jüdische Rundschau*, November 1, 1935.

49. Advertisement, *Israelitisches Familienblatt*, March 15, 1938.

50. Cohn, *Kein Recht*, p. 155 (September 9, 1934). For another, more profound account of a visit to the cemetery prior to Rosh Hashanah, see p. 465 (September 5, 1937).

51. Cohn, *Kein Recht*, p. 314 (March 22, 1936).

52. For his account of his last visit, with Ruth, see Cohn, *Kein Recht*, p. 564 (December 11, 1938); for accounts of his visits to the cemetery with Susannah, see pp. 725 (December 3, 1939), 788 (May 2, 1940), 852–52 (October 2, 1940), and 955 (July 16, 1941).

53. Norbert Elias, *The Loneliness of the Dying* (Oxford, UK, and New York: B. Blackwell, 1985), pp. 29–32.

54. "The Executive of the Jewish Community of Berlin Reports on Vocational Training and Retraining Measures in 1937," in Wolf Gruner, ed., *The Persecution and Murder of the European Jews by Nazi Germany, 1933–1945* (hereafter *PMJ*), vol. 1, *German Reich, 1933–1937* (Berlin and Boston: Walter de Gruyter, 2019), doc. 319, p. 793.

55. Elisabeth Freund, *Als Zwangsarbeiterin 1941 in Berlin: Die Aufzeichnungen der Volkswirtin Elisabeth Freund*, ed. and annotated by Carola Sachse (Berlin: Akademie, 1996), pp. 60–61.

56. Freund, *Als Zwangsarbeiterin 1941 in Berlin*, pp. 116–17. Marion Kaplan, Moshe Zimmermann, and Jacob Borut have noted this phenomenon. See Kaplan, *Between Dignity and Despair*, p. 163; Moshe Zimmermann, *Deutsche gegen Deutsche: Das Schicksal der Juden 1938–1945* (Berlin: Aufbau, 2008), p. 65; Jacob Borut, "Struggles for Spaces," p. 349.

57. Cohn, *Kein Recht*, pp. 854–55 (October 2, 1940), citation from p. 855; pp. 955–56 (July 16, 1941), citation from p. 956. See also pp. 983 (September 23, 1941) and 989 (October 6, 1941).

58. "War Diary, 1939–1942" of Philipp Manes, WL (Wiener Library, London), doc. 1346, box 10 4.5a, pp. 105 (October 2, 1940), 229 (April 1, 1942), and 232–33 (April 14, 1942).

59. Arno Nadel, [*Tagebuch*] [2 volumes; copies of originals], 1941–42; AR 4314; Leo Baeck Institute, p. 20 (April 18, 1942).

60. Victor Klemperer, *I Will Bear Witness: A Diary of the Nazi Years, 1942–1945* (New York: Modern Library, 2001), p. 145 (September 12, 1942).

61. Klemperer, *I Will Bear Witness*, p. 159 (October 29, 1942).

62. For the quote "almost at home," see Klemperer, *I Will Bear Witness*, p. 197 (February 5, 1943). On "the place to get news," see p. 330 (July 1, 1944). See also p. 317 (May 23, 1944).

63. Michael Brenner, *The Renaissance of Jewish Culture in Weimar Germany* (New Haven, CT: Yale University Press, 1996).

64. Jacob Borut, "Struggles for Spaces," pp. 309–13.

65. Rivka Elkin, *The Heart Beats On: Continuity and Change in Social Work and Welfare Activities of German Jews under the Nazi Regime, 1933–1945* [in Hebrew] (Jerusalem: Yad Vashem, 2004), pp. 31–66.

66. Kerstin von der Krone, "The Representation and Creation of Spaces through Print Media: Some insights from the History of the Jewish Press," in Lässig and Rürup, eds., *Space and Spatiality in Modern German Jewish History*, pp. 125–39.

67. Lm., "Vom jüdischen Lehrhaus in Stuttgart," *Jüdische Rundschau*, October 31, 1933.

68. See, for example, the description of the Berlin house of study in an article published to mark the opening of its winter semester: "Eröffnung des Berliner Lehrhauses," *CV-Zeitung*, October 24, 1935.

69. On this, see Wolf Gruner, *Öffentliche Wohlfahrt und Judenverfolgung: Wechselwirkungen lokaler und zentraler Politik im NS-Staat 1933–1942* (Munich: R. Oldenbourg, 2002).

70. Elkin, *The Heart Beats On*, pp. 184–85.

71. For a description of this activity, see Käte Marcus, "Die Hoffnung von Tausenden: Rundgang bei der Berliner Jüdischen Winterhilfe," *CV-Zeitung*, January 28, 1937.

72. L. B. Aschheim, "Das Jüdische Museum in Breslau," *Jüdische Rundschau*, April 20, 1934.

73. Cohn, *Kein Recht*, p. 102 (November 15, 1933).

74. "Das jüdische Museum eröffnet," *Jüdische Rundschau*, January 27, 1933.

75. "Jüdisches Museum unter neuer Leitung: Professor Franz Landsberger, über seine Pläne," *Berliner Blatt der CV-Zeitung*, June 6, 1935.

76. Max Reinheimer, "Die Not der Kleingemeinden: Was wird aus den jüdischen Landbewohnern?" *Jüdische Rundschau*, August 25, 1933.

77. Hans Buxman, "Der jüdische Kulturbund Hamburg: Zugleich Wanderbühne für Mittel-, Süd und Ostdeutschland," *CV-Zeitung*, August 19, 1937. Until 1935 the organization was called the Kulturbund Deutscher Juden (the Cultural Federation of German Jews).

78. Martha Wertheimer, "Dazwischen notiert . . . ," *Israelitisches Familienblatt*, February 11, 1937.

79. See for example, Cohn, *Kein Recht*, pp. 97 (November 1, 1933), 107 (November 26–27, 1933), and 129 (February 4, 1934); On the spiritual isolation of peripheral communities, see, for example, p. 160 (September 30, 1934). On the opening of the new synagogue, see p. 180 (November 17, 1934). On the combination of the synagogue and community center in the same building, see p. 184 (November 25, 1934). On the vital cultural activity in synagogues in peripheral communities, see also the reports of Rabbi Nachum Wahrmann, the district rabbi of Oels in Upper Silesia: "On 5 February 1934 Rabbi Wahrmann Reports on the Mounting Social and Pastoral Problems in His Silesian District," *PMJ*, vol. 1, doc. 101, pp. 322–24.

80. Cohn, *Kein Recht*, p. 183 (November 25, 1934).

81. Cohn, *Kein Recht*, p. 197 (January 4, 1935).

82. Cohn, *Kein Recht*, p. 215 (April 18, 1935). See also p. 320 (May 10, 1936). For a description of the atmosphere in a synagogue where there was an atmosphere of warmth (*Wärme*) and security (*Geborgenheit*), see also Lise Lewinneck, "Abend in eine alten Synagoge: Vortragsabend Edith Hernstadt-Oettingen," *CV-Zeitung*, April 17, 1935.

83. On the activities of Jewish youth groups in Germany prior to the Nazi regime, see Yehoyakim Doron, *The Jewish Youth Movements in Germany* [in Hebrew] (Jerusalem: Rubin Mass, 1996).

84. Hagit Lavsky, "Jewish Agricultural Training in Germany: Its Context and Changing Role," in Tal Alon-Mozes, Irene Aue-Ben-David, and Joachim Wolschke Bulmahn, eds., *Jewish Horticultural Schools and Training Centers in Germany and Their Impact on Horticulture, Agriculture and Landscape Architecture in Palestine/Israel* (Munich: AVM. edition, 2020), pp. 13–22.

85. Kaplan, *Between Dignity and Despair*, p. 94. And see also Werner T. Angress, *Between Fair and Hope: Jewish Youth in the Third Reich* (New York: Columbia University Press, 1988), pp. 1–42.

86. Joachim Prinz, "Tag der Jugend: Eine Chance für unsere Kinder," *Jüdische Rundschau*, June 22, 1934.

87. Kaplan, *Between Dignity and Despair*, p. 109. For the Gestapo's discussion of imposing limits on Jewish youth movement activity in the German public space, and forbidding Jewish youth to wear uniforms, see "On 2 August 1934 the Gestapo Prohibits Members of Jewish Youth Organizations from Wearing Uniforms and Participating in Military Sports Training," *PMJ*, vol.1, doc. 130, pp. 387–88.

88. "Die Zeit der Vorbereitung, Jüdische Jugend lernt für ein Arbeitsleben in Palästina," *Jugend Rundschau, Jüdische Rundschau*, December 19, 1933. As Ulrike Pilarczyk has shown, the communal aspect of the Zionist training farms was very prominent in the rich visual documentation they produced. See Ulrike Pilarczyk, *Gemeinschaft in Bildern: Jüdische Jugendbewegung und zionistische Erziehungspraxis in Deutschland und Palästina/Israel* (Göttingen, Germany: Wallstein, 2009). On the Zionist training farms in the Brandenburg area, see also Andreas Paetz and Karin Weiss, "Auf Hachschara in Brandenburg: Stätten jüdischer Berufsausbildung in der früheren Provinz Brandenburg," in Andreas Paetz and Karin Weiss, eds., *Hachschara: Die Vorbereitung junger Juden auf die Auswanderung nach Palästina* (Potsdam, Germany: Verlag für Berlin-Brandenburg, 1999), pp. 47–88.

89. Cohn, *Kein Recht*, p. 143 (August 5, 1934).

90. Tamar Cohen Gazit, "From Diary's Notebook to a Book," in Cohen Gazit, ed., *In the Talons of the Third Reich* [in Hebrew] pp. xiii–xv. Before his deportation, Cohn gave the diaries to his friends Else and Paul Zeitz, who kept them in Berlin until 1945. Later, their son Wolfgang sent the diaries to London. Ernst Abraham Cohn brought the diaries from London to Israel in 1960. Cohen Gazit, Ernst Abraham's daughter, published the diary in her father's Hebrew translation and also wrote a comprehensive study of it.

91. "Jüdische Landwirte auf deutsche Erde," *CV-Zeitung*, October 4, 1933.

92. "Tage in Lehnitz," "Leben jetzt und hier," *CV-Zeitung, Seite der Jugend*, November 8, 1934.

93. Vera Craner, "Hauswirtschaftsschülerinnen in Lehnitz," *CV-Zeitung*, February 4, 1937.

94. Later, following the promulgation of the Nuremberg Laws, its name was changed to the German-Jewish Youth Ring (*Ring, Bund der Jewish Jugend*).

95. Diary of Ilse Strauss née Gimnicher, 1935–39; Ilse Strauss Collection; AR 3273, box 1, folder 4, Leo Baeck Institute, June 6–13, 1935.

96. Diary of Ilse Strauss née Gimnicher, late February 1939.

97. Lavsky, "Jewish Agricultural Training in Germany."

98. "On 13 June 1934 State Secretary Hans Pfundtner Writes to the Reich Minister of

Agriculture Proposing the Creation of Closed Camps for the Agricultural Retraining of Jews," *PMJ*, vol. 1, doc. 122, pp. 372–74, here p. 374.

99. Ilana Michaeli and Irmgard Klönne, eds., *Gut Winkel: Die schützende Insel; Hachschara 1933–1941* (Berlin: Lit, 2007) p. 30.

100. Werner T. Angress, *Between Fair and Hope*, pp. 43–76.

101. Werner T. Angress, *Witness to the Storm: A Jewish Journey from Nazi Berlin to the 82nd Airborne 1920–1945* (Bloomington: Indiana University Press, 2019), p. 154.

102. Daniel Fraenkel, *Jewish Sports in Nazi Germany as Reflected in the Jewish Press* [in Hebrew] (Jerusalem: Yad Vashem, 2016), pp. 17–22. Citation from p. 22. I am grateful to Daniel Fraenkel for the sources he made available to me for this discussion.

103. Meta Fuß-Opet, "Abschied vom Turnverein," *Israelitisches Familienblatt*, May 11, 1933.

104. Fraenkel, *Jewish Sports in Nazi Germany*, pp. 24–25.

105. Wertheimer, Goldschmidt, and Yogi Mayer, *Das jüdische Sportbuch*, p. 14. Fraenkel, who cited these numbers on p. 25 of his book, remarked there that this level of participation was especially impressive given the aging of the Jewish population during the early years of the Nazi regime, as a result of emigration by young people.

106. "On 29 December 1933 Fritz Wolfes Asks the Mayor of Hanover to Lease a Sports Hall to the Jewish Gymnastics Association," *PMJ*, vol. 1, doc. 92, pp. 300–301, here p. 300.

107. "Jüdischer Sport im Jahre 1933," *Jüdische Rundschau*, December 1, 1933.

108. "Jungs, Wir brauchen einen Sportplatz," *CV-Zeitung*, July 20, 1933.

109. "Das erste Sportfest des Reichsaüsschüsses," *CV-Zeitung*, August 23, 1934.

110. K. J. R., "Der 'Bund' marschiert . . . , Das Sportfest des Bundes Deutsch-Jüdischer Jugend," *CV-Zeitung*, August 30, 1934.

111. Neumann, *Nazi Weltanschauung*, p. 103.

112. Inge Deutschkron, *Ich trug den gelben Stern* (Cologne: Verlag Wissenschaft und Politik, 1978), p. 26.

113. "Berliner Sportplatz in neuen Gewande," *CV-Zeitung*, July 9, 1936.

114. Deutschkron, *Ich trug den gelben Stern*, p. 27.

115. Fraenkel, *Jewish Sports in Nazi Germany*, p. 49.

116. N. N. "Begeisterung um die Palästinenser," *Jüdische Rundschau*, *Berliner Rundschau*, June 29, 1937. On the visit by the Petah Tikva team to Danzig and Berlin, see also Eyal Gertmann and Lorenz Peiffer, "Im Schatten antisemitischer Diskriminierung und Verfolgung: Sportliche Begegnungen zwischen jüdischen Mannschaften aus Nazi-deutschland und Erez Israel im Jahre 1937," in Lorenz Peiffer and Moshe Zimmerman, eds., *Sport als Element des Kulturtransfers: Jüdische Sportler zwischen NS-Deutschland und Palästina* (Göttingen, Germany: Wallstein, 2013), pp. 115–26.

117. Fraenkel, *Jewish Sports in Nazi Germany*, p. 37.

118. Jim H. Kroner, "Sport mit einfachen Mitteln," *Israelitisches Familienblatt*, December 7, 1933.

119. Turnlehrer Erich Sonn, "Schulturnen ohne Geräte and ohne Raum," *Die jüdische Schule: Jüdische Rundschau*, April 13, 1934.

120. Hajo Bernett, *Der jüdische Sport im nationalsozialistischen Deutschland 1933–1938* (Schorndorf, Germany: K. Hofmann, 1978), p. 90.

121. "Das Ziel bleibt," *Israelitisches Familienblatt, Der jüdische Sport*, March 25, 1937. Another article in the same issue stressed that the need to adjust to holding athletic activities anywhere, even in a room, was especially urgent for small communities. See "Es

geht auch so! Anregungen für den Turn- und Sportbetrieb in den kleinen Gemeinden," *Israelitisches Familienblatt, Der jüdische Sport*, March 25, 1937.

122. Wertheimer, Goldschmidt, and Yogi Mayer, *Das jüdische Sportbuch*, p. 43.

123. See an account of the refurbishing of the ruins of a synagogue in Hanover as a gymnasium, a project that met no opposition and was even welcomed by the community's rabbi. Lorenz Pfeiffer and Henry Wahlig, *Juden im Sport während des Nationalsozialismus: Ein historisches Handbuch für Niedersachsen und Bremen* (Göttingen, Germany: Wallstein, 2012), pp. 208–9.

124. L. L., "Jüdisches Leben in Königsberg," *Israelitisches Familienblatt*, September 1, 1938.

125. "Wer reist mit? Eine Reise durch jüdische Kulturstätten in Deutschland und jenseits zur Grenzen," *Kinderblatt*, supplement of *CV-Zeitung*, June 14, 1934.

126. "Wir reisen nach Australien," *Kinderblatt*, supplement of *CV-Zeitung*, October 21, 1937.

127. On the public discourse in the press about the issue of whether to emigrate or remain, see Herbert Freeden, *The Jewish Press in the Third Reich* (Providence, RI: Berg 1993), pp. 49–74. For a comprehensive scholarly discussion of plans for emigration and the debate about it among Germany's Jews in the 1930s, see David Jünger, *Jahre der Ungewissheit: Emigrationspläne deutscher Juden 1933–1938* (Göttingen, Germany: Vandenhoeck & Ruprecht, 2016).

128. Hugo Rosenthal, "Unser 'Jetzt und Hier,'" *Jüdische Rundschau*, September 8, 1933.

129. "Kundgebung der neuen Reichsvertretung der deutschen Juden," *Jüdische Rundschau*, September 29, 1933.

130. Ernst G. Löwethal and Hans Oppenheimer, eds., *Philo-Atlas: Handbuch für die jüdische Auswanderung* (Berlin: Philo, 1938).

131. For a study of the *Philo-Atlas*, see Karl Schlögel, "Philo-Atlas: Escape Routes," in *In Space We Read Time*, pp. 93–96.

132. For a detailed discussion of this subject, see Yael Dinur, "'Treue um Treue': Advertisements in the Jewish Press in Nazi Germany, 1933–1938," MA thesis [in Hebrew], Hebrew University of Jerusalem 2017. See also Christoph Kreutzmüller, *Printed under Pressure: Newspaper Advertisements of Jewish-Owned Businesses in Nazi Germany 1933–1942* [in Hebrew] (Jerusalem: Yad Vashem, 2019), pp. 38, 40–42.

133. Hilde Cohn, "Gehen und Kommen," *Der Morgen* 12 (March 1937): 571–73.

134. Cohn, "Gehen und Kommen," pp. 571, 572.

135. Marc Augé, *Non-Places: Introduction to an Anthropology of Supermodernity* (New York: Verso, 1995), p. 31.

136. For Augé's definition of anthropological places, see Augé, *Non-Places*, pp. 42–74. For his discussion of the transition from anthropological places to non-places, see pp. 75–115.

137. A. H., "Rosch Haschana 5699, Die Grundlage," *CV-Zeitung*, September 22, 1938.

138. Kerstin Schoor, *Vom literarischen Zentrum zum literarischen Ghetto* (Göttingen, Germany: Wallstein, 2010), p. 328.

139. Meta Samson, *Spatz macht sich* (Berlin: Altberliner Verlag, 1990), p. 142.

140. Hertha Rosenfeld, "Erlebnis am Hauptbahnhof," *Israelitisches Familienblatt*, November 3, 1938.

141. Ulrich Alexander Boschwitz, *The Passenger: A Novel* (New York: Metropolitan Books: 2021), p. 179.

142. A. H. "Weite in der Enge," *CV-Zeitung*, November 14, 1935.

143. J. L., "Neues jüdisches Heim: Gemeinschaftshaus in Hamburg eröffnet," *Israelitisches Familienblatt*, January 13, 1938.

144. Martha Wertheimer, "Ghettogeist?" *Israelitisches Familienblatt*, June 17, 1937.

Chapter 3

1. "On 27 and 28 April 1938 Luise Solmitz Notes Her Reaction to the Instructions for the Registration of Assets," document 30 in Susanne Heim, ed., *The Persecution and Murder of the European Jews by Nazi Germany (PMJ), 1933–1945*, vol. 2, *German Reich 1938–August 1939* (Berlin and Boston: Walter de Gruyter, 2019), pp. 143–44, here p. 144.

2. Marc Fried, "Grieving for a Lost Home: Psychological Costs of Relocation," in L. J. Duhl, ed., *The Urban Condition* (New York: Basic Books, 1963), pp. 151–71. On spatial identity, see also Arijit Sen and Lisa Silverman, eds., *Making Place: Space and Embodiment in the City* (Bloomington: Indiana University Press, 2014).

3. Tiina Peil, "Home," in Nigel Thrift and Rob Kitchin, eds., *International Encyclopedia of Human Geography* (Amsterdam: Elsevier, 2009), p. 180.

4. Jonas Frykman and Orvar Löfgren, *Culture Builders: A Historical Anthropology of Middle-Class Life* (New Brunswick, NJ: Rutgers University Press, 1987), pp. 125–43; Catherine Hall, "The Sweet Delights of Home," in Michelle Perrot, ed., *A History of Private Life*, vol. 4: *From the Fires of Revolution to the Great War* (Cambridge, MA: Belknap Press, 1990), pp. 47–93; Moritz Föllmer, "Das Appartement," in Alexa Geisthövel and Habbo Knoch, eds., *Orte der Moderne: Erfahrungswelten des 19. und 20. Jahrhunderts* (Frankfurt am Main: Campus Verlag, 2005), pp. 325–34.

5. Brigitta Schmidt-Lauber, *Gemütlichkeit: Eine kulturwissenschaftliche Annäherung* (Frankfurt am Main: Campus Verlag, 2003).

6. Marion A. Kaplan, *The Making of the Jewish Middle Class: Women, Family and Identity in Imperial Germany* (New York: Oxford University Press, 1991), pp. 25–41, 117–26. On the development of the bourgeois culture of domesticity and its link to German nationalism, see Nancy R. Reagin, *Sweeping the German Nation: Domesticity and National Identity in Germany, 1870–1945* (Cambridge, UK: Cambridge University Press, 2007).

7. Tovi Fenster, *The Global City and the Holy City: Narratives on Knowledge, Planning and Diversity* (Harlow, UK, and New York: Prentice Hall / Pearson Education, 2004), p. 121.

8. Willy Frank, "Das eigene Heim," in Alexander Koch, ed., *Das schöne Heim: Ratgeber für die Ausgestaltung und Einrichtung der Wohnung* (Darmstadt, Germany: A. Koch, 1920), pp. 3–5. And see, in this context, Boaz Neumann, *Being-in-the-World: German Worlds at the Turn of the 20th Century* [in Hebrew] (Tel Aviv: Am Oved, 2014), pp. 46–52.

9. Frykman and Löfgren, *Culture Builders*, p. 140.

10. For a new study of this subject, see Wolf Gruner, "'Worse Than Vandals': The Mass Destruction of Jewish Homes and Jewish Responses during the 1938 Pogrom," in Wolf Gruner and Steve Ross, eds., *New Perspectives on Kristallnacht: After 80 Years, the Nazi Pogrom in Global Comparison* (West Lafayette, IN: Purdue University Press, 2019), pp. 25–49.

11. Marion A. Kaplan, *Between Dignity and Despair: Jewish Life in Nazi Germany* (New York: Oxford University Press, 1998), pp. 150–57; Moshe Zimmermann, *Deutsche gegen Deutsche: Das Schicksal der Juden, 1938–1945* (Berlin: Aufbau, 2008), pp. 102–4; Konrad Kwiet, "Without Neighbors: Daily Living in Judenhäuser," in Francis R. Nicosia and David Scrase, eds., *Jewish Life in Nazi Germany: Dilemmas and Responses* (New York: Berghahn Books, 2010), pp. 117–47.

12. See, on this subject, Doron Niederland, *The Jewish Home in Nazi Germany as Reflected in the German-Jewish Press, 1933–1938* [in Hebrew] (Jerusalem: Yad Vashem, 2018).

13. Fenster, *The Global City and the Holy City*, p. 122.

14. Willy Cohn, *Kein Recht, Nirgends: Tagebuch vom Untergang des Breslauer Judentums, 1933–1941*, ed. Norbert Conrads (Cologne: Böhlau, 2006), p. 40 (May 5, 1933).

15. Cohn, *Kein Recht*, p. 92 (October 17, 1933).

16. Cohn, *Kein Recht*, p. 126 (January 27, 1934).

17. For a detailed consideration of Cohn and his home life until the end of the 1930s, see Anja Schnabel, *Bleiben in Breslau: Jüdische Selbstbehauptung und Sinnsuche in den Tagebüchern Willy Cohns 1933 bis 1941* (Berlin: Be.bra Wissenschaft Verlag, 2018), pp. 170–83.

18. "On 9 May 1933 Heinrich Marx Reflects on His Personal Situation in Berlin and Conditions in Higher Education Institutions," in Wolf Gruner, ed., *The Persecution and Murder of the European Jews by Nazi Germany (PMJ), vol.1, German Reich 1933–1937* (Berlin and Boston: Walter de Gruyter, 2019), doc. 41, pp. 170–73; quote from p. 171.

19. On the shaping of "domestic Judaism" in the German Jewish bourgeois home, and the central role women played in this milieu, see Kaplan, *The Making of the Jewish Middle Class*, pp. 25–84.

20. Victor Klemperer, *I Will Bear Witness: A Diary of the Nazi Years, 1933–1941* (New York: Modern Library, 1999), p. 133 (September 16, 1935). On spending long periods at home, see also p. 6 (March 10, 1933).

21. Klemperer, *I Will Bear Witness*, pp. 128 (July 21, 1935) and 261 (July 12, 1938).

22. *Das Tagebuch der Hertha Nathorff*, ed. Wolfgang Benz (Munich: R. Oldenbourg, 1987), p. 61 (August 30, 1934).

23. Kurt F. Rosenberg, *"Einer, der nicht mehr dazugehört": Tagebücher 1933–1937*, ed. Beate Meyer and Björn Siegel (Göttingen, Germany: Wallstein Verlag, 2012), p. 228 (July 17, 1934).

24. And see, in this context, Leora Auslander, "Reading German Jewry through Vernacular Photography: From the Kaiserreich to the Third Reich," *Central European History* 48, no. 3 (2015): 300–334.

25. *Das Tagebuch der Hertha Nathorff*, p. 101 (Silvester 1937).

26. Meta Samson, *Spatz macht sich*, 2nd ed. (Berlin: Altberliner Verlag, 1990) [1st ed.: 1938].

27. Samson, *Spatz macht sich*, p. 22.

28. Samson, *Spatz macht sich*, p. 91.

29. Samson, *Spatz macht sich*, p. 92.

30. For a more detailed analysis of the story, with attention to the problem of overcrowding at home, see Hanna Livnat, *Jews and Proud: Shaping Identity for Jewish Children in Germany, 1933–1938* [in Hebrew] (Jerusalem: Yad Vashem, 2009), pp. 142–49.

31. Cohn, *Kein Recht*, p. 539 (November 11, 1938).

32. Elisabeth Block, *Erinnerungszeichen: Die Tagebücher der Elisabeth Block* (Augsburg, Germany: Bayerische Staatskanzlei, 1993), pp. 162–63 (November 17, 1938).

33. Peter Miesbeck, "Einführung," in Block, *Erinnerungszeichen*, p. 31.

34. Block, *Erinnerungszeichen*, p. 188 (October 4, 1939). Miesbeck, "Einführung," in Block, *Erinnerungszeichen*, pp. 33–34.

35. Cohn, *Kein Recht*, p. 605 (February 15, 1939).

36. Cohn, *Kein Recht*, p. 567 (December 17, 1938). And see also p. 836 (August 25, 1940).

37. Klemperer, *I Will Bear Witness*, pp. 312 (September 14, 1939) and 314 (September 29, 1939).

38. On Nadel's diary, see Kerstin Schoor, *Vom literarischen Zentrum zum literarischen Ghetto: Deutsch-jüdische literarische Kultur in Berlin zwischen 1933 und 1945* (Göttingen, Germany: Wallstein Verlag, 2010), pp. 450–57.

39. Arno Nadel, diary, 1941–42; AR 4314; Leo Baeck Institute, June 14, 1942.

40. Nadel, diary, June 1, 1942; July 2, 3, and 4, 1942; July 28, 1942; and August 3 and 23, 1942.

41. Philipp Manes, "War Diary, 1939–1942," Wiener Library, London, doc 1346, box 10 4.5a p. 150 (June 1941); pp. 158 (August 1941), 160 (August 16, 1941), and 163 (September 3, 1941).

42. Manes, "War Diary," p. 245 (June 1942).

43. Manes, "War Diary," p. 254 (July 4, 1942). From the context, apparently Manes worked on Sunday, but fewer hours than during the rest of the week.

44. Tiina Peil, "Home," p. 181.

45. Cohn, *Kein Recht*, p. 548 (November 17, 1938). His personal library, its arrangement, and its ultimate fate continued to preoccupy him thereafter as well. see pp. 616 (March 15, 1939), 836 (August 25, 1940), and 864 (October 31, 1941).

46. On his attempts to carry on with his teaching work, see Cohn, *Kein Recht*, pp. 588–89 (January 20, 1939). On his attempts to continue writing about history, see pp. 604 (February 14, 1939) and 633 (April 19, 1939).

47. For Cohn on his stamp collection, see, for example Cohn, *Kein Recht*, pp. 741 (January 9, 1940) and 883 (December 23, 1940). *CV-Zeitung* published a philately column; see, for example, "Der Briefmarkensammler," *CV-Zeitung* April 24, 1935; June 20, 1935; November 14, 1935; June 25, 1936; and December 24, 1936.

48. On the "little bit," see Victor Klemperer, *I Will Bear Witness: A Diary of the Nazi Years, 1942–1945*, (New York: Modern Library, 2001), p. 130 (June 14, 1942). For the second citation, see p. 157 (October 24, 1942).

49. Mary Douglas, "The Idea of a Home: A Kind of Space," *Social Research* 58, no. 1 (Spring 1991): 289.

50. Douglas, "The Idea of a Home," pp. 294–95.

51. Douglas, "The Idea of a Home," p. 298.

52. Mihaly Csikszentmihalyi and Eugene Halton, *The Meaning of Things: Domestic Symbols and the Self* (Cambridge, UK, and New York: Cambridge University Press, 1981), p. 139. On the role of domestic symbols and objects in maintaining the way in which Jews felt at home in Paris and Berlin, see Leora Auslander, "'Jewish Taste'? Jews and the Aesthetics of Everyday Life in Paris and Berlin, 1933–1942," in Rudy Koshar, ed., *Histories of Leisure* (Oxford, UK: Berg, 2002), pp. 299–318.

53. Quoted in Victoria Rosner, *Modernism and the Architecture of Private Life* (New York: Columbia University Press, 2008), pp. 128. See also Bill Brown, "Thing Theory," *Critical Inquiry* 28, no. 1 (2001): 1–22.

54. Kaplan, *Between Dignity and Despair*, p. 54.

55. Meta Samson, "Das möblierte Zimmer," *Der Morgen* 10, no. 2 (May 1934): 58.

56. Marc Fried, "Grieving for a Lost Home."

57. Samson, "Das möblierte Zimmer," pp. 58–59.

58. Samson, "Das möblierte Zimmer," p. 60.

59. Samson, "Das möblierte Zimmer," p. 61.

60. Joseph Rykwert, "House and Home," *Social Research* 58, no. 1 (Spring 1991): 54.

61. For a scholarly discussion of the subject, compare Joachim Schlör, "'Take Down Mezuzahs, Remove Name-Plates': The Emigration of Objects from Germany to Pales-

tine," in Simone J. Bronner, ed., *Jewish Cultural Studies, Vol. 1, Jewishness: Expression, Identity, and Representation* (Oxford, UK: Littman Library of Jewish Civilization, 2008), pp. 133–50.

62. Hetta Bamberger, "Vor dem Umzug," *CV-Zeitung, Beiblatt: Das Blatt der deutschen Jüdin*, March 22, 1934.

63. Walter Benjamin, "Unpacking My Library: A Talk about Book Collecting," in *Illuminations* (New York: Schocken Books, 1969), p. 60.

64. Benjamin, "Unpacking My Library," p. 66.

65. Frieda Vallentin, "Umziehen-Fortziehen," *Blätter des Jüdischen Frauenbundes* 3 (March 1938): 13.

66. Harold M. Proshansky, Abbe K. Fabian, and Robert Kaminoff, "Place-Identity: Physical World Socialization of the Self," *Journal of Environmental Psychology* 3 (1983): 66.

67. Vallentin, "Umziehen-Fortziehen."

68. Lise Lewinneck, "Wir räumen auf," *Israelitisches Familienblatt*, July 7, 1938.

69. Erich Seligmann, Tagebuch III (1938–1941), Erich Seligmann Collection, AR 4104, box 1, folder 2, Leo Baeck Institute, March 8, 1939.

70. Seligmann, Tagebuch III, May 9, 1939.

71. Klemperer, *I Will Bear Witness, 1933–1941*, p. 338 (May 21, 1940).

72. Amos Goldberg, *Trauma in First Person: Diary Writing during the Holocaust* (Bloomington: Indiana University Press, 2017), p. 119.

73. Manes, "War Diary," p. 31 (November 2, 1939).

74. Manes, "War Diary," p. 182 (October 26, 1941).

75. Kati Moses to Gerd Moses, August 14 1939, Yad Vashem Archives (YVA), Jerusalem, O.75/2484.

76. Daniel Roche, *The History of Everyday Life: The Birth of Consumption in France 1600–1800* (Cambridge, UK: Cambridge University Press, 2000), p. 16.

77. Werner M. Loval, *We Were Europeans: A Personal History of a Turbulent Century* (Jerusalem: Gefen, 2010), pp. 70–72 (photograph appears on page 72). Interview with Werner Loval (Karoline Lina Löbl's grandson), Jerusalem, August 6, 2017.

78. Mikołaj Szołtysek, "Households and Family Systems in Early Modern Europe," in Hamish Scott, ed., *The Oxford Handbook of Early Modern European History, 1350–1750, Volume I: Peoples and Place* (Oxford, UK: Oxford University Press, 2015), p. 313.

79. Judith Flanders, *The Making of Home: The 500-Year Story of How Our Houses Became Our Homes* (New York: Thomas Dunne Books / St. Martin's Press, 2015), pp. 23–54; Michelle Perrot, "The Family Triumphant," in Michelle Perrot, ed., *A History of Private Life*, vol. 4, pp. 99–129.

80. Csikszentmihalyi and Halton, *The Meaning of Things*, 104. See also David Sibley, *Geographies of Exclusion: Society and Difference in the West* (London: Routledge, 1995), p. 10.

81. Marion A. Kaplan, *The Making of the Jewish Middle Class*, pp. 25–63.

82. Kaplan, *Between Dignity and Despair*, pp. 129–44.

83. Kaplan, *Between Dignity and Despair*, pp. 117.

84. Cohn, *Kein Recht*, p. 655 (June 13, 1939).

85. Seligmann, Tagebuch III, February 22, 1939.

86. Anon., "Geselligkeit—aber wie?" *Israelitisches Familienblatt*, September 16, 1937.

87. Jewish Museum, Berlin, Fotografische Sammlung, inv-Nr. 2012/63/151.

88. Manes, "War Diary," pp. 38 (December 3, 1939) and 92 (August 25, 1940). See also p. 25 (November 25, 1939); p. 169 (September 21, 1941).

89. Manes, "War Diary," p. 204 (December 25, 1941). And see also p. 111 (October 20, 1940). His quote is from Schubert's lied "An die Musik," to a poem by Franz von Schober.

90. On the development of bourgeois *Geselligkeit* in Germany from the end of the eighteenth century through the beginning of the twentieth, and the changes that the concept underwent, see Gisela Mettele, "Der private Raum als öffentlicher Ort. Geselligkeit im bürgerlichen Haus," in Dieter Hein and Andreas Schulz, eds., *Bürgerkultur im 19. Jahrhundert: Bildung, Kunst und Lebenswelt* (Munich: Beck, 1996), pp. 155–69.

91. Attwood Lynne, *Gender and Housing in Soviet Russia: Private Life in a Public Space* (Manchester, UK: Manchester University Press, 2010), pp. 123–39.

92. Mark Peel, "On the Margins: Lodgers and Boarders in Boston, 1860–1900," *Journal of American History* 72, no. 4 (March 1986): 813–34; Richard Harris, "The End Justified the Means: Boarding and Rooming in a City of Homes, 1890–1951," *Journal of Social History* 26, no. 2 (1992): 331–58; Elia Etkin, "Neighborhood, Neighbors, and Neighborly Relations: Urban Life in the Yishuv and in Israel, during the British Mandate and Early Statehood," PhD diss., Tel Aviv University, 2019. I would like to thank Dr. Elia Etkin for sharing the concept of "intimate neighborly relations" with me.

93. Frieda Vallentin, "Probleme des Zusammenwohnens," *Blätter des Jüdischen Frauenbundes* 7 (July 1938): 13.

94. Vallentin, "Probleme des Zusammenwohnens." Emphasis in the original.

95. Iris Rachamimov, "Camp Domesticity, Shifting Gender Boundaries in WWI Internment Camps," in Gilly Carr and Harold Mytum, eds., *Cultural Heritage and Prisoners of War: Creativity behind Barbed Wire* (New York and London: Routledge, 2012), pp. 291–303.

96. Doris Wittner, "Zwischen Welt und Winkel," *Israelitisches Familienblatt*, January 21, 1937.

97. Wittner, "Zwischen Welt und Winkel."

98. Douglas, "The Idea of a Home," p. 299.

99. Klemperer, *I Will Bear Witness, 1933–1941*, p. 340 (May 26, 1940). See also Klemperer's depiction of promiscuity in his move to the *Judenhaus* in Zeughausstrasse 1. Klemperer, *I Will Bear Witness, 1942–1945*, p. 278 (December 14, 1943).

100. Collection of Jeanette Schocken's letters to her children Heinz Schocken and Hilda Schocken in Seattle, Yad Vashem Archives O.75 2774 and O.75 1010, June 2 and 12, 1939.

101. Jeanette Schocken's letters, September 24 and October 1, 1939.

102. Jeanette Schocken's letters, December 19, 1939.

103. Hans Schmoller family papers, Wiener Library, London, 1690, January 4, 6, 14, and 28, 1939.

104. Schmoller family papers, August 10, 1941.

105. Elizabeth H. Pleck, *Celebrating the Family, Ethnicity, Consumer Culture, and Family Rituals* (Cambridge, MA: Harvard University Press, 2000).

106. Schmoller family papers, January 2 and 27, 1939; January 16, 1942.

107. Jeanette Schocken's letters, January 9 and February 9, 1940.

108. Jeanette Schocken's letters, December 10, 1939. A year later they also celebrated Hanukah in what Schocken termed a *gemütlich* atmosphere: undated letter (Hanukah 1940).

109. Jeanette Schocken's letters, October 3, 1941.

110. Gertrud Kolmar, *Briefe*, ed. Johanna Woltmann (Göttingen, Germany: Wallstein Verlag, 2014), p. 30 (February 15, 1939).

111. Kolmar, *Briefe*, p. 110 (June 2, 1941). And see also, on this subject, pp. 44–45 (October 1, 1939) and 169 (August 8–10, 1942).

112. Kolmar, *Briefe*, pp. 37–38 (May 13–14, 1939). On German Jews' feeling of anonymity and alienation at this time, see Kerstin Schoor, *Vom literarischen Zentrum zum literarischen Ghetto*, pp. 322–55.

113. Kolmar, *Briefe*, p. 72 (February 22, 1940).

114. Kolmar, *Briefe*, pp. 60–61 (January 15, 1940).

115. Kolmar, *Briefe*, p. 146 (March 5, 1942).

116. Kolmar, *Briefe*, p. 108 (May 18, 1941).

117. Kolmar, *Briefe*, p. 119 (September 21, 1941).

118. Kolmar, *Briefe*, p. 145 (March 5, 1942).

119. Kolmar, *Briefe*, p. 119 (September 21, 1941).

120. Kolmar, *Briefe*, p. 189 (December 15, 1942).

121. Kolmar, *Briefe*, p. 169 (August 8–10, 1942).

122. Kolmar, *Briefe*, p. 165 (July 19, 1942).

123. Kolmar, *Briefe*, pp. 188–89 (December 15, 1942).

124. *Das Tagebuch der Hertha Nathorff*, p. 155 (April 7, 1939).

125. Martin Heidegger, "Building Dwelling Thinking," in *Poetry, Language, Thought* (New York: Harper & Row, 1971), p. 147.

Chapter 4

1. Walter Tausk, *Breslauer Tagebuch 1933–1940*, Ryszard Kincel ed, (Berlin: Aufbau Taschenbuch, 2000), p. 64, (April 23, 1933). On May Day's transformation into a national labor day in Nazi Germany, and on the way it was marked in the 1930s, see: Fritz Schellack, *Nationalfeiertage in Deutschland von 1871 bis 1945* (Frankfurt a.M: Peter Lang: 1990), pp. 287–92; 306–11.

2. Tausk, *Breslauer Tagebuch*, p. 68 (April 29, 1933).

3. Norbert Elias, *Time: An Essay* (Oxford, UK, and Cambridge, MA: B. Blackwell, 1992), pp. 1–34.

4. Elias, *Time: An Essay*, pp. 49–56, 121–22.

5. Elias, *Time: An Essay*, p. 136.

6. Eviatar Zerubavel, *Time Maps: Collective Memory and the Social Shape of the Past* (Chicago: University of Chicago Press, 2003), pp. 37–54

7. Arno Borst, *The Ordering of Time: From the Ancient Computus to the Modern Computer* (Chicago: University of Chicago Press, 1993).

8. David Cressy, *Bonfires and Bells: National Memory and the Protestant Calendar in Elizabethan and Stuart England* (Berkeley: University of California Press, 1989).

9. Mona Ozouf, *Festivals and the French Revolution* (Cambridge, MA: Harvard University Press, 1991).

10. Wolfgang Schivelbusch, *The Railway Journey: The Industrialization of Time and Space in the 19th Century* (Berkeley: University of California Press, 1986); Jürgen Osterhammel, *The Transformation of the World: A Global History of the Nineteenth Century* (Princeton, NJ: Princeton University Press, 2014), pp. 49–76.

11. John Gillis, *A World of Their Own Making: Myth, Ritual, and the Quest for Family Values* (New York: Basic Books, 1996), pp. 98–108.

12. Joe Perry, *Christmas in Germany: A Cultural History* (Chapel Hill: University of North Carolina Press, 2010), pp. 65–92, 139–88.

13. Benedict Anderson, *Imagined Communities: Reflections on the Origin and Spread of Nationalism* (London: Verso, 1983), p. 63.

14. On this, see also Stephen Kern, *The Culture of Time and Space, 1880–1918* (Cambridge, MA: Harvard University Press, 1983), pp. 65–88. On the role of the press in constituting modern German national identity, see Corey Ross, *Media and the Making of Modern Germany: Mass Communications, Society, and Politics from the Empire to the Third Reich* (New York: Oxford University Press, 2008).

15. For Katz's view, see Jacob Katz, *Die Entstehung der Judenassimilation in Deutschland und deren ideologie* (Darmstadt, Germany: Wissenschaftliche Buchgesellschaft, 1982). See also David Sorkin, *The Transformation of German Jewry 1780–1840* (New York: Oxford University Press, 1987); Simone Lässig, *Jüdische Wege ins Bürgertum: Kulturelles Kapital und sozialer Aufstieg im 19. Jahrhundert* (Göttingen, Germany: Vandenhoeck & Ruprecht, 2004).

16. Elisheva Carlebach, *Palaces of Time: Jewish Calendar and Culture in Early Modern Europe* (Cambridge, MA: Belknap Press of Harvard University Press, 2011).

17. Rahel Straus, *Wir lebten in Deutschland: Erinnerungen einer deutschen Jüdin 1880–1933* (Stuttgart, Germany: Deutsche Verlags-Anstalt, 1961), p. 54.

18. Michael Burleigh, *The Third Reich: A New History* (New York: Hill & Wang, 2000), p. 230, 248, 264; Hans-Jochen Gamm, *Der Braune Kult: Das Dritte Reich und seine Ersatzreligion* (Hamburg: Rütten & Loening, 1962), pp. 156–57.

19. Janosch Steuwer, "*Ein Drittes Reich, wie ich es auffasse*": *Politik, Gesellschaft und privates Leben in Tagebüchern 1933–1939* (Göttingen Germany: Wallstein Verlag, 2017), p. 64.

20. Willy Cohn, *Kein Recht, Nirgends: Tagebuch vom Untergang des Breslauer Judentums, 1933–1941*, ed. Norbert Conrads (Cologne: Böhlau, 2006), p. 33 (April 20, 1933).

21. Kurt F. Rosenberg, "*Einer, der nicht mehr dazugehört*": *Tagebücher 1933–1937*, ed. Beate Meyer and Björn Siegel (Göttingen, Germany: Wallstein Verlag, 2012), p. 87 (May 1, 1933).

22. Rosenberg, "*Einer, der nicht mehr dazugehört*," p. 89 (May 1, 1933).

23. Rosenberg, "*Einer, der nicht mehr dazugehört*," p. 103 (May 19, 1933).

24. Elisabeth Block, *Erinnerungszeichen: Die Tagebücher der Elisabeth Block* (Augsburg, Germany: Bayerische Staatskanzlei, 1993), p. 68 (May 1, 1934).

25. "Margot Littauer Describes Her Everyday School Life in Breslau in Mid 1934," in Wolf Gruner, ed., *The Persecution and Murder of the European Jews by Nazi Germany (PMJ), 1933–1945*, vol. 1, *German Reich, 1933–1937* (Berlin and Boston: Walter de Gruyter, 2019), doc. 128, pp. 383–85 (citation from p. 385).

26. On the exclusion experienced by Jewish children in Nazified German schools, see Marion A. Kaplan, *Between Dignity and Despair: Jewish Life in Nazi Germany*, (New York: Oxford University Press, 1998), pp. 94–99. Kaplan addresses the insults to which Jewish children were subject, especially at special events and on Nazi holidays—on Mother's Day, for example (p. 95).

27. Heinemann Stern, "Jüdische Schulen als Zuflucht," in Margarete Limberg and Hubert Rübsaat, eds., *Sie Durften nicht mehr Deutsche Sein: Jüdischer Alltag in Selbstzeugnissen 1933–1938* (Frankfurt: Campus Verlag, 1990), pp. 225–26.

28. Victor Klemperer, *I Will Bear Witness, A Diary of the Nazi Years, 1933–1941* (New York: Modern Library, 1999), p. 82 (August 11, 1934).

29. Klemperer, *I Will Bear Witness, 1933–1941*, pp. 114 (February 27, 1935) and 215–16 (April 25, 1937).

30. Klemperer, *I Will Bear Witness, 1933–1941*, pp. 260–61 (June 30, 1938).

31. A. H., "In geschichtlicher Stunde, Betrachtungen am 30. Januar," *CV-Zeitung*, February 1, 1934. Hirschberg's discussion of these issues, and especially his critical examination of the age of emancipation and the attempts to seek a new formula that would allow for the Jews' continued integration into German society, was in fact part of the liberal Jewish discourse in Nazi Germany, which spoke of a "new" or a "second" emancipation. See Abraham Margaliot, *Between Rescue and Annihilation: Studies in the History of German Jewry*, 1932–1938 [in Hebrew] (Jerusalem: Yad Vashem, 1990), pp. 183–93; Avraham Barkai, "*Wehr Dich*": *Der Centralverein deutscher Staatsbürger jüdischen Glaubens 1893–1938* (Munich: Beck, 2002), pp. 317–30; Guy Miron, *The Waning of the Emancipation, Jewish History, Memory, and the Rise of Fascism in Germany, France, and Hungary* (Detroit: Wayne State University Press, 2011), pp. 32–34.

32. A. H., "Die doppelte Aufgabe," *CV-Zeitung*, January 31, 1935.

33. "Ein Jahr Regierung Hitler," *Jüdische Rundschau*, January 30, 1934.

34. On the crystallization of this Memorial Day during the Weimar period, see Schellack, *Nationalfeiertage in Deutschland*, pp. 189–92; Thomas Peter Petersen, *Der Volkstrauertag—seine Geschichte und Entwicklung: Eine wissenschaftliche Betrachtung* (Bad Kleinen, Germany: T. P. Petersen, 1998), pp. 9–16; Alexandra Kaiser, *Von Helden und Opfern: Eine Geschichte des Volkstrauertags* (Frankfurt: Campus Verlag, 2010), pp. 24–175.

35. L. H. "Nach dem Volkstrauertag," *CV-Zeitung*, March 16, 1933.

36. A. H. "Heldengedenktag," *CV-Zeitung*, February 22, 1934.

37. On the transition from a day of mourning to Heroes' Memorial Day under the Third Reich, see Schellack, *Nationalfeiertage in Deutschland*, pp. 302–5; Petersen, *Der Volkstrauertag*, pp. 17–28; Kaiser, *Von Helden und Opfern*, pp. 176–209. In March 1935, Erich Seligmann wrote in his diary of the prohibition that forbade Berlin's Jews from participating in the raising of the flag on Memorial Day, when the wreath from the Reich Federation of Jewish Front-Line Soldiers was banned from one monument. See his entry in Diary II of Erich Seligmann (1908–38), Erich Seligmann collection, AR 4104, box 1, folder 1, Leo Baeck Institute, p. 64 (March 17, 1935).

38. A. H., "Feiertag der nationalen Arbeit," *CV-Zeitung*, April 27, 1933.

39. "Der Tag der Arbeit," *Jüdische Rundschau*, May 3, 1933.

40. The principle of "Distanz," according to which the Jews should of their own volition stand apart from the German world so as to maintain the boundaries of their own world, had been a central aspect of the German Zionist leadership's worldview since the Weimar Republic. Its most prominent spokesman was Kurt Blumenfeld. Jehuda Reinharz called the second generation of the German Zionist leadership, under Blumenfeld, "the 'distanz' generation." See Jehuda Reinharz, "Three Generations of German Zionism," *Jerusalem Quarterly* 9 (Fall 1978): 99–105.

41. A. H., "Zum 1. Mai," *CV-Zeitung*, April 26, 1934; A. H. "Die Arbeit bleibt," *CV-Zeitung*, May 3, 1935.

42. Rosenberg, "*Einer, der nicht mehr dazugehört*," p. 189 (May 1, 1934).

43. Cohn, *Kein Recht*, p. 220 (May 1, 1935); and see also his reference to another instance in which they canceled a trip because of a Nazi holiday: p. 633 (April 20, 1939).

44. Cohn, *Kein Recht*, pp. 272–73 (September 9, 1935).

45. Klemperer, *I Will Bear Witness, 1933–1941*, p. 253 (April 10, 1938).

46. Rosenberg, "*Einer, der nicht mehr dazugehört*," p. 308 (December 29, 1935).

47. Rosenberg, "*Einer, der nicht mehr dazugehört*," pp. 369–70 (September 15, 1936).

48. Cohn, *Kein Recht*, p. 489 (November 9, 1937).

49. Cohn, *Kein Recht*, p. 536 (November 9, 1938).

50. Tausk, *Breslauer Tagebuch*, p. 242 (November 12, 1939). See also Cohn, *Kein Recht*, pp. 868 (November 9, 1940) and 1005 (November 8, 1941).

51. Tausk, *Breslauer Tagebuch*, p. 206 (December 3, 1938).

52. Cohn, *Kein Recht*, p. 560 (December 3, 1938). And in a similar context, see also Klemperer, *I Will Bear Witness, 1933–1941*, p. 277 (December 3, 1938).

53. On the secularization of Christmas and its new guise as a bourgeois, national, and consumerist holiday in American society, see Elizabeth H. Pleck, *Celebrating the Family: Ethnicity, Consumer Culture, and Family Rituals* (Cambridge, MA: Harvard University Press, 2000), pp. 43–72.

54. Perry, *Christmas in Germany*, pp. 1–92.

55. Perry, *Christmas in Germany*, pp. 67–76. Nancy R. Reagin, *Sweeping the German Nation: Domesticity and National Identity in Germany 1870–1945* (New York: Cambridge University Press, 2007), p. 46. Marion Kaplan argues that the adoption of practices from Christian holidays—Christmas trees and Easter egg hunts—was restricted to a small minority of Jewish families during the imperial period. See Marion A. Kaplan, *The Making of the Jewish Middle Class: Women, Family and Identity in Imperial Germany* (New York: Oxford University Press, 1991), p. 76.

56. Perry, *Christmas in Germany*, pp. 189–238.

57. "Weihnachten und die deutsche Juden," *Jüdische Rundschau*, December 22, 1933.

58. And see also, in this context, "Makkabäertage," *Jüdische Rundschau*, December 12, 1933.

59. Wolfgang Salinger, "Von der neuen Aufgabe," in "Unsere Jüngeren suchen ein Fest," *CV-Zeitung, Seite der Jugend*, December 6, 1934.

60. Ignaz Maybaum, "Der Weihnachtsbaum," *CV-Zeitung*, December 28, 1934.

61. "Weniger Licht, aber eigenes!" *Der Israelit*, November 29, 1934.

62. Max Reiner, "Der Weg zum Paria," in *Sie Durften nicht mehr Deutsche Sein*, p. 153.

63. Seligmann, Diary II, December 24, 1934.

64. Lisbeth Schmidt, Diaries 1920–59, ME 1493, Leo Baeck Institute, June 9, 1936.

65. Rosenberg, "*Einer, der nicht mehr dazugehört*," pp. 298–307 (December 26, 1935). The quote is from pp. 301, 307.

66. Perry, *Christmas in Germany*, pp. 139–88.

67. Cohn, *Kein Recht*, p. 114 (December 24, 1933).

68. Cohn, *Kein Recht*, p. 310 (December 24, 1935).

69. Cohn, *Kein Recht*, p. 372 (December 25, 1936).

70. Cohn, *Kein Recht*, p. 571 (December 22, 1938).

71. Cohn, *Kein Recht*, p. 502 (December 25, 1937); and see also p. 734 (December 24, 1939).

72. Cohn, *Kein Recht*, p. 883 (December 24, 1940).

73. Block, *Erinnerungszeichen*, pp. 62–63 (Der Heilige Abend 1933).

74. Block, *Erinnerungszeichen*, pp. 162–63 (November 17, 1938). Citation from p. 163.

75. Block, *Erinnerungszeichen*, pp. 164–65 (December 24, 1938).

76. Block, *Erinnerungszeichen*, pp. 193–94 (Der Heilige Abend 1939), 230 (Weihnachten 1940), and 261–62 (December 24, 1941).

77. Hans Schmoller family papers, Wiener Library, London, 1690, January 18, 1942.

78. Klemperer, *I Will Bear Witness, 1933–1941*, p. 284 (December 25, 1938).

79. Victor Klemperer, *I Will Bear Witness: A Diary of the Nazi Years, 1942–1945* (New York: Modern Library, 2001), p. 385 (December 23, 1944).

80. Klemperer, *I Will Bear Witness, 1933–1941*, p. 284 (December 25, 1938).

81. Klemperer, *I Will Bear Witness, 1933–1941*, p. 366 (December 26, 1940).

82. Klemperer, *I Will Bear Witness, 1933–1941*, p. 451 (December 22, 1941).

83. On the routine confinement of Jews to their neighborhoods on Sundays and Christian holidays in the Holy Roman Empire during the modern age, see Lucia Raspe, "Die Lebensbedingungen des Ghettos in der jüdischen Brauchtumliteraur der frühen Neuzeit," in Fritz Backhaus, Gisela Engel, Gundula Grebner, and Robert Liberles, eds., *Frühneuzeitliche Ghettos in Europa im Vergleich* (Berlin: Trafo, 2012), p. 304.

84. A. H. "Silvestergedanken," *CV-Zeitung*, December 29, 1933.

85. A. H. "Die Sekunde der Jahreswende," *CV-Zeitung*, January 4, 1935; A. H. "1936," *CV-Zeitung*, January 3, 1936; A. H., "Zwischen zwei Jahre," *CV-Zeitung*, December 31, 1936.

86. Cohn, *Kein Recht*, p. 118 (December 31, 1933).

87. Cohn, *Kein Recht*, p. 373 (December 31, 1936).

88. Cohn, *Kein Recht*, p. 737 (December 31, 1939).

89. Cohn, *Kein Recht*, pp. 885 (December 31, 1940) and 886 (January 1, 1941).

90. Klemperer, *I Will Bear Witness, 1933–1941*, pp. 284–85 (New Year's Eve 1938).

91. Klemperer, *I Will Bear Witness, 1942–1945*, pp. 181–82 (December 31, 1942).

92. Carlebach, *Palaces of Time*, p. 74.

93. The drastic initiative to move the Jewish Sabbath to Sunday promoted by the radical Rabbi Samuel Holdheim won little support. See Michael A. Meyer, "Jewish Self-Understanding," in Michael Brenner, Stefi Jersch-Wenzel, and Michael A. Meyer, *Emancipation and Acculturation: 1780–1871*, vol. 2 in Michael Meyer, ed., *German-Jewish History in Modern Times* (New York: Columbia University Press, 1997), pp. 165–66.

94. Carlebach, *Palaces of Time*, pp. 207–11.

95. Kaplan, *Making of the Jewish Middle Class*, pp. 74–76.

96. Zerubavel, *Time Maps*, p. 4, 47.

97. "Stille Feiertage, Volk und Geschichte," *Jüdische Rundschau*, April 7, 1933.

98. Cohn, *Kein Recht*, p. 29 (April 11, 1933).

99. Max Wiener, "Pessach-Feier in dieser Zeit," *CV-Zeitung*, April 6, 1933.

100. Kurt Blumenfeld, "Die innerjüdische Seite," *Jüdische Rundschau*, April 7, 1933.

101. Etty Hirschfeld, "Wie die Berliner Pessach feierten: Seder wie noch nie," *Jüdisch-Liberale Zeitung*, April 6, 1934.

102. "Pessach in den jüdischen Gemeinden," *Gemeindeblatt der juedischen Gemeinde zu Berlin*, March 22, 1936. See also Jacob Borut, *Jewish Religious Practice under Nazi Rule (1933–1938) and Its Reflection in the German-Jewish Press* [in Hebrew] (Jerusalem: Yad Vashem, 2017), pp. 35–36.

103. Stadtrabbiner Dr. Schiff, Karlsruhe, "Pessach," *CV-Zeitung*, April 17, 1935. On the wave interpretation of Jewish history as voiced by liberal Jewish writers in this period, see Miron, *Waning of the Emancipation*, pp. 39–42.

104. Ignaz Maybaum, "Unsere Pessach," *CV-Zeitung*, April 2, 1936.

105. Alfred Hirschberg, "Gegürtet," *CV-Zeitung*, March 25, 1937.

106. Rabbiner Dr. L. Baerwald, München, "Pessach, das Fest des Übergangs," *CV-Zeitung*, March 25, 1937.

107. Borut, *Jewish Religious Practice under Nazi Rule*, sources 35–39 (pp. 120–23) and 66–71 (pp. 144–48).

108. C. Seligmann, "Zum Laubhüttenfest: Das ewige Haus der Väter," *CV-Zeitung*, October 11, 1933. See also Hermann Vogelstein, "Hüttenfest," *CV-Zeitung*, September 21, 1934.

109. Gemeinderabbiner Dr. Grün, "Laubhüttenfest," October 10, 1935; Manfred Swarsensky, "Fest unserer Freude," *CV-Zeitung*, October 1, 1936.

110. Manfred Swarsensky, "Die neue Lehre, Zu Schowuaus," *CV-Zeitung*, May 27, 1936.

111. The term "usable past" serves historians, in both Jewish and German history, in their discussions of the issues involved in the constitution of social memory and its adaptation to events in the past and the needs of the present. See, for example, David G. Roskies, *The Jewish Search for a Usable Past* (Bloomington: Indiana University Press, 1999); Robert G. Moeller, *War Stories, The Search for a Usable Past in the Federal Republic of Germany* (Berkeley: University of California Press, 2001).

112. Borut, *Jewish Religious Practice under Nazi Rule*, sources 62–65 (pp. 143–44).

113. *Israelitishes Familienblatt*, October 4, 1934, p. 12.

114. See, for example, Alfred Hirschberg, "Rosch Haschana 5694, An die Schwelle des Jahres . . . ," *CV-Zeitung*, September 20, 1933; Julius Brodnitz, "Rosch Haschana 5695, Festtags-Gruss an die Freunde," *CV-Zeitung*, September 6, 1934.

115. "Der Nationalismus der inneren Einkehr, Eine Neujahrbetrachtung 5695," *Jüdische Rundschau*, September 7, 1934.

116. Manfred Swarsensky, "Rosch Haschana 5696, Schicksal als Aufgabe," *CV-Zeitung*, September 26, 1935.

117. "Feiertagsgedenken," *Jüdische Rundschau*, September 29, 1933.

118. Rabbiner Dr. Eschelbacher, "Sendung, Schuld und Schicksal, Zum Versönungstag," *CV-Zeitung*, September 14, 1934.

119. The quote is from: Bezirksrabbiner Ernst Jacob–Augsburg, "Verlorenes Glück? Betrachtung zum Jom Kippur 5697," *CV-Zeitung*, September 24, 1936. See also M. Eschelbacher, "Gottes Joch, Zum Yom Hakkipurim 5696," *CV-Zeitung*, October 3, 1935; Rabbiner Dr. S. Ocs, Gleiwitz, "Der Versöhnungstag als Erlebnis und Forderung," *CV-Zeitung*, September 9, 1937.

120. Cohn, *Kein Recht*, p. 79 (September 20, 1933).

121. Cohn, *Kein Recht*, p. 155 (September 9, 1934).

122. Cohn, *Kein Recht*, p. 465 (September 5, 1937).

123. Cohn, *Kein Recht*, p. 285 (October 6, 1935).

124. Cohn, *Kein Recht*, p. 696 (September 22, 1939).

125. Eric Lucas, *The Sovereigns: A Jewish Family in the German Countryside* (Evanston, IL: Northwestern University Press, 2001), p. 122.

126. Max Wiener, "Jüdisches Volksgedächtnis, Zu Tisch'a b'aw 5693," *Jüdische Rundschau*, August 1, 1933. For another Zionist view of the Ninth of Av, see Erich Rosenblüth, "Gedanken zum Tisch'ah be'aw 5694," *Jüdische Rundschau*, July 20, 1934.

127. A. H. "Tisch'oh beaw," *CV-Zeitung*, July 19, 1934. Four years later, Hirschberg even more insistently demanded that his readers treat the recurrence of the Ninth of Av as an opportunity for self-examination. See A. H., "Glauben und Erkenntnisse, Gedanken zu Tischa beaw," *CV-Zeitung*, August 7, 1938.

128. Cohn, *Kein Recht*, p. 340 (July 27, 1936).

129. Cohn, *Kein Recht*, p. 830 (August 13, 1940).

130. On the Weimar period, see Trude Maurer, "From Everyday Life to a State of Emergency: Jews in Weimar and Nazi Germany," in Marion Kaplan, ed., *Jewish Daily Life in Germany 1618–1945*, (New York and Oxford, UK: Oxford University Press, 2005), p. 328. On the Nazi period, see Borut, *Jewish Religious Practice under Nazi Rule*, pp. 36–37.

131. For a range of reports on Hanukah parties, see Borut, *Jewish Religious Practice under Nazi Rule*, sources 73–74 (pp. 149–150) and 77–80 (pp. 153–55). On the diverse dis-

course of young Jews on this subject, see "Unsere Jüngern suchen ein Fest," *CV-Zeitung, Seite der Jugend*, December 6, 1934; "Jugend feiert Chanukkah," *Jüdische Rundschau*, December 7, 1934.

132. Hanna Livnat, *The Press for Jewish Children and Youth in Germany 1933–1938: Warning or Reassuring* [in Hebrew] (Jerusalem: Yad Vashem, 2017), p. 35. For the original tale, see Frieda Mehler, "Chanukka Märchen," *Kinderblatt, CV-Zeitung*, November 29, 1934.

133. "Das missverstandene Chanukafest," *Der Israelit*, December 6, 1934.

134. See, for example, Manfred Swarsensky, "Das 2001: Chanukka," *CV-Zeitung*, December 19, 1935; Julius Brodnitz, "Die Chanukka-Feier," *CV-Zeitung*, December 24, 1935; Fritz Friedländer, "Makkabäische Idee und Wirklichkeit," *CV-Zeitung*, November 25, 1937.

135. See, for example, Ludwig Feuchtwanger, "Weinen und Lachen, zum Purim Fest 5694," *Jüdische Rundschau*, February 27, 1934; Isch Yehudi, "Heute ist Purim, Morgen ist's aus!" *CV-Zeitung*, March 1, 1934.

136. Arno Herzberg, "The Jewish Press under the Nazi Regime: Its Mission, Suppression and Defiance; A Memoir," *Leo Baeck Institute Year Book* 36 (1991): 371.

137. Borut, *Jewish Religious Practice under Nazi Rule*, pp. 37–38. See also sources 82–87 (pp. 157–61) and 100 (pp. 173–74).

138. CV Wandkalender 5696 1935/36 *CV-Zeitung*, October 10, 1935.

139. On the pantheon of heroes, see Guy Miron, "The Emancipation Heroes' Pantheon in German-Jewish Public Memory of the 1930s," *German History* 21, no. 4 (2003): 476–504.

140. "Jüdischer C.V. Kalendar 5697," *CV-Zeitung*, September 16, 1936; "CV Kalender 5698," *CV-Zeitung*, September 9, 1937.

141. Zionistische Vereinigung für Deutschland, ed. (Redaktion Joachim Prinz), *Palästina Kalender* 5696, 5697 (Berlin: ZVfD, 1936).

142. Hans Oppenheimer, "Kalender–Kalender," *CV-Zeitung*, September 2, 1937.

143. Rosy Bodenheimer, "Vergangene Zeiten," *CV-Zeitung*, September 2, 1937.

144. "On 20 July 1938 Berlin's Chief of Police Issues Guidelines for the Discrimination against Jews," in Susanne Heim, ed., *The Persecution and Murder of the European Jews by Nazi Germany, vol. 2., German Reich 1938–August 1939* (Berlin and Boston: Walter de Gruyter, 2019), doc. 68, p. 240.

145. Klemperer, *I Will Bear Witness, 1942–1945*, p. 359 (September 18, 1944). And see an interesting previous reference by Klemperer to the Jewish calendar: Klemperer, *I Will Bear Witness, 1933–1941*, p. 134 (October 5, 1935).

146. Klemperer, *I Will Bear Witness, 1942–1945*, p. 359 (September 18, 1944).

147. See his attitude to January 30, the anniversary of the Nazi rise to power, a day on which he was particularly preoccupied with the question of how much longer the regime would last. Klemperer, *I Will Bear Witness, 1942–1945*, p. 294 (January 30, 1944).

148. Klemperer, *I Will Bear Witness, 1942–1945*, p. 452 (April 19, 1945).

149. Lothar Kroll, *Utopie als Ideologie: Geschichtsdenken und politisches Handeln im Dritten Reich* (Paderborn, Germany: Schöningh, 1999), pp. 32–37. On the unevenness of time as a characteristic of the magical premodern world, see Keith Thomas, *Religion and the Decline of Magic* (New York: Scribner's Sons, 1971), pp. 615–28.

Chapter 5

1. Kurt F. Rosenberg, *"Einer, der nicht mehr dazugehört": Tagebücher 1933–1937*, ed. Beate Meyer and Björn Siegel (Göttingen, Germany: Wallstein, 2012), p. 187 (April 18, 1934).

2. Rosenberg, "*Einer, der nicht mehr dazugehört*," p. 194 (May 13, 1934). The internal quotation marks are in the original.

3. Rosenberg, "*Einer, der nicht mehr dazugehört*," p. 208 (June 16, 1934).

4. Alberto Melucci, *The Playing Self: Person and Meaning in the Planetary Society* (Cambridge, UK: Cambridge Cultural Social Studies, 1996), p. 14.

5. Orvar Löfgren, "Rational and Sensitive: Changing Attitudes to Time, Nature and the Home," in Jonas Frykman and Orvar Löfgren, eds., *Culture Builders: A Historical Anthropology of Middle-Class Life* (New Brunswick, NJ, and London: Rutgers University Press, 1987), pp. 27–31.

6. Pitirim Sorokin, *Sociocultural Causality, Space and Time: A Study of Referential Principles of Sociology and Social Sciences* (New York: Russell and Russell, 1964), pp. 164–67, 190; Alberto Melucci, *The Playing Self*, p. 18.

7. Eugène Minkowski, *Lived Time: Phenomenological and Psychopathological Studies* (Evanston, IL: Northwestern University Press, 1970), pp. 6, 87–88.

8. Stephen Kern, *The Culture of Time and Space, 1880–1918* (London: Weidenfeld and Nicolson, 1983), pp. 89–91.

9. Lothar Kroll, *Utopie als Ideologie: Geschichtsdenken und politisches Handeln im Dritten Reich* (Paderborn, Germany: Schöningh, 1999), pp. 32–37. See also Dan Stone, *Histories of the Holocaust* (New York: Oxford University Press), 2010, pp. 255–56; Christopher Clark, *Time and Power: Visions of History in German Politics, from the Thirty Years' War to the Third Reich* (Princeton, NJ: Princeton University Press, 2019), pp. 171–210.

10. Ian Kershaw, *Hitler, 1889–1936: Hubris* (London: Allen Lane, 1998), p. 435.

11. Ian Kershaw, *Hitler, 1936–1945: Nemesis* (London: Allen Lane, 2000), pp. 64, 228–29, 276, 285.

12. Ian Kershaw, *Hitler, 1936–1945*, p. 28.

13. On the policy of patience as Russian Jewry's response to the pogroms of 1881, see Jonathan Frankel, *Prophecy and Politics: Socialism, Nationalism, and the Russian Jews* (Cambridge, UK: Cambridge University Press, 1981), p. 53. Frankel notes that it was a traditional Jewish response.

14. "Um Deutschland," *CV–Zeitung*, March 2, 1933.

15. "Zum 21. März," *Jüdische Rundschau*, March 21, 1933. Emphasis in the original.

16. Ismar Elbogen, "Haltung!" *CV–Zeitung*, April 6, 1933.

17. H. B., "Grenzen des Boykotts," *CV–Zeitung*, April 6, 1933.

18. "Verantwortung," *CV–Zeitung*, June 29, 1933. Emphasis in original.

19. Jewish history was frequently cited by such writers, especially those of the liberal camp, as they attempted to understand the fate of the Jews following the rise of the Nazi regime. Some went so far as to propose laws of Jewish history. See Guy Miron, *The Waning of Emancipation: Jewish History, Memory, and the Rise of Fascism in Germany, France and Hungary* (Detroit: Wayne State University Press, 2011), pp. 34–45. See also below, chapter 6.

20. Felix Goldmann, "Die Pfeiler unserer Zukunft," *CV–Zeitung*, October 11, 1934.

21. Felix Goldmann, "Die Pfeiler unserer Zukunft."

22. Hans Reichmann, "Geschichtsbewusstsein ist gefordert," *CV-Zeitung*, April 4, 1935.

23. "Juden und höhere Bildung: Was wird aus unseren Kindern?—Schafft jüdische Schulen!" *Jüdische Rundschau*, April 25, 1933. Emphasis in the original.

24. Kurt Blumenfeld, "Echte oder scheinbare Wandlung?" *Jüdische Rundschau*, May 9, 1933. Emphasis in original.

25. Daniel Frankel, *On the Edge of the Abyss: Zionist Policy and the Question of German Jewry, 1933–1938* [in Hebrew] (Jerusalem: Magnes, 1994), pp. 63–72.

26. Max Wiener, "Warten und Wirken," *Jüdische Rundschau*, December 12, 1933.

27. Wiener, "Warten und Wirken." Emphasis in the original. See also, in this context, Wiener's article on the Ninth of Av, discussed briefly in chapter 4: Max Wiener, "Jüdisches Volksgedächtnis, Zu Tisch'a b'aw 5693," *Jüdische Rundschau*, August 1, 1933. Wiener calls on his readers to turn the power of the sentimental pain of exile into a constructive force that unambiguously involves the transformation of waiting time into action time.

28. Leo Baeck, "Rosch Haschana 5694," *Jüdische Rundschau*, September 20, 1933.

29. On these changes for the Jewish press in Germany, see Thomas Pegelow Kaplan, *The Language of Nazi Genocide: Linguistic Violence and the Struggle of Germans of Jewish Ancestry* (Cambridge, UK: Cambridge University Press, 2009), pp. 121–24.

30. "Warten . . . ," *CV-Zeitung*, September 1, 1938.

31. Alberto Melucci, *The Playing Self*, pp. 18–19.

32. Eviatar Zerubavel, *Time Maps, Collective Memory and the Social Shape of the Past* (Chicago: University of Chicago Press, 2003), p. 26. See also Norbert Elias, *Time: An Essay* (Oxford, UK, and Cambridge, MA: B. Blackwell, 1992), p. 39.

33. This, for example, is the analysis offered by a prominent study of different forms of waiting among unemployed young members of the Indian middle class, which it argues reflect a range of processes of social and class dynamics. See Jeffrey Craig, *Timepass: Youth, Class, and the Politics of Waiting in India* (Stanford, CA: Stanford University Press, 2010). Experiences of imposed waiting (which are also described as being in the liminal state of limbo) and ways of coping with them are also discussed in the context of the lives of today's migrants and refugees at international border crossings. See Anne McNevin and Antje Missbach, "Luxury Limbo: Temporal Techniques of Border Control and the Humanitarianisation of Waiting," *International Journal for Migration and Border Studies* 4, nos. 1/2 (2018): 12–34.

34. Kern, *The Culture of Time and Space*, p. 34.

35. Iris Rachamimov, *Islands of Men: Shifting Gender Boundaries in WWI Internment Camps*, forthcoming. I am grateful to Iris Rachamimov for providing me with an advanced draft of her study. Ronit Or, "The Reconciliation Sphere of the Pacifist Carpenter: The Quaker James T. Baily's Relief Labour with Interned Enemy Aliens at Knockaloe Camp during World War I" [in Hebrew], *Zmanim: A Historical Quarterly* 141 (2019): 18–33.

36. Paul Cohen-Portheim, *Time Stood Still: My Internment in England, 1914–1918* (New York: E. P. Dutton, 1932), p. 48. Cited in Or, "The Reconciliation Sphere," p. 22.

37. On the effect that the career mentality has on the bourgeois male's experience of time, see Orvar Löfgren, "Rational and Sensitive," pp. 27–31.

38. Marion A. Kaplan, *Between Dignity and Despair: Jewish Life in Nazi Germany* (New York: Oxford University Press, 1998), pp. 50–54. For a new study of the way Jewish men coped with the crisis in their employment and work routine, see Sebastian Huebel, *Fighter, Worker, and Family Man: German-Jewish Men and Their Gendered Experiences in Nazi Germany, 1933–1941* (Toronto: University of Toronto Press, 2022), pp. 66–94.

39. Willy Cohn, *Kein Recht, Nirgends: Tagebuch vom Untergang des Breslauer Judentums, 1933–1941*, ed. Norbert Conrads (Cologne: Böhlau, 2006), p. 7 (January 31, 1933).

40. On the unique role played by this school in the fabric of the lives of Breslau's Jews, see Till van Rahden, *Jews and Other Germans: Civil Society, Religious Diversity, and Urban Politics in Breslau, 1860–1925* (Madison: University of Wisconsin Press, 2008), pp. 134–58.

41. Cohn, *Kein Recht*, p. 38 (May 2, 1933).

42. Cohn, *Kein Recht*, pp. 52–53 (June 18, 1933).

43. Cohn, *Kein Recht*, p. 56 (June 27, 1933).

44. Kaplan, *Between Dignity and Despair*, pp. 67–69.

45. Cohn, *Kein Recht*, p. 57 (June 28, 1933); see also p. 62 (July 20, 1933).

46. Rosenberg, "*Einer, der nicht mehr dazugehört*," p. 126 (June 25, 1933).

47. Rosenberg, "*Einer, der nicht mehr dazugehört*," p. 78 (April 7, 1933).

48. Rosenberg, "*Einer, der nicht mehr dazugehört*," p. 79 (April 11, 1933).

49. Rosenberg, "*Einer, der nicht mehr dazugehört*," p. 128 (August 7, 1933).

50. Rosenberg, "*Einer, der nicht mehr dazugehört*," p. 144 (September 6, 1933). And see similar depictions on pp. 164 (January 24, 1934) and 167 (February 4, 1934).

51. Victor Klemperer, *I Will Bear Witness: A Diary of the Nazi Years, 1933–1941* (New York: Modern Library, 1999), pp. 13–14 (April 12, 1933).

52. Victor Klemperer, *Ich will Zeugnis ablegen bis zum letzten: Tagebücher 1933–1941* (Berlin: Aufbau-Verlag, 1995), p. 27 (May 15, 1933). This quotation does not appear in the English edition.

53. Klemperer, *I Will Bear Witness, 1933–1941*, p. 17 (May 15, 1933).

54. Quotation marks in the original. Klemperer, *I Will Bear Witness, 1933–1941*, p.22 (June 30, 1933). Elsewhere, Klemperer links "empty and breathless busyness" to "absolute uncertainty"; see p. 280 (December 15, 1938).

55. Klemperer, *I Will Bear Witness, 1933–1941*, p. 76 (July 27, 1934).

56. Klemperer, *I Will Bear Witness, 1933–1941*, p. 108 (January 16, 1935).

57. Klemperer, *I Will Bear Witness, 1933–1941*, p. 241 (November 28, 1937).

58. Cohn, *Kein Recht*, p. 25 (April 1, 1933). On the closed horizon of the future and the experience of waiting, see also pp. 53 (June 18, 1933), 62 (July 20, 1933), and 69 (August 15, 1933).

59. Klemperer, *I Will Bear Witness, 1933–1941*, p. 128 (July 21, 1935).

60. Klemperer, *I Will Bear Witness, 1933–1941*, pp. 242–43 (December 28, 1937).

61. B. Brzg., "Der einsame Mensch," *Israelitisches Familienblatt*, June 30, 1938. For further discussion of loneliness in the Jewish press, see W. Blumenthal, "Erlebnis der Einsamkeit," *CV-Zeitung*, March 10, 1938, p. 3; "Uns fällt auf. . . . Vereinsamung," *Israelitisches Familienblatt*, April 12, 1934; Doris Wittner: "Zwischen Welt und Winkel," *Israelitisches Familienblatt*, January 21, 1937.

62. Cohn, *Kein Recht*, p. 238–39 (June 10, 1935).

63. Cohn, *Kein Recht*, p. 239 (June 10, 1935).

64. Rosenberg, "*Einer, der nicht mehr dazugehört*," p. 369 (September 15, 1936).

65. Klemperer, *I Will Bear Witness, 1933–1941*, p. 261 (July 12, 1938).

66. Beate Meyer, "'Ich leide als Deutscher wie als Jude,' Kurt F. Rosenberg: Seine Tagebücher 1933–1937, sein Leben und die Geschichte seiner Familie," in Rosenberg, "*Einer, der nicht mehr dazugehört*," p. 20.

67. Max Wiener, "Das Tempo unserer neueren Geschichte," *Jüdische Rundschau*, September 20, 1933. Emphasis in original.

68. Rosenberg, "*Einer, der nicht mehr dazugehört*," p. 250 (November 1, 1934).

69. Rosenberg, "*Einer, der nicht mehr dazugehört*," p. 264 (February 11, 1935).

70. Martha Wertheimer, "Freundschaft—jetzt," *Gemeindeblatt der israelitischen Religionsgemeinde zu Leipzig*, July 9, 1937.

71. A fundamentally similar insight can be found in an earlier piece by Wertheimer, in which she addressed the case of a teenage girl waiting for a permit ("certificate") to

immigrate to Palestine. Wertheimer called on the girl, living in a state of uncertainty, to make the most of the present.

72. Günter Friedländer, *Jüdische Jugend zwischen gestern und morgen* (Berlin, Jüdische Wirklichkeit Heute no. 2, 1938).

73. Friedländer, *Jüdische Jugend*, p. 27.

74. Friedländer, *Jüdische Jugend*, p. 30.

75. Kaplan, *Between Dignity and Despair*, pp. 129–44.

76. Hans Reichmann, *Deutscher Bürger und verfolgter Jude: Novemberpogrom und KZ Sachsenhausen 1937–1939* (Munich: R. Oldenburg Verlag, 1998), pp. 259–60.

77. Reichmann, *Deutscher Bürger und verfolgter Jude*, pp. 261, 266–67.

78. Klemperer, *I Will Bear Witness, 1933–1941*, p. 295 (March 6, 1939). See also Walter Tausk, *Breslauer Tagebuch 1933–1940*, ed. Ryszard Kincel (Berlin: Aufbau Taschenbuch Verlag, 2000), p. 220 (April 2, 1939). Tausk recounts how he received a *Wartenummer*, his number in line on the list for emigration to the United States, adding that it meant he would have to wait until the end of 1941 to be able to leave.

79. Sigmund-Shmuel and Gertrud Hirschberg, letter from Berlin to Palestine, March 19, 1939, in *From Berlin to Shanghai: Letters to Palestine* [in Hebrew] (Jerusalem: Yad Vashem, 2013), pp. 83–84.

80. Hirschberg, letters from Berlin to Palestine, March 29 and April 18, 1939, in *From Berlin to Shanghai*, pp. 89, 99.

81. Hirschberg, letter from Berlin to Palestine, April 20, 1939, in *From Berlin to Shanghai*, p. 102.

82. Hirschberg, letter from Berlin to Palestine, May 5 and May 11, 1939, in *From Berlin to Shanghai*, pp. 105, 107.

83. Hirschberg, letter from Lloyd Triestino to Palestine, May 11, 1939, in *From Berlin to Shanghai*, p. 107.

84. Phillip Maines, "War Diary, 1939–1942," Wiener Library, London, doc. 1346, box 10 4.5a, p. 56 (March 20, 1940).

85. Manes, "War Diary," p. 67 (May 1, 1940).

86. Thomas Mann, *The Magic Mountain*, trans. John E. Woods (New York: Vintage International, 1996), p. 102.

87. Moritz Föllmer, *Individuality and Modernity in Berlin: Self and Society from Weimar to the Wall* (Cambridge, UK: Cambridge University Press, 2013), pp. 133–55. See p. 145 on the tension between personal agency and reduced individuality.

88. Cohn, *Kein Recht*, p. 615 (March 15, 1939). And see the Hirschbergs' portrayal to their son: Hirschberg, letters from Berlin to Palestine, April 4, and 20, 1939, and more, in *From Berlin to Shanghai*, pp. 90, 102, etc.

89. "On 7 June 1940 Valerie Scheftel from Berlin Writes a Yearning Letter to Her Sweetheart Karl Wildmann in the USA," document 86, in Andrea Löw, ed., *The Persecution and Murder of the European Jews by Nazi Germany, Vol. 3: German Reich and Protectorate of Bohemia and Moravia September 1939–September 1941* (Berlin and Boston: Walter de Gruyter, 2020), p. 251.

90. Klemperer, *I Will Bear Witness, 1933–1941*, p. 323 (New Year's Eve 1939, Sunday evening).

91. Klemperer, *I Will Bear Witness, 1933–1941*, p. 328 (January 21, 1940).

92. Klemperer, *I Will Bear Witness, 1933–1941*, p. 353 (August 30, 1940).

93. Klemperer, *I Will Bear Witness, 1933–1941*, p. 381 (April 14, 1941).

94. The expression "snail's pace" (*Schneckentempo*) appears in Klemperer, *I Will Bear*

Witness, 1942–1945, p. 272 (November 14, 1943). For other examples, see pp. 242 (July 4, 1943), 256–57 (September 4, 1943), and 301 (March 10, 1944).

95. Emphasis in the original. For a description of waiting that becomes ever more excruciating, see Klemperer, *I Will Bear Witness, 1942–1945*, p. 372 (October 27, 1944). For the expressions "How much longer?" (*Wie lange noch?*) and "But when?" (*Aber wann?*), see, for example, pp. 6 (January 17, 1942), 258 (September 13, 1943), 324 (June 10, 1944), 351 (August 28, 1944), and 390 (January 6, 1945).

96. Klemperer, *I Will Bear Witness, 1942–1945*, p. 32 (March 24, 1942).

97. See for example, Cohn *Kein Recht*, p. 783 (April 19, 1940).

98. Klemperer, *I Will Bear Witness, 1942–1945*, p. 55 (May 19, 1942).

99. Klemperer, *I Will Bear Witness, 1942–1945*, p. 71 (June 9, 1942).

100. Kaplan, *Between Dignity and Despair*, pp. 173–79.

101. Elisabeth Freund, *Als Zwangsarbeiterin 1941 in Berlin: Die Aufzeichnungen der Volkswirtin Elisabeth Freund*, ed. and annotated by Carola Sachse (Berlin: Akademie, 1996), p. 53.

102. Freund, *Als Zwangsarbeiterin 1941*, p. 113.

103. Freund, *Als Zwangsarbeiterin 1941*, p. 121; and see additional references to the flow of time during her work in the armaments factory, pp. 108 and 129.

104. Arno Nadel, *Tagebuch* (2 volumes; copies of originals), 1941–42; AR 4314, Leo Baeck Institute, June 1942, p. 7.

105. Nadel, *Tagebuch*, pp. 50 (July 3, 1942) and 61 (July 10, 1942).

106. Minkowski, *Lived Time*; cited in Kern, *Culture of Time and Space*, p. 90.

107. Klemperer, *I Will Bear Witness, 1933–1941*, p. 446 (November 28, 1941).

108. Manes, *War Diary*, January 18, 1942, p. 209.

109. Klemperer, *I Will Bear Witness, 1942–1945*, p. 423 (February 27, 1945).

110. Hartmut Rosa, *Social Acceleration: A New Theory of Modernity* (New York: Columbia University Press, 2013).

111. Rosa addresses the issue of slowing time throughout his book, in different contexts; see p. 16 as well as pp. 80–93.

112. Klemperer, *I Will Bear Witness, 1933–1941*, pp. 393–94 (June 23–July 1, 1941).

113. Klemperer, *I Will Bear Witness, 1933–1941*, p. 399 (June 23–July 1, 1941).

114. Amos Goldberg has proposed an original interpretation of Klemperer's diary, using psychoanalytical theory to analyze the appearance of time standing still. In the diary, on his account, time standing in place represents death. Amos Goldberg, *Trauma in First Person: Diary Writing during the Holocaust* (Bloomington: Indiana University Press, 2017), pp. 114–17.

115. Hartmut Rosa, *Social Acceleration*, pp. 299–322.

Chapter 6

1. Fabius Schach, "Vergangenheit redet zur Gegenwart," *Israelitisches Familienblatt*, March 16, 1933.

2. C. Seligmann, (Gemeinderabbiner), "Ein Glück, Jude zu sein? Zum Schowusfest," *Frankfurter Israelitisches Gemeindeblatt*, June 1933.

3. Stephen Kern, *The Culture of Time and Space, 1880–1918* (London: Weidenfeld and Nicolson, 1983), pp. 36–64.

4. Alberto Melucci, *The Playing Self: Person and Meaning in the Planetary Society* (Cambridge, UK: Cambridge Cultural Social Studies, 1996), p. 20.

5. See, for example, Ismar Schorsch, *From Text to Context: The Turn to History in Mod-*

ern Judaism (Hanover, NH: University Press of New England, 1994); Michael A. Meyer, "The Emergence of Jewish Historiography: Motives and Motifs," in *Judaism within Modernity: Essays on Modern Jewish History and Religion* (Detroit: Wayne State University Press, 2001), pp. 44–63; Ernst Schulin, "Doppel-Nationalität? Die Integration der Juden in die deutsche Kulturnation und die neue Konstruktion der jüdischen Geschichte," in Peter Alter, Claus-Ekkehard Baersch, and Peter Berghoff, eds., *Die Konstruktion der Nation gegen die Juden* (Munich: W. Fink, 1999), pp. 243–59; Christhard Hoffmann, "Die Verbürgerlichung der jüdischen Vergangenheit: Formen, Inhalte, Kritik," in Ulrich Wyrwa, ed., *Judentum und Historismus: Zur Entstehung der jüdischen Geschichtswissenschaft in Europa* (Frankfurt am Main: Campus, 2003), pp. 149–71; Simone Lässig, *Jüdische Wege ins Bürgertum: Kulturelles Kapital und sozialer Aufstieg im 19. Jahrhundert* (Göttingen, Germany: Vandenhoeck & Ruprecht, 2004), pp. 278–89; Rachel Livneh-Freudenthal, *The Verein, Pioneers of the Science of Judaism in Germany* [in Hebrew] (Jerusalem: Leo Baeck Institute Jerusalem and Zalman Shazar Center, 2018).

6. Nitsa Ben-Ari, *Romance with the Past: The Nineteenth-Century German-Jewish Historical Novel and the Creation of a National Literature* [in Hebrew] (Tel Aviv: Dvir, 1997); Nils Roemer, *Jewish Scholarship and Culture in Nineteenth-Century Germany: Between History and Faith* (Madison: University of Wisconsin Press, 2005), pp. 66–78; Nils Roemer, "Between the Provinces and the City: Mapping German-Jewish Memories," *Leo Baeck Institute Year Book* 51 (2006): 61–77.

7. For a discussion of the historical discourse of the central current in German Jewry during the Weimar Republic, see Guy Miron, "Between History and 'Useful Past Picture': Representations of the Jewish and the German Past in the Jewish Liberal Historical Discourse in Weimar Germany," [in Hebrew] *Zion* 66 (2001): 297–330.

8. See, for example, Josef Kastein, *Eine Geschichte der Juden* (Berlin: E. Rowohlt, 1933); Joachim Prinz, *Wir Juden* (Berlin: E. Reiss, 1934); Bruno Weil, *Der Weg der deutschen Juden* (Berlin: n.p., 1934); Adolf Altmann, *Volk im Aufbruch, Diaspora in Bewegung, Reflexionen zur jüdischen Zeitgeschichte* (Frankfurt am Main: Hermon-Verlag, 1936); Emil Cohn, *Die jüdische Geschichte: Ein Gang durch Jahrtausende* (Berlin: Jüdische Buchvereinigung, 1936); Arthur Elösser, *Vom Ghetto nach Europe: Das Judentum im geistigen Leben des 19. Jahrhunderts* (Berlin: Jüdische Buchvereinigung, 1936).

9. On attempts to fashion a Nazi picture of the past, see Karl Ferdinand Werner, *Das NS Geschichtsbild und die deutsche Geschichtswissenschaft* (Stuttgart, Germany: Kohlhammer, 1967). On the Reich Institute for the History of the New Germany (Reichsinstitut für Geschichte des neuen Deutschlands), which sought to foster Nazi historical writing, see Helmut Heiber, *Walter Frank und sein Reichsinstitut für Geschichte des neuen Deutschlands* (Stuttgart, Germany: Deutsche Verlags-Anstalt, 1966). On the complex relations between the Nazi regime and the historians' guild, see Karen Schönwälder, *Historiker und Politik: Geschichtswissenschaft im Nationalsozialismus* (Frankfurt am Main: Campus, 1992).

10. Stefan Fraenkel, "Geschichte lehrt Gegenwart," *CV-Zeitung*, April 19, 1934.

11. M. Elias, "Rückblick und Ausblick," part 1, *Der Israelit*, January 3, 1935.

12. Trude Maurer, "From Everyday Life to a State of Emergency: Jews in Weimar and Nazi Germany," in Marion Kaplan, ed., *Jewish Daily Life in Germany 1618–1945* (New York and Oxford, UK: Oxford University Press, 2005), pp. 296–305; Marion A. Kaplan, *Between Dignity and Despair: Jewish Life in Nazi Germany* (New York: Oxford University Press, 1998), pp. 103–6.

13. Fritz Friedländer, "Der Geschichtsunterricht in der jüdische Schule," *CV-Zeitung*, May 10, 1934.

14. Fritz Friedländer, "Hemmung und Ziel jüdischen Geschichtsforschung," *CV-*

Zeitung, September 6, 1934. See also an article written in 1934 on Jewish emigration from Germany in the nineteenth century, in which the author states his belief that the subject will be of interest to contemporary readers because of the then-current wave of emigration: B. Weinryb, "Deutsch-jüdische Wanderungen im 19. Jahrhundert," *Der Morgen*, April 1934, pp. 4–10.

15. See, for example, Hans Grünfeld, "Warum und wie jüdische Geschichte?" *Jugend und Gemeinde: Beilage zum Frankfurter Israelitisches Gemeindeblatt*, June 1935; Realschuldirektor Dr. Elias, "Geschichtsunterricht an jüdischen Schulen," *Erziehung und Lehre: Pädagogische Beilage zum Israelit*, April 30, June 4, and August 27, 1936.

16. Willy Cohn, "Welche Ansprüche müssen an ein Werk über jüdische Geschichte gestellt werden?" *Frankfurter Israelitisches Gemeindeblatt*, November 1935.

17. See also, in this context, the claim that there was in fact a need at that time (1937) for history that was more than just a reverse-engineered explanation of how the current situation was the inevitable outcome of past events: Ernst Fraenkel, "Geschichtsbewusstsein und Geschichte," *Der Morgen*, March 1937, p. 575.

18. For a broader account of the varied attempts to discern historical laws and to find, in the past, the meaning of present events, see Guy Miron, *The Waning of the Emancipation: Jewish History, Memory, and the Rise of Fascism in Germany, France, and Hungary* (Detroit: Wayne State University Press, 2011), pp. 30–53.

19. Ismar Elbogen, *Geschichte der Juden in Deutschland* (Berlin: Erich Lichtenstein Verlag, 1935).

20. On such stoic restraint, see Fritz Friedländer, "Elbogens 'Geschichte der Juden in Deutschland,'" *Der Morgen*, November 1935, pp. 369–71. For further reactions to Elbogen's book, some of them even more critical, see Werner Cahnmann, "Ismar Elbogen, Geschichte der Juden in Deutschland," *CV-Zeitung*, May 3, 1935; Ludwig Feuchtwanger, "Geschichte der Juden in Deutschland," *Jüdische Rundschau*, June 6, 1935. And for a more detailed discussion, see Miron, *Waning of the Emancipation*, pp. 54–55.

21. For a detailed discussion of this issue, see Miron, *Waning of the Emancipation*, pp. 55–60. Events marking the birth and death of Mendelssohn had been reported in the Jewish press in Germany since the nineteenth century; see Christhard Hoffmann, "Constructing Jewish Modernity: Mendelssohn Jubilee Celebrations within German Jewry, 1829–1929," in Rainer Liedtke and David Rechter, eds., *Towards Normality? Acculturation and Modern German Jewry* (Tübingen, Germany: Mohr Siebeck, 2003), pp. 27–52.

22. Kurt F. Rosenberg, "*Einer, der nicht mehr dazugehört*": *Tagebücher 1933–1937*, ed. Beate Meyer and Björn Siegel (Göttingen, Germany: Wallstein Verlag, 2012), p. 64 (March 27, 1933).

23. Rosenberg, "*Einer, der nicht mehr dazugehört*," p. 114 (June 18, 1933).

24. Rosenberg, "*Einer, der nicht mehr dazugehört*," pp. 114–28 (June 18, 1933).

25. Rosenberg, "*Einer, der nicht mehr dazugehört*," p. 167 (February 4, 1934).

26. See, for example, Rosenberg, "*Einer, der nicht mehr dazugehört*," pp. 126 (June 25, 1933) and 128 (August 7, 1933). See also Ofer Ashkenazi and Guy Miron, "Jewish Vacations in Nazi Germany: Reflections on Time and Space amid an Unlikely Respite," *Jewish Quarterly Review* 110, no. 3 (Summer 2020): 536.

27. Willy Cohn, *Kein Recht, Nirgends: Tagebuch vom Untergang des Breslauer Judentums, 1933–1941*, ed. Norbert Conrads (Cologne: Böhlau, 2006), pp. 90 (October 14, 1933), 92 (October 20, 1933).

28. Cohn, *Kein Recht*, p. 271 (September 6, 1935).

29. Cohn, *Kein Recht*, p. 33 (April 20, 1933). Cohn also referred to this day on p. 511 (January 28, 1938). On Kaiser Wilhelm II's birthday on January 27, the way it was cel-

ebrated in Imperial Germany and during World War II, and the political uses that were made of it, see Fritz Schellack, *Nationalfeiertage in Deutschland von 1871 bis 1945* (Frankfurt am Main: Peter Lang, 1990), pp. 44–66.

30. Cohn, *Kein Recht*, p. 588 (January 18, 1939).

31. Cohn, *Kein Recht*, p. 827 (August 11, 1940); see also p. 457 (August 11, 1937).

32. Amos Goldberg, *Trauma in First Person: Diary Writing during the Holocaust* (Bloomington: University of Indiana Press, 2017), pp. 7–12. And see also Alexandra Garbarini, *Numbered Days: Diaries and the Holocaust* (New Haven: Yale University Press, 2006), pp. 129–67.

33. Steuwer presents the writing of diaries during this period as a means of consolidating what he calls *Positionierung* (positioning). See Janosch Steuwer, "*Ein Drittes Reich, wie ich es auffasse*": *Politik, Gesellschaft und privates Leben in Tagebüchern 1933–1939* (Göttingen, Germany: Wallstein Verlag, 2017), pp. 82–132.

34. Victor Klemperer, *I Will Bear Witness: A Diary of the Nazi Years, 1933–1941* (New York: Modern Library, 1999), p. 27 (July 28, 1933).

35. Klemperer, *I Will Bear Witness*, p. 111 (February 7, 1935).

36. Klemperer, *I Will Bear Witness*, p. 166 (May 24, 1936).

37. Klemperer, *I Will Bear Witness*, p. 233 (August 17, 1937).

38. Goldberg, *Trauma in First Person*, p. 125.

39. Rosenberg, "*Einer, der nicht mehr dazugehört*," pp. 205–6 (June 7, 1934).

40. Rosenberg, "*Einer, der nicht mehr dazugehört*," p. 274 (March 16, 1935).

41. Rosenberg, "*Einer, der nicht mehr dazugehört*," p. 320 (March 23, 1936).

42. Rosenberg, "*Einer, der nicht mehr dazugehört*," p. 381 (December 1, 1936).

43. Klemperer, *I Will Bear Witness*, p. 280 (December 6, 1938).

44. Klemperer, *I Will Bear Witness*, p. 381 (April 14, 1941). For Klemperer's memoir, see Victor Klemperer, *Curriculum Vitae: Erinnerungen 1881–1918* (Berlin: Berlin Aufbau-Verl, 1996).

45. Cohn, *Kein Recht*, p. 308 (December 17, 1935). In this entry, which refers to writing his memoirs, Cohn added that "It gives me great joy to once more delve into those times."

46. For Cohn's memoir, see Willy Cohn, *Verwehte Spuren: Erinnerungen an das Breslauer Judentum vor seinem Untergang* (Cologne: Böhlau Verlag, 1995).

47. Cohn, *Kein Recht*, pp. 962–63 (August 2, 1941). See also p. 857 (October 10, 1940).

48. Cohn, *Kein Recht*, p. 773 (March 29, 1940).

49. Philipp Manes, "War Diary, 1939–1942,"Wiener Library, London, doc 1346, box 10 4.5a, pp. 102–3 (September 22, 1940). Manes later also wrote a chronicle of the role Jews had played in the German fur industry, the field he worked in. See ibid., p. 133 (February 1, 1941).

50. Manes, "War Diary," p. 73 (May 25, 1940).

51. See also Manes, "War Diary," pp. 83 (June 30, 1940), 142 (early May 1941), and 160 (August 16, 1941).

52. Manes, "War Diary," pp. 208–9 (January 13, 1942).

53. Manes, "War Diary," p. 253 (July 4, 1942).

54. Gertrud Kolmar, *Briefe*, ed. Johanna Woltmann (Göttingen, Germany: Wallstein, 2014), p. 120 (September 21, 1941).

55. Kolmar, *Briefe*, p. 110 (June 2, 1941).

56. For a description of her withdrawal from present reality into "eternal flow" (*Ewigkeitsgeschehen*), see Kolmar, *Briefe*, pp. 44–45 (October 1, 1939).

57. Kolmar, *Briefe*, pp. 185–86 (December 4, 1942).

58. Eviatar Zerubavel, *Time Maps: Collective Memory and the Social Shape of the Past* (Chicago: University of Chicago Press, 2003), pp. 58–62.

59. "Gegen die ewig Gestrigen," *Jüdische Rundschau*, July 21, 1933.

60. Julius Brodnitz, "Rosch Haschana 5695: Festtags-Gruss an die Freunde," *CV-Zeitung*, September 6, 1934.

61. A. H., "Tradition," *CV-Zeitung*, March 11, 1937. For another connection that Hirschberg made between the community's conduct and the heritage of its "forefathers" (*Ahnen*), see A. H., "Gegürtet," *CV-Zeitung*, March 25, 1937.

62. Peter Fritzsche, *Life and Death in the Third Reich* (Cambridge, MA: Harvard University Press, 2008), pp. 77–78. See also Eric Ehrenreich, *The Nazi Ancestral Proof: Genealogy, Racial Science, and the Final Solution* (Bloomington: Indiana University Press, 2007).

63. Article by Martin Hirsch on his family's history in Germany and his documentation of the Hirsch family, Yad Vashem Archives, Jerusalem, 572/08.

64. Eugen Tannenbaum, "'Ich möchte einen Stammbaum . . .' Eine Stunde bei Dr. Jacob Jacobson," *CV-Zeitung*. March 15, 1934.

65. "Aus den Vitrinen der Ausstellung für Familienforschung, Urkunden und Jiskor-Bücher," *Berliner Rundschau*, supplement in *Jüdische Rundschau*, July 3, 1934.

66. Heinz Berggrün, "Wie lege ich eine Ahnentafel an?" *CV-Zeitung*, January 23, 1936. For another discussion of the subject, see "Arbeitsabend der Gesellschaft für jüdische Familienforschung," *Israelitisches Familienblatt*, March 26, 1936.

67. Cohn, *Kein Recht*, pp. 314 (March 22, 1936), 324 (May 17, 1936), 435 (May 23, 1937), 928 (April 20, 1941), and 939 (May 22, 1941).

68. Manes, "War Diary," p. 105 (October 2, 1940).

69. David Grünspecht, "Ein Viehhändler gibt auf," in Margarete Limberg and Hubert Rübsaat, eds., *Sie Durften nicht mehr Deutsche Sein: Jüdischer Alltag in Selbstzeugnissen 1933–1938* (Frankfurt and New York: Campus Verlag, 1990), pp. 120–21.

70. Hans Reichmann, *Deutscher Bürger und verfolgter Jude: Novemberpogrom und KZ Sachsenhausen 1937–1939* (Munich: R. Oldenburg Verlag, 1998), p. 58.

71. Cohn, *Kein Recht*, p. 32 (April 18, 1933).

72. Cohn, *Kein Recht*, p. 55 (June 24, 1933).

73. Cohn, *Kein Recht*, p. 564 (December 11, 1938).

74. Cohn, *Kein Recht*, pp. 788 (May 2, 1940), 852–53 (October 2, 1940), 928 (April 20, 1941), 939 (May 22, 1941), and 955 (July 16, 1941).

75. Cohn, *Kein Recht*, p. 968 (August 15, 1941).

76. Jean Améry, *On Aging, Revolt and Resignation* (Bloomington: Indiana University Press, 1994), pp. 13–15

77. Améry, *On Aging*, pp. 20–21.

78. Victor Klemperer, *Ich will Zeugnis ablegen bis zum letzten: Tagebücher 1933–1941* (Berlin: Aufbau-Verlag, 1995), pp. 217, 218 (September 16, 1935). Only part of this citation appears in the English translation, Klemperer, *I Will Bear Witness, 1933–41*, p. 133.

79. Klemperer, *I Will Bear Witness, 1933–41*, p. 110 (February 7, 1935).

80. For an especially interesting discussion of aging by Klemperer, see Klemperer, *I Will Bear Witness, 1933–41*, p. 226 (June 20, 1937).

Conclusion

1. Hannah Arendt, *The Origins of Totalitarianism* (San Diego: Harcourt, 1976), p. 296.

2. Boaz Neumann, *Being-in-the-World: German Worlds at the Turn of the 20th Century* [in Hebrew] (Tel Aviv: Am Oved, 2014), p. 66.

3. A. H. "1936," *CV-Zeitung*, January 3, 1936.

4. A. H., "Zwischen Pessach und Ostern," *CV-Zeitung*, April 24, 1935.

5. Compare with Neumann's argument in *Being-in-the-World*, pp. 87–90.

6. Kim Wünschmann, *Before Auschwitz: Jewish Prisoners in the Prewar Concentration Camps* (Cambridge, MA: Harvard University Press, 2015).

7. For a scholarly discussion of the experience of space and time in the concentration camps, as part of the distress experienced by the imates, see Wolfgang Sofsky, *The Order of Terror: The Concentration Camp* (Princeton, NJ: Princeton University Press, 1996), pp. 47–93.

8. Beate Meyer, ed., *Deutsche Jüdinnen und Juden in Ghettos und Lagern (1941–1945): Lodz. Chelmno. Minsk. Riga. Auschwitz. Theresienstadt* (Berlin: Metropol, 2017); Avraham Barkai, "Between East and West: Jews from Germany in the Lodz Ghetto," *Yad Vashem Studies* 16 (1984): 271–332; Shalom Cholawski, "The German Jews in the Minsk Ghetto," *Yad Vashem Studies* 17 (1986): 219–46.

9. For the estimates of numbers, see Abraham Barkai and Paul Mendes-Flohr, *Renewal and Destruction: 1918–1945*, vol. 4 in Michael Meyer, ed., *German-Jewish History in Modern Times* (New York: Columbia University Press, 1998), pp. 231–34. See also Marion A. Kaplan, *Between Dignity and Despair: Jewish Life in Nazi Germany* (New York: Oxford University Press, 1998), pp. 129–44; Trude Maurer, "From Everyday Life to a State of Emergency: Jews in Weimar and Nazi Germany," in Marion Kaplan, ed., *Jewish Daily Life in Germany 1618–1945* (New York: Oxford University Press, 2005), pp. 355–60; David Jünger, *Jahre der Ungewissheit: Emigrationspläne deutscher Juden 1933–1938* (Göttingen, Germany: Vandenhoeck & Ruprecht, 2016).

10. The research literature on the Jewish emigrants from Nazi Germany is wide-ranging. See, for example, Hagit Lavsky, *The Creation of the German-Jewish Diaspora: Interwar German-Jewish Immigration* (Berlin and Boston: De Gruyter & Magnes, 2017); Walter Laqueur, *Generation Exodus: The Fate of Young Jewish Refugees from Nazi Germany* (Hanover, NH, and London: Brandeis University Press, 2001); Mark M. Anderson, *Hitler's Exiles: Personal Stories of the Flight from Nazi Germany to America* (New York: New Press, 1998); Sibylle Quack, *Between Sorrow and Strength: Women Refugees of the Nazi Period* (New York: Cambridge University Press, 1995); Yoav Gelber, *New Homeland: Immigration and Absorption of Central European Jews 1933–1948* [In Hebrew] (Jerusalem: Yad Ben Zvi, 1990); Guy Miron, *German Jews in Israel: Memories and Past Images* [in Hebrew] (Jerusalem: Hebrew University Magnes Press, 2004) (Hebrew); Marion Berghahn, *Continental Britons: German-Jewish Refugees from Nazi Germany* (New York: Berghahn Books, 2007).

11. Georg Armbrüster, Michael Kohlsrtruck, and Sonja Mühlberger, eds., *Exil Shanghai, 1938–1947: Jüdisches Leben in der Emigration* (Berlin: Hentrich & Hentrich, 2000); Marcia Ristaino, *Port of Last Resort: The Diaspora Communities of Shanghai* (Stanford, CA: Stanford University Press, 2001); Steve Hochstadt, *Exodus to Shanghai: Stories of Escape from the Third Reich* (New York: Palgrave Macmillan, 2012).

12. Pitirim Sorokin, *Sociocultural Causality, Space and Time: A Study of Referential Principles of Sociology and Social Sciences* (New York: Russell & Russell, 1964), pp. 97–225.

13. Neumann, *Being-in-the-World*, pp. 20–24.

14. Compare with Sorokin's claim that, for a person isolated from society, the experience of time becomes more unstable: Sorokin, *Sociocultural Causality*, pp. 167–69.

Bibliography

Primary Sources

Archives

JEWISH MUSEUM, BERLIN

Fotografische Sammlung, inv-nr. 2012/63/151.

LEO BAECK INSTITUTE, NEW YORK (LBI)

Nadel, Arno. *Tagebuch* 1941–42 (2 volumes; copies of originals). LBI AR 4314.
Seligmann, Erich. Diary 1908–38. LBI Erich Seligmann collection, AR 4104, box 1b folder 1.
Strauss (*née* Gimnicher), Ilse. Diary 1935–39. LBI Ilse Strauss collection, AR 3273, box 1, folder 4.

WIENER LIBRARY, LONDON (WL)

Manes, Philip. "War Diary, 1939–1942." WL, box 10 4.5a, doc. 1346.
Schmoller, Hans, family papers. WL, 1690.

YAD VASHEM ARCHIVES, JERUSALEM (YVA)

Hirsch family collection. YVA O.8/572
Moses, Kati. Letters to son Gerd Moses, YVA O.75/2484.
Schocken, Janet. Letters to children Heinz Schocken and Hilda Schocken, YVA O.75 / 2774 and O.75 / 1010.

Published Collections of Documents

Gruner, Wolf, ed. *The Persecution and Murder of the European Jews by Nazi Germany, Vol. 1: German Reich 1933–1937*. Berlin and Boston: Walter de Gruyter, 2019.
Heim, Susanne, ed. *The Persecution and Murder of the European Jews by Nazi Germany, Vol. 2:, German Reich 1938–August 1939*. Berlin and Boston: Walter de Gruyter, 2019.
Löw, Andrea, ed. *The Persecution and Murder of the European Jews by Nazi Germany, Vol. 3: German Reich and Protectorate of Bohemia and Moravia September 1939–September 1941*. Berlin and Boston: Walter de Gruyter, 2020.

Periodicals

Blätter des Jüdischen Frauenbundes
CV-Zeitung
Frankfurter Israelitisches Gemeindeblatt
Gemeindeblatt der Jüdischen Gemeinde zu Berlin
Gemeindeblatt der Israelitischen Religionsgemeinde zu Leipzig
Der Israelit
Israelitisches Familienblatt
Jüdisch-Liberale Zeitung
Jüdische Rundschau
Der Morgen

Published Diaries, Memoirs, and other Primary Sources

Altmann, Adolf. *Volk im Aufbruch, Diaspora in Bewegung: Reflexionen zur jüdischen Zeitgeschichte*. Frankfurt am Main: Hermon Verlag, 1936.

Angress, Werner T. *Witness to the Storm: A Jewish Journey from Nazi Berlin to the 82nd Airborne, 1920–1945*. Bloomington: Indiana University Press, 2019.

Block, Elisabeth. *Erinnerungszeichen: Die Tagebücher der Elisabeth Block*. Augsburg, Germany: Bayerische Staatskanzlei, 1993.

Boschwitz, Ulrich Alexander. *The Passenger: A Novel*. New York: Metropolitan, 2021.

Cohn, Emil. *Die jüdische Geschichte: Ein Gang durch Jahrtausende*. Berlin: Jüdische Buchvereinigung, 1936.

Cohn, Willy. *Verwehte Spuren: Erinnerungen an das Breslauer Judentum vor seinem Untergang*. Cologne: Böhlau Verlag, 1995.

Cohn, Willy. *Kein Recht, Nirgends: Tagebuch vom Untergang des Breslauer Judentums, 1933–1941*. Edited by Norbert Conrads. Cologne: Böhlau, 2006.

Cohn, Willy. *In the Talons of the Third Reich: Willy Cohn's diary 1933–1941*. In Hebrew. Edited by Tamar Cohen Gazit. Jerusalem: Hebrew University Magnes Press, 2014.

Cohn, Willy. *No Justice in Germany: The Breslau Diaries 1933–1941*. Edited by Norbert Conrads. Stanford, CA: Stanford University Press, 2012.

C. V. Wegweiser durch Berlin. *Stadtplan mit Abbildungen jüdischer Einrichtungen und Gebäude aus der jüdischen Geschichte der Stadt Berlin*. Berlin: C. V., 1937.

Deutschkron, Inge. *Ich trug den gelben Stern*. Cologne: Verlag Wissenschaft und Politik, 1978.

Elbogen, Ismar. *Geschichte der Juden in Deutschland*. Berlin: Erich Lichtenstein Verlag, 1935.

Elösser, Arthur. *Vom Ghetto nach Europe: Das Judentum im geistigen Leben des 19. Jahrhunderts*. Berlin: Jüdische Buchvereinigung, 1936.

Freund, Elisabeth. *Als Zwangsarbeiterin 1941 in Berlin: Die Aufzeichnungen der Volkswirtin Elisabeth Freund*. Edited by Carola Sachse. Berlin: Akademie Verlag, 1996.

Friedländer, Günter. *Jüdische Jugend zwischen gestern und morgen*. Berlin: Jüdische Wirklichkeit Heute no. 2, 1938.

Goethe, Johann Wolfgang von. *Autobiography of Goethe: Truth and Poetry Relating to My Life*. Translated by John Oxenford. Auckland: Floating Press, 2008.

Hirsch, Frieda. *Mein Weg von Karlsruhe über Heidelberg nach Haifa 1890–1965*. Israel: n.p., 1965.

Hirschberg, Sigmund-Shmuel, and Gertrude Hirschberg. *From Berlin to Shanghai: Letters to Palestine*. In Hebrew. Jerusalem: Yad Vashem, 2013.

Kastein, Josef. *Eine Geschichte der Juden*. Berlin: E. Rowohlt, 1933.

Klemperer, Victor. *Curriculum Vitae: Erinnerungen 1881–1918*. Berlin: Berlin Aufbau Verlag, 1996.

Klemperer, Victor. *Ich will Zeugnis ablegen bis zum letzten: Tagebücher 1933–1941*. Berlin: Aufbau Verlag, 1995.

Klemperer, Victor. *Ich will Zeugnis ablegen bis zum letzten: Tagebücher (2) 1942–1945*. Berlin: AufbauVerlag, 1995.

Klemperer, Victor. *I Will Bear Witness: A Diary of the Nazi Years 1933–1941*. New York: Modern Library, 1999.

Klemperer, Victor. *I Will Bear Witness: A Diary of the Nazi Years 1942–1945*. New York: Modern Library, 2001.

Koch, Alexander, ed. *Das schöne Heim: Ratgeber für die Ausgestaltung und Einrichtung der Wohnung*. Darmstadt, Germany: A. Koch, 1920.

Kolmar, Gertrud. *Briefe*. Edited by Johanna Woltmann. Göttingen, Germany: Wallstein Verlag, 2014.

Lewissohn, Cäcilie. "Ich könnte immerzu heulen über die Aussichtslosigkeit, hier je wegzukommen." In Angela Martin and Claudia Schoppmann, eds., *"Ich fürchte die Menschen mehr als die Bomben": Aus den Tagebüchern von drei Berliner Frauen 1938–1946*, pp. 67–96. Berlin: Metropol, 1996.

Limberg, Margarete, and Hubert Rübsaat, eds., *Sie Durften nicht mehr Deutsche Sein: Jüdischer Alltag in Selbstzeugnissen 1933–1938*. Frankfurt: Campus Verlag, 1990. Esp. pp. 69–74 (Karl Friedländer), pp. 118–21 (David Grünspercht), pp. 140–42 (Gerta Pfeffer), pp. 150–52 (Hermann Klugmann), pp. 153–56 (Max Reiner), pp. 167–70 (Martin Andermann), pp. 171–74 (Heinemann Stern), pp. 175–77 (Friedrich Solon), pp. 191–93 (Ernst Marcus), pp. 212–16 (Hans Winterfeldt), and pp. 315–19 (Arthur Samuel).

Loval, Werner M. *We Were Europeans: A Personal History of a Turbulent Century*. Jerusalem: Gefen, 2010.

Lucas, Eric. *The Sovereigns: A Jewish Family in the German Countryside*. Evanston, IL: Northwestern University Press, 2001.

Nathorff, Hertha. *Das Tagebuch der Hertha Nathorff*. Edited by Wolfgang Benz. Munich: R. Oldenbourg, 1987.

Neumann, Siegfried. *Nacht über Deutschland: Vom Leben und Sterben einer Republik: Ein Tatsachenbericht*. Munich: Paul List Verlag, 1978.

Petersen, Jan. *Unsere Strasse: Eine Chronik Geschrieben im Herzen des faschistischen Deutschland 1933/34*. Berlin: Dietz, 1947.

Prinz, Joachim. *Wir Juden*. Berlin: E. Reiss, 1934.

Prinz, Joachim, ed. *Zionistische Vereinigung für Deutschland, Palästina Kalender 5696, 5697*. Berlin: ZVfD, 1936.

Reichmann, Hans. *Deutscher Bürger und verfolgter Jude: Novemberpogrom und KZ Sachsenhausen 1937–1939*. Munich: R. Oldenburg Verlag, 1998.

Richarz, Monika, ed. *Jewish Life in Germany: Memoirs from Three Centuries*. Translated by Stella P. Rosenfeld and Sidney Rosenfeld. Bloomington: Indiana University Press, 1991. Esp. pp. 306–15 (Edwin Landau), pp. 342–51 (Alexander Szanto), and pp. 351–61 (Marta Appel).

Rosenberg, Kurt F. *"Einer, der nicht mehr dazugehört," Tagebücher 1933–1937*. Edited by Beate Meyer and Björn Siegel. Göttingen, Germany: Wallstein Verlag, 2012.

Samson, Meta. *Spatz macht sich*. 2nd ed. (Berlin: Altberliner Verlag, 1990).

Straus, Rahel. *Wir lebten in Deutschland: Erinnerungen einer deutschen Jüdin 1880–1933*. Stuttgart, Germany: Deutsche Verlags-Anstalt, 1961.

Tausk, Walter. *Breslauer Tagebuch 1933–1940*. Edited by Ryszard Kincel. Berlin: Aufbau Taschenbuch Verlag, 2000.

Wahrman, Shlomo. *Lest We Forget: Growing Up in Nazi Leipzig 1933–1939*. New York: Mesorah Publications, 1991.

Weil, Bruno. *Der Weg der deutschen Juden*. Berlin: n.p., 1934.

Wertheimer, Martha. *In mich ist die große dunkle Ruhe gekommen, Briefe an Siegfried Guggenheim*. Frankfurt am Main: Arbeitsstelle zur Vorbereitung des Frankfurter Lern- und Dokumentationszentrum des Holocaust, 1993.

Wertheimer, Martha, Siddy Goldschmidt, and Paul Yogi Mayer. *Das Jüdische Sportbuch, Weg, Kampf und Sieg*. Berlin: Verlag Atid, 1937.

Research and Secondary Literature

Améry, Jean. *On Aging: Revolt and Resignation*. Bloomington: Indiana University Press, 1994.

Anderson, Benedict. *Imagined Communities: Reflections on the Origin and Spread of Nationalism*. London and New York: Verso, 1991.

Anderson, Mark M. *Hitler's Exiles: Personal Stories of the Flight from Nazi Germany to America*. New York: The New Press, 1998.

Angress, Werner T. *Between Fair and Hope: Jewish Youth in the Third Reich*. New York: Columbia University Press, 1988.

Arendt, Hannah. *The Human Condition*. Chicago: University of Chicago Press, 1998.

Arendt, Hannah. *The Origins of Totalitarianism*. San Diego: Harcourt, 1976.

Armbrüster, Georg, Michael Kohlsrtruck, and Sonja Mühlberger, eds. *Exil Shanghai 1938–1947: Jüdisches Leben in der Emigration*. Berlin: Hentrich & Hentrich, 2000.

Ascher, Abraham. *A Community under Siege: The Jews of Breslau under Nazism*. Stanford, CA: Stanford University Press, 2007.

Ashkenazi, Ofer, and Guy Miron. "Jewish Vacations in Nazi Germany: Reflections on Time and Space amid an Unlikely Respite." *Jewish Quarterly Review* 110, no. 3 (Summer 2020): 523–52.

Attwood, Lynne. *Gender and Housing in Soviet Russia: Private Life in a Public Space*. Manchester, UK: Manchester University Press, 2010.

Augé, Marc. *Non-Places: Introduction to an Anthropology of Supermodernity*. New York: Verso, 1995.

Auslander, Leora. "'Jewish Taste'? Jews and the Aesthetics of Everyday Life in Paris and Berlin 1933–1942." In Rudy Koshar, ed., *Histories of Leisure*, pp. 299–318. Oxford, UK: Berg, 2002.

Auslander, Leora. "Reading German Jewry through Vernacular Photography: From the Kaiserreich to the Third Reich." *Central European History* 48, no. 3 (2015): 300–334.

Barkai, Avraham. "Between East and West: Jews from Germany in the Lodz Ghetto." *Yad Vashem Studies* 16 (1984): 271–332.

Barkai, Abraham, and Paul Mendes-Flohr. *Renewal and Destruction: 1918–1945*. Vol. 4 in Michael Meyer, ed., *German-Jewish History in Modern Times*. New York: Columbia University Press, 1998.

Barkai, Avraham. "*Wehr Dich*": *Der Centralverein deutscher Staatsbürger jüdischen Glaubens 1893–1938*. Munich: Beck, 2002.

Barkow, Ben. *Alfred Wiener and the Making of the Holocaust Library*. London: Vallentine, Mitchell, 1997.

Bar-Levav, Avriel. "Another Place: The Cemetery in Jewish Culture." In Hebrew. *Pe'amim* 98–99 (2003): 5–38.

Bauer, Yehuda. *Rethinking the Holocaust*. New Haven, CT, and London: Yale University Press, 2001.

Ben-Ari, Nitsa. *Romance with the Past: The Nineteenth-Century German-Jewish Historical Novel and the Creation of a National Literature*. In Hebrew. Tel Aviv: Dvir, 1997.

Benjamin, Walter. "The Flaneur's Return," In *Selected Writings*, vol. 2, pp. 262–67. Cambridge, MA: Harvard University Press, 2005.

Benjamin, Walter. "Unpacking My Library: A Talk About Book Collecting." In *Illuminations*, pp. 59–67. New York: Schocken, 1969.

Benz, Wolfgang. *Die Juden in Deutschland 1933–1945: Leben unter nationalsozialistischer Herrschaft*. Munich: C. H. Beck, 1988.

Berghahn, Marion. *Continental Britons: German-Jewish Refugees from Nazi Germany*. New York: Berghahn Books, 2007.

Borst, Arno. *The Ordering of Time: From the Ancient Computus to the Modern Computer*. Chicago: University of Chicago Press, 1993.

Borut, Jacob. *Jewish Religious Practice under Nazi Rule (1933–1938) and Its Reflection in the German-Jewish Press*. In Hebrew. Jerusalem: Yad Vashem, 2017.

Borut, Jacob. "Struggles for Spaces: Where Could Jews Spend Free Time in Nazi Germany?" *Leo Baeck Institute Year Book* 56 (2011): 307–50.

Brauch, Julia, Anna Lipphardt, and Alexandra Nocke, eds. *Jewish Topographies: Visions of Space, Traditions of Place*. Aldershot, UK, and Burlington VT: Ashgate, 2008.

Brenner, Michael, Stefi Jersch-Wenzel, and Michael A. Meyer. *Emancipation and Acculturation: 1780–1871*. Vol. 2 in Michael Meyer, ed., *German-Jewish History in Modern Times*. New York: Columbia University Press, 1997.

Brenner, Michael. *The Renaissance of Jewish Culture in Weimar Germany*. New Haven, CT: Yale University Press, 1996.

Breuer, Mordechai, and Michael Graetz. *Tradition and Enlightenment: 1600–1780*. Vol. 1 in Michael Meyer, ed., *German-Jewish History in Modern Times*. New York: Columbia University Press, 1996.

Brown, Bill. "Thing Theory." *Critical Inquiry* 28, no. 1 (2001): 1–22.

Burleigh, Michael. *The Third Reich: A New History*. New York: Hill & Wang, 2000.

Carlebach, Elisheva. *Palaces of Time: Jewish Calendar and Culture in Early Modern Europe*. Cambridge, MA: Belknap Press of Harvard University Press, 2011.

Cholawski, Shalom. "The German Jews in the Minsk Ghetto." *Yad Vashem Studies* 17 (1986): 219–46.

Clark, Christopher. *Time and Power: Visions of History in German Politics, from the Thirty Years' War to the Third Reich*. Princeton, NJ: Princeton University Press, 2019.

Coenen Snyder, Saskia. *Building a Public Judaism: Synagogues and Jewish Identity in Nineteenth-Century Europe*. Cambridge, MA, Harvard University Press, 2013.

Confino, Alon. *A World Without Jews: Nazi Imagination From Persecution to Genocide*. New Haven, CT: Yale University Press, 2014.

Confino, Alon. "Memory as Historical Narrative and Method." In *Germany as a Culture of Remembrance: Promises and Limits of Writing History*, pp. 153–58. Chapel Hill: University of North Carolina Press.

Craig, Jeffrey. *Timepass: Youth, Class, and the Politics of Waiting in India*. Stanford, CA: Stanford University Press, 2010.

Cressy, David. *Bonfires and Bells: National Memory and the Protestant Calendar in Elizabethan and Stuart England*. Berkeley: University of California Press, 1989.

Csikszentmihalyi, Mihaly, and Eugene Halton. *The Meaning of Things: Domestic Symbols and the Self*. Cambridge, UK and New York: Cambridge University Press, 1981.

Dant, Tim. "The Driver-Car." *Theory, Culture & Society* 21, no. 4/5 (August-October 2004): 61–79.

Dekker, Rudolf, ed. *Egodocuments and History: Autobiographical Writing in Its Social Context since the Middle Ages*. Hilversum, Netherlands: Verloren, 2002.

Diehl, Katrin. *Die jüdische Presse im Dritten Reich: Zwischen Selbstbehauptung und Fremdbestimmung*. Tübingen, Germany: M. Niemeyer, 1997.

De Certeau, Michel. *The Practice of Everyday Life*. Berkeley: University of California Press, 1984.

Dinur, Yael. "'Treue um Treue': Advertisements in the Jewish Press in Nazi Germany 1933–1938." MA thesis, Hebrew University of Jerusalem, 2017.

Doron, Yehoyakim. *The Jewish Youth Movements in Germany*. In Hebrew. Jerusalem: Rubin Mass, 1996.

Douglas, Mary. "The Idea of a Home: A Kind of Space." *Social Research* 58, no. 1 (Spring 1991): 287–307.

Ehrenreich, Eric. *The Nazi Ancestral Proof: Genealogy, Racial Science, and the Final Solution*. Bloomington: Indiana University Press, 2007.

Elias, Norbert. *The Loneliness of the Dying*. Oxford, UK: B. Blackwell, 1985.

Elias, Norbert. *Time: An Essay*. Oxford, UK, and Cambridge, MA: B. Blackwell: 1992.

Elkin, Rivka. *The Heart Beats On: Continuity and Change in Social Work and Welfare Activities of German Jews under the Nazi Regime 1933–1945*. In Hebrew. Jerusalem: Yad Vashem, 2004.

Etkin, Elia. "Neighborhood, Neighbors, and Neighborly Relations: Urban Life in the Yishuv and in Israel, during the British Mandate and Early Statehood." PhD dissertation, Tel Aviv University, 2019.

Fenster, Tovi. *The Global City and the Holy City: Narratives on Knowledge, Planning and Diversity*. Harlow, UK: Prentice Hall / Pearson Education, 2004.

Flanders, Judith. *The Making of Home: The 500-Year Story of How Our Houses Became Our Homes*. New York: Thomas Dunne Books / St. Martin's Press, 2015.

Föllmer, Moritz. "Das Appartement." In Alexa Geisthövel and Habbo Knoch, eds., *Orte der Moderne: Erfahrungswelten des 19. und 20. Jahrhunderts*, pp. 325–34. Frankfurt am Main: Campus Verlag, 2005.

Föllmer, Moritz. *Individuality and Modernity in Berlin: Self and Society from Weimar to the Wall*. Cambridge, UK: Cambridge University Press, 2013.

Foucault, Michel. "Of Other Spaces." *Diacritics* 16, no. 1 (Spring 1986): 22–27.

Fraenkel, Daniel. *Jewish Sports in Nazi Germany as Reflected in the Jewish Press*. In Hebrew. Jerusalem: Yad Vashem, 2016.

Frankel, Daniel. *On the Edge of the Abyss: Zionist Policy and the Question of German Jewry, 1933–1938*. In Hebrew. Jerusalem: Magnes, 1994.

Frankel, Jonathan. *Prophecy and Politics: Socialism, Nationalism, and the Russian Jews*. Cambridge, UK: Cambridge University Press, 1981.

Freeden, Herbert. *The Jewish Press in the Third Reich*. Providence, RI: Berg, 1993.

Fried, Marc. "Grieving for a Lost Home: Psychological Costs of Relocation." In L. J. Duhl, ed., *The Urban Condition*, pp. 151–71. New York: Basic Books, 1963.

Friedländer, Saul. *Nazi Germany and the Jews, Vol. 1: The Years of Persecution 1933–1939*. New York: Harper & Collins, 1997.

Fritzsche, Peter. *Life and Death in the Third Reich*. Cambridge, MA: Harvard University Press, 2008.

Frykman, Jonas, and Orvar Löfgren. *Culture Builders: A Historical Anthropology of Middle-Class Life*. New Brunswick, NJ: Rutgers University Press, 1987.

Fryxell, A. R. P. "Time and the Modern: Current Trends in the History of Modern Temporalities." *Past and Present* 243, no. 1 (2019): 285–98.

Gamm, Hans-Jochen. *Der Braune Kult: Das Dritte Reich und seine Ersatzreligion*. Hamburg: Rütten & Loening, 1962.

Garbarini, Alexandra. *Numbered Days: Diaries and the Holocaust*. New Haven, CT: Yale University Press, 2006.

Gazit, Tamar Cohen. "From Diary's Notebook to a Book." In Cohen Gazit, ed., *In the Talons of the Third Reich*, pp. xiii–xv. In Hebrew. Jerusalem: Hebrew University Magnes Press, 2014.

Gay, Peter. *The Bourgeois Experience: Victoria to Freud*, vol. 2, *The Tender Passion*. New York: Oxford University Press, 1986.

Gelber, Yoav. *New Homeland: Immigration and Absorption of Central European Jews 1933–1948*. In Hebrew. Jerusalem: Yad Ben Zvi, 1990.

Gertmann, Eyal, and Lorenz Peiffer. "Im Schatten antisemitischer Diskriminierung und Verfolgung, Sportliche Begegnungen zwischen jüdischen Mannschaften aus Nazideutschland und Erez Israel im Jahre 1937." In Lorenz Peiffer and Moshe Zimmerman, eds., *Sport als Element des Kulturtransfers: Jüdische Sportler zwischen NS-Deutschland und Palästina*, pp. 115–26. Göttingen, Germany: Wallstein, 2013.

Giaccaria, Paolo, and Claudio Minca, eds. *Hitler's Geographies: The Spatialities of the Third Reich*. Chicago: University of Chicago Press, 2016.

Gillis, John. *A World of Their Own Making: Myth, Ritual, and the Quest for Family Values*. New York: Basic Books, 1996.

Goldberg, Amos. *Trauma in First Person: Diary Writing during the Holocaust*. Bloomington: Indiana University Press, 2017.

Goldberg, Sylvie-Anne. *Crossing the Jabbok: Illness and Death in Ashkenazi Judaism in Sixteenth- through Nineteenth-Century Prague*. Berkeley: University of California Press, 1996.

Gotzmann, Andreas. "Out of the Ghetto, into the Middle Class, Changing Perspectives on Jewish Spaces in Nineteenth-Century Germany: The Case of Synagogues and Jewish Burial Grounds." In Simone Lässig and Miriam Rürup, eds., *Space and Spatiality in Modern German Jewish History*, pp. 140–59. New York and Oxford, UK: Berghahn, 2017.

Gruner, Wolf. "Defiance and Protest: A Comparative Micro-Historical Re-evaluation of Individual Jewish Responses towards Nazi Persecution." In Claire Zalc and Tal Bruttmann, eds., *Microhistories of the Holocaust*, pp. 209–26. New York: Berghahn, 2017).

Gruner, Wolf. "Die NS-Judenverfolgung und die Kommunen, Zur wechselseitigen Dynamisierung von zentraler und lokaler Politik 1933–1941." *Vierteljahrshefte für Zeitgeschichte* 48, no. 1 (2000): 75–126.

Gruner, Wolf. *Öffentliche Wohlfahrt und Judenverfolgung: Wechselwirkungen lokaler und zentraler Politik im NS-Staat 1933–1942*. Munich: R. Oldenbourg, 2002.

Gruner, Wolf. "'Worse Than Vandals': The Mass Destruction of Jewish Homes and Jewish Responses during the 1938 Pogrom." In Wolf Gruner and Steve Ross, eds., *New*

Perspectives on Kristallnacht after 80 Years: The Nazi Pogrom in Global Comparison, pp. 25–49. West Lafayette, IN: Purdue University Press, 2019.

Hagen, Joshua, and Robert C. Ostergen. *Nazi Germany: Place, Space, Architecture and Ideology*. Lanham, MD: Rowman & Littlefield, 2020.

Hajo, Bernett. *Der jüdische Sport im nationalsozialistischen Deutschland 1933–1938*. Schorndorf, Germany: K. Hofmann, 1978.

Hall, Catherine. "The Sweet Delights of Home." In Michelle Perrot, ed., *A History of Private Life*, vol. 4: *From the Fires of Revolution to the Great War*, pp. 47–93. Cambridge, MA: Belknap Press, 1990.

Harris, Richard. "The End Justified the Means: Boarding and Rooming in a City of Homes 1890–1951." *Journal of Social History* 26, no. 2 (1992): 331–58.

Heiber, Helmut. *Walter Frank und sein Reichsinstitut für Geschichte des neuen Deutschlands*. Stuttgart, Germany: Deutsche Verlags-Anstalt, 1966.

Heidegger, Martin. "Building Dwelling Thinking." In *Poetry, Language, Thought*, pp. 143–59. New York: Harper & Row, 1971.

Herzberg, Arno, "The Jewish Press under the Nazi Regime—Its Mission, Suppression and Defiance: A Memoir." *Leo Baeck Institute Year Book* 36 (1991): 367–88.

Hessel, Franz. *Walking in Berlin: A Flaneur in the Capital*. Cambridge: MIT Press, 2017.

Hochstadt, Steve. *Exodus to Shanghai: Stories of Escape from the Third Reich*. New York: Palgrave Macmillan, 2012.

Hoffmann, Christhard. "Constructing Jewish Modernity: Mendelssohn Jubilee Celebrations within German Jewry, 1829–1929." In Rainer Liedtke and David Rechter, eds., *Towards Normality? Acculturation and Modern German Jewry*, pp. 27–52. Tübingen, Germany: Mohr Siebeck, 2003.

Hoffmann, Christhard. "Die Verbürgerlichung der jüdischen Vergangenheit: Formen, Inhalte, Kritik." In Ulrich Wyrwa, ed., *Judentum und Historismus: Zur Entstehung der jüdischen Geschichtswissenschaft in Europa*, pp. 149–71. Frankfurt am Main: Campus, 2003.

Huebel, Sebastian. *Fighter, Worker, and Family Man: German-Jewish Men and Their Gendered Experiences in Nazi Germany, 1933–1941*. Toronto: University of Toronto Press, 2022.

Imort, Michael. "'Eternal Forest–Eternal Volk': The Rhetoric and Reality of National Socialist Forest Policy." In Thomas Zeller, Franz-Josef Brüggemeier, and Mark Cioc, eds., *How Green Were the Nazis? Nature, Environment, and Nation in the Third Reich*, pp. 43–72. Athens: Ohio University Press, 2005.

Jünger, David. *Jahre der Ungewissheit: Emigrationspläne deutscher Juden 1933–1938*. Göttingen, Germany: Vandenhoeck & Ruprecht, 2016.

Kaiser, Alexandra. *Von Helden und Opfern: Eine Geschichte des Volkstrauertags*. Frankfurt: Campus Verlag, 2010.

Kaplan, Marion A. *The Making of the Jewish Middle Class: Women, Family and Identity in Imperial Germany*. New York: Oxford University Press, 1991.

Kaplan, Marion A. *Between Dignity and Despair: Jewish Life in Nazi Germany*. New York: Oxford University Press, 1998.

Katz, Jacob. *Die Entstehung der Judenassimilation in Deutschland und deren ideologie*. Darmstadt, Germany: Wissenschaftliche Buchgesellschaft, 1982.

Kern, Stephen. *The Culture of Time and Space 1880–1918*. Cambridge, MA: Harvard University Press, 1983.

Kershaw, Ian. *Hitler 1889–1936: Hubris*. London: Allen Lane, 1998.

Kershaw, Ian. *Hitler 1936–1945: Nemesis*. London: Allen Lane, 2000.
Koshar, Rudy. "Cars and Nations: Anglo-German Perspectives on Automobility between the World Wars." *Theory, Culture & Society* 21, no. 4/5 (August-October 2004): 121–44.
Koshar, Rudy. *German Travel Cultures*. New York: Berg, 2000.
Krauss, Samuel. *History of Jewish Houses of Prayer*, pp. 302–16. In Hebrew. New York: Ogen, 1955.
Kreutzmüller, Christoph, Ingo Loose, and Benno Nietzel. "Nazi Persecution and Strategies for Survival: Jewish Businesses in Berlin, Frankfurt am Main, and Breslau, 1933–1942." *Yad Vashem Studies* 39, no. 1 (2011): 31–70.
Kreutzmüller, Christoph. *Printed under Pressure: Newspaper Advertisements of Jewish-Owned Businesses in Nazi Germany 1933–1942*. In Hebrew. Jerusalem: Yad Vashem, 2019.
Kroll, Lothar. *Utopie als Ideologie: Geschichtsdenken und politisches Handeln im Dritten Reich*. Paderborn, Germany: Schöningh, 1999.
Kulka, Otto Dov, ed. *Deutsches Judentum unter dem Nationalsozalismus*, vol. 1. Tübingen, Germany: Mohr Siebeck, 1997.
Kwiet, Konrad. "Without Neighbors: Daily Living in Judenhäuser." In Francis R. Nicosia and David Scrase, eds., *Jewish Life in Nazi Germany: Dilemmas and Responses*, pp. 117–47. New York: Berghahn Books, 2010.
Laqueur, Walter. *Generation Exodus: The Fate of Young Jewish Refugees from Nazi Germany*. Hanover and London: Brandeis University Press, 2001.
Lässig, Simone. *Jüdische Wege ins Bürgertum: Kulturelles Kapital und sozialer Aufstieg im 19. Jahrhundert*. Göttingen, Germany: Vandenhoeck & Ruprecht, 2004.
Lässig, Simone, and Miriam Rürup. "Introduction: What Made a Space 'Jewish'? Reconsidering a Category of Modern German History." In Lässig and Rürup, eds., *Space and Spatiality in Modern German Jewish History*, pp. 1–20. New York and Oxford, UK: Berghahn, 2017.
Lavsky, Hagit. "Jewish Agricultural Training in Germany: Its Context and Changing Role." In Tal Alon-Mozes, Irene Aue-Ben-David, and Joachim Wolschke Bulmahn, eds., *Jewish Horticultural Schools and Training Centers in Germany and Their Impact on Horticulture, Agriculture and Landscape Architecture in Palestine/Israel*, pp. 13–22. Munich: AVM.edition, 2020.
Lavsky, Hagit. *The Creation of the German-Jewish Diaspora: Interwar German-Jewish Immigration*. Berlin and Boston: De Gruyter & Magnes, 2017.
Lefebvre, Henri. *The Production of Space*. Oxford, UK: Blackwell, 1991.
Lekan, Thomas. *Imagining the Nation in Nature: Landscape Preservation and German Identity 1885–1945*. Cambridge, MA: Harvard University Press, 2004.
Livnat, Hanna. *Jews and Proud: Shaping Identity for Jewish Children in Germany 1933–1938*. In Hebrew. Jerusalem: Yad Vashem, 2009.
Livnat, Hanna. *The Press for Jewish Children and Youth in Germany 1933–1938: Warning or Reassuring*. In Hebrew. Jerusalem: Yad Vashem, 2017.
Livneh-Freudenthal, Rachel. *The Verein: Pioneers of the Science of Judaism in Germany*. In Hebrew. Jerusalem: Leo Baeck Institute Jerusalem and the Zalman Shazar Center, 2018.
Lowenstein, Steven M. "The Beginning of Integration 1780–1870." In Marion Kaplan, ed., *Jewish Daily Life in Germany 1618–1945*, pp. 93–171. New York: Oxford University Press, 2005.

Mann, Thomas. *The Magic Mountain*, translated by John E. Woods. New York: Vintage International, 1996.

Margaliot, Abraham. *Between Rescue and Annihilation: Studies in the History of German Jewry 1932–1938*. In Hebrew. Jerusalem: Yad Vashem, 1990.

Margaliot, Abraham, and Yehoyakim Cochavi, eds. *History of the Holocaust: Germany*. In Hebrew, 2 volumes. Jerusalem: Yad Vashen, 1998.

Maurer, Trude. "From Everyday Life to a State of Emergency: Jews in Weimar and Nazi Germany." in Marion Kaplan, ed., *Jewish Daily Life in Germany 1618–1945*, pp. 271–373. New York: Oxford University Press, 2005.

McNevin, Anne, and Antje Missbach. "Luxury Limbo: Temporal Techniques of Border Control and the Humanitarianisation of Waiting." *International Journal for Migration and Border Studies* 4, no. 1/2 (2018): 12–34.

Melucci, Alberto. *The Playing Self: Person and Meaning in the Planetary Society*. Cambridge, UK: Cambridge University Press, 1996.

Mettele, Gisela. "Der private Raum als öffentlicher Ort: Geselligkeit im bürgerlichen Haus." In Dieter Hein and Andreas Schulz, eds., *Bürgerkultur im 19. Jahrhundert: Bildung, Kunst und Lebenswelt*, pp. 155–69. Munich: Beck, 1996.

Meyer, Beate, ed. *Deutsche Jüdinnen und Juden in Ghettos und Lagern (1941–1945): Lodz. Chelmno. Minsk. Riga. Auschwitz. Theresienstadt*. Berlin: Metropol, 2017.

Meyer, Michael. "The Emergence of Jewish Historiography: Motives and Motifs." In *Judaism within Modernity: Essays on Modern Jewish History and Religion*, pp. 44–63. Detroit: Wayne State University Press, 2001.

Meyer, Michael. "'How Awesome is this Place!' The Reconceptualization of the Synagogue in Nineteenth-Century Germany." *Leo Baeck Institute Year Book* 41 (1996): 51–63.

Meyer, Michael. "Liberal Judaism in Nazi Germany." In Moshe Zimmermann, ed., *On Germans and Jews under the Nazi Regime: Essays by Three Generations of Historians; A Festschrift in Honor of Otto Dov Kulka*, pp. 281–95. Jerusalem: Hebrew University Magnes Press, 2006.

Michaeli, Ilana, and Irmgard Klönne, eds. *Gut Winkel—die schützende Insel: Hachschara 1933–1941*. Berlin: Lit, 2007.

Mikota, Jana. "Jüdische Schriftstellerinnen—wieder entdeckt: 'Sollte sich Spatz nun freuen oder traurig sein, daß die großen Geschwister so weit fort waren?' Die Schriftstellerin, Journalistin und Pädagogin Meta Samson." *Medaon* 6 (2010): 1–7.

Minkowski, Eugène. *Lived Time: Phenomenological and Psychopathological Studies*. Evanston, IL: Northwestern University Press, 1970.

Miron, Guy. "Between History and 'Useful Past Picture': Representations of the Jewish and the German Past in the Jewish Liberal Historical Discourse in Weimar Germany." In Hebrew. *Zion* 66 (2001): 297–330.

Miron, Guy. "From 'Public Space' to 'Space of Writing': Jewish Diarists in Nazi Germany." *Yearbook for European Jewish Literature Studies* 6, no. 1 (2019): 90–107.

Miron, Guy. "The Emancipation Heroes' Pantheon in German-Jewish Public Memory of the 1930s." *German History* 21, no. 4 (2003): 476–504.

Miron, Guy. *German Jews in Israel: Memories and Past Images*. In Hebrew. Jerusalem: Hebrew University Magnes Press, 2004.

Miron, Guy. *The Waning of the Emancipation: Jewish History, Memory, and the Rise of Fascism in Germany, France, and Hungary*. Detroit: Wayne State University Press, 2011.

Moeller, Robert G. *War Stories: The Search for a Usable Past in the Federal Republic of Germany*. Berkeley: University of California Press, 2001.

Nagel, Michael. *1933 as a Watershed? Form and Function of the German-Jewish Press before and after the Nazi Takeover*. In Hebrew. Jerusalem: Yad Vashem, 2015.

Neumann, Boaz. *Being-in-the-World: German Worlds at the Turn of the 20th Century*. In Hebrew. Tel Aviv: Am Oved, 2014.

Neumann, Boaz. *Nazi Weltanschauung: Space, Body, Language*. In Hebrew. Haifa and Tel Aviv: University of Haifa Press, 2002.

Niederland, Doron. *The Jewish Home in Nazi Germany as Reflected in the German-Jewish Press 1933–1938*. In Hebrew. Jerusalem: Yad Vashem, 2018.

Nielsen, Philipp. *Between Heimat and Hatred: Jews and the Right in Germany 1871–1935*. New York: Oxford University Press, 2019.

Or, Ronit. "The Reconciliation Sphere of the Pacifist Carpenter: The Quaker James T. Baily's Relief Labour with Interned Enemy Aliens at Knockaloe Camp during World War I." In Hebrew. *Zmanim, A Historical Quarterly* 141 (2019): 18–33.

Osterhammel, Jürgen. *The Transformation of the World: A Global History of the Nineteenth Century*. Princeton, NJ: Princeton University Press, 2014.

Ozouf, Mona. *Festivals and the French Revolution*. Cambridge, MA: Harvard University Press, 1991.

Paetz, Andreas, and Karin Weiss, eds. *Hachschara: Die Vorbereitung junger Juden auf die Auswanderung nach Palästina*. Potsdam, Germany: Verlag für Berlin-Brandenburg, 1999.

Paucker, Arnold, ed. *The Jews in Nazi Germany 1933–1943*. Tübingen, Germany: J. C. B. Mohr, 1986.

Peel, Mark. "On the Margins: Lodgers and Boarders in Boston 1860–1900." *Journal of American History* 72, no. 4 (March 1986): 813–34.

Pegelow Kaplan, Thomas. *The Language of Nazi Genocide: Linguistic Violence and the Struggle of Germans of Jewish Ancestry*. New York: Cambridge University Press, 2009.

Peil, Tiina. "Home." In Nigel Thrift and Rob Kitchin, eds., *International Encyclopedia of Human Geography*, Amsterdam: Elsevier, 2009.

Perrot, Michelle. "The Family Triumphant." In Michelle Perrot, ed., *A History of Private Life*, vol. 4, *From the Fires of Revolution to the Great War*, pp. 99–129. Cambridge, MA: Belknap Press of Harvard University Press, 1990.

Perry, Joe. *Christmas in Germany: A Cultural History*. Chapel Hill: University of North Carolina Press, 2010.

Petersen, Thomas Peter. *Der Volkstrauertag, seine Geschichte und Entwicklung: Eine wissenschaftliche Betrachtung*. Bad Kleinen, Germany: T. P. Petersen, 1998.

Pfeiffer, Lorenz, and Henry Wahlig. *Juden im Sport während des Nationalsozialismus: Ein historisches Handbuch für Niedersachsen und Bremen*, Göttingen, Germany: Wallstein, 2012.

Pilarczyk, Ulrike. *Gemeinschaft in Bildern: Jüdische Jugendbewegung und zionistische Erziehungspraxis in Deutschland und Palästina/Israel*, Göttingen, Germany: Wallstein, 2009.

Pleck, Elizabeth H. *Celebrating the Family: Ethnicity, Consumer Culture and Family Rituals*. Cambridge, MA: Harvard University Press, 2000.

Proshansky, Harold M., Abbe K. Fabian, and Robert Kaminoff. "Place-Identity: Physical World Socialization of the Self." *Journal of Environmental Psychology* 3 (1983): 57–83.

Quack, Sibylle. *Between Sorrow and Strength: Women Refugees of the Nazi Period.* New York: Cambridge University Press, 1995.

Rachamimov, Iris. "Camp Domesticity: Shifting Gender Boundaries in WWI Internment Camps." In Gilly Carr and Harold Mytum, eds., *Cultural Heritage and Prisoners of War: Creativity behind Barbed Wire*, pp. 291–305. New York and London: Routledge, 2012.

Rachamimov, Iris. *Islands of Men: Shifting Gender Boundaries in WWI Internment Camps.* Forthcoming.

Raspe, Lucia. "Die Lebensbedingungen des Ghettos in der jüdischen Brauchtumsliteraur der frühen Neuzeit." In Fritz Backhaus et al., eds., *Frühneuzeitliche Ghettos in Europa im Vergleich*, pp. 303–31. Berlin: Trafo, 2012.

Reagin, Nancy R. *Sweeping the German Nation: Domesticity and National Identity in Germany 1870–1945.* New York: Cambridge University Press, 2007.

Reinharz, Jehuda. "Three Generations of German Zionism." *Jerusalem Quarterly* 9 (Fall 1978): 99–105.

Richarz, Monika. "Demographic Developments." In Michael A. Meyer, ed., *German-Jewish History in Modern Times. Volume 3: Integration in Dispute 1871–1918*, pp. 7–34. New York: Columbia University Press, 1997.

Ristaino, Marcia. *Port of Last Resort: The Diaspora Communities of Shanghai.* Stanford, CA: Stanford University Press, 2001.

Roche, Daniel. *The History of Everyday Life: The Birth of Consumption in France 1600–1800.* Cambridge, UK: Cambridge University Press, 2000.

Roemer, Nils. "Between the Provinces and the City: Mapping German-Jewish Memories." *Leo Baeck Institute Year Book* 51 (2006): 61–77.

Roemer, Nils. *German City, Jewish Memory: The Story of Worms.* Waltham, MA: Brandeis University Press, 2010.

Roemer, Nils. *Jewish Scholarship and Culture in Nineteenth-Century Germany: Between History and Faith.* Madison: University of Wisconsin Press, 2005.

Rosa, Hartmut. *Social Acceleration: A New Theory of Modernity.* New York: Columbia University Press, 2013.

Roskies, David G. *The Jewish Search for a Usable Past.* Bloomington: Indiana University Press, 1999.

Rosner, Victoria. *Modernism and the Architecture of Private Life.* New York: Columbia University Press, 2008.

Ross, Corey. *Media and the Making of Modern Germany: Mass Communications, Society, and Politics from the Empire to the Third Reich.* New York: Oxford University Press, 2008.

Rykwert, Joseph. "House and Home." *Social Research* 58, no. 1 (Spring 1991): 51–62.

Schellack, Fritz. *Nationalfeiertage in Deutschland von 1871 bis 1945.* Frankfurt am Main: Peter Lang, 1990.

Schivelbusch, Wolfgang. *The Railway Journey: The Industrialization of Time and Space in the 19th Century.* Berkeley: University of California Press, 1986.

Schlögel, Karl. *In Space We Read Time: On the History of Civilization and Geopolitics.* New York: Bard Graduate Center, 2016.

Schnabel, Anja. *Bleiben in Breslau: Jüdische Selbstbehauptung und Sinnsuche in den Tagebüchern Willy Cohns 1933 bis 1941.* Berlin: Be.bra Wissenschaft Verlag, 2018.

Schönwälder, Karen. *Historiker und Politik: Geschichtswissenschaft im Nationalsozialismus.* Frankfurt am Main: Campus, 1992.

Schoor, Kerstin. *Vom literarischen Zentrum zum literarischen Ghetto*. Göttingen, Germany: Wallstein Verlag, 2010.

Schlör, Joachim. "'Take Down Mezuzahs, Remove Name-Plates': The Emigration of Objects from Germany to Palestine." In Simone J. Bronner, ed., *Jewish Cultural Studies, Vol. 1, Jewishness: Expression, Identity, and Representation*, pp. 133–50. Oxford, UK: Littman Library of Jewish Civilization, 2008.

Schmidt-Lauber, Brigitta. *Gemütlichkeit: Eine kulturwissenschaftliche Annäherung*. Frankfurt am Main: Campus Verlag, 2003.

Schorsch, Ismar. *From Text to Context: The Turn to History in Modern Judaism*. Hanover, NH: University Press of New England, 1994.

Schulin, Ernst. "Doppel-Nationalität? Die Integration der Juden in die deutsche Kulturnation und die neue Konstruktion der jüdischen Geschichte." In Peter Alter, Claus-Ekkehard Baersch, and Peter Berghoff, eds., *Die Konstruktion der Nation gegen die Juden*, pp. 243–59. Munich: W. Fink, 1999.

Sen, Arijit, and Lisa Silverman, eds. *Making Place: Space and Embodiment in the City*. Bloomington: Indiana University Press, 2014.

Sheller, Mimi. "Automotive Emotions: Feeling the Car." *Theory, Culture & Society* 21, no. 4/5 (August-October 2004): 221–42.

Sibley, David. *Geographies of Exclusion: Society and Difference in the West*. London: Routledge, 1995.

Siemens, Daniel. *Stormtroopers: A New History of Hitler's Brownshirts*. New Haven, CT: Yale University Press, 2017.

Simmel, Georg. "Metropolis and Mental Life." In David Frisby and Mike Featherstone, eds., *Simmel on Culture: Selected Writings*, pp. 174–85. London: Sage Publications.

Sofsky, Wolfgang. *The Order of Terror: The Concentration Camp*. Princeton, NJ: Princeton University Press, 1996.

Soja, Edward W. "Taking Space Personally." In Barney Warf and Santa Arias, eds., *The Spatial Turn: Interdisciplinary Perspectives*, pp. 11–35. London and New York: Routledge, 2009.

Soja, Edward W. *Postmodern Geographies: The Reassertion of Space in Critical Social Theory*. London and New York: Verso, 1989.

Sorkin, David. *The Transformation of German Jewry 1780–1840*. New York: Oxford University Press, 1987.

Sorokin, Pitirim. *Sociocultural Causality, Space and Time: A Study of Referential Principles of Sociology and Social Sciences*. New York: Russell & Russell, 1964.

Spiegel, Gabrielle M. "Memory and History: Liturgical Time and Historical Time." *History and Theory* 41, no. 2 (2002): 149–62.

Steber, Martina, and Bernhard Gotto, eds. *Visions of Community in Nazi Germany: Social Engineering and Private Lives*. New York: Oxford University Press, 2014.

Steuwer, Janosch. "*Ein Drittes Reich, wie ich es auffasse*": *Politik, Gesellschaft und privates Leben in Tagebüchern 1933–1939*. Göttingen, Germany: Wallstein Verlag, 2017.

Stone, Dan. *Histories of the Holocaust*. New York: Oxford University Press, 2010.

Szołtysek, Mikołaj. "Households and Family Systems in Early Modern Europe." In Hamish Scott, ed., *The Oxford Handbook of Early Modern European History 1350–1750, Volume I: Peoples and Place*, pp. 313–41. Oxford, UK: Oxford University Press, 2015.

Thomas, Keith. *Religion and the Decline of Magic*. New York: Scribner's Sons, 1971.

Tuan, Yi-Fu. *Space and Place: The Perspective of Experience*. Minneapolis: University of Minnesota Press, 2001.

Van Rahden, Till. *Jews and Other Germans: Civil Society, Religious Diversity and Urban Politics in Breslau 1860–1925*. Madison: University of Wisconsin Press, 2008.

Volkov, Shulamit. *Germans, Jews, and Antisemites: Trials in Emancipation*. Cambridge, UK: Cambridge University Press, 2006.

Von der Krone, Kerstin. "The Representation and Creation of Spaces through Print Media: Some Insights from the History of the Jewish Press." In Simone Lässig and Miriam Rürup, eds., *Space and Spatiality in Modern German Jewish History*, pp. 125–39. New York: Berghahn, 2017.

Walch, Teresa. "Degenerate Spaces: The Coordination of Space in Nazi Germany." PhD dissertation, University of California, San Diego, 2018.

Walch, Teresa. "With an Iron Broom: Cleansing Berlin's Bülowplatz of 'Judeo-Bolshevism,' 1933–1936." *German History* 40 (2022): 61–87.

Werner, Karl Ferdinand. *Das NS Geschichtsbild und die deutsche Geschichtswissenschaft*. Stuttgart, Germany: Kohlhammer, 1967.

Wildt, Michael. *Volksgemeinschaft als Selbstermächtigung: Gewalt gegen Juden in der deutschen Provinz 1919 bis 1939*. Hamburg: Hamburger Edition, 2007.

Wobick-Segev, Sarah. "Buying, Selling, Being, Drinking; or, How the Coffeehouse Became a Site for the Consumption of New Jewish Modalities of Belonging." In Gideon Reuveni and Sarah Wobick-Segev, eds., *The Economy in Jewish History: New Perspectives on the Interrelationship between Ethnicity and Economic Life*, pp. 115–34. New York: Berghahn, 2011.

Wobick-Segev, Sarah. *Homes Away from Home: Jewish Belonging in Twentieth-Century Paris, Berlin, and St. Petersburg*. Stanford, CA: Stanford University Press, 2018.

Wünschmann, Kim. *Before Auschwitz: Jewish Prisoners in the Prewar Concentration Camps*. Cambridge, MA: Harvard University Press, 2015.

Zadoff, Mirjam. *Next Year in Marienbad: The Lost World of Jewish Spa Culture*. Philadelphia: University of Pennsylvania Press, 2012.

Zeller, Thomas. *Driving Germany: The Landscape of the German Autobahn 1930–1970*. New York: Berghahn, 2007.

Zerubavel, Eviatar. *Time Maps: Collective Memory and the Social Shape of the Past*. Chicago: University of Chicago Press, 2003.

Zimmermann, Moshe. *Deutsche gegen Deutsche: Das Schicksal der Juden 1938–1945*. Berlin: Aufbau, 2008.

Zimmermann, Moshe. *Die deutschen Juden 1914–1945*. Berlin: Oldenbourg Wissenschaftsverlag, 2010.

Index

Page numbers in italics refer to figures.